MYTH, LEG
FOLKLORE S

The Phantom World

APPENDIX:

CALENDAR YEAR JEEP SALES

A word of caution is always in order when it comes to discussing Jeep sales figures. Due to the frequent change of corporate parent, plus some years for which the records were destroyed, a completely accurate listing of Jeep sales or production numbers is not possible at this time. However, over the years the good folks at the *Automotive News* have published calendar year sales for most makes, Jeep included, and they can be considered a good source. We list their numbers here:

Year   Calendar Year Retail Sales (USA only)

1946	44,464	
1947	73,219	
1948	97,892	
1949	61,341	
1950	58,566	
1951	50,341	
1952	61,372	includes Willys cars
1953	60,145	includes Willys cars
1954	34,535	includes Willys cars
1955	33,519	includes Willys cars
1956	23,488	
1957	22,005	
1958	22,178	
1959	30,626	
1960	31,385	
1961	32,644	
1962	30,426	
1963	44,339	
1964	44,385	
1965	42,415	

1953 Jeep CJ-3B

1966 Jeep Gladiator J-200

1966	42,860
1967	39,757
1968	38,486
1969	36,017
1970	33,984
1971	35,925
1972	50,926
1973	68,227
1974	96,835
1975	85,111
1976	107,487
1977	124,843
1978	163,548
1979	145,214
1980	77,852
1981	63,275
1982	63,761
1983	82,140
1984	153,801
1985	181,389
1986	207,514
1987	208,440
1988	253,454
1989	249,170
1990	196,863
1991	177,775
1992	268,724
1993	408,323
1994	436,445
1995	426,628
1996	509,183
1997	472,872

1967 Jeepster Commando station wagon

1972 Jeepster Commando roadster

1973 Jeep J-4000 pickup

1977 Jeep Cherokee station wagon

BIBLIOGRAPHY

BOOKS:
Ackerson, Robert C. *Jeep-the 50 year history.* Haynes Pub., 1988
Ackerson, Robert C., ed. *Standard Catalog of 4X4s—1945-1993.* Krause Publications, 1993
Borth, Christy. *Masters Of Mass Production.* The Bobbs-Merrill Co., 1945
Brown, Arch. *Jeep-The Unstoppable Legend.* Publications International, 1994
Conde, John A. *American Motors Family Album.* American Motors, 1976 ed.
Fetherston, David. *Jeep-Warhorse, Workhorse & Boulevard Cruiser.* Motorbooks International, 1995
Fowler, William. *Jeep Goes To War.* Brompton Books, 1993
Gunnell, John, ed. *Standard Catalog of Trucks 1896-1986.* Krause Publications, 1987
Heiner, Albert P. *Western Colossus-Henry J. Kaiser* Halo Books, 1991
Lichty, Robert C. and Terry V. Boyce. *The Hurst Heritage.* Dobbs Publications, 1983
Rifkind, Herbert. *Jeep Genesis-The Rifkind Report.* Iso-Galago, 1943
Scott, Graham. *Essential Military Jeep.* Bay View Books, 1996
Wells, Wade A. *Hail to the Jeep.* Harper & Brothers, 1946
Willinger, Kurt and Gene Gurney. *The American Jeep in War and Peace.* Crown Publishers, 1983
Zeicher, Walter. *Jeep-Willys, Kaiser, AMC 1942-1986.* Schiffer Publishing, Inc., 1990

PERIODICALS:
"Aero Eagle." *Special Interest Autos* magazine # 18 Feb./Mar. 1973
"Jeep Collectors Edition." *Peterson's 4 Wheel and Off-Road* 1986
"Truck of the Year." *Motor Trend* Dec. 1992
"Willys New 140 hp Bomb." *Four Wheeler* June 1962
"World News this Week." *AutoWeek* Dec. 29, 1997
Burck, Charles G. "A Fresh Start-Again-For American Motors." *Fortune* July 16, 1979
Gross, Ken. "The Man Who Never Failed." *Special Interest Autos* #27 Mar./Apr.1975
Koblenz, Jay. "Jeep CJ 1946-1986." *Collectible Automobile* Aug. 1986
Lamm, Michael. "Jeep Station Wagon 1946-1965." *Collectible Automobile* Feb. 1991
Langworth, Richard M. "1952-1955 Willys." *Collectible Automobile* Feb. 1990
MacDonald, Don. "AMC's Struggle for Survival." *Road Test* Apr. 1973
Probst, Karl with Charles Probst. "One Summer in Butler." *Automobile Quarterly*
Sanders, Bill. "Rip Roaring Renegade." *Four Wheeler* Aug. 1972
Stevens, Brooks. "He Made Milwaukee Cars Famous." *Car Classics* Dec. 1974
Ward's Auto World Dec. 1977, Dec. 1978, Dec.1979, Dec.1980, Dec.1981, Dec.1982, Dec.1983, and Dec. 1984, Dec. 1985, Dec. 1986, Dec. 1987, Dec. 1988, Dec. 1989, Dec. 1990, Dec. 1991 issues
Whiteside, David E. "Jumpin' Jeep." *Ward's Auto World* July 1977

ANNUAL REPORTS AND ETC.:
Annual Report to the Stockholders of American Motors Corporation 1970-1986 editions
Annual Report to the Stockholders of Chrysler Corporation 1987-1997 editions
Annual Report to the Stockholders of Kaiser Industries 1968 edition
Annual Report to the Stockholders of Willys-Overland 1951 edition
Automotive News 100 Year Almanac
Automotive News 1990, 1991, 1992, 1993, 1994, 1995, 1996 Market Data Books.

In addition to the above, the author utilized dozens of Jeep sales catalogs and brochures, as well as hundreds of company memos, letters, press releases, and newspaper clippings, (all from the Patrick R. Foster Historical Collection), which the listing of in detail would consume a great many pages the author believes wouldn't interest the average reader. Also referenced were recorded interviews with several former members of Jeep management, and retired Jeep designers, the audio tapes of which all reside in the Patrick R. Foster Historical Collection.

ABOUT THE AUTHOR

Patrick R. Foster's name is familiar to most automotive enthusiasts. His award-winning books *American Motors, The Last Independent* and *The Metropolitan Story* have become the standard texts for those two marques, and there is every expectation that *The Story of Jeep* will follow that pattern of success.

Pat can claim at least one advantage over most authors who have tackled the writing of Jeep history—as a former Jeep salesman he played a small part in making Jeep what it is today. As one of America's best-known automotive historians, Pat brings a wealth of experience to the task of telling the story of Jeep in a way that everyone can understand and appreciate.

Pat has lived most of his life in Milford, Connecticut, a picturesque town situated on the shores of Long Island Sound. He lives there today with his lovely wife Diane, daughter Caitlin, and Samantha the cat. Pat would like to extend his thanks to all the readers who have supported him over the years.

THE PHANTOM WORLD

Concerning Apparitions and Vampires

('Traité sur les apparitions et sur les vampires')

Augustin Calmet

With an Introduction by

GILLIAN BENNETT

WORDSWORTH EDITIONS
in association with
THE FOLKLORE SOCIETY

This edition published 2001 by Wordsworth Editions Limited
Cumberland House, Crib Street, Ware, Hertfordshire SG12 9ET
in association with FLS Books, The Folklore Society,
c/o The Warburg Institute, Woburn Square, London WC1H 0AB

Editor FLS Books: Jennifer Chandler

ISBN 1 84022 508 4

Typeset by Antony Gray
Printed and bound in Great Britain by
Mackays of Chatham plc, Chatham, Kent

This exciting new series is made possible by a unique partnership between Wordsworth Editions and The Folklore Society.

Among the major assets of The Folklore Society is its unparalleled collection of books, in the making since 1878. The library and archives have, over the years, formed an invaluable specialist resource. Now, Wordsworth Editions, which is committed to opening up whole areas of culture through good-looking, good-value books and intelligent commentary, make these riches widely available.

Individual introductions by acknowledged experts place each work in historical context and provide commentaries from the perspective of modern scholarship.

PROFESSOR W. F. H. NICOLAISEN
President, The Folklore Society

Contents

Introduction

Augustin Calmet, born in 1672 in Lorraine, was a churchman, biblical scholar and man of letters, with an abiding interest in history and antiquities, especially those of his birthplace. He joined the Benedictine order at the age of sixteen and by twenty-two was appointed sub-Prior of the monastery of Münster in Alsace. In 1718 he became Abbot of St Leopold's in Nancy, and ten years later became Abbot at Senones where he remained until his death. Rational and erudite, during a long and distinguished life (he lived to be 85) he wrote in the region of 82 works. He is best known for his Bible commentaries (1707–16) which were translated into six languages in the space of ten years, and his *Dictionary of the Bible*, of which there were six editions and an English translation in 1732. He was also author of a *History of the Life and Miracles of Jesus* (Paris 1720); *Antiquities, Sacred and Profane* (translated into English in 1727); the seventeen-volume *Histoire universelle, sacreé et profane, depuis le commencement du monde jusqu'à nos jours* (Strasbourg 1735–71); and local histories such as his ecclesiastical and civil history of Lorraine (Nancy 1728) and his *Dissertations sur les grands chemins de Lorraine* (1727) which was translated into English in 1729 as *A Dissertation upon the High-Roads of the Duchy of Lorraine*. His commentary on the rule of St Benedict (1734) is full of antiquarian and folkloric detail, and when he died he left manuscripts of essays on many subjects some of which are of definite interest to folklorists. These include essays on the origin of playing cards, ancient divinities once worshipped in Lorraine, customs and usages of Lorraine, and the ceremony of 'The King of the Bean'. His fame and influence well-outlived his life: the British Library catalogue lists fifty-six, mainly nineteenth-century, works containing extracts from Calmet's Bible commentaries, treatises and histories.

Dissertations sur les apparitions des anges, des démons et des esprits. Et sur les revenans et vampires de Hongrie, de Boheme, de Moravie et de Silésie was first published in Paris in 1746, and updated in 1749. A revised and augmented edition was published in Senones in 1751 under the title *Traité sur les apparitions et sur les vampires ou les revenans de Hongrie, de Bohème, de Moravie et de Silésie*. In 1850, London clergyman and scholar, Henry

Christmas, edited and translated the 1751 edition and re-titled it *The Phantom World: The Philosophy of Spirits, Apparitions etc.* and added a substantial introduction of his own. For the present edition Christmas's text has been used, but the supplementary material added to the 1751 edition (correspondence, refutations of correspondents' arguments and so) has been removed, and so have Christmas's introduction and footnotes which today make wearisome reading. Calmet's own prefaces have, however, been retained to help contextualise the mass of stories and discussion he presents. There has been no change to the text apart from the substitution of the word 'spirit' for Christmas's preferred term 'genius' (which nowadays is almost exclusively used in a different sense) and the addition of the letter 't' to the word 'revenan' to bring the spelling into line with present-day usage.

The title of the 1850 translation into English seems to have been Henry Christmas's own invention. It's catchy but misleading. Whereas it implies that the book is going to be about ghosts and that it will be presented from a believer's perspective, Calmet's actual aim was to explore popular beliefs about a wide variety of supernatural occurrences, and his dominant stance is that of the logician or scientific enquirer. True, volume one does indeed have a good many chapters devoted to people who encounter ghosts, but the subject is treated within the prevailing philosophical/religious framework which interpreted such occurrences as most likely to be visitations from good or bad angels, as the title of the first edition indicates. Also, Calmet does not confine himself to ghosts; he considers magic and oracles, possession by demons, and the witches' sabbath. Again, volume two deals with the return of the dead; but what Calmet is interested in here are not ghosts but the undead, the vampires of Eastern Europe. For this edition, therefore, we have preferred to subtitle the volume with Calmet's own title for the 1751 edition, both in translation and in the original French, 'Concerning Apparitions and Vampires *(Traité sur les apparitions et sur les vampires)*'.

Like his near-contemporary the English clergyman-antiquary Henry Bourne, who wrote his celebrated *Antiquitates Vulgares* in 1725, Calmet aims to examine a variety of familiar supernatural stories and beliefs and to determine which are false and harmful, and which are consistent with religion and good sense. His data are stories circulating in the oral tradition, or familiar to educated people via the classics, the Bible, and the works of the Christian Fathers. His overwhelmingly rational temperament leads him to discount or redefine almost everything that comes his way. The pagan oracles were deceptions of the priests, he alleges; the witches' sabbath cannot be described because one can never describe 'what has no existence and has never existed except in . . . craving and deluded imaginations . . . '; 'magic, impiety, enchantments, are often the effects of a diseased imagination.' Ghosts cannot exist, he says, because how can 'those who have been buried and turned to dust for a long time find themselves to be able to walk about with their chains? How do they drag them? How do they speak? What do they want?' In examining haunted houses (chapter 36), he explains that it is commonly thought there are three kinds of spirit – 'sprites or elves which divert themselves by troubling the quiet of those who dwell there' (what we would probably now call 'poltergeists'), spectres of the dead who seek burial or continue to haunt the place where they died until they receive burial or are avenged, and those who make the world of the living their personal Purgatory. 'So many stories are told concerning these things,' he says, that 'nobody will believe any of them.' Most are hoaxes: a tenant perhaps wants to protect his lease from others who might offer more rent, or maybe the building is the headquarters of coiners: other 'hauntings' are natural effects misunderstood – rats, perhaps, or owls.

To his mind, none of these stories can be true because they are not logically possible. In the first place, if spirits are the souls of the dead and the soul is incorporeal, how can spirits appear in corporeal form? What do they use for bodies? In the second place, if they are not actually the dead, but only appearances of the dead, they cannot appear by their own volition, they must be emissaries or emanations of some outside power or force. Effectively this means that they must either be good angels sent from God or bad angels sent by the devil. However, it's not logical to suppose that they are sent from God, he argues, because they are intrinsically deceptive and, moreover, often lead people into error (especially the error of thinking that rituals after death can redeem a damned soul). But it's not logical to think that all of them come from the devil either, because they often ask for prayers to be said for their souls or for alms to be given to the poor. Moreover, unless the devil is as powerful as God, God would have to permit the Devil to send evil angels about the mundane world, and why would he do that?

Nevertheless, unsatisfactory as he obviously finds this explanation, it is the one he has to keep falling back on, as in his treatment of the famous story of the Pied Piper of Hamelin (chapter 33). He dates this story to the year 1384 and interprets the Pied Piper as an evil spirit 'who, by God's permission, punished the bad faith of the burghers.' Only diabolical malice, he argues, 'would cause so many innocent children to perish.' Among other stories he dissects are Pliny's account of the chain-clanking ghost that haunted the philosopher Athendorus until he found its bones and buried them, and the famous Old Testament case of the Witch of Endor who conjured up the ghost of the prophet Samuel to advise King Saul. By way of a large number of stories like this – some familiar, others famous in their day but now forgotten – Calmet attempts to sift sense from nonsense and develop a rational stance on the supernatural which is consistent with the evidence, the Bible and Christian teaching, but dismissive of all forms of credulity and superstition.

The thread that runs through the whole of this discussion is that some of the stories might be true and others are indubitably false. Consequently, everything must be examined on its merits: 'There are two dangers to avoid: a too great credulity, and an excessive difficulty in believing . . . It is allowable to examine, prove and select; we must never form our judgement, but with knowledge of the case; a story may be false in many of its circumstances . . . but true in its foundation.'

Calmet has particular difficulty with biblical accounts. One feels that his naturally sceptical temperament should lead him to dismiss many of them, but this course of action is closed to him as a Benedictine monk. He escapes from this dilemma by attempting to redefine the most awkward cases: 'It is not permitted us to dispute the truth of the apparitions noted in the Old and the New Testament,' he says, 'but we may be permitted to explain them.' As far as popular traditions are concerned, he has fewer qualms; genuine cases are rare, he thinks. So, for example, of flight to the witches' sabbath, he writes: 'It is . . . not absolutely impossible, that a person may be raised in the air and transported to some very high and distant place, by order or permission of God, by good or evil spirits; but we must own that the thing is of rare occurrence, and that in all that is related of sorcerers and witches, and their assembly at the witches' sabbath, there is an infinity of stories which are false, absurd, ridiculous, and even destitute of probability.' Similarly, of the possibility that the dead might return to visit past scenes and loved ones, he observes that, if this were possible, the world would be full of spirits: 'there would be few persons who would not come back to visit the things or persons which have been dear to them during this life . . . It is a pure favour of the mercy or the power of God, and which he grants to very few . . . and we should be very much on our guard against all that is said, and all that we find written on the subject in books.' So, throughout volume one, he presents, weighs, judges, and delivers his verdict – in all but a few cases coming out in favour of caution, common sense and scepticism.

In volume two he turns to a subject that was a prime subject for scholarly discussion in his day. In the later seventeenth century, the debate about the reality of supernatural entities and operations had largely centred on witchcraft, with ghosts drawn in as subsidiary arguments This, for example, is very much the position in classic British polemics such as Joseph Glanvil's *Sadducismus Triumphatus* (1681) and Richard Baxter's *The Certainty of the World of Spirits Fully Evinced* (1691). In the 1730s, however, a large number of publications appeared reporting the cases of vampires in Hungary. These reports refocused the argument from witches to vampires, enabling the debate about the reality of the supernatural to continue for some time after witch prosecutions had ceased in Western Europe. In his *The Uses of Supernatural Power* (Cambridge 1990) Gábor Klaniczay suggests that it was the intellectual puzzles presented by the vampire reports that inspired many of the scientific and theological meditations on the subject. Popular reactions to suspected vampires fed into enlightened rationalists' arguments against the superstitions of ignorant peasants. Physicians reflected on possible natural causes for the undecayed corpses, and writers of the eighteenth-century occult revival speculated on the mystical 'forces of human fantasy' that might give rise to vampires.

The *vroucolacas* was the vampire, whose corpse did not decay properly and continued to show signs of life after death, and who would rise from the grave to harm the living by sucking their blood or inflicting diseases until finally laid to rest by exhumation and staking, decapitation or extraction and burning of the heart. Though there are references to these evil dead in medieval literature, reports of them only began to proliferate from the late sixteenth century, increasing during the seventeenth and reaching a peak in the Hungarian cases of the early eighteenth century. As Gábor Klaniczay remarks, the East European vampire was a synthesis of characteristics of five different sets of magical beliefs: 'the revenants, the . . . nightly pressing spirits, the blood-sucking *stryge* of Antiquity, those witches from Slavic and Balkan territories who were said to persist in harmful activities after their deaths, and finally the werewolf, a person capable of adopting the form of a wolf in order to attack and devour humans' (Klaniczay 1990, pp. 168–88, esp. p. 178).

For religious writers like Calmet, vampires represented a blasphemous parody of Christian doctrines. Like the uncorrupted remains of saints, the corpses of vampires refused to decay and resurrected themselves every night instead of waiting for the Day of Judgement. Aping the sacrament of the mass they drank the blood of the living, and strange lights like unholy haloes were seen round their graves. It was these grotesque perversions that prompted Calmet to write the treatise which forms volume 2 of *The Phantom World*. To safeguard Catholic doctrines concerning miracles, the resurrection, the veneration of the saints, and the efficacy of the sacraments, he sought to distinguish these from the blasphemous vanities of peasant beliefs about vampires, and to expose the ignorance that led to mistaken assumptions about phenomena that really had natural causes. Calmet was not only trying to rescue Catholic doctrine from superstitious perversions but also from the onslaughts of atheists and materialists who saw no difference between religious doctrine and popular superstitions.

Unfortunately, Calmet failed to walk this tightrope successfully. His vampire treatise was condemned as uncritical and credulous. Voltaire, who had initially treated Calmet with respect, thereby gaining access to the riches of the library at Senones, later decided that Calmet was a credulous fool. This is a judgement which Henry Christmas, the anti-Catholic translator and editor of *The Phantom World*, seems to have supported. His introduction (not reprinted here) has some very harsh things to say about 'popery', 'superstition', and 'human error'. This, however, is both to misunderstand Calmet's intention and to underestimate his abilities. It's as useless for Voltaire to criticise him for not being a materialist as for Christmas to find him at fault for being a Catholic. Calmet's mind is clear, he writes with incisive wit and logic, it is a delight to see him deconstructing a story or destroying an argument. Necessarily he brings to his task the constraints of his position and his time, but for anyone interested in the history of ideas that is a bonus not a fault.

One can read this book just for the stories – for there are plenty – but it is perhaps best appreciated as a portrait of the thinking of an educated person at a time when the old supernatural worldview was giving way to the new scientific materialism. Calmet's personality comes clearly through his prose, presenting a portrait of a sharply rigorous scholar trying to reconcile the worldview of the classics, the Bible and the Christian Fathers, which he must venerate, with his natural scepticism and the changing intellectual climate. His attempts to square the circle – often convoluted and sometimes verging on the comical – might seem unnecessary to modern readers. But, acutely aware that the tenor of the age led directly from scepticism, to materialism, to atheism ('a greater heresy,' he says, 'even than Calvinism or Lutheranism'), Calmet must defend biblical accounts. Nevertheless, he comes as close to rejecting all instances of the supernatural as his calling and his times could allow.

Intelligent people, he says, should: 'Keep the medium between excessive credulity and extreme incredulity; we must be prudent, moderate, and enlightened; we must test everything, examine everything, yield only to evidence and known truth.' Remarkably, this is what Augustin Calmet consistently does throughout the whole of this justly famous work

GILLIAN BENNETT
Editor of *Folklore*
Manchester Metropolitan University

The Phantom World

VOLUME ONE

Author's Preface to the first volume

The great number of authors who have written upon the apparitions of angels, demons, and disembodied souls is not unknown to me; and I do not presume sufficiently on my own capacity to believe that I shall succeed better in it than they have done, and that I shall transcend their knowledge and their discoveries. I am perfectly sensible that I expose myself to criticism, and perhaps to the mockery of many readers, who regard this matter as done with, and settled in the minds of philosophers, learned men, and many theologians. I must not reckon either on the approbation of the people, whose want of discernment prevents their being competent judges of this same. My aim is not to foment superstition, nor to feed the vain curiosity of visionaries, and those who believe without examination everything that is related to them as soon as they find therein anything marvellous and supernatural. I write only for reasonable and unprejudiced minds, which examine things seriously and coolly; I speak but for those who assent even to known truth only after mature reflection, who know how to doubt of what is uncertain, to suspend their judgment on what is doubtful, and to deny what is manifestly false.

As for pretended freethinkers, who reject everything in order to distinguish themselves, and to place themselves above the common herd, I leave them in their elevated sphere; they will think of this work as they may consider proper, and as it is not calculated for them, will not probably take the trouble to read it.

I undertook it for my own information, and to form to myself a just idea of all that is said on the apparitions of angels, of the demon, and of disembodied souls. I wished to see how far that matter was certain or uncertain, true or false, known or unknown, clear or obscure.

In this great number of facts which I have collected I have endeavoured to make a choice, and not to heap together too great a multitude of them, for fear that in the too numerous examples the doubtful might harm the certain, and in wishing to prove too much I might prove absolutely nothing. There will, even amongst those I have cited, be found some which will not easily be credited by many readers, and I allow them to regard such as not related.

I beg those readers, nevertheless, to discern justly amongst these facts and instances; after which they can with me form their opinion – affirm, deny, or remain in doubt.

From the respect which every man owes to truth, and the veneration which a Christian and a Priest owes to religion, it appeared to me very important to undeceive people respecting the opinion which they have of apparitions, if they believe them all to be true; or to instruct them and show them the truth and reality of a great number, if they think them all false. It is always shameful to be deceived; and dangerous, in regard to religion, to believe on light grounds, to remain wilfully in doubt, or to maintain oneself without any reason in superstition and illusion; it is already much to know how to doubt wisely, and not to form a decided opinion beyond what one really knows.

I never had any idea of treating profoundly the matter of apparitions; I have treated of it, as it were, by chance, and occasionally. My first and principal object was to discourse of the vampires of Hungary. In collecting my materials on that subject, I found many things concerning apparitions; the great number of these embarrassed this treatise on vampires. I detached some of them, and thus have composed this treatise on apparitions: there still remains a large number of them, which I might have separated for the better arrangement of this treatise. Many persons here have taken the accessory for the principal, and have paid more attention to the first part than to the second, which was, however, the first and the principal in my design. For I own I have always been much struck with what was related of the vampires or ghosts of Hungary, Moravia, and Poland; of the vroucolacas of Greece; and of the excommunicated, who are said not to be subject to decomposition after death. I thought I ought to bestow on it all the attention in my power; and I have deemed it right to treat on this subject in a particular dissertation. After having deeply studied it, and obtaining as much information as I was able, I found little solidity and certainty on the subject; which, joined to the opinion of some prudent and respectable persons whom I consulted, had induced me to give up my design entirely, and to renounce labouring on a subject which is so contradictory, and embraces so much uncertainty.

But looking at the matter in another point of view, I resumed my pen, decided upon undeceiving the public, if I found that what was said of it was absolutely false; to show that what is uttered on this subject is uncertain, and that we ought to be very reserved in pronouncing on these vampires, which have made so much noise in the world for a certain time, and still divide opinions at this day, even in the countries which are the scene of their pretended return, and where they appear; or to show that what has been said and written on this subject is not destitute of probability, and that the subject of the return of vampires is worthy the attention of the curious and the learned, and deserves to be seriously studied, to have the facts related of it examined, and the causes, circumstances, and means sounded deeply.

I am then about to examine this question as a historian, philosopher, and theologian. As a historian, I shall endeavour to discover the truth of the facts; as a philosopher, I shall examine the causes and circumstances; lastly, the knowledge or light of theology will cause me to deduce consequences as relating to religion. Thus I do not write in the hope of convincing freethinkers and pyrrhonians, who will not allow the existence of ghosts or vampires, nor even of the apparitions of angels, demons, and spirits; nor to intimidate those weak and credulous, by relating to them extraordinary stories of apparitions. I do not reckon either on curing the superstitious of their errors, nor the people of their prepossessions; not even on correcting the abuses which arise from this unenlightened belief, nor of doing away all the doubts which may be formed on apparitions; still less do I pretend to erect myself as a judge and censor of the works and sentiments of others, nor to distinguish myself, make myself a name, or divert myself, by spreading abroad dangerous doubts upon a subject which concerns religion, and from which they might make wrong deductions against the certainty of the Scriptures, and against the unshaken dogmas of our creed. I shall treat it as solidly and gravely as it merits; and I pray God to give me that knowledge which is necessary to do it successfully.

I exhort my reader to distinguish between the facts related, and the manner in which they happened. The fact may be certain, and the way in which it occurred unknown. Scripture relates certain apparitions of angels and disembodied souls; these instances are indubitable and found in the revelations of the holy books; but the manner in which God operated the resurrections, or in which he permitted these apparitions to take place, is hidden among his secrets. It is allowable for us to examine them, to seek out the circumstances, and propound some conjectures on the manner in which it all came to pass; but it would be rash to decide upon a matter which God has not thought proper to reveal to us. I say us much in proportion, concerning the stories related by sensible, contemporary, and judicious authors, who simply relate the facts without entering into the examination of the circumstances, of which, perhaps, they themselves were not well informed.

It has already been objected to me, that I cited poets and authors of little credit, in support of a thing so grave and so disputed as the apparition of spirits: such authorities, they say, are more calculated to cast a doubt on apparitions, than to establish the truth of them.

But I cite those authors as witnesses of the opinions of nations; and I count it not a small thing in the extreme licence of opinions, which at this day predominates in the world, amongst those even who make a profession of Christianity, to be able to show that the ancient Greeks and Romans thought that souls were immortal, that they subsisted after the death of the body, and that there was another life, in which they received the reward of their good actions, or the chastisement of their crimes.

Those sentiments which we read in the poets, are also repeated in the fathers of the Church, and the Pagan and Christian historians; but as they did not pretend to think them weighty, nor to approve them in repeating them, it must not be imputed to me either, that I have any intention of authorising them. For instance, what I have related of the manes, or lares; of the evocation of souls after the death of the body; of the avidity of these souls to suck the blood of the immolated animals; of the shape of the soul separated from the body; of the inquietude of souls which have no rest until their bodies are under ground; of those superstitious statues of wax which are devoted and consecrated under the name of certain persons whom the magicians pretended to kill by burning and stabbing their effigies; of the transportation of wizards and witches through the air, and of their assemblies on the Sabbath; all these things are related both in the works of the philosophers and pagan historians, as well as in the poets.

I know the value of one and the other, and I esteem them as they deserve; but I think that in treating this matter, it is important to make known to our readers the ancient superstitions, the vulgar or common opinions, and the prejudices of nations, to be able to refute them, and bring back the figures to truths, by freeing them from what poesy had added for the embellishment of the poem, and the amusement of the reader.

Moreover, I generally repeat this kind of thing, only when it is apropos of certain facts avowed by historians, and by other grave and rational authors; and sometimes rather as an ornament of the discourse, or to enliven the matter, than to derive thence certain proofs and consequences necessary for the dogma, or to certify the facts and give weight to my recital.

I know how little we must depend on what Lucian says on this subject; he only speaks of it to ridicule it. Philostratus, Jamblicus, and some others, do not merit more consideration; therefore I quote them only to refute them, or to show how far idle and ridiculous credulity has been carried on these matters, which were laughed at by the most sensible among the heathens themselves.

The consequences which I deduce from all these stories, and these poetical fictions, and the manner in which I speak of them in the course of this dissertation, sufficiently vouch that esteem, and give as true and certain only what is so in fact; and that I do not wish to impose on my reader, by relating many things which I myself regard as false, or as doubtful, or even as fabulous. But this ought not to be prejudicial to the dogma of the immortality of the soul, and to that of another life, nor to the truth of certain apparitions related in Scripture, or proved elsewhere by good testimony.

The first edition of this work having been printed in my absence, and upon an incorrect copy, several misprints have occurred, and even expressions and phrases displeasing and interrupted. I have tried to remedy this in a second edition, and to cast light on those passages which they noticed as demanding explanation, and correcting what might offend scrupulous readers, and prevent the bad consequences which might be derived from what I had said. I have even done more in this third edition. I have retrenched several passages; others I have suppressed; I have profited by the advice which has been given me; and I have replied to the objections which have been made.

People have complained that I took no part, and did not come to a decision on several difficulties which I propose, and that I leave my reader in uncertainty.

I make but little defence against this reproach; I should require more justification if I decided without a perfect knowledge of causes, for one side of the question, at the risk of embracing an error, and of falling into a still greater impropriety. There is wisdom in suspending our judgment till we have succeeded in finding the very truth.

I have also been told, that certain persons have made a joke of some facts which I have related. If I related them as certain, and they afford just cause for pleasantry, let the condemnation pass; but if I cited them as fabulous and false, they present no subject for pleasantry; *Falsum non est de ratione faceti.*

There are certain persons who delight in jesting on the most serious things, and who spare nothing, either sacred or profane. The histories of the Old and New Testament, the most sacred ceremonies of our religion, the lives of the most respectable saints, are not safe from their dull, tasteless pleasantry.

I have been reproached for having related several false histories, several doubtful facts, and several fabulous events. This is true; but I give them for what they are. I have declared several times, that I did not vouch for their truth, that I repeated them to show how false and ridiculous they were, and to deprive them of the credit they might have with the people; and if I have not gone at length into their refutation, I thought it right to let my reader have the pleasure of refuting them, supposing him to possess enough good sense and self-sufficiency to form his own judgment upon them, and feel the same contempt for such stories that I do myself. It is doing too much honour to certain things to refute them seriously.

But another objection, and a much more serious one, is said to be, what

I say of the illusions of the demon, leading some persons to doubt of the truth of the apparitions related in Scripture, as well as of the others suspected of falsehood.

I answer, that the consequences deduced from principles are not right, except when things are equal, and the subjects and circumstances the same; without which there can be no application of principles. The facts to which my reasoning applies, are related by authors of small authority, by ordinary or commonplace historians, bearing no character which deserves a belief of any thing superhuman. I may, without attacking their person or their merit, advance that they may have been badly informed, prepossessed, and mistaken; that the spirit of seduction may have been of the party; that the senses, the imagination, and superstition, may have made them take that for truth, which was only seeming.

But, in regard to the apparitions related in the Holy Scriptures, they borrow their infallible authority from the sacred and inspired authors who wrote them; they are verified by the events which followed them, by the execution or fulfilment of predictions made many ages previously; and which could neither be done, nor foreseen, nor performed, either by the human mind, or by the strength of man, not even by the angel of darkness.

I am but little concerned at the opinion passed on myself and my intentions in the publication of this treatise. Some have thought that I did it to destroy the popular and common idea of apparitions, and to make it appear ridiculous; and I acknowledge that those who read this work attentively and without prejudice, will remark in it more arguments for doubting what the people believe on this point, than they will find to favour the contrary opinion. If I have treated this subject seriously, it is only in what regards those facts in which religion and the truth of Scripture is interested; those which are indifferent, I have left to the censure of sensible people, and the criticism of the learned, and of philosophical minds.

I declare that I consider as true all the apparitions related in the sacred books of the Old and New Testament; without pretending, however, that it is not allowable to explain them. On this point I may apply the principle of St Paul: 'The letter killeth, and the Spirit giveth life.'

As to the other apparitions and visions related in Christian, Jewish, or heathen authors, I do my best to discern amongst them, and I exhort my readers to do the same; but I blame and disapprove the outrageous criticism of those who deny everything, and make difficulties of everything, in order to distinguish themselves by their pretended strength of mind, and to authorise themselves thus to deny everything, dispute the most certain facts, and in general all that savours of the marvellous. St Paul permits us to examine and prove everything; but he desires us to hold fast that which is good.

Advertisement

Every body talks of apparitions of angels and demons, and of souls separated from the body. The reality of these apparitions is considered as certain by many persons, while others deride them and treat them as altogether visionary.

I have determined to examine this matter, just to see what certitude there can be on this point; and I shall divide this Dissertation into four parts. In the first, I shall speak of good angels; in the second, of the appearances of bad angels; in the third, of the apparitions of souls of the dead; and in the fourth, of the appearance of living men to others living, absent, distant, and this unknown to those who appear. I shall occasionally add something on magic, wizards, and witches; on the Sabbath, oracles, and obsession and possession by demons.

CHAPTER 1

The Appearance of Good Angels Proved by the Books of the Old Testament

The apparitions or appearances of good angels are frequently mentioned in the books of the Old Testament. He who was stationed at the entrance of the terrestrial Paradise, was a cherub, armed with a flaming sword; those who appeared to Abraham, and who promised that he should have a son; those who appeared to Lot, and predicted to him the ruin of Sodom, and other guilty cities; he who spoke to Hagar in the desert, and commanded her to return to the dwelling of Abraham, and to remain submissive to Sarah, her mistress; those who appeared to Jacob, on his journey into Mesopotamia, ascending and descending the mysterious ladder; he who taught him how to cause his sheep to bring forth young differently marked; he who wrestled with Jacob on his return from Mesopotamia – were angels of light, and benevolent ones; the same as he who spoke with Moses from the burning bush on Horeb, and who gave him the tables of the law on Mount Sinai. That Angel who takes generally the name of God, and acts in his name, and with his authority; who served as a guide to the Hebrews in the desert, hidden during the day in a dark cloud, and shining during the night; he who spoke to Balaam, and threatened to kill his she-ass; he, lastly, who contended with Satan for the body of Moses – all these angels were without doubt good angels.

We must think the same of him who presented himself armed to Joshua on the plain of Jericho, and who declared himself head of the army of the Lord; it is believed, with reason, that it was the angel Michael. He who showed himself to the wife of Manoah, the father of Samson, and afterwards to Manoah himself. He who announced to Gideon that he should deliver Israel from the power of the Midianites. The angel Gabriel, who appeared to Daniel, at Babylon; and Raphael who conducted the young Tobias to Rages, in Media.

The prophecy of the Prophet Zechariah is full of visions of angels. In the books of the Old Testament, the throne of the Lord is described as resting on cherubim; and the God of Israel is represented as having before his throne seven principal angels, always ready to execute his orders, and four cherubim singing his praises, and adoring his sovereign holiness; the whole making a sort of allusion to what they saw in the court of the ancient Persian kings, where there were seven principal officers who saw his face, approached his person, and were called the eyes and ears of the king.

CHAPTER 2

The Appearance of Good Angels Proved by the Books of the New Testament

The books of the New Testament are in the same manner full of facts which prove the apparition of good angels. The angel Gabriel appeared to Zachariah, the father of John the Baptist, and predicted to him the future birth of the Fore-runner. The Jews, who saw Zachariah come out of the temple, after having remained within it a longer time than usual, having remarked that he was struck dumb, had no doubt but that he had seen some apparition of an angel. The same Gabriel announced to Mary the future birth of the Messiah. When Jesus was born in Bethlehem, the angel of the Lord appeared to the shepherds in the night, and declared to them that the Saviour of the world was born at Bethlehem. There is every reason to believe that the star which appeared to the Magi in the East, and which led them straight to Jerusalem, and thence to Bethlehem, was directed by a good angel. St Joseph was warned by a celestial spirit to retire into Egypt, with the mother and the infant Christ, for fear that Jesus should fall into the hands of Herod, and be involved in the massacre of the Innocents. The same angel informed Joseph of the death of King Herod, and told him to return to the land of Israel.

After the temptation of Jesus Christ in the wilderness, angels came and brought him food. The demon tempter said to Jesus Christ, that God had commanded his angels to lead him, and to prevent him from stumbling against a stone; which is taken from the 92nd Psalm, and proves the belief of the Jews on the article of guardian angels. The Saviour confirms the same truth when he says that the angels of children constantly behold the face of the celestial Father. At the last judgment, the good angels will separate the just, and lead them to the kingdom of heaven, while they will precipitate the wicked into eternal fire.

At the agony of Jesus Christ in the garden of Olives, an angel descended from heaven to console him. After his resurrection, angels appeared to the holy women who had come to his tomb to embalm him. In the Acts of the Apostles, they appeared to the Apostles as soon as Jesus had ascended into heaven; and the angel of the Lord came and opened the doors of the prison where the Apostles were confined, and set them at liberty. In the same book St Stephen tells us that the law was given to Moses by the ministration of angels; consequently, those were angels who appeared on Sinai and Horeb, and who spoke to him in the name of God, as his ambassadors, and as invested with his authority; also, the same Moses, speaking of the angel of the Lord, who was to introduce Israel into the Promised Land, says that 'the name of God is in him'. St Peter, being in prison, is delivered from thence by an angel, who conducted him the length of a street, and disappeared. St Peter, knocking at the door of the house in which his brethren were, they could not believe that it was he; they thought that it was his angel who knocked and spoke. St Paul, instructed in the school of the Pharisees, thought as they did on the subject of angels; he believed in their existence, in opposition to the Sadducees, and supposed that they could appear. When this Apostle, having been arrested by the Romans, related to the people how he had been overthrown at Damascus, the Pharisees, who were present, replied to those who exclaimed against him – 'How do we know, if an angel or a spirit hath not spoken to him?' St Luke says, that a Macedonian, (apparently the angel of Macedonia,) appeared to St Paul, and begged him to come and announce the Gospel in that country.

St John, in the Apocalypse, speaks of the seven angels, who presided over the Churches in Asia. I know that these seven angels are the Bishops of these Churches, but the ecclesiastical tradition will have it, that every Church has its tutelary angel. In the same book, the Apocalypse, are related divers appearances of angels. All Christian antiquity has recognised them, the Synagogue also has recognised them; so that it may be affirmed that nothing is more certain than the existence of good angels and their apparitions.

I place in the number of apparitions, not only those of good or bad angels, and the spirits of the dead who show themselves to the living, but also those of the living who show themselves to the angels or souls of the dead; whether these apparitions are seen in dreams, or during sleep, or awaking; whether they manifest themselves to all those who are present, or only to the persons to whom God judges proper to manifest them. For instance, in the Apocalypse, St John saw the four animals, and the four-and-twenty elders, who were clothed in white garments and wore crowns of gold upon their heads, and were seated on thrones around that of the

Almighty, who prostrated themselves before the throne of the Eternal, and cast their crowns at his feet.

And, elsewhere: 'I saw four angels standing at the four corners of the world, who held back the four winds and prevented them from blowing on the earth; then I saw another angel, who rose on the side of the east, and who cried out to the four angels who had orders to hurt the earth, "Do no harm to the earth, or the sea, or the trees, until we have impressed a sign on the foreheads of the servants of God." And I heard that the number of those who received this sign (or mark) was a hundred and forty-four thousand. Afterwards I saw an innumerable multitude of all nations, tribes, people and languages, standing before the throne of the Most High, arrayed in white garments, and having palms in their hands.'

And in the same book St John says, after having described the majesty of the throne of God, and the adoration paid to him by the angels and saints prostrate before him, one of the elders said to him – ' Those whom you see covered with white robes, are those who have suffered great trials and afflictions, and have washed their robes in the blood of the Lamb; for which reason they stand before the throne of God, and will do so night and day in his temple; and He who is seated on the throne will reign over them, and the angel which is in the midst of the throne will conduct them to the fountains of living water.' And, again, 'I saw under the altar of God the souls of those who have been put to death for defending the word of God, and for the testimony which they have rendered; they cried with a loud voice, saying, "When, O Lord, wilt thou not avenge our blood upon those who are on the earth?" ' etc.

All these apparitions, and several others similar to them, which might be related as being derived from the holy books as well as from authentic histories, are true apparitions, although neither the angels, nor the martyrs, spoken of in the Apocalypse, came and presented themselves to St John; but, on the contrary, this Apostle was transported in spirit to heaven, to see there what we have just related. These are apparitions which may be called passive on the part of the angels and holy martyrs, and active on the part of the holy Apostle who saw them.

CHAPTER 3

Under what Form have Good Angels Appeared?

The most usual form in which good angels appear, both in the Old Testament and the New, is the human form. It was in that shape they showed themselves to Abraham, Lot, Jacob, Moses, Joshua, Manoah the father of Samson, to David, Tobit, the Prophets; and in the New Testament they appeared in the same form to the Holy Virgin, to Zachariah the father of John the Baptist, to Jesus Christ after his fast of forty days, and to him again in his agony in the Garden of Olives. They showed themselves in the same form to the holy women after the resurrection of the Saviour. The one who appeared to Joshua on the plain of Jericho, appeared apparently in the guise of a warrior, since Joshua asks him, 'Art thou for us, or for our adversaries?'

Sometimes they hide themselves under some form which has resemblance to the human shape, like him who appeared to Moses in the burning bush, and who led the Israelites in the desert in the form of a cloud, dense and dark during the day, but luminous at night. The Psalmist tells us, that God makes his angels serve as a piercing wind and a burning fire, to execute his orders.

The cherubim, so often spoken of in the Scriptures, and who are described as serving for a throne to the majesty of God, were hieroglyphical figures, something like the sphinx of the Egyptians; those which are described in Ezekiel are like animals composed of the figure of a man, having the wings of an eagle, the feet of an ox; their heads were composed of the face of a man, an ox, a lion, and an eagle, two of their wings were spread towards their fellows, and two others covered their body; they were brilliant as burning coals, as lighted lamps, as the fiery heavens when they send forth the lightning's flash – they were terrible to look upon.

The one who appeared to Daniel was different from those we have just described; he was in the shape of a man, covered with a linen garment, and round his loins a girdle of very fine gold; his body was shining as a chrysolite, his face as a flash of lightning; his eyes darted fire like a lamp; his arms and all the lower part of his body was like brass melted in the furnace; his voice was loud as that of a multitude of people.

St John, in the Apocalypse, saw around the throne of the Most High four animals, which doubtless were four angels; they were covered with eyes before and behind. The first resembled a lion, the second an ox, the third had the form of a man, and the fourth was like an eagle with outspread wings; each of them had six wings, and they never ceased to cry night and day, 'Holy, holy, holy, Lord God Almighty, who was, and is, and is to come.'

The angel who was placed at the entrance of the terrestrial paradise was armed with a shining sword, as well as the one who appeared to Balaam, and who threatened, or was near killing, both himself and his ass; and so, apparently, was the one who showed himself to Joshua in the plain of Jericho, and the angel who appeared to David, ready to smite all Israel. The angel Raphael guided the young Tobias to Ragès under the human form of a traveller. The angel who was seen by the holy woman at the sepulchre of the Saviour, who overthrew the large stone which closed the mouth of the tomb, and who was seated upon it, had a countenance which shone like lightning, and garments white as snow.

In the Acts of the Apostles, the angel who extricated them from prison, and told them to go boldly and preach Jesus Christ in the temple, also appeared to them in a human form. The manner in which he delivered them from the dungeon is quite miraculous; for the chief priests having commanded that they should appear before them, those who were sent found the prison securely closed, the guards wide awake; but having caused the doors to be opened, they found the dungeon empty. How could an angel, without opening, or any fracture of the doors, thus extricate men from prison without either the guards or the gaoler perceiving anything of the matter? The thing is beyond any known powers of nature; but it is no more impossible than to see our Saviour after his resurrection, invested with flesh and bones, as he himself says, come forth from his sepulchre, without opening it, and without breaking the seals, enter the chamber wherein were the Apostles without opening the doors, and speak to the disciples going to Emmaus without making himself known to them; then, after having opened their eyes, disappear and become invisible. During the forty days that he remained upon earth till his ascension, he drank and ate with them, he spoke to them, he appeared to them; but he showed himself only to those witnesses who were preordained by the eternal Father to bear testimony to his resurrection.

The angel who appeared to the centurion, Cornelius, a pagan, but fearing God, answered his questions, and discovered to him unknown things, which things came to pass.

Sometimes the angels, without assuming any visible shape, give proofs of their presence by intelligible voices, by inspirations, by sensible effects, by dreams, or by revelations of things unknown, whether future or past. Sometimes by striking with blindness, or infusing a spirit of uncertainty or stupidity in the minds of those whom God wills should feel the effects of his wrath; for instance, it is said in the Scriptures that the Israelites heard no distinct speech, and beheld no form on Horeb when God spoke to Moses, and gave him the Law.

The angel, who might have killed Balaam's ass, was not at first perceived by the prophet; Daniel was the only one who beheld the angel Gabriel, who revealed to him the mystery of the great empires which were to succeed each other.

When the Lord spoke for the first time to Samuel, and predicted to him the evils which he would inflict on the family of the High-priest, Eli, the young prophet saw no visible form; he only heard a voice, which he at first mistook for that of the high priest, Eli, not being yet accustomed to distinguish the voice of God from that of a man.

The angels who guided Lot and his family from Sodom and Gomorrah were at first perceived under a human form by the inhabitants of the city; but afterwards, these same angels struck the men with blindness, and thus prevented them from finding the door of Lot's house, into which they would have entered by force.

Thus, then, angels do not always appear under a visible or sensible form, nor in a figure uniformly the same; but they give proofs of their presence by an infinity of different ways – by inspirations, by voices, by prodigies, by miraculous effects, by predictions of the future, and other things hidden and impenetrable to the human mind.

St Cyprian relates, that an African bishop, falling ill during the persecution, earnestly requested to have the viaticum administered to him; at the same time he saw, as it were, a young man, with a majestic air, and shining with such extraordinary lustre, that the eyes of mortals could not have beheld him without terror; nevertheless, the bishop was not alarmed. This angel said to him angrily, and in a menacing tone, 'You fear to suffer. You do not wish to leave this world. What would you have me do for you?' (or 'What can I do for you?') The good bishop comprehended that these words alike regarded him and the other Christians who feared persecution and death. The bishop talked to them, encouraged them, and exhorted them to arm themselves with patience to support the tortures with which they were threatened. He received the communion, and died in peace. We shall find in different histories an infinite number of other apparitions of angels under a human form.

CHAPTER 4

Opinions of the Jews, Christians, Mahometans,
and Oriental Nations, concerning the
Apparitions of Good Angels.

After what we have just related from the books of the Old and New
Testament, it cannot be disavowed that the Jews in general, the Apostles,
the Christians, and their disciples, have commonly believed in the apparitions of good angels. The Sadducees, who denied the existence and the
apparition of angels, were commonly considered by the Jews as heretics,
and as supporting an erroneous doctrine. Jesus Christ refutes them in the
Gospel. The Jews of our days believe literally what is related in the Old
Testament, concerning the angels who appeared to Abraham, Lot, and
other patriarchs. It was the belief of the Pharisees and of the Apostles in the
time of our Saviour, as may be seen by the writings of the Apostles and by
the whole of the Gospel.

The Mahometans believe, as do the Jews and Christians, that good
angels appear to men sometimes, under a human form; that they appeared
to Abraham and Lot; that they punished the inhabitants of Sodom; that
the archangel Gabriel appeared to Mahomet, and revealed to him all that is
laid down in his Koran: that the Genii are of a middle nature, between man
and angel; that they eat, drink, beget children, that they die, and can
foresee things to come. In consequence of this principle or idea, they
believe that there are male and female Genii; that the males, whom the
Persians call by the name of *Dives*, are bad, very ugly, and mischievous,
making war against the *Peris*, who are the females. The Rabbis will have it
that these Genii were born of Adam alone, without any concurrence of his
wife Eve, or of any other woman, and that they are what we call *ignis fatuii*
(or wandering lights).

The antiquity of these opinions touching the corporality of angels,
appears in several old writers, who, deceived by the apocryphal book
which passes under the name of the *Book of Enoch*, have explained of the
angels what is said in Genesis, '*That the children of God, having seen the*
daughters of men, fell in love with their beauty, wedded them, and begot giants
of them.' Several of the ancient Fathers have adopted this opinion, which is

now given up by everybody, with the exception of some new writers, who desired to revive the idea of the corporality of angels, demons, and souls – an opinion which is absolutely incompatible with that of the Catholic Church, which holds that angels are of a nature entirely distinct from matter.

I acknowledge that, according to their system, the affair of apparitions could be more easily explained; it is easier to conceive that a corporeal substance should appear, and render itself visible to our eyes, than a substance purely spiritual; but this is not the place to reason on a philosophical question, on which different hypotheses could be freely grounded, and to choose that which should explain these appearances in the most plausible manner, even though it answer in the most satisfactory manner the questions asked, and the objections formed against the facts, and against the proposed manner of stating them.

The question is resolved, and the matter decided. The Church and the Catholic schools, hold that angels, demons, and reasonable souls, are disengaged from all matter; the same Church and the same school hold it as certain, that good and bad angels, and souls separated from the body, sometimes appear by the will and with the permission of God: there we must stop; as to the manner of explaining these apparitions, we must, without losing sight of the certain principle of the immateriality of these substances, explain them according to the analogy of the Christian and Catholic faith, acknowledge sincerely that in this matter there are certain depths which we cannot sound, and confine our mind and information within the limits of that obedience which we owe to the authority of the Church, that can neither err nor deceive us.

The apparitions of good angels, and of guardian angels, are frequently mentioned in the Old as in the New Testament. When the Apostle St Peter had left the prison by the assistance of an angel, and went and knocked at the door where the brethren were, they believed that it was his angel and not himself who knocked. And when Cornelius the centurion prayed to God in his own house, an angel (apparently his good angel) appeared to him, and told him to send and fetch Peter, who was then at Joppa.

St Paul desires that at Church no woman should appear among them without her face being veiled, because of the angels, doubtless from respect to the good angels who presided in these assemblies. The same St Paul reassures those who were with him in danger of almost inevitable shipwreck, by telling them that his angel had appeared to him, and assured him that they should arrive safe at the end of their voyage.

In the Old Testament we likewise read of several apparitions of angels, which can hardly be explained but as of guardian angels; for instance, the one who appeared to Hagar in the wilderness, and commanded her to return and submit herself to Sarah her mistress; and the angel who appeared to Abraham, as he was about to immolate Isaac his son, and told him that God was satisfied with his obedience; and when the same Abraham sent his servant Eleazer into Mesopotamia, to ask for a wife for his son Isaac, he told him that the God of heaven, who had promised to give him the land of Canaan, would send his angel to dispose all things according to his wishes. Examples of similar apparitions of tutelary angels, derived from the Old Testament, might here be multiplied, but the circumstance does not require a greater number of proofs.

Under the new dispensation, the apparitions of good angels, of guardian spirits, are not less frequent in most authentic stories; there are few saints to whom God has not granted similar favours: we may cite in particular St Frances, a Roman lady of the sixteenth century, who saw her guardian angel, and he talked to her, instructed her, and corrected her.

CHAPTER 5

Opinion of the Greeks and Romans on the Apparitions of Good Genii

Jamblichus, a disciple of Porphyry, has treated the matter of Genii and their apparition more profoundly than any other author of antiquity. It would seem, to hear him discourse, that he knew both the Genii and their qualities, and that he had with them the most intimate and continual converse. He affirms that our eyes are delighted by the appearance of the gods, that the apparitions of the archangels are terrible; those of angels are milder; but when demons and heroes appear, they inspire terror; the archontes, who preside over this world, cause at the same time an impression of grief and fear. The apparition of souls is not quite so disagreeable as that of heroes. In the appearance of the gods there is order and mildness, confusion and disorder in that of demons, and tumult in that of the archontes.

When the gods show themselves, it seems as if the heavens, the sun and moon, were all about to be annihilated; one would think that the earth could not support their presence. On the appearance of an archangel, there is an earthquake in every part of the world; it is preceded by a stronger light than that which accompanies the apparition of the angels; at the appearance of a demon it is less strong, and diminishes still more when it is a hero who shows himself.

The apparitions of the gods are very luminous; those of angels and archangels less so; those of demons are dark, but less dark than those of heroes. The archontes who preside over the brightest things in this world, are luminous; but those which are occupied only with what is material, are dark. When souls appear, they resemble a shade. He continues his description of these apparitions, and enters into tiresome details on the subject; one would say, to hear him, that there was a most intimate and habitual connexion between the gods, the angels, the demons, and the souls separated from the body, and himself. But all this is only the work of his imagination; he knew no more than any other concerning a matter which is above the reach of man's understanding. He had never seen any apparitions of gods, or heroes, or archontes; unless we say that there are veritable demons which sometimes appear to men. But to discern them one from the other, as Jamblichus pretends to do, is mere illusion.

The Greeks and Romans, like the Hebrews and Christians, acknowledged two sorts of genii, some good and beneficent, the others bad and causing evil. The ancients even believed, that everyone of us received at our birth a good and an evil spirit; the former procured us happiness and prosperity, the latter engaged us in unfortunate enterprises, inspired us with unruly desires, and cast us into the worst misfortunes. They assigned genii, not only to every person, but also to every house, every city, and every province. These genii are considered as good, beneficent and worthy of the worship of those who invoke them. They were represented sometimes under the form of a serpent, sometimes as a child or a youth. Flowers, incense, cakes, and wine were offered to them. Men swore by the names of the genii. It was a great crime to perjure one's self after having sworn by the spirit of the emperor, says Tertullian; *Citius apud vos per omnes Deos, quàm per unicum Genium Caesaris perjuratur.*

We often see on medals the inscription, GENIO POPULI ROMANI; and when the Romans landed in a country, they failed not to salute and adore its spirit, and to offer him sacrifices. In short, there was neither kingdom, nor province, nor town, nor house, nor door, nor edifice, whether public or private, which had not its spirit.

We have seen above, what Jamblichus informs us concerning apparitions of the gods, genii, good and bad angels, heroes, and the archontes who preside over the government of the world.

Homer, the most ancient of Greek writers, and the most celebrated theologian of Paganism, relates several apparitions both of gods and heroes, and also of the dead. In the Odyssey, he represents Ulysses going to consult the sorcerer Tiresias; and this diviner having prepared a grave or trench full of blood to evoke the manes, Ulysses draws his sword to prevent them from coming to drink this blood, for which they thirst, but which they were not allowed to taste before they had answered the questions put to them. They believed also, that the souls of the dead could not rest, and that they wandered around their dead bodies so long as the corpse remained uninhumed.

Even after they were interred, food was offered them; above everything honey was given, as if leaving their tomb they came to taste what was offered them. They were persuaded that the demons loved the smoke of sacrifices, melody, the blood of victims, and intercourse with women; that they were attached for a time to certain spots and certain edifices which they infested. They believed that souls separated from the gross and terrestrial body, preserved after death one more subtle and elastic, having the form of that they had quitted; that these bodies were luminous, and like the stars; that they retained an inclination for those things which they had loved during their life on earth, and that often they appeared gliding around their tombs.

To bring back all this to the matter here treated of, that is to say, to the appearance of good angels, we may note, that in the same manner that we attach to the apparitions of good angels the idea of tutelary spirits of kingdoms, provinces, and nations, and of each of us in particular – as for instance, the Prince of the kingdom of Persia, or the angel of that nation, who resisted the Archangel Gabriel during twenty-one days, as we read in Daniel; the angel of Macedonia, who appeared to St Paul, and of whom we have spoken before; the archangel St Michael, who is considered as the chief of the people of God, and the armies of Israel; and the guardian angels deputed by God to guide us and guard us all the days of our life; so we may say, that the Greeks and Romans being gentiles, believed that certain sorts of spirits, which they imagined were good and beneficent, protected their kingdoms, provinces, towns, and private houses.

They paid them a superstitious and idolatrous worship, as to domestic divinities; they invoked them, offered them a kind of sacrifice and offerings of incense, cakes, honey, and wine, etc. – but not bloody sacrifices.

The Platonicians taught, that carnal and voluptuous men could not see their genii, because their mind was not sufficiently pure, nor enough disengaged from sensual things; but that men who were wise, moderate, and temperate, and who applied themselves to serious and sublime subjects, could see them; as Socrates, for instance, who had his familiar spirit, whom he consulted, to whose advice he listened, and whom he beheld, at least with the eyes of the mind.

If the oracles of Greece and other countries are reckoned in the number of apparitions of bad spirits, we may also recollect the good spirits who have announced things to come, and have assisted the prophets and inspired persons, whether in the Old Testament or the New. The angel Gabriel was sent to Daniel, to instruct him concerning the vision of the four great monarchies, and the accomplishment of the seventy weeks, which were to put an end to the captivity. The prophet Zechariah says expressly, that the angel who appeared unto him, revealed to him what he must say – he repeats it in five or six places; St John, in the Apocalypse, says the same thing, that God had sent his angel to inspire him with what he was to say to the Churches. Elsewhere he again makes mention of the angel who talked with him, and who took in his presence the dimensions of the heavenly Jerusalem. And again, St Paul in his Epistle to the Hebrew, 'If what has been predicted by the angels may pass for certain.'

From all we have just said, it results, that the apparitions of good angels are not only possible, but also very real; that they have often appeared, and under diverse forms; that the Hebrews, Christians, Mahometans, Greeks, and Romans, have believed in them; that when they have not sensibly appeared, they have given proofs of their presence in several different ways. We shall examine elsewhere how we can explain the kind of apparition, whether of good or bad angels, or souls separated from the body.

CHAPTER 6

The Apparition of Bad Angels Proved by the Holy Scriptures – under what Form they have Appeared

The books of the Old and New Testament, together with sacred and profane history, are full of relations of the apparition of bad spirits. The first, the most famous, and the most fatal apparition of Satan, is that of the appearance of this evil spirit to Eve, the first woman, in the form of a serpent, which animal served as the instrument of that seducing demon in order to deceive her and induce her to sin. Since that time he has always chosen to appear under that form rather than any other; so in Scripture he is often termed the Old Serpent; and it is said, that the infernal dragon fought against the woman who figured or represented the Church; that the archangel St Michael vanquished him and cast him down from heaven. He has often appeared to the servants of God in the form of a dragon, and he has caused himself to be adored by unbelievers in this form, in a great number of places: at Babylon, for instance, they worshipped a living dragon, which Daniel killed by making it swallow a ball or bolus, composed of ingredients of a mortally poisonous nature. The Serpent was consecrated to Apollo, the god of physic and of oracles, and the pagans had a sort of divination by means of serpents, which they called *Ophiomantia*.

The Egyptians, Greeks, and Romans worshipped serpents, and regarded them as divine. They brought to Rome the serpent of Epidaurus, to which they paid divine honours. The Egyptians considered vipers as divinities. The Israelites adored the brazen serpent elevated by Moses in the desert, and which was in after times broken in pieces by the holy king Hezekiah.

St Augustine assures us that the Manichaeans regarded the serpent as the Christ, and said that this animal had opened the eyes of Adam and Eve, by the bad counsel which he gave them. We almost always see the form of the serpent in the magical figures *Abraxas* and *Abrachadabra*, which were held in veneration among the Basilidian heretics, who like the Manichaeans acknowledge two principles in all things – the one good, the other bad; *Abraxas* in Hebrew signifies *that bad principle*, or the father of evil; *ab-ra-achad-ab-ra, the father of evil, the sole father of evil,* or the only bad principle.

St Augustine remarks that no animal has been more subject to the effects of enchantment and magic than the serpent, as if to punish him for having seduced the first woman by his imposture.

However, the demon has usually assumed the human form when he would tempt mankind; it was thus that he appeared to Jesus Christ in the desert; that he tempted him and told him to change the stones into bread that he might satisfy his hunger; that he transported him, the Saviour, to the highest pinnacle of the temple, and showed him all the kingdoms of the world, and offered him the enjoyment of them.

The angel who wrestled with Jacob at Peniel on his return from his journey into Mesopotamia, was a bad angel according to some ancient writers; others, as Severus Sulpicius and some Rabbis, have thought that it was the angel of Esau, who had come to combat with Jacob; but the greater number believe that it was a good angel. And would Jacob have asked him for his blessing had he deemed him a bad angel? But however that fact may be taken, it is not doubtful that the demon has appeared in a human form.

Several stories, both ancient and modern, are related, which inform us that the demon has appeared to those whom he wished to seduce, or who have been so unhappy as to invoke his aid, or make a compact with him, as a man taller than the common stature, dressed in black, and with a rough ungracious manner; making a thousand fine promises to those to whom he appeared, but which promises were always deceitful, and never followed by a real effect. I can even believe that they beheld what existed only in their own confused and deranged ideas.

At Molsheim, in the chapel of St Ignatius in the Jesuits' Church, may be seen a celebrated inscription, which contains the history of a young German gentleman, named Michael Louis, of the house of Boubenhoren, who having been sent by his parents when very young to the court of the Duke of Lorraine, to learn the French language, lost all his money at cards; reduced to despair, he resolved to give himself to the demon, if that bad spirit would or could give him some good money; for he doubted that he would only furnish him with counterfeit and bad coin. As he was meditating on this idea, suddenly he beheld before him a youth of his own age, well made, well dressed, who having asked him the cause of his uneasiness, presented him with a handful of money, and told him to try if it was good. He desired him to meet him at that place the next day.

Michael returned to his companions, who were still at play, and not only regained all the money he had lost, but won all that of his companions. Then he went in search of his demon, who asked as his reward three drops of his blood, which he received in an acorn-cup; after which, presenting a pen to Michael, he desired him to write what he should dictate. He then dictated some unknown words, which he made him write on two different bits of paper, one of which remained in the possession of the demon, the other was inserted in Michael's arm, at the same place whence the demon had drawn the blood. And the demon said to him, 'I engage myself to serve you during seven years, after which you will unreservedly belong to me.'

The young man consented to this, though with a feeling of horror; and the demon never failed to appear to him day and night under various forms, and taught him many unknown and curious things, but which always tended to evil. The fatal termination of the seven years was approaching, and the young man was then about twenty years old. He returned to his father's house, when the demon to whom he had given himself inspired him with the idea of poisoning his father and mother, of setting fire to their château, and then killing himself. He tried to commit all these crimes, but God did not allow him to succeed in these attempts. The gun with which he wished to kill himself missed fire twice, and the poison did not take effect on his father and mother.

More and more uneasy, he revealed to some of his father's domestics the miserable state in which he found himself, and entreated them to procure him some succour. At the same time the demon seized him, and bent his body back, so that he was near breaking his bones. His mother, who had adopted the heresy of Suenfeld, and had induced her son to follow it also, not finding in her sect any help against the demon that possessed, or obseded [obsessed] him, was constrained to place him in the hands of some monks. But he soon withdrew from them and retired to Islade, from whence he was brought back to Molsheim by his brother, a canon of Wurzburg, who put him again into the hands of fathers of the society. Then it was that the demon made still more violent efforts against him, appearing to him in the form of ferocious animals. One day, amongst others, the demon, wearing the form of a hairy savage, threw on the ground a schedule, or compact, different from the true one which he had extorted from the young man, to try by means of this false appearance to withdraw him from the hands of those who kept him, and prevent his making his general confession. At last they fixed on the 20th October 1603, as the day for being in the Chapel of St Ignatius, and to cause to be brought the true schedule containing the compact made with the demon. The young man there made profession of the Catholic and orthodox faith, renounced the demon, and received the holy sacrament. Then, uttering horrible cries, he said he saw as it were two he-goats of immeasurable size, which, holding up their fore-feet, (standing on their hind-legs,) held between their claws, each one separately, one of the schedules or agreements. But as soon as the exorcisms were begun, and the priests invoked the name of St Ignatius, the two he-goats fled away, and there came from the left arm or hand of the young man, almost without pain, and without leaving any scar, the compact, which fell at the feet of the exorcist.

There now wanted only the second compact, which had remained in the power of the demon. They recommenced their exorcisms, and invoked St Ignatius, and promised to say a mass in honour of the saint; at the same moment there appeared a tall stork, deformed and badly made, who let fall the second schedule from his beak, and they found it on the altar.

The pope, Paul V, caused information of the truth of these facts to be taken by the commissary deputies, M. Adam, Suffragan of Strasburg, and George, Abbot of Altorf, who were juridically interrogated, and who affirmed that the deliverance of this young man was principally due, after God, to the intercession of St Ignatius.

The same story is related rather more at length in Bartoli's *Life of St Ignatius Loyola*.

Melancthon owns that he has seen several spectres, and conversed with them several times; and Jerome Cardan affirms, that his father, Fassius Cardanus, saw demons whenever he pleased, apparently in a human form. Bad spirits sometimes appear also under the figure of a lion, a dog, or a cat, or some other animal – as a bull, a horse, or a raven; for the pretended sorcerers and sorceresses relate that at the (witches') sabbath he is seen under several different forms of men, animals, and birds; whether he takes the shape of these animals, or whether he makes use of the animals themselves as instruments to deceive or harm, or whether he simply affects the senses and imagination of those whom he has fascinated and who give themselves to him; for in all the appearances of the demon we must always be on our guard, and mistrust his stratagems and malice. St Peter tells us that Satan is always roaming round about us, like a roaring lion, seeking whom he may devour. And St Paul, in more places than one, warns us to mistrust the snares of the devil, and to hold ourselves on our guard against him.

Sulpicius Severus, in the life of St Martin, relates a few examples of persons who were deceived by apparitions of the demon, who transformed himself into an angel of light. A young man of very high rank, and who was afterwads elevated to the priesthood, having devoted himself to God in a monastery, imagined that he held converse with angels; and as they would not believe him, he said that the following night God would give him a white robe, with which he would appear amongst them. In fact, at midnight the monastery was shaken as with an earthquake, the cell of the young man was all brilliant with light, and they heard a noise like that of many persons going to and fro, and speaking.

After that, coming forth from his cell, he showed to the Brothers (of the convent) the tunic with which he was clothed: it was made of a stuff of admirable whiteness, shining as purple, and so extraordinarily fine in texture, that they had never seen anything like it, and could not tell from what substance it was woven.

They passed the rest of the night in singing psalms of thanksgiving, and in the morning they wished to conduct him to St Martin. He resisted as much as he could, saying that he had been expressly forbidden to appear in his presence. As they were pressing him to come, the tunic vanished, which led everyone present to suppose that the whole thing was an illusion of the demon.

Another solitary suffered himself to be persuaded that he was Eli; another, that he was St John the Evangelist. One day, the demon wished to mislead St Martin himself, appearing to him, having on a royal robe, wearing on his head a rich diadem, ornamented with gold and precious stones, golden sandals, and all the apparel of a great prince. Addressing himself to Martin, he said to him, 'Acknowledge me, Martin – I am Jesus Christ, who, wishing to descend to earth, have resolved to manifest myself to thee first of all.' St Martin remained silent at first, fearing some snare; and the phantom having repeated to him that he was the Christ, Martin replied: 'My Lord Jesus Christ did not say that he should come clothed in purple, and decked with diamonds. I shall not acknowledge him unless he appears in that same form in which he suffered death, and unless I see the marks of his cross and passion.'

At these words the demon disappeared; and Sulpicius Severus affirms that he relates this as he heard it from the mouth of St Martin himself. A little before this, he says that Satan showed himself to him sometimes under the form of Jupiter, or Mercury, or Venus, or Minerva; and sometimes he was to reproach Martin greatly because, by baptism, he had converted and regenerated so many great sinners. But the saint despised him, drove him away by the sign of the cross, and answered him, that baptism and repentance effaced all sins in those who were sincere converts.

All this proves the malice, envy, and fraud of the devil against the saints, on the one side; and on the other, the weakness and uselessness of his efforts against the true servants of God, and that it is but too true he often appears in a visible form.

In the histories of the saints we sometimes see that he hides himself under the form of a woman, to tempt pious hermits, and lead them into evil; sometimes in the form of a traveller, a priest, a monk, or an angel of light, to mislead simple-minded people, and cause them to err; for everything suits his purpose, provided he can exercise his malice and hatred against men.

When Satan appeared before the Lord in the midst of his holy angels, and asked permission of God to tempt Job, and try his patience through everything that was dearest to that holy man, he doubtless presented himself in his natural state, simply as a spirit, but full of rage against the saints, and in all the deformity of his sin and rebellion.

But when he says, in the Books of Kings, that he will be a lying spirit in the mouth of false prophets, and that God allows him to put in force his ill will, we must not imagine that he shows himself corporeally to the eyes of the false prophets of King Ahab; he only inspired the falsehood in their minds – they believed it, and persuaded the king of the same. Amongst the visible appearances of Satan may be placed mortalities, wars, tempests, public and private calamities, which God sends upon nations, provinces, cities, and families, whom the Almighty causes to feel the terrible effects of his wrath and just vengeance. Thus the exterminating angel kills the first-born of the Egyptians. The same angel strikes with death the inhabitants of the guilty cities of Sodom and Gomorrah. He does the same with Onan, who committed an abominable action. The wicked man seeks only division and quarrels, says the sage; and the cruel angel shall be sent against him. And the Psalmist, speaking of the plagues which the Lord inflicted upon Egypt, says, that he sent evil angels among them.

When David, in a spirit of vanity, caused his people to be numbered, God showed him an angel hovering over Jerusalem, ready to smite and destroy it. I do not say decidedly whether it was a good or a bad angel, since it is certain that sometimes the Lord employs good angels to execute his vengeance against the wicked. But it is thought that it was the devil who slew eighty-five thousand men of the army of Sennacherib. And in the Apocalypse, those are also evil angels who pour out on the earth the phials of wrath, and caused all the scourges set down in that holy book.

We shall also place amongst the appearances and works of Satan, false Christs, false prophets, pagan oracles, magicians, sorcerers, and sorceresses, those who are inspired by the spirit of Python, the obsession and possession of demons, those who pretend to predict the future, and whose predictions are sometimes fulfilled; those who make compacts with the devil, to discover treasures and enrich themselves; those who make use of charms; evocations by means of magic; enchantment; the being devoted to death by a vow; the deceptions of idolatrous priests, who feigned that their gods ate and drank and had commerce with women – all these can only be the work of Satan, and must be ranked with what the Scripture calls the depths of Satan. We shall say something on this subject in the course of the Treatise.

CHAPTER 7

Of Magic

Many persons regard magic, magicians, witchcraft, and charms, as fables and illusions, the effects of imagination in weak minds, who, foolishly persuaded of the excessive power possessed by the devil, attribute to him a thousand things which are purely natural, but the physical reasons for which are unknown to them, or which are the effects of the art of certain charlatans, who make a trade of imposing on the simple and ignorant. These opinions are supported by the authority of the principal parliaments of the kingdom, who acknowledge neither magicians nor sorcerers, and who never punish those accused of magic, or sorcery, unless they are convicted also of some other crimes. As, in short, the more they punish and seek out magicians and sorcerers, the more they abound in a country; and, on the contrary, experience proves that in places where nobody believes in them, none are to be found, the most efficacious means of uprooting this fancy is to despise and neglect it.

It is said that magicians and sorcerers themselves, when they fall into the hands of judges and inquisitors, are often the first to maintain that magic and sorcery are merely imaginary, and the effect of popular prejudices and errors. Upon that footing, Satan would destroy himself, and overthrow his own empire, if he were thus to decry magic, of which he is himself the author and support. If the magicians really, and of their own good will, independently of the demon, make this declaration, they betray themselves most lightly, and do not make their cause better; since the judges, notwithstanding their disavowal, prosecute them, and always punish them without mercy, being well persuaded that it is only the fear of execution and the hope of remaining unpunished which makes them say so.

But would it not rather be a stratagem of the evil spirit, who endeavours to render the reality of magic doubtful, to save from punishment those who are accused of it, and to impose on the judges, and make them believe that magicians are only madmen and hypochondriacs, worthy rather of compassion than chastisement? We must then return to the deep examination of the question, and prove that magic is not a chimera, neither has it aught to do with reason. We can neither rest on a sure foundation, nor derive any certain argument for or against the reality of magic, either from the opinion of pretended *esprits forts*, who deny because they think proper to do so, and because the proofs of the contrary do not appear to them sufficiently clear or demonstrative; nor from the declaration of the demon, of magicians and sorcerers, who maintain that magic and sorcery are only the effects of a disturbed imagination; nor from minds foolishly and vainly prejudiced on the subject, that these declarations are produced simply by the fear of punishment; nor by the subtlety of the malignant spirit, who wishes to mask his play, and cast dust in the eyes of the judges and witnesses, by making them believe that what they regard with so much horror, and what they so vigorously prosecute, is anything but a punishable crime, or at least a crime deserving of punishment.

We must then prove the reality of magic by the Holy Scriptures, by the authority of the Church, and by the testimony of the most grave and sensible writers; and, lastly, show that it is not true that the most famous parliaments acknowledge neither sorcerers nor magicians.

The teraphim which Rachel the wife of Jacob brought away secretly from the house of Laban, her father, were doubtless superstitious figures, to which Laban's family paid a worship, very like that which the Romans rendered to their household gods, *Penates* and *Lares*, and whom they consulted on future events. Joshua says very distinctly, that Terah the father of Abraham adored strange gods in Mesopotamia. And in the prophets Hosea and Zechariah, the Seventy translate *teraphim* by the word *oracles*. Zechariah and Ezekiel show that the Chaldeans and the Hebrews consulted these teraphim to learn future events.

Others believe that they were talismans or preservatives; everybody agrees as to their being superstitious figures (or idols), which were consulted in order to find out things unknown, or that were to come to pass.

The patriarch Joseph, speaking to his own brethhren according to the idea which they had of him in Egypt, says to them: 'Know ye not that in all the land there is not a man who equals me in the art of divining and predicting things to come?' And the officer of the same Joseph, having found in Benjamin's sack, Joseph's cup, which he had purposely hidden in it, says to them: 'It is the cup of which my master makes use to discover hidden things.'

By the secret of their art, the magicians of Pharaoh imitated the true miracles of Moses; but not being able like him to produce gnats (English version lice), they were constrained to own that the finger of God was in what Moses had hitherto achieved.

After the departure of the Hebrews from Egypt, God expressly forbids his people to practise any sort of magic or divination. He condemns to death magicians, and those who make use of charms.

Balaam the Diviner, being invited by Balak the king to come and devote [doom] the Israelites to destruction, God put blessings into his mouth instead of curses; and this bad prophet, amongst the blessings which he bestows on Israel, says, there is among them neither augury, nor divination, nor magic.

In the time of the Judges, the idol of Micah was consulted as a kind of oracle. Gideon made, in his house and his city, an Ephod, accompanied by a superstitious image, which was for his family, and to all the people, the occasion of scandal and ruin.

The Israelites went sometimes to consult Beelzebub, god of Ekron, to know if they should recover from their sickness. The history of the evocation of Samuel by the witch of Endor is well known. I am aware that some difficulties are raised concerning this history. I shall deduce nothing from it here, except that this woman passed for a witch, that Saul esteemed her such, and that this prince had exterminated the magicians in his own states, or, at least, that he did not permit them to exercise their art.

Manasses, king of Judah, is blamed for having introduced idolatry into his kingdom, and particularly for having allowed there diviners, aruspices, and those who predicted things to come. King Josiah, on the contrary, destroyed all these superstitions.

The prophet Isaiah, who lived at the same time, says that they wished to persuade the Jews then in captivity at Babylon to address themselves, as did other nations, to diviners and magicians; but they ought to reject these pernicious counsels, and leave those abominations to the Gentiles, who knew not the Lord. Daniel speaks of the magicians, or workers of magic among the Chaldeans, and of those amongst them who interpreted dreams, and predicted things to come.

In the New Testament, the Jews accused Jesus Christ of casting out devils in the name of Beelzebub, the prince of the devils; but he refutes them by saying, that being come to destroy the empire of Beelzebub, it was not to be believed that Beelzebub would work miracles to destroy his own power, or kingdom. St Luke speaks of Simon the sorcerer, who had for a long time bewitched the inhabitants of Samaria with his sorceries; and also of a certain Bar-Jesus of Paphos, who professed sorcery, and boasted he could predict future events. St Paul, when at Ephesus, caused a number of books of magic to be burned. Lastly, the Psalmist and the author of the Book of Ecclesiasticus, speak of charms with which they enchanted serpents.

In the Acts of the Apostles, the young girl of the town of Philippi, who was a Pythoness, for several successive days rendered testimony to Paul and Silas, saying that they were 'the servants of the Most High, and that they announced to men the way of salvation'. Was it the devil who inspired her with these words, to destroy the fruit of the preaching of the Apostles, by making the people believe that they acted in concert with the spirit of evil? Or was it the Spirit of God which put these words into the mouth of this young girl, as he put into the mouth of Balaam prophecies concerning the Messiah? There is reason to believe that she spoke through the inspiration of the evil spirit, since St Paul imposed silence on her, and expelled the spirit of Python, by which she had been possessed, and which had inspired the predictions she uttered, and the knowledge of hidden things. In what way soever we may explain it, it will always follow that magic is not a chimera, that this maiden was possessed by an evil spirit, and that she predicted and revealed things hidden and to come, and brought her masters considerable gain by soothsaying; for those who consulted her would, doubtless, not have been so foolish as to pay for these predictions, had they not experienced the truth of them by their success and by the event.

From all this united testimony it results that magic, enchantments, sorcery, divination, the interpretation of dreams, auguries, oracles, and the magical figures which announced things to come, are very real, since they are so severely condemned by God, and that He wills that those who practise them should be punished with death.

CHAPTER 8

Objections to the Reality of Magic

I shall not fail to be told that all these testimonies from Scripture do not prove the reality of magic, sorcery, divination, and the rest; but only that the Hebrews and Egyptians, I mean the common people among them, believed that there were people who had intercourse with the Divinity, or with good and bad angels, to predict the future, explain dreams, devote their enemies to the direst misfortunes, cause maladies, raise storms, and call forth the souls of the dead; if there was any reality in all this, it was not in the things themselves, but in their imaginations and prepossessions.

Moses and Joseph were regarded by the Egyptians as great magicians. Rachel, it appears, believed that the teraphim of her father Laban were capable of giving her information concerning things hidden and to come. The Israelites might consult the idol of Micah, and Beelzebub the god of Ekron; but the sensible and enlightened people of those days, like similar persons in our own, considered all this as the sport and knavery of pretended magicians, who derived much emolument from maintaining these prejudices among the people.

Moses most wisely ordained the penalty of death against those persons who abused the simplicity of the ignorant to enrich themselves at their expense, and turned away the people from the worship of the true God, in order to keep up among them such practices as were superstitious and contrary to true religion.

Besides, it was necessary to good order, the interests of the commonwealth and of true piety, to repress those abuses which are in opposition to them, and to punish with extreme severity those who draw away the people from the true and legitimate worship due to God, lead them to worship the devil, and place their confidence in the creature, in prejudice to the right of the Creator; inspiring them with vain terrors, where there is nothing to fear, and maintaining their minds in the most dangerous errors. If amongst an infinite number of false predictions, or vain interpretations of dreams, some of them are fulfilled, either this is occasioned by chance, or it is the work of the devil, who is often permitted by God to deceive those whose foolishness and impiety lead them to address themselves to him and place their confidence in him, all which the wise lawgiver, animated by the divine Spirit, justly repressed by the most rigorous punishment.

All histories and experience on this subject, demonstrate that those who make use of the art of magic, charms, and spells, only employ their art, their secret, and their power, to corrupt and mislead; for crime and vice; thus they cannot be too carefully sought out or too severely punished.

We may add, that what is often taken for black or diabolical magic, is nothing but natural magic, or art and cleverness on the part of those who perform things which appear above the force of nature. How many marvellous effects are related of the divining rod, sympathetic powder, phosphoric lights, and mathematical secrets! How much knavery is now well known in the priests of idols, and in those of Babylon, who made the people believe that the god Bel drank and ate; that a large living dragon was a divinity; that the god Anubis desired to have certain women, who were thus deceived by the priests; that the ox Apis gave out oracles, and that the serpent of Alexander of Abonotiche knew the sickness, and gave remedies to the patient without opening the billet which contained a description of the illness! We may possibly speak more fully on this subject hereafter.

In short, the most judicious and most celebrated parliaments have recognised neither magicians nor sorcerers, at least, they have not condemned them to death unless they were convicted of other crimes, such as theft, bad practices, poisoning, or criminal seduction; for instance, in the affair of Gaufredi, a priest of Marseilles, who was condemned by the parliament of Aix to be torn with hot pincers, and burnt alive. The heads of that company, in the account which they render to the chancellor of this their sentence, testify that this curé was in truth accused of sorcery, but that he had been condemned to the flames as guilty and convicted of spiritual incest with his penitent, Madelaine de la Palud. From all this it is concluded that there is no reality in what is called magic.

CHAPTER 9

Reply to the Objections

In answer to these, I allow that there is indeed very often a great deal of illusion, prepossession, and imagination in all that is termed magic and sorcery; and sometimes the devil by false appearances combines with them to deceive the simple; but oftener, without the evil spirit being any otherwise a party to it, wicked, corrupt, and interested men, artful and deceptive, abuse the simplicity both of men and women, so far as to persuade them that they possess supernatural secrets for interpreting dreams and foretelling things to come, for curing maladies, and discovering secrets unknown to anyone; I can easily agree to all that. All kinds of histories are full of facts which demonstrate what I have just said. The devil has a thousand things imputed to him in which he has no share; they give him the honour of predictions, revelations, secrets, and discoveries, which are by no means the effect of his power, or penetration; as in the same manner he is accused of having caused all sorts of evils, tempests, and maladies, which are purely the effect of natural but unknown causes.

It is very true that there are really many persons who are persuaded of the power of the devil, of his influence over an infinite number of things, and of the effects which they attribute to him; that they have consulted him to learn future events, or to discover hidden things; that they have addressed themselves to him for success in their projects, for money, or favour, or to enjoy their criminal pleasures. All this is very real. Magic, then, is not a simple chimera, since so many persons are infatuated with the power of charms and convicted of holding commerce with the devil, to procure a number of effects which pass for supernatural. Now it is the folly, the vain credulity, the prepossession of such people that the law of God interdicts, that Moses condemns to death, and that the Christian Church punishes by its censures, and which the secular judges repress with the greatest rigour. If in all these things there was nothing but a diseased imagination, weakness of the brain, or popular prejudices, would they be treated with so much severity? Do we put to death hypochondriacs, maniacs, or those who imagine themselves ill? No, they are treated with compassion, and every effort is made to cure them. But in the other case, it is impiety, or superstition, or vice, in those who consult, or believe they consult the devil, and place their confidence in him, against which the laws are put in force and ordain chastisement.

Even if we could deny and contest the reality of augurs, diviners, and magicians, and look on all these kind of persons, as seducers, who abuse the simplicity of those who betake themselves to them, could we deny the reality of the magicians of Pharaoh, that of Simon, of Bar-Jesus, of the Pythoness of the Acts of the Apostles? Did not the first mentioned perform many wonders before Pharaoh? Did not Simon the magician rise into the air by means of the devil? Did not St Paul impose silence on the Pythoness of the city of Philippi in Macedonia? Will it be said that there was any collusion between St Paul and the Pythoness? Nothing of the kind can be maintained by any reasonable argument.

A small volume was published at Paris in 1732, by a new author, who conceals himself under the two initials M. D.; it is entitled, *Treatise on*

Magic, Witchcraft, Possessions, Obsessions and Charms; in which their truth and reality are demonstrated. He shows that he believes there are magicians; he shows by Scripture, both in the Old and New Testament, and by the authority of the ancient fathers, some passages from whose works are cited in that of Father Debrio, entitled *Disquisitiones Magicoe.* He proves it by the rituals of all the dioceses, and by the examinations which are found in the printed 'Hours,' wherein they suppose the existence of sorcerers and magicians.

The civil laws of the emperors, whether pagan or christian, those of the kings of France, both ancient and modern, jurisconsult, physicians, historians both sacred and profane, concur in maintaining this truth. In all kinds of writers we may remark an infinity of stories of magic, spells, and sorcery. The parliaments of France, and the tribunals of justice in other nations, have recognised magicians, the pernicious effects of their art, and condemned them personally to the most rigorous punishments.

He relates at full length the remonstrances made to King Louis XIV in 1670 by the parliament at Rouen, to prove to that monarch, that it was not only the parliament of Rouen, but also all the other parliaments of the kingdom, which followed the same rules of jurisprudence in what concerns magic and sorcery, that they acknowledged the existence of such things, and condemn them. This author cites several facts, and several sentences given on this matter in the parliaments of Paris, Aix, Toulouse, Rennes, Dijon, etc. etc.; and it was upon these remonstrances that the same king in 1682 made his declaration concerning the punishment of various crimes, and in particular, of sorcery, diviners or soothsayers, magicians, and similar crimes.

He also cites the treaty of M. de la Marre, commissary at the *châtelet* of Paris, who speaks largely of magic, and proves its reality, origin, progress, and effects. Would it be possible that the sacred authors, laws divine and human, the greatest men of antiquity, jurisconsults, the most enlightened historians, bishops in their councils, the Church in her decisions, her practices and prayers, should have conspired to deceive us, and to condemn those who practise magic, sorcery, spells, and crimes of the same nature, to death, and the most rigorous punishments, if they were merely illusive, and the effect only of a diseased and prejudiced imagination? Father le Brun, of the Oratoire, who has written so well upon the subject of superstitions, substantiates the fact that the parliament of Paris recognises that there are sorcerers, and that it punishes them severely when they are convicted. He proves it by a decree issued in 1601 against some inhabitants of Champagne accused of witchcraft. The decree wills that they shall be sent to the Conciergerie by the subaltern judges on pain of being deprived of their charge. It supposes that they must be rigorously punished, but it desires that the proceedings against them for their discovery and punishment may be exact and regular.

M. Servin, advocate general and councillor of state, fully proves from the Old and New Testament, from tradition, laws and history, that there are diviners, enchanters, and sorcerers, and refutes those who would maintain the contrary. He shows that magicians and those who make use of charms, ought to be punished and held in execration; but he adds that no punishment must be inflicted till after certain and evident proofs have been obtained; and this is what must be strictly attented to by the parliament of Paris, for fear of punishing madmen for guilty persons, and taking illusions for realities.

The parliament leaves it to the Church to inflict excommunication, both on men and women who have recourse to charms, and who believe they go in the night to nocturnal assemblies, there to pay homage to the devil. The Capitularies of the kings recommend the pastors to instruct the faithful on the subject of what is termed the Sabbath; at any rate they do not command that these persons should receive corporeal punishment, but only that they should be undeceived and prevented from misleading others in the same manner.

And there the parliament stops, so long as the case goes no further than simply misleading; but when it goes so far as to injure others, the kings have often commanded the judges to punish these persons with fines and banishment. The Ordonnances of Charles VIII in 1490, and of Charles IX in the states of Orleans in 1560, express themselves formally on this point, and they were renewed by King Louis XIV in 1682. The third article of these Ordonnances, bears, that if it should happen '*there were persons to be found wicked enough to add impiety and sacrilege to superstition, those who shall be convicted of these crimes shall be punished with death.*'

When, therefore, it is evident that some person has inflicted injury on his neighbour by malpractices, the parliament punishes them rigorously, even to the pain of death, conformably to the ancient Capitularies of the kingdom, and the royal Ordonnances. Bodin, who wrote in 1680, has collected a great number of decrees, to which may be added those which the reverend Father le Brun reports, given since that time.

He afterwards relates a remarkable instance of a man named Hocque, who was condemned to the galleys, the 2nd September 1687, by sentence of the high court of justice at Passy, for having made use of malpractices towards animals, and having thus killed a great number in Champagne. Hocque died suddenly, miserably, and in despair, after having discovered, when drunken with wine, to a person named Beatrice, the secret which he made use of to kill the cattle; he was not ignorant that the demon would cause his death, to revenge the discovery which he had made of this spell.

Some of the accomplices of this wretched man were condemned to the galleys by divers decrees; others were condemned to be hanged and burnt, by order of the Baillé of Passy, the 26th October 1691, which sentence was confirmed by decree of the parliament of Paris, the 18th December 1691. From all which we deduce that the parliament of Paris acknowledges that the spells by which people do injury to their neighbours ought to be rigorously punished; that the devil has very extensive power which he too often exercises over men and animals, and that he would exercise it oftener, and with greater extension and fury, if he were not limited and hindered by the power of God, and that of good angels, who set bounds to his malice. St Paul warns us to put on the armour of God, to be able to resist the snares of the devil: for, adds he, 'we have not to war against flesh and blood: but against princes and powers, against the bad spirits who govern this dark world, against the spirits of malice who reign in the air.'

CHAPTER 10

Examination of the Affair of Hocque, Magician

Monsieur de St André, consulting physician in ordinary to the king, in his sixth letter against magic, maintains that in the affair of Hocque which has been mentioned, there was neither magic, nor sorcery, nor any operation of the demon; that the venomous drug which Hocque placed in the stables, and by means of which he caused the death of the cattle stalled therein, was nothing but a poisonous compound which, by its smell and the diffusion of its particles, poisoned the animals and caused their death; it required only for these drugs to be taken away, for the cattle to be safe, or else to keep the cattle from the stable in which the poison was placed. The difficulty lay in discovering where these poisonous drugs were hidden; the shepherds, who were the authors of the mischief, taking all sorts of precautions to conceal them, knowing that their lives were in danger if they should be discovered.

He further remarks, that these *gogues* or poisoned drugs lose their effects after a certain time, unless they are renewed or watered with something to revive them and make them ferment again. If the devil had any share in this mischief, the drug would always possess the same virtue, and it would not be necessary to renew it and refresh it, to restore it to its pristine power.

In all this, M. de St André supposes that if the demon had any power to deprive animals of their lives, or to cause them fatal maladies, he could do so independently of secondary causes; which will not be easily granted him by those who hold that God alone can give life and death by an absolute power, independently of all secondary causes and of any natural agent. The demon might have revealed to Hocque the composition of this fatal and poisonous drug – he might have taught him its dangerous effects, after which the venom acts in a natural way; it recovers and resumes its pristine strength when it is watered; it acts only at a certain distance, and according to the reach of the corpuscules which exhale from it. All these effects have nothing supernatural in them, nor which ought to be attributed to the demon; but it is credible enough, that he inspired Hocque with the pernicious design to make use of a dangerous drug, which the wretched man knew how to make up, or the composition of which was revealed to him by the evil spirit.

M. de St André continues, and says, that there is nothing in the death of Hocque which ought to be attributed to the demon; it is, says he, a purely natural effect, which can proceed from no other cause than the venomous effluvia which came from the poisonous drug when it was taken up, and which were carried towards the malefactor by those which proceeded from his own body while he was preparing it, and placing it in the ground, which remained there and were preserved in that spot, so that none of them had been dissipated.

These effluvia proceeding from the person of Hocque, then finding themselves liberated, returned to whence they originated, and drew with them the most malignant and corrosive particles of the charge or drug, which acted on the body of this shepherd as they did on those of the animals who smelled them. He confirms what he has just said, by the example of sympathetic powder which acts upon the body of a wounded person, by the immersion of small particles of the blood, or the pus of the wounded man upon whom it is applied, which particles draw with them the spirit of the drugs of which it (the powder) is composed, and carry them to the wound.

But the more I reflect on this pretended evaporation of the venomous effluvia emanating from the poisoned drug, hidden at Passy en Brie, six leagues from Paris, which are supposed to come straight to Hocque, shut up at la Tournelle, borne by the animal effluvia proceeding from this malefactor's body at the time he made up the poisonous drug and put it in the ground, so long before the dangerous composition was discovered; the more I reflect on the possibility of these evaporations, the less I am persuaded of them; I could wish to have proofs of this system, and not instances of the very doubtful and very uncertain effects of sympathetic powder, which can have no place in the case in question. It is proving the obscure by the obscure, and the uncertain by the uncertain; and even were we to admit generally some effects of the sympathetic powder, they could not be applicable here; the distance between the places is too great, and the time too long; and what sympathy can be found between this shepherd's poisonous drug and his person, for it to be able to return to him who is imprisoned at Paris, when the *gogue* is discovered at Passy?

The account composed and printed on this event, bears, that the fumes of the wine which Hocque had drank, having evaporated, and he reflecting on what Beatrice had made him do, began to agitate himself, howled, and complained most strangely, saying that Beatrice had taken him by surprise, that it would occasion his death, and that he must die the instant that Bras-de-fer, another shepherd, to whom Beatrice had persuaded Hocque to write word to take off the poisoned drug, which he had scattered on the ground, at Passy, should take away the dose. He attacked Beatrice, whom he wanted to strangle, and even excited the other felons who were with him in prison, and condemned to the galleys, to maltreat her, through the pity they felt for the despair of Hocque, who, at the time the dose was taken off the land, had died in a moment, in strange convulsions, and agitating himself like one possessed.

M. de St André would again explain all this, by supposing Hocque's imagination being struck with the idea of his dying, which he was persuaded would happen at the time they carried away the poison, had a great deal to do with his sufferings and death. How many people have been known to die at the time they had fancied they should, when struck with the idea of their approaching death. The despair and agitation of Hocque had disturbed the mass of his blood, altered the humours, deranged the motion of the effluvia, and rendered them much susceptible of the actions of the vapours proceeding from the poisonous composition.

M. de St André adds, that if the devil had had any share in this kind of mischievous spell, it could only be in consequence of some compact, either expressed or tacit, that as soon as the poison should be taken up, he who had put it there should die immediately. Now what likelihood is there that the person who should make this compact with the devil, should have made use of such a stipulation, which would expose him to a cruel and inevitable death?

1 We may reply, that fright can cause death; but that it is not possible for it to produce it at a given time, nor can he who falls into a paroxysm of grief, say that he shall die at such a moment: the moment of death is not in the power of man in similar circumstances.

2 That so corrupt a character as Hocque, a man who without provocation, and to gratify his ill will, kills an infinite number of animals, and causes great damage to innocent persons, is capable of the greatest excess, may

give himself up to the evil spirit, by implicated or explicit compacts, and engage, on pain of losing his life, never to take off the charge he had thrown upon a village. He believed he should risk nothing by this stipulation, since he was free to take it away or to leave it, and it was not probable that he should ever lightly thus expose himself to certain death. That the demon had some share in this virtue of the poisonous composition is very likely, when we consider the circumstances of its operations, and those of the death and despair of Hocque. This death is the just penalty of his crimes, and of his confidence in the exterminating angel to whom he had yielded himself.

It is true that impostors, weak minds, heated imaginations, ignorant and superstitious persons, have been found, who have taken for black magic, and operations of the demon, what was quite natural, and the effect of some subtlety of philosophy or mathematics, or even an illusion of the senses, or a secret which deceives the eye and the senses. But to conclude from thence that there is no magic at all, and that all that is said about it is pure prejudice, ignorance, and superstition, is to conclude what is general from what is particular, and to deny what is true and certain, because it is not easy to distinguish what is true from what is false, and because men will not take the trouble to examine into causes. It is far easier to deny everything than to enter upon a serious examination of facts and circumstances.

CHAPTER 11

Magic of the Egyptians and Chaldeans

All Pagan antiquity speaks of magic and magicians, of magical operations, and of superstitious, curious, and diabolical books. Historians, poets, and orators, are full of things which relate to this matter; some believe in it, others deny it; some laugh at it, others remain in uncertainty and doubt. Are they bad spirits, or deceitful men, impostors and charlatans, who, by the subtleties of their art, make the ignorant believe that certain natural effects are produced by supernatural causes? That is the point on which men differ. But in general, the name of magic and magician is now taken in these days in an odious sense, for an art which produces marvellous effects, that appear above the common course of nature; and that by the operation of the bad spirit.

The author of the celebrated *Book of Enoch*, which had so great a vogue, and has been cited by some ancient writers as inspired Scripture, says that the eleventh of the watchers, or of those angels who were in love with women, was called Pharmacius or Pharmachus; that he taught men, before the flood, enchantments, spells, magic arts, and remedies against enchantments. St Clement of Alexandria, in his Recognitions, says that Ham the son of Noah received that art from heaven, and taught it to Misraim his son, the father of the Egyptians.

In the Scripture, the name of *Mage* or *Magus* is never used in a good sense as signifying philosophers who studied astronomy, and were versed in divine and supernatural things, except in speaking of the Magi who came to adore Jesus Christ at Bethlehem. Everywhere else the Scriptures condemn and abhor magic and magicians. They severely forbid the Hebrews to consult such persons and things. They speak with abhorrence of Simon and of Elymas, well-known magicians, in the Acts of the Apostles; and of the magicians of Pharaoh, who counterfeited by their illusions the true miracles of Moses. It seems likely that the Israelites had taken the habit in Egypt, where they then were, of consulting such persons, since Moses forbids them in so many different places, and so severely, either to listen to them, or to place confidence in their predictions.

The Chevalier Marsham shows very clearly that the school for magic among the Egyptians, is the most ancient ever known in the world; that from thence it spread amongst the Chaldeans, the Babylonians, the Greeks and Persians. St Paul informs us that Jannès and Jambrès, famous magicians of the time of Pharaoh, resisted Moses. Pliny remarks, that anciently, there was no science more renowned, or more in honour, than that of magic: *Summam litterarum claritatem gloriamque ex ea scientia antiquitùs et penè semper petitam.*

Porphyry says that King Darius, son of Hystaspes, had so high an idea of the art of magic, that he caused to be engraved on the mausoleum of his father Hystaspes, 'That he had been the chief and the master of the magi of Persia.'

The embassy that Balak, king of the Moabites, sent to Balaam the son of Beor, who dwelt in the mountains of the East, towards Persia and Chaldea, to entreat him to come and curse and devote to death the Israelites, who threatened to invade his country, shows the antiquity of magic, and of the magical superstitions of that country. For will it be said that these maledictions and inflictions were the effect of the inspiration of the good Spirit, or the work of good angels? I acknowledge that Balaam was inspired by God in the blessings which he gave to the people of the Lord, and in the prediction which he made of the coming of the Messiah; but we must acknowledge, also, the extreme corruption of his heart, his avarice, and all that he would have been capable of doing, if God had permitted him to follow his bad inclination and the inspiration of the evil spirit.

Diodorus of Sicily, on the tradition of the Egyptians, says, that the Chaldeans who dwelt at Babylon and in Babylonia, were a kind of colony of the Egyptians, and that it was from these last that the sages, or magi of Babylon, learned the astronomy which gave them such celebrity.

We see, in Ezekiel, the king of Babylon, marching against his enemies at the head of his army, stop short where two roads meet, and mingle the darts, to know by magic art, and the flight of these arrows, which road he must take. In the ancients, this manner of consulting the demon by divining wands is known – the Greeks call it *Rhabdomanteia*.

The prophet Daniel speaks more than once of the magicians of Babylon; King Nebuchadnezzar having been frightened in a dream, sent for the magi, or magicians, diviners, aruspices, and Chaldeans, to interpret the dream he had had.

King Belshazzar in the same manner convoked the magicians, Chaldeans, and aruspices of the country, to explain to him the meaning of these words which he saw written on the wall: *Mene, Tekel, Perez*. All this indicates the habit of the Babylonians to exercise magic art, and consult magicians, and that this pernicious art was held in high repute among them. We read in the same Prophet, of the trickery made use of by the priests to deceive the people, and make them believe that their gods lived, ate, drunk, spoke, and revealed to them hidden things.

I have already mentioned the magi who came to adore Jesus Christ; there is no doubt that they came from Chaldea or the neighbouring country, but differing from those of whom we have just spoken, by their piety, and having studied the true religion.

We read in books of travels, that superstition, magic, and fascinations, are still very common in the East, both among the fire-worshippers, descended from the ancient Chaldeans, and among the Persians, sectaries of Mahomet. St Chrysostom had sent into Persia a holy bishop, named Maruthas, to have the care of the Christians who were in that country; the king Isdegerde having discovered him, treated him with much consideration. The magi, who adore and keep up the perpetual fire, which is regarded by the Persians as their principal divinity, were jealous at this, and concealed underground an apostate, who, knowing that the king was to come and pay his adoration to the sacred fire, was to cry out from the depth of his cavern, that the king must be deprived of his throne because he esteemed the Christian priest as a friend of the gods. The king was alarmed at this, and wished to send Maruthas away; but the latter discovered to him the imposture of the priests: he caused the ground to be turned up where the man's voice had been heard, and there they found him from whom it proceeded.

This example, and those of the Babylonish priests spoken of by Daniel, and that of some others, who, to satisfy their irregular passions, pretended that their God required the company of certain women, prove that what is usually taken for the effect of the black art, is only produced by the knavishness of priests, magicians, diviners, and all kinds of persons who impose on the simplicity and credulity of the people; I do not deny that the devil sometimes takes part in it, but more rarely than is imagined.

CHAPTER 12

Magic Among the Greeks and Romans

The Greeks have always boasted that they received the art of magic from the Persians, or the Bactrians. They affirm that Zoroaster communicated it to them; but when we wish to know the exact time at which Zoroaster lived, and when he taught them these pernicious secrets, they wander widely from the truth, and even from probability; some placing Zoroaster 600 years before the expedition of Xerxes into Greece, which happened in the year of the world 3523, and before Jesus Christ 477; others 500 years before the Trojan war; others 5000 years before that famous war; others 6000 years before that great event. Some believe that Zoroaster is the same as Ham, the son of Noah. Lastly, others maintain that there were several Zoroasters. What appears indubitably true, is, that the worship of a plurality of gods, as also magic, superstition, and oracles, came from the Egyptians and Chaldeans, or Persians, to the Greeks, and from the Greeks to the Latins.

From the time of Homer, magic was quite common among the Greeks. That poet speaks of the cure of wounds, and of blood staunched by the secrets of magic, and by enchantment. St Paul, when at Ephesus, caused to be burned there books of magic and curious secrets, the value of which amounted to the sum of 50,000 pieces of silver. We have before said a few words concerning Simon the magician, and the magician Elymas, known in the Acts of the Apostles. Pindar says, that the centaur Chiron cured several enchantments. When they say that Orpheus rescued from hell his wife Eurydice, who had died from the bite of a serpent, they simply mean that he cured her by the power of charms. The poets have employed magic verses to make themselves beloved, and they have taught them to others for the same purpose; they may be seen in Theocritus, Catullus, and Virgil.

Theophrastus affirms that there are magical verses which cure sciatica. Cato mentions (or repeats) some against luxations [dislocation of joints]. Varro admits that there are some powerful against the gout.

The sacred books testify that enchanters have the secret of putting serpents to sleep, and of charming them, so that they can never either bite again, or cause any more harm. The crocodile, that terrible animal, fears even the smell and voice of the Tentyriens. Job, speaking of the leviathan, which we believe to be the crocodile, says, 'Shall the enchanter destroy it?' And in Ecclesiasticus, 'Who will pity the enchanter that has been bitten by the serpent?'

Everybody knows what is related of the Marsi, people of Italy, and of the Psyllae, who possessed the secret of charming serpents. One would say, says St Augustine, that these animals understand the languages of the Marsi, so obedient are they to their orders; we see them come out of their caverns as soon as the Marsian has spoken. All this can only be done, says the same Father, by the power of the malignant spirit, whom God permits to exercise this empire]absolute control] over venomous reptiles, above all, the serpent, as if to punish him for what he did to the first woman. In fact, it may be remarked, that no animal is more exposed to charms, and the effects of magic art, than the serpent.

The laws of the Twelve Tables forbid the charming of a neighbour's crops, *qui fruges excantâsset*. Valerius Flaccus quotes authors who affirm, that when the Romans were about to besiege a town, they employed their priests to evoke the divinity who presided over it, promising him a temple in Rome, either like the one dedicated to him in the besieged place, or on a rather larger scale, and that the proper worship should be paid to him. Pliny says, that the memory of these evocations is preserved among the priests.

If that which we have just related, and what we read in ancient and modern writers, is at all real, and produces the effects attributed to it, it cannot be doubted that there is something supernatural in it, and that the devil has a great share in the matter.

The Abbot Trithemius speaks of a sorceress who, by means of certain beverages, changed a young Burgundian into a beast.

Everybody knows the fable of Circé, who changed the soldiers or companions of Ulysses into swine. We know also the fable of the Golden Ass, by Apuleius, which contains the account of a man metamorphosed into an ass. I bring forward these things merely as what they are, that is to say, simply poetic fictions.

But it is very credible that these fictions are not destitute of some foundation, like many other fables, which contain not only a hidden and moral sense, but which have also some relation to an event really historical: for instance, what is said of the Golden Fleece carried away by Jason; of the Wooden Horse, made use of to surprise the city of Troy; the Twelve Labours of Hercules; the metamorphoses related by Ovid. All fabulous as those things appear in the poets, they have, nevertheless, their historical truth. And thus the Pagan poets and historians have travestied and disguised the stories of the Old Testament, and have attributed to Bacchus, Jupiter, Saturn, Apollo, and Hercules, what is related of Noah, Moses, Aaron, Samson, and Jonah, etc.

Origen, writing against Celsus, supposes the reality of magic, and says, that the magi who came to adore Jesus Christ at Bethlehem, wishing to perform their accustomed operations, not being able to succeed, a superior power preventing the effect and imposing silence on the demon, they sought out the cause, and beheld at the same time a divine sign in the heavens, whence they concluded that it was the Being spoken of by Balaam, and that the new King whose birth he had predicted was born in Judea, and immediately they resolved to go and seek him. Origen believes that magicians, according to the rules of their art, often foretell the future, and that their predictions are followed by the event, unless the power of God, or that of the angels, prevents the effect of their conjurations, and puts them to silence.

CHAPTER 13

Examples which Prove the Reality of Magic

St Augustine remarks, that not only the poets, but the historians even, relate that Diomede, of whom the Greeks have made a divinity, had not the happiness to return to his country with the other princes who had been at the siege of Troy; that his companions were changed into birds, and that these birds have their dwelling in the environs of the Temple of Diomede, which is situated near Mount Garganos; that these birds caress the Greeks who come to visit this temple, but fly at and peck the strangers who arrive there.

Varro, the most learned of Romans, to render this more credible, relates what everybody knows about Circé, who changed the companions of Ulysses into beasts; and what is said of the Arcadians, who, after having drawn lots, swam over a certain lake, after which they were metamorphosed into wolves, and ran about in the forests like other wolves. If during the time of their transmutation they did not eat human flesh, at the end of nine years they repassed the same lake, and resumed their former shape.

The same Varro relates of a certain Demenotas, that, having tasted the flesh of a child which the Arcadians had immolated to their god Lycaea, he had also been changed into a wolf, and ten years after he had resumed his natural form, had appeared at the Olympic games, and won the prize for pugilism.

St Augustine testifies, that in his time many believed that these transformations still took place, and some persons even affirmed that they had experienced them in their own persons. He adds, that when in Italy, he was told that certain women gave cheese to strangers who lodged at their houses, when these strangers were immediately changed into beasts of burden, without losing their reason, and carried the loads which were placed upon them; after which they returned to their former state. He says, moreover, that a certain man, named Praestantius, related that his father, having eaten of this magic cheese, remained lying in bed, without anyone being able to awaken him, for several days, when he awoke, and said that he had been changed into a horse, and had carried victuals to the army; and the thing was found to be true, although it appeared to him to be only a dream.

St Augustine, reasoning on all this, says, that either these things are false, or else so extraordinary that we cannot give faith to them. It is not to be doubted that God, by his almighty power, can do anything that he thinks proper, but that the devil, who is of a spiritual nature, can do nothing without the permission of God, whose decrees are always just; that the demon can neither change the nature of the spirit or the body of a man, to transform him into a beast; but that he can only act upon the fancy or imagination of a man, and persuade him that he is what he is not, or that he appears to others different from what he is; or that he remains in a deep sleep, and believes during that slumber that he is bearing loads which the devil carries for him; or that he (the devil) fascinates the eyes of those who believe they see them borne by animals, or by men metamorphosed into animals.

If we consider it only a change arising from fancy or imagination, as it happens in the disorder called lycanthropy, in which a man believes himself changed into a wolf, or into any other animal, as Nebuchadnezzar, who believed himself changed into an ox, and acted for seven years as if he had really been metamorphosed into that animal, there would be nothing in that more marvellous than what we see in hypochondriacs, who persuade themselves that they are kings, generals, popes, and cardinals; that they are snow, glass, pottery, etc. Like him who, being alone at the theatre, believed that he beheld there actors and admirable representations; or the man who imagined that all the vessels which arrived at the port of Pireus, near Athens, belonged to him; or, in short, what we see every day in dreams, and which appear to us very real during our sleep. In all this, it is needless to have recourse to the devil, or to magic, fascination, or illusion; there is nothing above the natural order of things. But that, by means of certain beverages, certain herbs, and certain kinds of food, a person may disturb the imagination, and persuade another that he is a wolf, a horse, or an ass, appears more difficult of explanation, although we are aware that plants, herbs, and medicaments possess great power over the bodies of men, and are capable of deranging the brain, constitution, and imagination. We have but too many examples of such things.

Another circumstance, which, if true, deserves much reflection, is that of Apollonius of Tyana, who, being at Ephesus during a great plague which desolated the city, promised the Ephesians to cause the pest to cease the very day on which he was speaking to them, and which was that of his second arrival in their town. He assembled them at the theatre, and ordered them to stone to death a poor old man, covered with rags, who asked alms. 'Strike,' cried he, 'that enemy of the gods! Heap stones upon him.' They could not make up their minds to do so, for he excited their pity, and asked mercy in the most touching manner. But Apollonius pressed it so much, that at last they slew him, and amassed over him an immense heap of stones. A little while after he told them to take away these stones, and they would see what sort of an animal they had killed. They found only a great dog, and were convinced that this old man was only a phantom who had fascinated their eyes, and caused the pestilence in their town.

We here see five remarkable things: 1. The demon who causes the plague in Ephesus; 2. This same demon, who, instead of a dog, causes the appearance of a man; 3. The fascination of the senses of the Ephesians, who believe that they behold a man instead of a dog; 4. The proof of the magic of Apollonius, who discovers the cause of this pestilence; 5. And who makes it cease at the given time.

Aeneas Sylvius Picolomini, who was afterwards Pope by the name of Pius II writes, in his *History of Bohemia*, that a woman predicted to a soldier of King Wratislaus, that the army of that prince would be cut in pieces by the Duke of Bohemia, and that, if this soldier wished to avoid death, he must kill the first person he should meet on the road, cut off their ears, and put them in his pocket; that with the sword he had used to pierce them he must trace on the ground a cross between his horse's legs; that he must kiss it, and then take flight. All this the young soldier performed. Wratislaus gave battle, lost it, and was killed. The young soldier escaped; but on entering his house, he found that it was his wife whom he had killed and run his sword through, and whose ears he had cut off.

This woman was, then, strangely disguised and metamorphosed, since her husband could not recognise her, and she did not make herself known to him in such perilous circumstances, when her life was in danger. These two were, then, apparently magicians; both she who made the prediction, and the other on whom it was exercised. God permits, on this occasion, three great evils. The first magician counsels the murder of an innocent person; the young man commits it on his own wife without knowing her; and the latter dies in a state of condemnation, since by the secrets of magic she had rendered it impossible to recognise her.

A butcher's wife of the town of Jena, in the duchy of Wiemar in Thuringia, having refused to let an old woman have a calf's head for which she offered very little, the old woman went away grumbling and muttering. A little time after this the butcher's wife felt violent pains in her head. As the cause of this malady was unknown to the cleverest physicians, they could find no remedy for it; from time to time a substance like brains came from this woman's left ear, and at first it was supposed to be her own brain. But as she suspected that old woman of having cast a spell upon her on account of the calf's head, they examined the thing more minutely, and they saw that these were calf's brains; and what strengthened this opinion was, that splinters of calf's-head bones came out with the brains. This disorder continued some time; at last the butcher's wife was perfectly cured. This happened in 1685. M. Hoffman, who relates this story in his dissertation *On the Power of the Demon over Bodies*, printed in 1736, says that the woman was perhaps still alive.

One day they brought to St Macarius the Egyptian a virtuous woman who had been transformed into a mare, by the pernicious arts of a magician. Her husband, and all those who saw her, thought that she really was changed into a mare. This woman remained three days and three nights without tasting any food, proper either for man or horse. They showed her to the priests of the place, who could apply no remedy.

Then they led her to the cell of St Macarius, to whom God had revealed that she was to come; his disciples wanted to send her back, thinking that it was a mare. They informed the saint of her arrival, and the subject of her journey. 'He said to them, "You are downright animals yourselves, thinking you see what is not; that woman is not changed, but your eyes are fascinated." At the same time he sprinkled holy water on the woman's head, and all present beheld her in her former state. He gave her something to eat, and sent her away safe and sound with her husband. As he sent her away the saint said to her. "Do not keep from church, for this has happened to you for having been five weeks without taking the Sacrament of our Lord, or attending divine service." '

St Hilarion, much in the same manner, cured by virtue of holy water a young girl, whom a magician had rendered most violently amorous of a young man. The demon who possessed her cried aloud to St Hilarion, 'You make me endure the most cruel torments, for I cannot come out till the young man who caused me to enter shall unloose me, for I am enchained under the threshold of the door by a band of copper covered with magical characters, and by the tow which envelopes it.' Then St Hilarion said to him, 'Truly your power is very great, to suffer yourself to be bound by a bit of copper and a little thread;' at the same time, without permitting these things to be taken from under the threshold of the door, he chased away the demon and cured the girl.

In the same place, St Jerome relates that one Italicus, a citizen of Gaza and a Christian, who brought up horses for the games in the Circus, had a pagan antagonist who hindered and held back the horses of Italicus in their course, and gave most extraordinary celerity to his own. Italicus came to St Hilarion, and told him the subject he had for uneasiness. The saint laughed and said to him, 'Would it not be better to give the value of your horses to the poor, rather than employ them in such exercises?' 'I cannot do as I please,' said Italicus; 'it is a public employment which I fill, because I cannot help it, and as a Christian I cannot employ malpractices against those used against me.' The brothers, who were present, interceded for him; and St Hilarion gave him the earthen vessel out of which he drank, filled it with water, and told him to sprinkle his horses with it. Italicus not only sprinkled his horses with this water, but likewise his stable and chariot all over; and the next day the horses and chariot of this rival were left far behind his own; which caused the people to shout in the theatre, 'Marnas is vanquished – Jesus Christ is victorious!' And this victory of Italicus produced the conversion of several persons at Gaza.

Will it be said that this is only the effect of imagination, prepossession, or the trickery of a clever charlatan? How can you persuade fifty people that a woman who is present before their eyes can be changed into a mare, supposing that she has retained her own natural shape? How was it that the soldier mentioned by Aeneas Sylvius did not recognise his wife, whom he pierced with his sword, and whose ears he cut off? How did Apollonius of Tyana persuade the Ephesians to kill a man, who really was only a dog? How did he know that this dog, or this man, was the cause of the pestilence which afflicted Ephesus? It is then very credible that the evil spirit often acts on bodies, on the air, the earth, and on animals, and produces effects which appear above the power of man.

It is said that in Lapland they have a school for magic, and that fathers send their children to it, being persuaded that magic is necessary to them, that they may avoid falling into the snares of their enemies, who are themselves great magicians. They make the familiar demons, whose services they command, pass as an inheritance to their children, that they may make use of them to overcome the demons of other families who are adverse to their own. They often make use of a certain kind of drum for their magical operations; for instance, if they wish to know what is passing in a foreign country, one amongst them beats this drum, placing upon it at the part where the image of the sun is represented, a quantity of pewter rings attached together with a chain of the same metal; then they strike the drum with a forked hammer made of bone, so that these rings move; at the same time they sing distinctly a song, called by the Laplanders *Jonk*; and all those of their nation who are present, men and women, add their own songs, expressing from time to time the name of the place whence they desire to have news.

The Laplander having beaten the drum for some time, places it on his head in a certain manner, and falls down directly motionless on the ground, and without any sign of life. All the men and all the women continue singing, till he revives; if they cease to sing, the man dies, which happens also if anyone tries to awaken him by touching his hand or his foot. They even keep the flies from him, which by their humming might awaken him and bring him back to life.

When he is recovered he replies to the questions they ask him concerning the place he has been at. Sometimes he does not awake for four-and-twenty hours, sometimes more, sometimes less, according to the distance he has gone; and in confirmation of what he says, and of the distance he has been, he brings back from the place he has been sent to, the token demanded of him, a knife, a ring, shoes, or some other object.

These same Laplanders make use also of this drum, to learn the cause of any malady, or to deprive their enemies of their life or their strength. Moreover, amongst them are certain magicians, who keep in a kind of leathern game-bag magic flies, which they let loose from time to time against their enemies or against their cattle, or simply to raise tempests and hurricanes. They have also a sort of dart which they hurl into the air, and which causes the death of anyone it falls upon. They have also a sort of little ball called *tyre*, almost round, which they send in the same way against their enemies to destroy them; and if by ill luck this ball should hit on its way some other person, or some animal, it will inevitably cause its death.

Who can be persuaded that the Laplanders who sell fair winds, raise storms, relate what passes in distant places, where they go, as they say, in the spirit, and bring back things which they have found there – who can persuade themselves that all this is done without the aid of magic? It has been said that in the circumstance of Apollonius of Tyana, they contrived to send away the man all squalid and deformed, and put in his place a dog which was stoned, or else they substituted a dead dog. All which would require a vast deal of preparation, and would be very difficult to execute in sight of all the people. It would perhaps be better to deny the fact altogether, which certainly does appear very fabulous, than to have recourse to such explanations.

CHAPTER 14

Effects of Magic According to the Poets

Were we to believe what is said by the poets concerning the effects of magic, and what the magicians boast of being able to perform by their spells, nothing would be more marvellous than their art, and we should be obliged to acknowledge that the power of the demon was greatly shown thereby. Pliny relates, that Appian evoked the spirit of Homer, to learn from him which was his country, and who were his parents. Philostratus says, that Apollonius of Tyana went to the tomb of Achilles, evoked his manes, and implored them to cause the figure of that hero to appear to him; the tomb trembled, and afterwards he beheld a young man, who at first appeared about five cubits, or seven and a half feet high – after which, the phantom dilated to twelve cubits, and appeared of a singular beauty. Apollonius asked him some frivolous questions, and as the young man jested indecently with him, he comprehended that he was possessed by a demon; this demon he expelled, and cured the young man. But all this is fabulous.

Lactantius, refuting the philosophers Democritus, Epicurus, and Dicearchus, who denied the immortality of the soul, says, they would not dare to maintain their opinion before a magician, who, by the power of his art, and by his spells, possessed the secret of bringing souls from Hades, of making them appear, speak, and foretell the future, and give certain signs of their presence.

St Augustine, always circumspect in his decisions, dare not pronounce whether magicians possess the power of evoking the spirits of saints by the might of their enchantments. But Tertullian is bolder, and maintains that no magical art has power to bring the souls of the saints from their rest; but that all the necromancers can do, is to call forth some phantoms with a borrowed shape, which fascinate the eyes, and make those who are present believe that to be a reality which is only appearance. In the same place he quotes Heraclius, who says, that the Nasamones, people of Africa, pass the night by the tombs of their near relations to receive oracles from the latter; and that the Celts, or Gauls, do the same thing in the mausoleums of great men, as related by Nicander.

Lucan says, that the magicians by their spells cause thunder in the skies unknown to Jupiter; that they tear the moon from her sphere, and precipitate her to earth; that they disturb the course of nature, prolong the nights, and shorten the days; that the universe is obedient to their voice, and that the world is chilled as it were when they speak and command. They were so well persuaded that the magicians possessed power to make the moon come down from the sky, and they so truly believed that she was evoked by magic art whenever she was eclipsed, that they made a great noise by striking on copper vessels, to prevent the voice which pronounced enchantments from reaching her.

These popular opinions and poetical fictions deserve no credit, but they show the force of prejudice. It is affirmed that, even at this day, the Persians think they are assisting the moon when eclipsed, by striking violently on brazen vessels, and making a great uproar.

Ovid attributes to the enchantments of magic, the evocation of the infernal powers, and their dismissal back to hell; storms, tempests, and the return of fine weather. They attributed to it the power of changing men into beasts by means of certain herbs, the virtues of which are known to them.

Virgil speaks of serpents put to sleep and enchanted by the magicians. And Tibullus says, that he has seen the enchantress bring down the stars from heaven, and turn aside the thunderbolt ready to fall upon the earth – and that she has opened the ground and made the dead come forth from their tombs.

As this matter allows of poetical ornaments, the poets have vied with each other in endeavouring to adorn their pages with them, not that they were convinced there was any truth in what they said; they were the first to laugh at it when an opportunity presented itself, as well as the gravest and wisest men of antiquity. But neither princes nor priests took much pains to undeceive the people, or to destroy their prejudices on those subjects. The Pagan religion allowed them, nay, authorised them, and part of its practices were founded on similar superstitions.

CHAPTER 15

Of the Pagan Oracles

If it were well proved that the oracles of Pagan antiquity were the work of the evil spirit, we could give more real and palpable proofs of the apparition of the demon among men than these boasted oracles, which were given in almost every country in the world, among the nations which passed for the wisest and most enlightened, as the Egyptians, Chaldeans, Persians, Syrians, even the Hebrews, Greeks, and Romans. Even the most barbarous people were not without their oracles.

In the Pagan religion, there was nothing esteemed more honourable, or more complacently boasted of.

In all their great undertakings they had recourse to the oracle; by that was decided the most important affairs between town and town, or province and province. The manner in which the oracles were rendered, was not everywhere the same. It is said, the bull Apis, whose worship was anciently established in Egypt, gave out his oracles on his receiving food from the hand of him who consulted. If he received it, say they, it was considered a good omen; if he refused it, this was a bad augury. When this animal appeared in public, he was accompanied by a troop of children, who sang hymns in his honour; after which these boys were filled with sacred enthusiasm, and began to predict future events. If the bull went quietly into his lodge, it was a happy sign; if he came out, it was the contrary. Such was the blindness of the Egyptians.

There were other oracles also in Egypt: as those of Mercury, Apollo, Hercules, Diana, Minerva, Jupiter Ammon, etc. which last was consulted by Alexander the Great. But Herodotus remarks, that in his time there were neither priests nor priestesses who uttered oracles. They were derived from certain presages, which they drew by chance, or from the movements of the statues of the gods, or from the first voice which they heard after having consulted. Pausanias says, that he who consults whispers in the ear of Mercury what he requires to know, then he stops his ears, goes out of the temple, and the first words which he hears from the first person he meets, are held as the answer of the god.

The Greeks acknowledge that they received from the Egyptians both the names of their gods and their most ancient oracles; amongst others that of Dodona, which was already much resorted to in the time of Homer, and which came from the oracle of Jupiter of Thebes: for the Egyptian priests related that two priestesses of that god had been carried off by Phoenician merchants, who had sold them, one into Libya and the other into Greece. Those of Dodona related, that two black doves had flown from Thebes of Egypt – that the one which had stopped at Dodona had perched upon a beech-tree, and had declared in an articulate voice that the gods willed that an oracle of Jupiter should be established in this place; and that the other, having flown into Libya, had there formed or founded the oracle of Jupiter Ammon. These origins are certainly very frivolous and very fabulous. The oracle of Delphi is more recent and more celebrated. Phemonoé was the first priestess of Delphi, and began in the time of Acrisius, twenty-seven years before Orpheus, Musaeus, and Linus. She is said to have been the inventress of hexameters.

But I think I can remark vestiges of oracles in Egypt, from the time of the patriarch Joseph, and from the time of Moses. The Hebrews had dwelt for 215 years in Egypt, and having multiplied there exceedingly, had begun to form a separate people and a sort of republic. They had imbibed a taste for the ceremonies, the superstitions, the customs, and the idolatry of the Egyptians.

Joseph was considered the cleverest diviner and the greatest expounder of dreams in Egypt. They believed that he derived his oracles from the inspection of the liquor which he poured into his cup. Moses, to cure the Hebrews of their leaning to the idolatry and superstitions of Egypt, prescribed to them laws and ceremonies which favoured his design; the first, diametrically opposite to those of the Egyptians; the second, bearing some resemblance to theirs in appearance, but differing both in their aim and circumstances.

For instance, the Egyptians were accustomed to consult diviners, magicians, interpreters of dreams, and augurs; all which things are forbidden to the Hebrews by Moses, on pain of rigorous punishment; but in order that they might have no room to complain that their religion did not furnish them with the means of discovering future events and hidden things, God, with condescension worthy of reverential admiration, granted them the *Urim and Thummim*, or the Doctrine and the Truth, with which the high priest was invested according to the ritual in the principal ceremonies of religion, and by means of which he rendered oracles, and discovered the will of the Most High. When the Ark of the Covenant and the tabernacle were constructed, the Lord, consulted by Moses, gave out his replies from between the two cherubim which were placed upon the mercy-seat above the Ark. All which seems to insinuate, that from the time of the patriarch Joseph, there had been oracles and diviners in Egypt, and that the Hebrews consulted them.

God promised his people, to raise up a prophet among them, who should declare to them his will: in fact, we see in almost all ages among them, prophets inspired by God; and the true prophets reproached them vehemently for their impiety, when instead of coming to the prophets of the Lord, they went to consult strange oracles, and divinities equally powerless and unreal.

We have spoken before of the teraphim of Laban, of the idols or pretended oracles of Micah and Gideon. King Saul, who, apparently by the advice of Samuel, had exterminated diviners and magicians from the land of Israel, desired in the last war to consult the Lord, who would not reply to him. He then afterwards addressed himself to a witch, who promised him she would evoke Samuel for him. She did, or feigned to do so, for the thing offers many difficulties, into which we shall not enter here.

The same Saul having consulted the Lord on another occasion, to know whether he must pursue the Philistines whom he had just defeated, God refused also to reply to him, because his son Jonathan had tasted some honey, not knowing that the king had forbidden his army to taste anything whatever before his enemies were entirely overthrown.

The silence of the Lord on certain occasions, and his refusal to answer sometimes when He was consulted, are an evident proof that He usually replied, and that they were certain of receiving instructions from Him, unless they raised an obstacle to it by some action which was displeasing to Him.

CHAPTER 16

The Certainty of the Event Predicted, is not always a Proof that the Prediction Comes from God

Moses had foreseen, that so untractable and superstitious a people as the Israelites would not rest satisfied with the reasonable, pious, and supernatural means which he had procured them for discovering future events, by giving them prophets and the oracle of the high priest. He knew that there would arise among them false prophets and seducers, who would endeavour by their illusions and magical secrets to mislead them into error; whence it was that he said to them: 'If there should arise among you a prophet, or anyone who boasts of having had a dream, and he foretells a wonder, or anything which surpasses the ordinary power of man, and what he predicts shall happen; and after that he shall say unto you, Come, let us go and serve the strange gods, which you have not known; you shall not hearken unto him, because the Lord your God will prove you, to see whether you love Him with all your heart and with all your soul.'

Certainly, nothing is more likely to mislead us, than to see what has been foretold by anyone come to pass.

'Shew the things that are to come,' says Isaiah, 'that we may know that ye are gods. Let them come, let them foretell what is to happen, and what has been done of old, and we will believe in them,' etc. *Idoneum testimonium divinationis*, says Tertullian, *veritas divinationis*. And St Jerome, *Confitentur magi, confitentur arioli, et omnis scientia saecularis litteraturae, praescientiam futurorum non esse hominum, sed Dei.*

Nevertheless, we have just seen that Moses acknowledges that false prophets can predict things which will happen. And the Saviour warns us in the Gospel, that at the end of the world several false prophets will arise, who will seduce many, 'They shall shew great signs and wonders, insomuch that, if it were possible, they shall deceive even the elect.' It is not, then, precisely either the successful issue of the event, which decides in favour of the false prophet – nor the default of the predictions made by true prophets, which proves that they are not sent by God.

Jonah was sent to foretell the destruction of Nineveh, which did not come to pass; and many other threats of the prophets were not put into execution, because God, moved by the repentance of the sinful, revoked or commuted his former sentence. The repentance of the Ninevites guaranteed them against the last misfortune.

Isaiah had distinctly foretold to King Hezekiah, that he would not recover from his illness: 'Set thine house in order, for thou shalt die, and not live.' Nevertheless God, moved with the prayer of this prince, revoked the sentence of death; and before the prophet had left the court of the king's house, God commanded him to return and tell the king, that God would add yet fifteen years to his life.

Moses assigns the mark of a true prophet to be, when he leads us to God and his worship – and the mark of a false prophet is, when he withdraws us from the Lord, and inclines us to superstition and idolatry. Balaam was a true prophet inspired by God, who foretold things which were followed up by the event; but his morals were very corrupt, and he was extremely self-interested. He did everything he could to deserve the recompense promised him by the king of Moab, and to curse and immolate Israel. God did not permit him to do so, he put into his mouth blessings instead of curses; he did not induce the Israelites to forsake the Lord; but he advised the Moabites to seduce the people of God, and cause them to commit fornication, and to worship the idols of the country, and by that means to irritate God against them, and draw upon them the effects of his vengeance. Moses caused the chiefs among the people, who had consented to this crime, to be hung; and caused to perish the Midianites who had led the Hebrews into it. And lastly, Balaam, who was the first cause of this evil, was also punished with death.

In all the predictions of diviners or oracles, when they are followed by fulfilment, we can hardly disavow that the evil spirit intervenes, and discovers the future to those who consult him. St Augustine in his book *de Divinatione Daemonum*, or of predictions made by the evil spirit, when they are fulfilled, supposes that the demons are of an aerial nature, and much more subtle than bodies in general; insomuch, that they surpass beyond comparison the lightness both of men and the swiftest animals, and even the flight of birds, which enables them to announce things that are passing in very distant places, and beyond the common reach of men. Moreover, as they are not subject to death as we are, they have acquired infinitely more experience than even those who possess the most among mankind, and are the most attentive to what happens in the world. By that means they can sometimes predict things to come, announce several things at a distance, and do some wonderful things; which has often led mortals to pay them divine honours, believing them to be of a nature much more excellent than their own.

But when we reflect seriously on what the demons predict, we may remark, that often they announce nothing but what they are to do themselves. For God permits them sometimes to cause maladies, corrupt the air and produce in it qualities of an infectious nature, and to incline the wicked to persecute the worthy. They perform these operations in a hidden manner, by resources unknown to mortals, and proportionate to the subtlety of their own nature. They can announce what they have foreseen must happen, by certain natural tokens unknown to men, like as a physician foresees by the secret of his art, the symptoms and the consequences of a malady which no one else can. Thus, the demon, who knows our constitution and the secret tendency of our humours, can foretell the maladies which are the consequences of them. He can also discover our thoughts and our secret wishes, by certain external motions, and by certain expressions we let fall by chance, whence he infers that men would do or undertake certain things, consequent upon these thoughts or inclinations.

But his predictions are far from being comparable with those revealed to us by God, through his angels, or the prophets; these are always certain and infallible, because they have for their principle God, who is truth; while the predictions of the demons are often deceitful, because the arrangements on which they are founded can be changed and deranged, when they least expect it, by unforeseen and unexpected circumstances, or by the authority of superior powers overthrowing the first plans, or by a peculiar disposition of Providence, who sets bounds to the power of the Prince of Darkness. Sometimes also, demons purposely deceive those who have the weakness to place confidence in them. But usually, they throw the fault upon those who have taken on themselves to interpret their discourses and predictions.

So says St Augustine; and although we do not quite agree with him, but hold the opinion that souls, angels, and demons are disengaged from all matter or substance, still we can apply his reasoning to evil spirits, even upon the supposition that they are immaterial – and own that sometimes they can predict the future, and that their predictions may be fulfilled; but that is not a proof of their being sent by God, or inspired by his Spirit. Even were they to work miracles, we must anathematise them, as soon as they turn us from the worship of the true God, or incline us to irregular lives.

CHAPTER 17

Reasons which Lead us to Believe that the Greater Part of the Ancient Oracles were only Impositions of the Priests and Priestesses, who Feigned that they were Inspired by God

If it is true, as has been thought by many, both among the ancients and the moderns, that the oracles of Pagan antiquity were only illusions and deceptions on the part of the priests and priestesses, who said that they were possessed by the spirit of Python, and filled with the inspiration of Apollo, who discovered to them internally things hidden and past, or present and future, I must not place them here in the rank of evil spirits. The devil has no other share in the matter than he has always in the crimes of men, and in that multitude of sins which cupidity, ambition, interest, and self-love produce in the world; the demon being always ready to seize an occasion to mislead us, and draw us into irregularity and error, employing all our passions to lead us into these snares. If what he has foretold is followed by fulfilment, either by chance, or because he has foreseen certain circumstances unknown to men, he takes to himself all the credit of it, and makes use of it to gain our confidence and conciliate credit for his predictions; if the thing is doubtful, and he knows not what the issue of it will be, the demon, the priest or priestess, will pronounce an equivocal oracle, in order that at all events they may appear to have spoken true.

The ancient legislators of Greece, the most skilful politicians, and generals of armies, dexterously made use of the prepossession of the people in favour of oracles, to persuade them that what they had concerted was approved of by the gods, and announced by the oracle. These things and these oracles were often followed by success, not because the oracle had predicted or ordained it, but because the enterprise being well concerted and well conducted, and the soldiers also perfectly persuaded that God was on their side, fought with more than ordinary valour. Sometimes they gained over the priestess by the aid of presents, and thus disposed her to give favourable replies. Demosthenes haranguing at Athens against Philip, king of Macedon, said, that the priestess of Delphi *Philippised*, and only pronounced oracles conformable to the inclinations, advantage, and interest of that prince.

Porphyry, the greatest enemy of the Christian name, makes no difficulty of owning that these oracles were dictated by the spirit of falsehood, and that the demons are the true authors of enchantments, philtres, and spells; that they fascinate or deceive the eyes by the spectres and phantoms which they cause to appear; that they ambitiously desire to pass for gods; that their aerial and spiritual bodies are nourished by the smell and smoke of the blood and fat of the animals which are immolated to them; and that the office of uttering oracles replete with falsehood, equivocation, and deceit, has devolved upon them. At the head of these demons he places Hecate and Serapis. Jamblichus, another pagan author, speaks of them in the same manner, and with as much contempt.

The ancient fathers who lived so near the times when these oracles existed, several of whom had forsaken paganism and embraced Christianity, and who consequently knew more about the oracles than we can, speak of them as things invented, governed, and maintained by the demons. The most sensible among the heathens do not speak of them otherwise, but also they confess that often the malice, imposition, servility and interest of the priests had great share in the matter, and that they abused the simplicity, credulity and prepossessions of the people.

Plutarch says, that a governor of Cilicia having sent to consult the oracle of Mopsus, as he was going to Malle in the same country, the man who carried the billet fell asleep in the temple, where he saw in a dream a handsome looking man, who said to him the single word *black*. He carried this reply to the governor, whose mysterious question he knew nothing about. Those who heard this answer laughed at it, not knowing what was the in billet: but the governor having opened it showed them these words written in it; *Shall I immolate to thee a black ox, or a white one?* and that the oracle had thus answered his question without opening the note. But who can answer for their not having deceived the bearer of the billet in this case, as did Alexander of Abonotiche, a town of Paphlagonia, in Asia Minor. This man had the art to persuade the people of his country, that he had with him the god Esculapius, in the shape of a tame serpent, who pronounced oracles, and replied to the consultations addressed to him on divers diseases, without opening the billets they placed on the altar of the temple of this pretended divinity; after which, without opening them, they found the next morning the reply written below. All the trick consisted in the seal being raised artfully by a heated needle, and then replaced after having written the reply at the bottom of the note, in an obscure and enigmatical style, after the manner of other oracles. At other times he used mastic, which being yet soft, took the impression of the seal, then when that was hardened he put on another seal with the same impression. He received about ten sols (five-pence) per billet, and this game lasted all his life, which was a long one; for he died at the age of seventy, being struck by lightning, near the end of the second century of the Christian era: all which may be found more at length in the book of Lucian entitled, *Pseudo Manes*, or the false Diviner. The priest of the oracle of Mopsus could by the same secret open the billet of the governor who consulted him, and showing himself during the night to the messenger, declare to him the above-mentioned reply.

Macrobius relates that the Emperor Trajan, to prove the oracle of Heliopolis in Phoenicia, sent him a well sealed letter in which nothing was written; the oracle commanded that a blank letter should also be sent to the emperor. The priests of the oracle were much surprised at this, not knowing the reason of it. Another time the same emperor sent to consult this same oracle, to know whether he should return safe from his expedition against the Parthians. The oracle commanded that they should send him some branches of a knotted vine, which was sacred in his temple. Neither the emperor nor anyone else could guess what that meant; but his body, or rather his bones, having been brought to Rome after his death, which happened during his journey, it was supposed that the oracle had intended to predict his death, and designate his fleshless bones, which somewhat resemble the branches of a vine.

It is easy to explain this quite otherwise. If he had returned victorious, the vine being the source of wine which rejoices the heart of man, and is agreeable to both gods and men, would have typified his victory – and if the expedition had proved fruitless, the wood of the vine, which is useless for any kind of work, and only good for burning as firewood, might in that case signify the inutility of this expedition. It is allowed that the artifice, malice, and inventions of the heathen priests had much to do with the oracles, but are we to infer from this that the demon had no part in the matter?

We must allow that as by degrees the light of the gospel was spread in the world, the reign of the demon, ignorance, corruption of morals, and crime, diminished. The priests who pretended to predict, by the inspiration of the evil spirit, things concealed from mortal knowledge, or who misled the people by their illusions and impostures, were obliged to confess that the Christians imposed silence on them, either by the empire they exercised over the devil, or else by discovering the malice and knavishness of the priests, which the people had not dared to sound, from a blind respect which they had for this mystery of iniquity.

If in our days anyone would deny that in former times there were oracles which were rendered by the inspiration of the demon, we might convince him of it by what is still practised in Lapland, and by what missionaries relate, that in India the demon reveals things hidden and to come, not by the mouth of idols, but by that of the priests, who are present when they interrogate either the statues or the demon. And they remark that there the demon becomes mute and powerless, in proportion as the light of the gospel is spread among these nations. Thus then the silence of the oracles may be attributed – 1. To a superhuman cause, which is the power of Jesus Christ, and the publication of the gospel. 2. Mankind are become less superstitious, and bolder in searching out the cause of these pretended revelations. 3. To their having become less credulous, as Cicero says. 4. Because princes have imposed silence on the oracles, fearing that they might inspire the nation with rebellious principles. For which reason Lucan says, that princes feared to discover the future.

Strabo conjectures that the Romans neglected them, because they had the Sibylline books, and their auspices (aruspices or haruspices,) which stood them instead of oracles. M. Vandale demonstrates that some remains of the oracles might yet be seen under the Christian emperors. It was then only in process of time that oracles were entirely abolished, and it may be boldly asserted that sometimes the evil spirit revealed the future, and inspired the ministers of false gods, by permission of the Almighty, who wished to punish the confidence of the infidels in their idols. It would be going too far, if we affirmed that all that was said of the oracles was only the effect of the artifices or the malice of the priests, who always imposed on the credulity of mankind. Read on this subject, the learned reply of Father Balthus to the treatises of MM. Vandale and Fontenelle.

CHAPTER 18

On Sorcerers and Sorceresses, or Witches

The empire of the devil nowhere shines forth with more lustre than in what is related of the Sabbath (witches' sabbath or assembly), where he receives the homage of those of both sexes who have abandoned themselves to him. It is there, the wizards and witches say, that he exercises the greatest authority, and appears in a visible form, but always hideous, misshapen, and terrible; always during the night in out-of-the-way places, and arrayed in a manner more gloomy than gay, rather sad and dull, than majestic and brilliant. If they pay their adoration in that place to the Prince of Darkness, he shows himself there in a despicable posture, and in a base, contemptible and hideous form; if people eat there, the viands of the feast are dirty, insipid, and destitute of solidity and substance, they neither satisfy the appetite, nor please the palate; if they dance there, it is without order, without skill, without propriety.

To endeavour to give a description of the infernal sabbath, is to aim at describing what has no existence and never has existed, except in the craving and deluded imagination of sorcerers and sorceresses; the paintings we have of it are conceived after the reveries of those who fancy they have been transported through the air to the sabbath, both in body and soul.

People are carried thither, say they, sitting on a broomstick, sometimes on the clouds or on a he-goat. Neither the place, the time, nor the day when they assemble is fixed. It is sometimes in a lonely forest, sometimes in a desert, usually on the Wednesday or the Thursday night; the most solemn of all is that of the eve of St John the Baptist: they there distribute to every sorcerer, the ointment with which he must anoint himself when he desires to go to the sabbath, and the spell-powder he must make use of in his magic operations. They must all appear together in this general assembly, and he who is absent is severely ill-used both in word and deed. As to the private meetings, the demon is more indulgent to those who are absent for some particular reason.

As to the ointment with which they anoint themselves, some authors, amongst others, John Baptista Porta, and John Wierius, boast that they know the composition. Amongst other ingredients there are many narcotic drugs, which cause those who make use of it to fall into a profound slumber, during which they imagine that they are carried to the sabbath up the chimney, at the top of which they find a tall black man, with horns, who transports them where they wish to go, and afterwards brings them back again by the same chimney. The accounts given by these people, and the description which they give of their assemblies, are wanting in unity and uniformity.

The demon, their chief, appears there, either in the shape of a he-goat, or as a great black dog, or as an immense raven; he is seated on an elevated throne, and receives there the homage of those present in a way which decency does not allow us to describe. In this nocturnal assembly they sing, they dance, they abandon themselves to the most shameful disorder; they sit down to table, and indulge in good cheer; while at the same time they see on the table neither knife nor fork, salt nor oil; they find the viands devoid of savour, and quit the table without their hunger being satisfied.

One would imagine that the attraction of a better fortune, and a wish to enrich themselves, drew thither men and women; the devil never fails to make them magnificent promises, at least the sorcerers say so, and believe it, deceived, without doubt, by their imagination; but experience shows us that these people are always ragged, despised, and wretched, and usually end their lives in a violent and dishonourable manner.

When they are admitted for the first time to the sabbath, the demon inscribes their name and surname on his register, which he makes them sign; then he makes them forswear cream and baptism, makes them renounce Jesus Christ and his Church; and, to give them a distinctive character and make them known for his own, he imprints on their bodies a certain mark with the nail of the little finger of one of his hands; this mark, or character, thus impressed, renders the part insensible to pain. They even pretend that he impresses this character in three different parts of the body, and at three different times. The demon does not impress these characters, say they, before the person has attained the age of twenty-five.

But none of these things deserve the least attention. There may happen to be in the body of a man, or a woman, some benumbed part, either from illness, or the effect of remedies, or drugs, or even naturally; but that is no proof that the devil has anything to do with it. There are even persons accused of magic and sorcery, on whom no part thus characterised has been found, nor yet insensible to the touch, however exact the search. Others have declared that the devil has never made any such marks upon them. Consult on this matter the second letter of M. de St André, Physician to the King, in which he well develops what has been said about these characters of sorcerers.

The word sabbath, taken in the above sense, is not to be found in ancient writers; neither the Hebrews nor the Egyptians, the Greeks nor the Latins, have known it.

The thing itself, I mean the *sabbath* taken in the sense of a nocturnal assembly of persons devoted to the devil, is not remarked in antiquity, although magicians, sorcerers, and witches are spoken of often enough – that is to say, people who boasted that they exercised a kind of power over the devil, and by his means, over animals, the air, the stars, and the lives and fortunes of men.

Horace makes use of the word *coticia* to indicate the nocturnal meetings of the magicians – *Tu riseris coticia;* which he derives from *Cotys* or *Cotto*, Goddess of Vice, who presided in the assemblies which were held at night, and where the Bacchantes gave themselves up to all sorts of dissolute pleasures; but this is very different from the witches' sabbath.

Others derive this term from *Sabbatius*, which is an epithet given to the god Bacchus, whose nocturnal festivals were celebrated in debauchery. Arnobius, and Julius Firmicus Maternus, inform us that in these festivals they slipped a golden serpent into the bosoms of the initiated, and drew it downwards; but this etymology is too far-fetched; the people who gave the name of *sabbath* to the assemblies of the sorcerers, wished apparently to compare them in derision to those of the Jews, and to what they practised in their synagogues on sabbath days.

The most ancient monument in which I have been able to remark any express mention of the nocturnal assemblies of the sorcerers is in the Capitularies, wherein it is said that women led away by the illusions of the demons, say that they go in the night with the goddess Diana and an infinite number of other women, borne through the air on different animals, that they go in a few hours a great distance, and obey Diana as their queen. It was therefore to the goddess Diana, or the Moon, and not to Lucifer, that they paid homage. The Germans call witches' dances what we call the sabbath. They say that these people assemble on Mount Bructere.

The famous Agobard, Archbishop of Lyons, who lived under the Emperor Louis the Debonair, wrote a treatise against certain superstitious persons in his time, who believed that storms, hail, and thunder were caused by certain sorcerers whom they called tempesters, (*tempestarios*, or storm-brewers), who raised the rain in the air, caused storms and thunder, and brought sterility upon the earth. They called these extraordinary rains *aura lavatitia*, as if to indicate that they were raised by magic power. In this place the people still call these violent rains *alvace*. There were even persons sufficiently prejudiced to boast that they knew of *tempêtiers*, who had to conduct the tempests where they chose, and to turn them aside when they pleased. Agobard interrogated some of them, but they were obliged to own that they had not been present at the things they related.

Agobard maintains that this is the work of God alone; that in truth, the saints, with the help of God, have often performed similar prodigies; but that neither the devil nor sorcerers can do anything like it. He remarks that there were among his people, superstitious persons, who would pay very punctually what they called *canonicum*, which was a sort of tribute which they offered to these tempest-brewers, that they might not hurt them, while they refused the tithe to the priest, and alms to the widow, orphan, and other indigent persons.

He adds, that he had of late found people sufficiently foolish enough to spread a report that Grimaldus, Duke of Benevento, had sent persons into France, carrying certain powders which they had scattered over the fields, mountains, meadows and springs, and had thus caused the death of an immense number of animals. Several of these persons were taken up, and they owned that they carried such powders about with them, and though they made them suffer various tortures, they could not force them to retract what they had said.

Others affirmed that there was a certain country named Mangonia, where there were vessels which were borne through the air and took away the productions; that certain wizards had cut down trees to carry them to their country. He says, moreover, that one day three men and a woman were presented to him, who they said had fallen from these ships which floated in the air. They were kept some days in confinement, and at last having been confronted with their accusers, the latter were obliged, after contesting the matter, and making several depositions, to avow that they knew nothing certain concerning their being carried away, or of their pretended fall from the ship in the sky.

Charlemagne in his Capitularies, and the authors of his time, speak also of these wizard tempest-brewers, enchanters, etc., and commanded that they should be reprimanded and severely chastised.

Pope Gregory IX in a letter addressed to the Archbishop of Mayence, the Bishop of Hildesheim, and Doctor Conrad, in 1234, thus relates the abominations of which they accused the heretic Stadingians. 'When they receive,' says he, 'a novice, and when he enters their assemblies for the first time, he sees an enormous toad, as big as a goose, or bigger. Some kiss it on the mouth, some kiss it behind. Then the novice meets a pale man with very black eyes, and so thin that he is only skin and bones. He kisses him, and feels that he is cold as ice. After this kiss, the novice easily forgets the Catholic faith; afterwards they hold a feast together, after which a black cat comes down behind a statue, which usually stands in the room where they assemble.

'The novice first of all kisses the cat on the back, then he who presides over the assembly, and the others who are worthy of it. The imperfect receive only a kiss from the master; they promise obedience; after which they extinguish the lights, and commit all sorts of disorders. They receive every year, at Easter, the Lord's Body, and carry it in their mouth to their own houses, when they cast it away. They believe in Lucifer, and say that the Master of Heaven has unjustly and fraudulently thrown him into hell. They believe also that Lucifer is the creator of celestial things, that will re-enter into glory, after having thrown down his adversary, and that through him they will gain eternal bliss.' This letter bears date the 13th June 1233.

CHAPTER 19

Instances of Sorcerers and Witches being, as they said, Transported to the Sabbath

All that is said about witches going to the sabbath is treated as a fable, and we have several examples which prove that they do not stir from their bed or their chamber. It is true that some of them anoint themselves with a certain grease or unguent, which makes them sleepy, and renders them insensible; and during this swoon they fancy that they go to the sabbath, and there see and hear what everyone says is there seen and heard.

We read in the book entitled *Malleus Maleficorum*, or the *Hammer of the Sorcerers*, that a woman who was in the hands of the Inquisitors assured them that she repaired really and bodily whither she would, and that even were she shut up in prison and strictly guarded, and let the place be ever so far off.

The Inquisitors ordered her to go to a certain place, to speak to certain persons, and bring back news of them; she promised to obey, and was directly locked up in a chamber, where she laid down, extended as if dead; they went into the room, and moved her; but she remained motionless, and without the least sensation, so that when they put a lighted candle to her foot and burnt it she did not feel it. A little after, she came to herself, and gave an account of the commission they had given her, saying she had had a great deal of trouble to go that road. They asked her what was the matter with her foot; she said it hurt her very much since her return, and knew not whence it came.

Then the Inquisitors declared to her what had happened; that she had not stirred from her place, and that the pain in her foot was caused by the application of a lighted candle during her pretended absence. The thing having been verified, she acknowledged her folly, asked pardon, and promised never to fall into it again.

Other historians relate, that, by means of certain drugs with which both wizards and witches anoint themselves, they are really and corporally transported to the sabbath. Torquemada relates, on the authority of Paul Grilland, that a husband suspecting his wife of being a witch, desired to know if she went to the sabbath, and how she managed to transport herself thither. He watched her so narrowly, that he saw her one day anoint herself with a certain unguent, and then take the form of a bird and fly away, and he saw her no more till the next morning, when he found her by his side. He questioned her very much, without making her own anything; at last he told her what he had himself seen, and by dint of beating her with a stick, he constrained her to tell him her secret, and to take him with her to the sabbath.

Arrived at this place, he sat down to table with the others; but as all the viands which were on the table were very insipid, he asked for some salt; they were some time before they brought any; at last, seeing a salt-cellar, he said, 'God be praised, there is some salt at last!' At the same instant he heard a very great noise, all the company disappeared, and he found himself alone and naked in a field among the mountains. He went forward and found some shepherds; he learned that he was more than three leagues from his dwelling. He returned thither as he could, and having related the circumstance to the Inquisitors, they caused the woman and several others, her accomplices, to be taken up and chastised as they deserved.

The same author relates that a woman returning from the sabbath and being carried through the air by the evil spirit, heard in the morning the bell for the *Angelus*. The devil let her go immediately, and she fell into a quickset hedge on the bank of a river, her hair fell dishevelled over her neck and shoulders. She perceived a young lad, who after much entreaty came and took her out and conducted her to the next village, where her house was situated; it required most pressing and repeated questions on the part of the lad, before she would tell him truly what had happened to her; she made him presents, and begged him to say nothing about it, nevertheless the circumstance got spread abroad.

If we could depend on the truth of these stories, and an infinite number of similar ones, which books are full of, we might believe that sometimes sorcerers are carried bodily to the sabbath; but on comparing these stories with others which prove that they go thither only in mind and imagination, we may say boldly, that what is related of wizards and witches who go or think they go to the sabbath, is usually only illusion on the part of the devil, and seduction on the part of those of both sexes who fancy they fly and travel, while they in reality do not stir from their places. The spirit of malice and falsehood being mixed up in this foolish prepossession, they confirm themselves in their follies and engage others in the same impiety; for Satan has a thousand ways of deceiving mankind and of retaining them in error. Magic, impiety, enchantments, are often the effects of a diseased imagination. It rarely happens that these kind of people do not fall into every excess of licentiousness, irreligion, and theft, and into the most outrageous consequences of hatred to their neighbours.

Some have believed that demons took the form of the sorcerers and sorceresses who were supposed to be at the sabbath, and that they maintained the simple creatures in their foolish belief, by appearing to them sometimes in the shape of those persons who were reputed witches, while they themselves were quietly asleep in their beds. But this belief contains difficulties as great, or perhaps greater, than the opinion we would combat. It is far from easy to understand that the demon takes the form of pretended sorcerers and witches, that he appears under this shape, that he eats, drinks, and travels, and does other actions to make simpletons believe that sorcerers go to the sabbath. What advantage does the devil derive from making idiots believe these things, or maintaining them in such an error?

Nevertheless it is related, that St Germain, Bishop of Auxerre, travelling one day, and passing through a village in his diocese, after having taken some refreshment there, remarked that they were preparing a great supper, and laying out the table anew; he asked if they expected company, and they told him it was for those good women who go by night. St Germain well understood what was meant, and resolved to watch to see the end of this adventure.

Sometime after he beheld a multitude of demons who came in the form of men and women, and sat down to table in his presence. St Germain forbade them to withdraw, and calling the people of the house, he asked them if they knew those persons. They replied, that they were such and such among their neighbours. 'Go,' said he, 'and see if they are in their houses.' They went, and found them asleep in their beds. The saint conjured the demons, and obliged them to declare that it is thus they mislead mortals, and make them believe that there are sorcerers and witches who go by night to the sabbath; they obeyed, and disappeared, greatly confused.

This history may be read in old manuscripts, and is to be found in Jacques de Varasse, Pierre de Noëls, in St Antonine, and in old Breviaries of Auxerre, as well printed, as manuscript. I by no means guarantee the truth of this story; I think it is absolutely apocryphal; but it proves that those who wrote and copied it, believed that these nocturnal journeys of sorcerers and witches to the sabbath, were mere illusions of the demon. In fact it is hardly possible to explain all that is said of sorcerers and witches going to the sabbath, without having recourse to the ministry of the demon; to which we must add a disturbed imagination, with a mind misled, and foolishly prepossessed, and, if you will, a few drugs which affect the brain, excite the humours, and produce dreams relative to impressions already in their minds.

In John Baptist Porta, Cardan, and elsewhere, may be found the composition of those ointments with which witches are said to anoint themselves, to be able to transport themselves to the sabbath; but the only real effect they produce is to send them to sleep, disturb their imagination, and make them believe they are going long journeys, while they remain profoundly sleeping in their beds.

The fathers of the council of Paris, of the year 829, confess that magicians, wizards, and people of that kind, are the ministers and instruments of the demon in the exercise of their diabolical art; that they trouble the minds of certain persons by beverages calculated to inspire impure love; that they are persuaded they can disturb the sky, excite tempests, send hail, predict the future, ruin and destroy the fruit, and take away the milk of cattle belonging to one person, in order to give it to cattle the property of another.

The bishops conclude, that all the rigour of the laws enacted by princes against such persons ought to be put in force against them, and so much the more justly, that it is evident they yield themselves up to the service of the devil.

Sprenger, in the *Malleus Maleficarum*, relates, that in Suabia, a peasant who was walking in his fields with his little girl, a child about eight years of age, complained of the drought, saying, 'Alas! when will God give us some rain?' Immediately the little girl told him that she could bring him some down whenever he wished it. He answered, 'And who has taught you that secret?' 'My mother,' said she, 'who has strictly forbidden me to tell anybody of it.'

'And what did she do to give you this power?'

'She took me to a master, who comes to me as many times as I call him.'

'And have you seen this master?'

'Yes,' said she, 'I have often seen men come to my mother's house; she has devoted me to one of them.'

After this dialogue, the father asked her how she could do to make it rain upon his field only? She asked but for a little water; he led her to a neighbouring brook, and the girl having called the water in the name of him to whom she had been devoted by her mother, they beheld directly abundance of rain falling on the peasant's field.

The father, convinced that his wife was a sorceress, accused her before the judges, who condemned her to be burnt. The daughter was baptised and vowed to God, but she then lost the power of making it rain at her will.

CHAPTER 20

Story of Louis Gaufredi and Magdalen de la Palud, Owned by Themselves to be a Sorcerer and Sorceress

This is an unheard-of example; a man and woman who declared themselves to be a sorcerer and sorceress. Louis Gaufredi, Curé of the parish of Accouls, at Marseilles, was accused of magic, and arrested at the beginning of the year 1611. Christopher Gaufredi, his uncle, of Pourrieres, in the neighbourhood of Beauversas, sent him, six months before he (Christopher) died, a little paper book, in 16mo, with six leaves written upon; at the bottom of every leaf were two verses in French, and in the other part were characters or ciphers, which contained magical mysteries. Louis Gaufredi at first thought very little of this book, and kept it for five years.

At the end of that time, having read the French verses, the devil presented himself under a human shape, and by no means deformed, and told him that he was come to fulfil all his wishes, if he would give *him* credit for all his good works. Gaufredi agreed to the condition. He asked of the demon that he might enjoy a great reputation for wisdom and virtue among persons of probity, and that he might inspire with love all the women and young girls he pleased, by simply breathing upon them.

Lucifer promised him all this in writing, and Gaufredi very soon saw the perfect accomplishment of his designs. He inspired with love a young lady named Magdalen, the daughter of a gentleman whose name was Mandole de la Palud. This girl was only nine years old, when Gaufredi, on pretence of devotion and spirituality, gave her to understand that, as her spiritual father, he had a right to dispose of her, and persuaded her to give herself to the devil; and some years afterwards, he obliged her to give a schedule, signed with her own blood, to the devil, to deliver herself up to him still more. It is even said, that he made her give from that time seven or eight other schedules.

After that, he breathed upon her, inspired her with a violent passion for himself, and took advantage of her; he gave her a familiar demon, who served her and followed her everywhere. One day he transported her to the witches' sabbath, held on a high mountain near Marseilles; she saw there people of all nations, and in particular Gaufredi, who held there a distinguished rank, and who caused characters to be impressed or stamped on her head and in several other parts of her body. This girl afterwards became a nun of the order of St Ursula, and passed for being possessed by the devil.

Gaufredi also inspired several other women with an irregular passion, by breathing on them; and this diabolical power lasted for six years. For at last they found out that he was a sorcerer and magician; and Mademoiselle de Mandole having been arrested by the Inquisition, and interrogated by father Michael Jacobin, owned a great part of what we have just told, and during the exorcisms discovered several other things. She was then nineteen years of age.

All this made Gaufredi known to the Parliament of Provence. They arrested him; and proceedings against him commenced February, 1611. They heard in particular the deposition of Magdalen de la Palud, who gave a complete history of the magic of Gaufredi, and the abominations he had committed with her. That for the last fourteen years he had been a magician, and head of the magicians; and if he had been taken by the justiciary power, the devil would have carried him body and soul to hell.

Gaufredi had voluntarily gone to prison; and from the first examination which he underwent, he denied everything and represented himself as an upright man. But from the depositions made against him, it was shown that his heart was very corrupted, and that he had seduced Mademoiselle de Mandole, and other women whom he confessed. This young lady was heard juridically the 21st February, and gave the history of her seduction, of Gaufredi's magic, and of the sabbath whither he had caused her to be transported several times.

Some time after this, being confronted with Gaufredi, she owned that he was a worthy man, and that all which had been reported against him was imaginary, and retracted all she herself had avowed. Gaufredi on his part acknowledged his illicit connexion with her, denied all the rest, and maintained that it was the devil, by whom she was possessed, that had suggested to her all she had said. He owned that having resolved to reform his life, Lucifer had appeared to him, and threatened him with many misfortunes; that in fact he had experienced several; that he had burnt the magic book in which he had placed the schedules of Mademoiselle de la Palud and his own, which he had made with the devil; but that when he afterwards looked for them, he was much astonished not to find them. He spoke at length concerning the sabbath, and said there was near the town of Nice, a magician, who had all sorts of garments ready for the use of the sorcerers; that on the day of the sabbath, there is a bell weighing a hundred pounds, four ells in width, and with a clapper of wood, which made the sound dull and lugubrious. He related several horrors, impieties, and abominations, which were committed at the sabbath. He repeated the schedule which Lucifer had given him, by which he bound himself to cast a spell on those women who should be to his taste.

After this exposition of the things related above, the Attorney General drew his conclusions: As the said Gaufredi has been convicted of having divers marks in several parts of his body, where if pricked he has felt no pain, neither has any blood come; that he has been illicitly connected with Magdalen de la Palud, both at church and in her own house, both by day and by night, by letters in which were amorous or love characters, invisible to any other but herself; that he had induced her to renounce her God and her Church – and that she had received on her body several diabolical characters; that he has owned himself to be a sorcerer and magician; that he had kept by him a book of magic, and had made use of it to conjure and invoke the evil spirit; that he has been with the said Magdalen to the sabbath, where he had committed an infinite number of scandalous, impious, and abominable actions, such as having worshipped Lucifer: for these causes, the said Attorney General requires, that the said Gaufredi be declared attainted and convicted of the circumstances imputed to him, and as reparation of them, that he be previously degraded from sacred orders, by the Lord Bishop of Marseilles, his diocesan, and afterwards condemned to make honourable amends one audience day, having his head and feet bare, a cord about his neck, and holding a lighted taper in his hands – to ask pardon of God, the king, and the court of justice – then, to be delivered into the hands of the executioner of the high court of law, to be taken to all the chief places and cross-roads of this city of Aix, and torn with red-hot pincers in all parts of his body; and after that, in the *Place des Jacobins*, burned alive, and his ashes scattered to the wind; and before being executed, let the question be applied to him, and let him be tormented as grievously as can be devised, in order to extract from him the names of his other accomplices. Deliberated the 18th April 1611, and the decree in conformity given the 29th April 1611.

The same Gaufredi having undergone the question ordinary and extraordinary, declared that he had seen at the sabbath no person of his acquaintance except Mademoiselle de Mandole; that he had seen there also certain monks of certain orders, which he did not name, neither did he know the names of the monks. That the devil anointed the heads of the sorcerers with certain unguents, which quite effaced everything from their memory.

Notwithstanding this decree of the Parliament of Provence, many people believed that Gaufredi was a sorcerer only in imagination; and the author from whom we derive this history says, that there are some parliaments, amongst others the Parliament of Paris, which do not punish sorcerers, when no other crimes are combined with magic; and that experience has proved, that in not punishing sorcerers, but simply treating them as madmen, it has been seen in time that they were no longer sorcerers, because they no longer fed their imagination with these ideas; while in those places where sorcerers were burnt, they saw nothing else, because everybody was strengthened in this prejudice. That is what this writer says.

But we cannot conclude from thence, that God does not sometimes permit the demon to exercise his power over men, and lead them to the excess of malice and impiety, and shed darkness over their minds and corruption in their hearts, which hurry them into an abyss of disorder and misfortune. The demon tempted Job by the permission of God. The messenger of Satan and the thorn in the flesh wearied St Paul; he asked to be delivered from them; but he was told that the grace of God would enable him to resist his enemies, and that virtue was strengthened by infirmities and trials. Satan took possession of the heart of Judas, and led him to betray Jesus Christ his Master to the Jews his enemies. The Lord wishing to warn his disciples against the impostors who would appear after his ascension, says, that by God's permission, these impostors would work such miracles as might mislead the very elect themselves, were it possible. He tells them elsewhere, that Satan has asked permission of God to sift them as wheat, but that He has prayed for them that their faith may be steadfast.

Thus then with permission from God, the devil can lead men to commit such excesses as we have just seen in Mademoiselle de la Palud and in the priest Louis Gaufredi, perhaps even so far as really to take them through the air to unknown spots, and to what is called the witches' sabbath; or, without really conducting them thither, so strike their imagination and mislead their senses, that they think they move, see, and hear, when they do not stir from their places, see no object and hear no sound.

Observe also, that the Parliament of Aix did not pass any sentence against even that young girl, it being their custom to inflict no other punishment on those who suffered themselves to be seduced and dishonoured, than the shame with which they were loaded ever after. In regard to the curé Gaufredi, in the account which they render to the chancellor of the sentence given by them, they say that this curé was in truth accused of sorcery; but that he had been condemned to the flames as being arraigned and convicted of spiritual incest with Magdalen de la Palud, his penitent.

CHAPTER 21

Reasons which Prove the Possibility of Sorcerers and Witches being Transported to the Sabbath

All that has just been said is more fitted to prove, that the going of sorcerers and witches to the sabbath is only an illusion and a deranged imagination on the part of these persons, and malice and deceit on that of the devil, who misleads them, and persuades them to yield themselves to him, and renounce true religion, by the lure of vain promises that he will enrich them, load them with honours, pleasures, and prosperity, rather than to convince us of the reality of the corporeal transportation of these persons to what they call the sabbath.

Here are some arguments and examples which seem to prove, at least, that the transportation of sorcerers to the sabbath is not impossible; for the impossibility of this transportation is one of the strongest objections which is made to the opinion that supposes it.

There is no difficulty in believing that God may allow the demon to mislead men, and carry them on to every excess of irregularity, error, and impiety; and that he may also permit him to perform some things which to us appear astonishing, and even miraculous; whether the devil achieves them by natural power, or by the supernatural concurrence of God, who employs the evil spirit to punish his creature, who has willingly forsaken Him to yield himself up to his enemy. The prophet Ezekiel was transported through the air from Chaldea, where he was a captive, to Judea, and into the temple of the Lord, where he saw the abominations which the Israelites committed in that holy place; and thence he was brought back again to Chaldea by the ministration of angels, as we shall relate in another chapter. We know by the Gospel that the devil carried our Saviour to the highest point of the temple at Jerusalem. We know also that the prophet Habakkuk was transported from Judea to Babylon, to carry food to Daniel in the lions' den. St Paul informs us that he was carried up to the third heaven, and that he heard ineffable things; but he owns that he does not know whether it was in the body or only in the spirit. He therefore doubted not the possibility of a man being transported in body and soul through the air. The deacon St Philip was transported from the road from Gaza to Azotus in a very little time by the Spirit of God. We learn by ecclesiastical history, that Simon the magician was carried by the demon up into the air, whence he was precipitated, through the prayers of St Peter. John the Deacon, author of the Life of St Gregory the Great, relates, that one Farold having introduced into the monastery of St Andrew, at Rome, some women who led disorderly lives, in order to divert himself there with them, and offer insult to the monks, that same night Farold, having occasion to go out, was suddenly seized and carried up into the air by demons, who held him there suspended by his hair, without his being able to open his mouth to utter a cry, till the hour of matins, when Pope St Gregory, the founder and protector of that monastery, appeared to him, reproached him for his profanation of that holy place, and foretold that he would die within the year – which did happen.

I have been told by a magistrate, as incapable of being deceived by illusions, as of imposing any such on other people, that on the 16th October 1716, a carpenter, who inhabited a village near Bar, in Alsace, called Heiligenstein, was found at five o'clock in the morning in the garret of a cooper at Bar. This cooper having gone up to fetch the wood for his trade that he might want to use during the day, and having opened the door, which was fastened with a bolt *on the outside*, perceived a man lying at full length upon his stomach, and fast asleep. He recognised him, and having asked him what he did there, the carpenter in the greatest surprise told him he knew neither by what means, nor by whom, he had been taken to that place.

The cooper, not believing this, told him that assuredly he was come thither to rob him, and had him taken before the magistrate of Bar, who having interrogated him concerning the circumstance just spoken of, he related to him with great simplicity, that having set off about four o'clock in the morning to come from Heiligenstein to Bar – there being but a quarter of an hour's distance between those two places – he saw on a sudden, in a place covered with verdure and grass, a magnificent feast, brightly illuminated, where a number of persons were highly enjoying themselves with a sumptuous repast and by dancing; that two women of his acquaintance, inhabitants of Bar, having asked him to join the company, he sat down to table and partook of the good cheer, for a quarter of an hour at the most; after that, one of the guests having cried out 'Citò, citò,' he found himself carried away gently to the cooper's garret, without knowing how he had been transported there.

This is what he declared in presence of the magistrate. The most singular circumstance of this history is, that hardly had the carpenter deposed what we read, than those two women of Bar who had invited him to join their feast hung themselves, each in her own house.

The superior magistrates, fearing to carry things so far as to compromise perhaps half the inhabitants of Bar, judged prudently, that they had better not inquire further; they treated the carpenter as a visionary, and the two women who hung themselves were considered as lunatics; thus the thing was hushed up, and the matter ended.

If this is what they call the witches' sabbath, neither the carpenter, nor the two women, nor apparently the other guests at the festival, had need to come mounted on a demon; they were too near their own dwellings to have recourse to superhuman means in order to have themselves transported to the place of meeting. We are not informed how these guests repaired to this feast, nor how they returned each one to their home; the spot was so near the town, that they could easily go and return without any extraneous assistance.

But if secrecy was necessary, and they feared discovery, it is very probable that the demon transported them to their homes through the air before it was day, as he had transported the carpenter to the cooper's garret. Whatever turn may be given to this event, it is certainly difficult not to recognise a manifest work of the evil spirit in the transportation of the carpenter through the air, who finds himself, without being aware of it, in a well-fastened garret. The women who hung themselves, showed clearly that they feared something still worse from the law, had they been convicted of magic and witchcraft. And had not their accomplices also, whose names must have been declared, as much to fear?

William de Neubridge relates another story, which bears some resemblance to the preceding. A peasant having heard, one night as he was passing near a tomb, a melodious concert of different voices, drew near, and finding the door open, put in his head, and saw in the middle a grand feast, well lighted, and a well-covered table, round which were men and women making merry. One of the attendants having perceived him, presented him with a cup filled with liquor; he took it, and having spilled the liquor, he fled with the cup to the first village, where he stopped. If our carpenter had done the same, instead of amusing himself at the feast of the witches of Bar, he would have spared himself much uneasiness.

We have in history several instances of persons full of religion and piety, who, in the fervour of their orisons, have been taken up into the air, and remained there for some time. We have known a good monk, who rises sometimes from the ground, and remains suspended without wishing it, without seeking to do so, especially on seeing some devotional image, or on hearing some devout prayer, such as '*Gloria in excelsis Deo*'. I know a nun to whom it has often happened in spite of herself, to see herself thus raised up in the air to a certain distance from the earth; it was neither from choice, nor from any wish to distinguish herself, since she was truly confused at it. Was it by the ministration of angels, or by the artifice of the seducing spirit, who wished to inspire her with sentiments of vanity and pride? Or was it the natural effect of Divine love, or fervour of devotion in these persons?

I do not observe that the ancient fathers of the desert, who were so spiritual, so fervent, and so great in prayer, experienced similar ecstasies. These risings up in the air are more common among our new saints, as we may see in the Life of St Philip of Neri, where they relate his ecstasies and his elevations from earth into the air, sometimes to the height of several yards, and almost to the ceiling of his room, and this quite involuntarily. He tried in vain to hide it from the knowledge of those present, for fear of attracting their admiration, and feeling in it some vain complacency. The writers who give us these particulars do not say what was the cause, whether these ecstatic elevations from the ground were produced by the fervour of the Holy Spirit, or by the ministry of good angels, or by a miraculous favour of God, who desired thus to do honour to his servants in the eyes of men. God had moreover favoured the same St Philip de Neri, by permitting him to see the celestial spirits and even the demons, and to discover the state of holy spirits, by supernatural knowledge.

St John Columbino, teacher of the Jesuits, made use of St Catherine Columbina, a maiden of extraordinary virtue, for the establishment of nuns of his order. It is related of her, that sometimes she remained in a trance, and raised up two yards from the ground, motionless, speechless, and insensible.

The same thing is said of St Ignatius de Loyola, who remained entranced by God, and raised up from the ground to the height of two feet, while his body shone like light. He has been seen to remain in a trance insensible, and almost without respiration, for eight days together.

St Robert de Palentin rose also from the ground, sometimes to the height of a foot and a half, to the great astonishment of his disciples and assistants. We see similar trances and elevations in the Life of St Bernard Ptolomei, teacher of the congregation of Notre Dame of Mount Olivet; of St Philip Benitas, of the order of Servites; of St Cajetanus, founder of the Théatins; of St Albert of Sicily, confessor, who, during his prayers, rose three cubits from the ground; and lastly of St Dominic, the founder of the order of Preaching Brothers.

It is related of St Christina, Virgin at S. Tron, that being considered dead, and carried into the church in her coffin, as they were performing for her the usual service, she arose suddenly, and went as high as the beams of the church, as lightly as a bird. Being returned into the house with her sisters, she related to them that she had been led first to purgatory, and thence to hell, and lastly to paradise, where God had given her the choice of remaining there, or of returning to this world and doing penance for the souls she had seen in purgatory. She chose the latter, and was brought back to her body by the holy angels. From that time she could not bear the effluvia of the human body, and rose up into trees and on the highest towers with incredible lightness, there to watch and pray. She was so light in running, that she outran the swiftest dogs. Her parents tried in vain all they could do to stop her, even to loading her with chains, but she always escaped from them. So many other almost incredible things are related of this saint, that I dare not repeat them here.

M. Nicole, in his letters, speaks of a nun named Seraphina, who, in her ecstasies, rose from the ground with so much impetuosity, that five or six of the sisters could hardly hold her down.

This doctor, reasoning on the fact, says, that it proves nothing at all for Sister Seraphina; but the thing well verified proves God and the devil – that is to say, the whole of religion; that the circumstance being proved, is of very great consequence to religion; that the world is full of certain persons who believe only what cannot be doubted; that the great heresy of the world is no longer Calvinism and Lutheranism, but Atheism. There are all sorts of Atheists – some real, others pretended; some determined, others vacillating, and others tempted to be so. We ought not to neglect this kind of people; the grace of God is all-powerful; we must not despair of bringing them back by good arguments, and by solid and convincing proofs. Now, if these facts are certain, we must conclude that there is a God, or bad angels who imitate the works of God, and perform by themselves or their subordinates works capable of deceiving even the elect.

One of the oldest instances I remark of persons thus raised from the ground without anyone touching them, is that of St Dunstan, Archbishop of Canterbury, who died in 988, and who, a little time before his death, as he was going up stairs to his apartment, accompanied by several persons, was observed to rise from the ground; and as all present were astonished at the circumstance, he took occasion to speak of his approaching death.

Trithemius, speaking of St Elizabeth, Abbess of Schonau, in the diocese of Treves, says, that sometimes she was in an ecstatic trance, so that she would remain motionless and breathless during a long time. In these intervals she learned, by revelation and by the intercourse she had with blessed spirits, admirable things; and when she revived, she would discourse divinely, sometimes in German, her native language, sometimes in Latin, though she had no knowledge of that language. Trithemius did not doubt her sincerity and the truth of her discourse. She died in 1165.

St Richard, Abbot of S. Vanne de Verdun, appeared in 1036 elevated from the ground while he was saying mass in presence of the Duke Galizon, his sons, and a great number of lords and soldiers.

In the last century, the reverend Father Dominic Carme Déchaux was raised from the ground before the King of Spain, the Queen, and all the court, so that they had only to blow upon his body to move it about like a soap-bubble.

CHAPTER 22

Continuation of the Same Subject

We cannot reasonably dispute the truth of these ecstatic trances and elevations of the body of some saints, to a certain distance from the ground, since these circumstances are supported by so many witnesses. To apply this to the matter we here treat of, might it not be said that sorcerers and witches by the operation of the demon, and with God's permission, by the help of a lively and subtle temperament, are rendered light and rise into the air; where their heated imagination and prepossessed mind lead them to believe that they have done, seen, and heard, what has no reality except in their own brain?

I shall be told that the parallel I make between the actions of saints, which can only be attributed to angels and the operation of the Holy Spirit, or to the fervour of their charity and devotion, with what happens to wizards and witches, is injurious and odious; I know how to make a proper distinction between them: do not the books of the Old and New Testament, place in parallel lines the true miracles of Moses, with those of the magicians of Pharaoh; those of antichrist and his subordinates, with those of the saints and apostles; and does not St Paul inform us, that the angel of darkness often transforms himself into an angel of light?

In the first edition of this work, we spoke very fully of certain persons, who boast of having what they call 'the garter', and by that means are able to perform with extraordinary quickness in a very few hours, what would naturally take them several days journeying. Almost incredible things are related on that subject, nevertheless the details are so circumstantial, that it is hardly possible there should not be some foundation for them; and the demon may transport these people in a forced and violent manner, which causes them a fatigue similar to what they would have suffered, had they really performed the journey with more than ordinary rapidity.

For instance, the two circumstances related by Torquemada: the first of a poor scholar of his acquaintance, a clever man, who at last rose to be physician to Charles V; when studying at Guadalupe, was invited by a traveller who wore the garb of a monk, and to whom he had rendered some little service, to mount up behind him on his horse, which seemed a sorry animal and much tired; he got up and rode all night, without perceiving that he went at an extraordinary pace, but in the morning he found himself near the City of Granada; the young man went into the town, but the conductor passed onwards.

Another time, the father of a young man, known to the same Torquemada, and the young man himself, were going together to Granada, and passing through the village of Almeda, met a man on horseback like themselves and going the same way; after having travelled two or three leagues together, they halted, and the cavalier spread his cloak on the grass, so that there was no crease in the mantle; they all placed what provisions they had with them on this extended cloak, and let their horses graze. They drank and ate very leisurely, and having told their servants to bring their horses, the cavalier said to them, 'Gentlemen, do not hurry, you will reach the town early', at the same time he showed them Granada, at not a quarter of an hour's distance from thence.

Something equally marvellous is said of a canon of the cathedral of Beauvais. The Chapter of that church had been charged for a long time to acquit itself of a certain personal duty to the Church of Rome; the canons having chosen one of their brethren to repair to Rome for this purpose, the canon deferred his departure from day to day, and set off after matins on Christmas Day – arrived that same day at Rome, acquitted himself there of his commission, and came back from thence with the same despatch, bringing with him the original of the bond, which obliged the canons to send one of their body to make this offering in person.

However fabulous and incredible this story may appear, it is asserted that there are authentic proofs of it in the archives of the cathedral; and that upon the tomb of the canon in question, may still be seen the figures of demons engraved at the four corners in memory of this event. They even affirm, that the celebrated Father Mabillon saw the authentic voucher.

Now, if this circumstance and the others like it are not absolutely fabulous, we cannot deny that they are the effects of magic, and the work of the evil spirit.

Peter, the venerable Abbot of Cluny, relates so extraordinary a thing which happened in his time, that I should not repeat it here, had it not been seen by the whole town of Mâcon. The count of that town, a very violent man, exercised a kind of tyranny over the ecclesiastics, and against whatever belonged to them, without troubling himself either to conceal his violence, or to find a pretext for it; he carried it on with a high hand and gloried in it. One day when he was sitting in his palace in company with several nobles and others, they beheld an unknown person enter on horseback, who advanced to the count and desired him to follow him. The count rose and followed him, and having reached the door, he found there a horse ready caparisoned; he mounts it, and is immediately carried up into the air, crying out in a terrible tone to those who were present, 'Here, help me!' All the town ran out at the noise, but they soon lost sight of him; and no doubt was entertained that the devil had flown away with him to be the companion of his tortures, and to bear the pain of his excesses and his violence.

It is then not absolutely impossible, that a person may be raised into the air and transported to some very high and distant place, by order or by permission of God, by good or evil spirits; but we must own that the thing is of rare occurrence, and that in all that is related of sorcerers and witches, and their assemblings at the witches' sabbath, there is an infinity of stories, which are false, absurd, ridiculous, and even destitute of probability. M. Remi, attorney-general of Lorraine, author of a celebrated work, entitled *Demonology*, who tried a great number of sorcerers and sorceresses, with which Lorraine was then infested, produces hardly any proof whence we can infer the truth and reality of witchcraft, and of wizards and witches being transported to the sabbath.

CHAPTER 23

Obsession and Possession of the Devil

It is with reason that obsessions and possessions of the devil are placed in the rank of apparitions of the evil spirit among men. We call it *obsession* when the demon acts externally against the person whom he besets, and *possession* when he acts internally, agitates them, excites their ill humour, makes them utter blasphemy, speak tongues they have never learnt, discovers to them unknown secrets, and inspires them with the knowledge of the obscurest things in philosophy or theology. Saul was agitated and possessed by the evil spirit, who at intervals excited his melancholy humour, and awakened his animosity and jealousy against David, or who on occasion of the natural movement or impulsion of these dark moods, seized him, agitated him, and disturbed from his usual tenor of mind. Those whom the Gospel speaks of as being possessed, and who cried aloud that Jesus was the Christ, and that he was come to torment them before the time, that he was the Son of God, are instances of possession. But the demon Asmodeus, who beset Sara, the daughter of Raguel, and who killed her first seven husbands; those spoken of in the Gospel, who were simply struck with maladies or incommodities which were thought to be incurable; those whom the Scripture sometimes calls *lunatics*, who foamed at the mouth, who were convulsed, who fled the presence of mankind, who were violent and dangerous, so that they were obliged to be chained to prevent them from striking and maltreating other people; these kinds of persons were simply beset, or obseded by the devil.

Opinions are much divided on the matter of obsessions and possessions of the devil. The hardened Jews, and the ancient enemies of the Christian religion, convinced by the evidence of the miracles which they saw worked by Jesus Christ, by his Apostles, and by Christians, dared neither dispute their truth nor their reality; but they attributed them to magic, to the prince of the devils, or to the virtue of certain herbs, or of certain natural secrets.

St Justin, Tertullian, Lactantius, St Cyprian, Minutius, and the other fathers of the first ages of the church, speak of the power which the Christian exorcists exercised over the possessed, so confidently and so freely, that we can doubt neither the certainty, nor the evidence of the thing. They call upon their adversaries to bear witness, and pique themselves on making the experiment in their presence, and of forcing to come out of the bodies of the possessed, to declare their names, and acknowledge that those they adore in the Pagan temples are but devils.

Some opposed to [contrasted] the true miracles of the Saviour [with] those of their false gods, their magicians, and their heroes of paganism, such as those of Esculapius, and the famous Apollonius of Tyana. The pretended freethinkers dispute them in our days upon philosophical principles; they attribute them to a diseased imagination, the prejudices of education, and hidden springs of the constitution; they reduce the expressions of Scripture to hyperbole; they maintain that Jesus Christ condescended to the understanding of the people, and their prepossessions or prejudices; that demons being purely spiritual substances could not by themselves act immediately upon bodies; and that it is not at all probable God should work miracles to allow of their doing so.

If we examine closely those who have passed for being possessed, we shall not perhaps find one amongst them, whose mind had not been deranged by some accident, or whose body was not attacked by some infirmity either known or hidden, which had caused some ferment in the blood or the brain, and which, joined to prejudice, or fear, had given rise to what was termed in their case obsession or possession.

The possession of King Saul is easily explained by supposing that he was naturally an atrabilarian, and that in his fits of melancholy he appeared mad, or furious; therefore they sought no other remedy for his illness than music, and the sound of instruments proper to enliven or calm him. Several of the obsessions and possessions noted in the New Testament were simple maladies, or fantastic fancies, which made it believed that such persons were possessed by the devil. The ignorance of the people maintained this prejudice, and their being totally unacquainted with physics and medicine served to strengthen such ideas.

In one it was a sombre and melancholy temper, in another the blood was too fevered and heated; here the bowels were burnt up with heat, there a concentration of diseased humour, which suffocated the patient, as it happens with those subject to epilepsy and hypochondria, who fancy themselves gods, kings, cats, dogs, and oxen. There were others who, disturbed at the remembrance of their crimes, fell into a kind of despair, and into fits of remorse, which irritated their mind and constitution, and made them believe that the devil pursued and beset them. Such, apparently, were those women who followed Jesus Christ, and who had been delivered by him from the unclean spirits that possessed them, and partly so Mary Magdalen, from whom he expelled seven devils. The Scripture often speaks of the spirit of impurity, of the spirit of falsehood, of the spirit of jealousy; it is not necessary to have recourse to a particular demon to excite these passions in us; St James tells us that we are enough tempted by our own concupiscence which leads us to evil, without seeking after external causes.

The Jews attributed the greater part of their maladies to the demon: they were persuaded that they were a punishment for some crime either known or unrevealed. Jesus Christ and his Apostles wisely supposed these prejudices, without wishing to attack them openly and reform the old opinions of the Jews; they cured the diseases, and chased away the evil spirits who caused them, or who were said to cause them. The real and essential effect was the cure of the patient; no other thing was required to confirm the mission of Jesus Christ, his divinity, and the truth of the doctrine which he preached. Whether he expelled the demon, or not, is not essentially necessary to his first design; it is certain that he cured the patient either by expelling the devil, if it be true that this evil spirit caused the malady, or by replacing the inward springs and humours in their regular and natural state, which is always miraculous, and proves the Divinity of the Saviour.

Although the Jews were sufficiently credulous concerning the operations of the evil spirit, they at the same time believed that in general the demons who tormented certain persons were nothing else than the souls of some wretches, who fearing to repair to the place destined for them, took possession of the body of some mortal whom they tormented and endeavoured to deprive of life.

Josephus the historian relates that Solomon composed some charms against maladies, and some formulae of exorcism to expel evil spirits. He says besides, that a Jew named Eleazar cured in the presence of Vespasian some possessed persons by applying under their nose a ring, in which was enchased a root, pointed out by that prince. They pronounced the name of Solomon with a certain prayer, and an exorcism; directly, the person possessed fell on the ground, and the devil left him. The generality of common people among the Jews had not the least doubt that Beelzebub, prince of the devils, had the power to expel other demons, for they said that Jesus Christ only expelled them in the name of Beelzebub. We read in history that sometimes the pagans expelled demons; and the physicians boast of being able to cure some possessed persons, as they cure hypochondriacs, and imaginary disorders.

These are the most plausible things that are said against the reality of the possessions and obsessions of the devil.

CHAPTER 24

*The Truth and Reality of Possession and Obsession
by the Devil Proved from Scripture*

But the possibility, the verity and reality of the obsessions and possessions of the devil are indubitable, and proved by the Scripture, and by the authority of the Church, the Fathers, the Jews, and the Pagans. Jesus Christ and the Apostles believed this truth, and taught it publicly. The Saviour gives us a proof of his mission that he cures the possessed; he refutes the Pharisees, who asserted that he expelled the demons only in the name of Beelzebub; and maintains that he expels them by the virtue of God. He speaks to the demons; he threatens them, and puts them to silence. Are these equivocal marks of the reality of obsessions? The Apostles do the same, as did the early Christians their disciples. All this was done before the eyes of the heathen, who could not deny it, but who eluded the force and evidence of these things, by attributing this power to other demons, or to certain divinities, more powerful than ordinary demons; as if the kingdom of Satan were divided, and the evil Spirit could act against himself, or as if there were any collusion between Jesus Christ and the demons whose empire he had just destroyed.

The seventy disciples on their return from their mission came to Jesus Christ to give him an account of it, and tell him that the demons themselves are obedient to them. After his resurrection, the Saviour promises to his Apostles that they shall work miracles in his name, *that they shall cast out devils*, and receive the gift of tongues. All which was literally fulfilled.

The exorcisms used at all times in the Church against the demons are another proof of the reality of possessions; they show that at all times the Church and her ministers have believed them to be true and real, since they have always practised these exorcisms. The ancient fathers defied the heathen to produce a demoniac before the Christians; they pride themselves on curing them, and expelling the demon. The Jewish exorcists employed even the name of Jesus Christ to cure demoniacs; they found it efficacious in producing this effect; it is true that sometimes they employed the name of Solomon, and some charms said to have been invented by that prince, or roots and herbs to which they attributed the same virtues, like as a clever physician by the secret of his art can cure a hypochondriac or a maniac, or a man strongly persuaded that he is possessed by the devil, or as a wise confessor will restore the mind of a person disturbed by remorse, and agitated by the reflection of his sins, or the fear of hell. But we are speaking now of real possessions and obsessions which are cured only by the power of God, by the name of Jesus Christ, and by exorcisms. The son of Sceva, the Jewish priest, having undertaken to expel a devil in the name of Jesus Christ, whom Paul preached, the demoniac threw himself upon him, and would have strangled him, saying that he knew Jesus Christ, and Paul, but that for him, he feared him not. We must then distinguish well between possessions and possessions, exorcists and exorcists. There may be found demoniacs who counterfeit the possessed, to excite compassion and obtain alms. There may even be exorcists who abuse the name and power of Jesus Christ to deceive the ignorant; and how do I know that there are not even impostors to be found, who would place pretended possessed persons in the way, in order to pretend to cure them, and thus gain a reputation?

I do not enter into longer details on this matter; I have treated it formerly in a particular dissertation on the subject, printed apart with other dissertations on Scripture, and I have therein replied to the objections which were raised on this subject.

CHAPTER 25

Examples of Real Possessions Caused by the Devil

We must now report some of the most famous instances of the possession and obsession of the demon. Everybody is talking at this time of the possession (by the devil) of the nuns of Loudun, on which such different opinions were given, both at the time and since. Martha Brossier, daughter of a weaver of Romorantin, made as much noise in her time; but Charles Miron, Bishop of Orleans, discovered the fraud, by making her drink holy water as common water; by making them present to her a key wrapped up in red silk, which was said to be a piece of the true cross; and in reciting some lines from Virgil, which Martha Broissier's demon took for exorcisms, agitating her very much at the approach of the hidden key, and at the recital of the verses from Virgil. Henri de Gondi, Cardinal Bishop of Paris, had her examined by five of the faculty; three were of opinion that there was a great deal of imposture and a little disease. The parliament took notice of the affair, and nominated eleven physicians, who reported unanimously that there was nothing demoniacal in this matter.

In the reign of Charles IX, or a little before, a young woman of the town of Vervins, fifteen or sixteen years of age, named Nicola Aubry, had different apparitions of a spectre, who called itself her grandfather, and asked her for masses and prayers for the repose of his soul. Very soon after, she was transported to different places by this spectre, and sometimes even was carried out of sight, and from the midst of those who watched over her.

Then, they had no longer any doubt that it was the devil, which they had a great deal of trouble to make her believe. The Bishop of Laon gave his power (of attorney) for conjuring the spirit, and commanded them to see that the proces-verbaux were exactly drawn up by the notaries nominated for that purpose. The exorcisms lasted more than three months, and only serve to prove more and more the fact of the possession. The poor sufferer was torn from the hands of nine or ten men, who could hardly retain their hold of her: and on the last day of the exorcisms sixteen could not succeed in so doing. She had been lying on the ground, when she stood upright and stiff as a statue, without those who held her being able to prevent it. She spoke divers languages, revealed the most secret things, announced others at the moment they were being done, although at a great distance; she discovered to many the secret of their conscience, uttered at once three different voices, or tones, and spoke with her tongue hanging half a foot out of her mouth. After some exorcisms had been made at Vervins, they took her to Laon, where the Bishop undertook her. He had a scaffolding erected for this purpose in the cathedral. Such immense numbers of people went there, that they saw in the church ten or twelve thousand persons at a time; some even came from foreign countries. Consequently France could not be less curious; so the princes and great people, and those who could not come there themselves, sent persons who might inform them of what passed. The Pope's nuncios, the parliamentary deputies, and those of the university were present.

The devil, forced by the exorcisms, rendered such testimony to the truth of the Catholic religion, and, above all, to the reality of the Holy Eucharist, and at the same time to the falsity of Calvinism, that the irritated Calvinists no longer kept within bounds. From the time the exorcisms were made at Vervins, they wanted to kill the possessed, with the priest who exorcised her, in a journey they made her take to Nôtre Dame de Liesse. At Laon it was still worse; as they were the strongest in numbers there, a revolt was more than once apprehended. They so intimidated the Bishop and the magistrates, that they took down the scaffold, and did not have the general procession usually made before exorcisms. The devil became prouder thereupon, insulted the Bishop, and laughed at him. On the other hand, the Calvinists having obtained the suppression of the procession, and that she should be put in prison to be more nearly examined, Carlier, a Calvinist doctor, suddenly drew from his pocket something which was averred to be a most violent poison, which he threw into her mouth, and she kept it on her stomach whilst the convulsion lasted, but she threw it up of herself when she came to her senses.

All these experiments decided them on recommencing the processions, and the scaffold was replaced. Then the outraged Calvinists conceived the idea of a writing from M. de Montmorency, forbidding the continuation of the exorcisms, and enjoining the King's officers to be vigilant. Thus they abstained a second time from the procession, and again the devil triumphed at it. Nevertheless, he discovered to the Bishop the trick of this suppositious writing, named those who had taken part in it, and declared that he had again gained time by this obedience of the Bishop to the will of man rather than that of God. Besides that, the devil had already protested publicly that it was against his own will that he remained in the body of this woman; that he had entered there by the order of God; that it was to convert the Calvinists or to harden them, and that he was very unfortunate in being obliged to act and speak against himself.

The chapter then represented to the Bishop that it would be proper to make the processions and the conjurations twice a day, to excite still more the devotion of the people. The prelate acquiesced in it, and everything was done with the greatest éclat, and in the most orthodox manner. The devil declared again more than once that he had gained time; once because the Bishop had not confessed himself; another time because he was not fasting; and lastly, because it was requisite that the chapter and all the dignitaries should be present, as well as the court of justice and the King's officers, in order that there might be sufficient testimony; that he was forced to warn the Bishop thus of his duty, and that accursed was the hour when he entered into the body of this person; at the same time he uttered a thousand imprecations against the Church, the Bishop, and the clergy.

Thus at the last day of possession, everybody being assembled in the afternoon, the Bishop began the last conjurations, when many extraordinary things took place; amongst others, the Bishop desiring to put the Holy Eucharist near the lips of this poor woman, the devil in some way seized hold of his arm, and at the same moment raised this woman up, as it were, out of the hands of sixteen men who were holding her. But at last, after much resistance, he came out, and left her perfectly cured, and thoroughly sensible of the goodness of God. The *Te Deum* was sung to the sound of all the bells in the town; nothing was heard among the Catholics but acclamations of joy, and many of the Calvinists were converted, whose descendants still dwell in the town. Florimond de Raimond, counsellor of the parliament of Bordeaux, had the happiness to be of the number, and has written the history of it. For nine days they made the procession, to return thanks to God; and they founded a perpetual mass, which is celebrated every year on the 8th February, and they represented this story in bas-relief round the choir, where it may be seen at this day.

In short, God, as if to put the finishing stroke to so important a work, permitted that the Prince of Condé, who had just left the Catholic religion, should be misled on this subject by those of his new communion. He sent for the poor woman, and also the Canon d'Espinois, who had never forsaken her during all the time of the exorcisms. He interrogated them separately, and at several different times, and made every effort, not to discover if they had practised any artifice, but to find out if there was any in the whole affair. He went so far as to offer the canon very high situations if he would change his religion. But what can you obtain in favour of heresy from sensible and upright people, to whom God has thus manifested the power of his Church? All the efforts of the prince were useless; the firmness of the canon, and the simplicity of the poor woman, only served to prove to him still more the certainty of the event which displeased him, and he sent them both home.

Yet a return of ill-will caused him to have this woman again arrested, and he kept her in one of his prisons until her father and mother having entreated an inquiry into this injustice to King Charles IX, she was set at liberty by order of his majesty.

An event of such importance, and so carefully attested, both on the part of the Bishop and the chapter, and on that of the magistrates, and even by the violence of the Calvinistic party, ought not to be buried in silence. King Charles IX, on making his entry into Laon some time after, desired to be informed about it by the dean of the cathedral, who had been an ocular witness of the affair. His majesty commanded him to give publicity to the story, and it was then printed, first in French, then in Latin, Spanish, Italian and German, with the approbation of the Sorbonne, supported by the rescripts of Pope Pius V and Gregory XIII his successor. And they made after that a pretty exact abridgment of it, by order of the Bishop of Laon, printed under the title of *Le Triomphe du S. Sacrament sur le Diable*.

These are facts which have all the authenticity that can be desired, and such as a man of honour cannot with any good breeding affect to doubt, since he could not after that consider any facts as certain without being in shameful contradiction with himself.

CHAPTER 26

Continuation of the same Subject

There was in Lorraine, about the year 1620, a woman, possessed by the devil, who made a great noise in the country, but whose case is much less known among foreigners. I mean Mademoiselle Elizabeth de Ranfaing, the story of whose possession was written and printed at Nancy in 1622, by M. Pichard, a doctor of medicine, and physician in ordinary to their highnesses of Lorraine. Mademoiselle de Ranfaing was a very virtuous person, through whose agency God established a kind of order of nuns *of the Refuge*, the principal object of which is to withdraw from profligacy the girls or women who have fallen into libertinism. M. Pichard's work was approved by doctors of theology, and authorised by M. de Porcelets, Bishop of Toul, and in an assembly of learned men whom he sent for to examine the case, and the reality of the possession. It was ardently attacked and loudly denied by a monk of the Minimite order, named Claude Pithoy, who had the temerity to say that he would pray to God to send the devil into himself, in case the woman whom they were exorcising at Nancy was possessed; and again, that God was not God, if he did not command the devil to seize his body, if the woman they exorcised at Nancy was really possessed.

M. Pichard refutes him fully; but he remarks that persons who are weak minded, or of a dull and melancholy character, heavy, taciturn, stupid, and who are naturally disposed to frighten and disturb themselves, are apt to fancy that they see the devil, that they speak to him, and even that they are possessed by him; above all, if they are in places where others are possessed, whom they see, and with whom they converse. He adds, that thirteen or fourteen years ago, he remarked at Nancy a great number of this kind, and with the help of God he cured them. He says the same thing of atrabilarians, and women who suffer from *furor uterine*, who sometimes do such things and utter such cries, that anyone would believe they were possessed.

Mademoiselle Ranfaing having become a widow in 1617, was sought in marriage by a physician named Poviot. As she would not listen to his addresses, he first of all gave her philtres to make her love him, which occasioned strange derangements in her health. At last he gave her some magical medicaments; (for he was afterwards known to be a magician, and burnt as such by a judicial sentence). The physicians could not relieve her, and were quite at fault with her extraordinary maladies. After having tried all sorts of remedies, they were obliged to have recourse to exorcisms.

Now these are the principal symptoms which made it believed that Mademoiselle Ranfaing was really possessed. They began to exorcise her the 2nd September 1619, in the town of Remirémont, whence she was transferred to Nancy; there she was visited and interrogated by several clever physicians, who after having minutely examined the symptoms of what happened to her, declared that the casualties they had remarked in her had no relation at all with the ordinary course of known maladies, and could only be the result of diabolical possession.

After which, by order of M. de Porcelets, Bishop of Toul, they nominated for the exorcists M. Viardin, a doctor of divinity, counsellor of state of the Duke of Lorraine, a Jesuit and Capuchin. Almost all the monks in Nancy, the said lord bishop, the Bishop of Tripoli, suffragan of Strasburg, M. de Sancy, formerly ambassador from the most Christian king at Constantinople, and then priest of the *Oratoire*, Charles de Lorraine, Bishop of Verdun; two doctors of the Sorbonne sent on purpose to be present at the exorcisms, often exorcised her in Hebrew, Greek, and Latin, and she always replied pertinently to them, she who could hardly read Latin.

They report the certificate given by M. Nicolas de Harley, very well skilled in the Hebrew tongue, who avowed that Mademoiselle Ranfaing was really possessed, and had answered him from the movement of his lips alone, without his having pronounced any words, and had given several proofs of her possession. The Sieur Garnier, a doctor of the Sorbonne, having also given her several commands in Hebrew, she replied pertinently, but in French, saying that the compact was made that he should speak only in the usual tongue. The demon added, 'Is it not enough that I show thee that I understand what thou sayest?' The same M. Garnier, speaking to him in Greek, inadvertently put one case for another; the possessed, or rather the devil, said to him, 'Thou hast committed an error.' The doctor said to him in Greek, 'Point out my fault;' the devil replied, 'Let it suffice thee that I point out an error; I shall tell thee no more concerning it.' The doctor telling him in Greek to hold his tongue, he answered, 'Thou commandest me to hold my tongue, and I will not do so.'

M. Midot Ecolâtre de Toul said to him in the same language, 'Sit down;' he replied, 'I will not sit down.' M. Midot said to him moreover in Greek, 'Sit down on the ground and obey;' but as the demon was going to throw the possessed by force on the ground, he said to him in the same tongue, 'Do it gently;' he did so. He said in Greek, 'Put out the right foot;' he extended it; he said also in the same language, 'Cause her knees to be cold,' the woman replied that she felt them very cold.

The Sieur Mince, a doctor of the Sorbonne, holding a cross in his hand, the devil whispered to him in Greek, 'Give me the cross,' which was heard by some persons who were near him. M. Mince desired to make the devil repeat the same sentence; he answered, 'I will not repeat it all in Greek;' but he simply said in French, 'Give me,' and in Greek, 'the cross.'

The Reverend Father Albert, Capuchin, having ordered him in Greek to make the sign of the cross seven times with his tongue, in honour of the seven joys of the Virgin, he made the sign of the cross three times with his tongue, and then twice with his nose; but the holy man told him anew to make the sign of the cross seven times with his tongue; he did so; and having been commanded in the same language to kiss the feet of the lord Bishop of Toul, he prostrated himself and kissed his feet.

The same father having observed that the demon wished to overturn the *Bénitier*, or basin of holy water which was there, he ordered him to take the holy water and not spill it, and he obeyed. The Father commanded him to give marks of the possession; he answered, 'The possession is sufficiently known;' he added in Greek, 'I command thee to carry some holy water to the governor of the town.' The demon replied, 'It is not customary to exorcise in that tongue.' The father answered in Latin, 'It is not for thee to impose laws on us; but the Church has power to command thee in whatever language she may think proper.'

Then the demon took the basin of holy water and carried it to the keeper of the Capuchins, to the Duke Eric of Lorraine, to the Counts of Brionne, Remonville, la Vaux, and other lords.

The physician, M. Pichard having told him in a sentence, partly Hebrew, and partly Greek, to cure the head and eyes of the possessed woman; hardly had he finished speaking the last words, when the demon replied: 'Faith, we are not the cause of it; her brain is naturally moist: that proceeds from her natural constitution,' then M. Pichard said to the assembly, 'Take notice, gentlemen, that he replies to Greek and Hebrew at the same time.' 'Yes,' replied the demon, 'you discover the pot of roses, and the secret; I will answer you no more.' There were several questions and replies in foreign languages, which showed that he understood them very well.

M. Viardin having asked him in Latin, 'Ubi censebaris quandò mane oriebaris?' He replied, 'Between the seraphim.' They said to him, 'Pro signo exhibe nobis patibulum fratris Cephae.' The devil extended his arms in the form of a St Andrew's cross. They said to him, 'Applica carpum carpo.' He did so, placing the wrist of one hand over the other. Then, 'Admove tarsum tarso et metatarsum metatarso.' He crossed his feet and raised them one upon the other. Then afterwards he said, 'Excita in calcaneo qualitatem congregantem heterogenea.' The possessed said she felt her heel cold; after which, 'Repraesenta nobis labarum Venetorum.' He made the figure of the cross. Afterwards they said, 'Exhibe nobis videntum Deum benèprecantem nepotibus ex salvatore Egypti.' He crossed his arms as did blessing to the sons of Joseph; and then, 'Exhibe crucem conterebrantem stipiti,' he represented the cross of St Peter. The exorcist having by mistake said, 'Per eum qui adversus te praeliavit,' the demon did not give him time to correct himself; he said to him, 'O the ass! instead of *proeliatus est*.' He was spoken to in Italian and German, and he always answered accordingly.

They said to him one day, 'Sume encolpium ejus qui hodieè functus est officio illius de quo cecinit Psaltes: pro patribus tuis nati sunt tibi filii.' He went directly and took the cross hanging round the neck and resting on the breast of the Prince Eric de Lorraine, who that same day had filled the office of Bishop in giving orders, because the Bishop of Toul was indisposed. He discovered secret thoughts, and heard words that were said in the ear of some persons which he was not possibly near enough to overhear, and declared that he had known the mental prayer that a good priest had made before the Holy Sacrament.

Here is a trait still more extraordinary. They said to the demon, speaking Latin and Italian in the same sentence: 'Adi scholastrum seniorem et osculare ejus pedes, la cui scarpa ha più di sugaro,' that very moment he went and kissed the foot of the Sieur Juillet, ecolâtre of St George, the Elder of M. Viardin, ecolâtre of the Primitiale. M. Juillet's right let was shorter than the left, which obliged him to wear a shoe with a cork heel, (or raised by a piece of cork, called in Italian *sugaro*.)

They proposed to him very difficult questions concerning the Trinity, the Incarnation, the Holy Sacrament of the altar, the grace of God, free will, the manner in which angels and demons know the thoughts of men, etc., and he replied with much clearness and precision. She discovered things unknown to everybody, and revealed to certain persons, but secretly and in private, some sins of which they had been guilty.

The demon did not obey the voice only of the exorcists; he obeyed even when they simply moved their lips, or held their hand, or a handkerchief, or a book upon the mouth. A Calvinist having one day mingled secretly in the crowd, the exorcist, who was warned of it, commanded the demon to go and kiss his feet; he went immediately, rushing through the crowd.

An Englishman having come from curiosity to the exorcist, the devil told him several particulars relating to his country and religion; he was a Puritan; and the Englishman owned that everything he had said was true. The same Englishman said to him in his language, 'As a proof of thy possession, tell me the name of my master who formerly taught me embroidery,' he replied, 'William.' They commanded him to recite the *Ave Maria;* he said to a Huguenot gentleman who was present, 'Do you say it, if you know it; for they don't say it amongst your people.' M. Pichard relates several unknown and hidden things which the demon revealed, and that he performed several feats which it is not possible for any person, however agile and supple he may be, to achieve by natural strength or power; such as crawling on the ground without making use of hands or feet, appearing to have the hair standing erect like serpents.

After all the details concerning the exorcisms, marks of possession, questions and answers of the possessed, M. Pichard reports the authentic testimony of the theologians, physicians, of the Bishops Eric of Lorraine, and Charles of Lorraine, Bishop of Verdun, of several monks of every order, who attest the said possession to be real and veritable; and lastly, a letter from the Revd Father Cotton, a Jesuit, who certifies the same thing. The said letter bears the date 5th June 1621, and is in reply to the one which the Prince Eric of Lorraine had written to him.

I have omitted a great many particulars related in the recital of the exorcisms, and the proofs of the possession of Mademoiselle de Ranfaing. I think I have said enough to convince any persons who are sincere and unprejudiced, that her possession is as certain as these things can be. The affair occurred at Nancy, the capital of Lorraine, in the presence of a great number of enlightened persons, two of whom were of the house of Lorraine, both bishops, and well informed; in presence and by the orders of my Lord de Porcelets, Bishop of Toul, a most enlightened man, and of distinguished merit; of two doctors of the Sorbonne, called thither expressly to judge of the reality of the possession; in presence of people of the so-called Reformed religion, and much on their guard against things of this kind. It has been seen how far Father Pithoy carried his temerity against the possession in question; he has been reprimanded by his diocesan and his superiors, who have imposed silence on him.

Mademoiselle de Ranfaing is known to be personally a woman of extraordinary virtue, prudence, and merit. No reason can be imagined for her feigning a possession which has pained her in a thousand ways. The consequence of this terrible trial has been the establishment of a kind of religious order, from which the Church has received much edification, and from which God has providentially derived glory.

M. Nicolas de Harlay Sancy and M. Viardin, are persons highly to be respected both for their personal merit, their talent, and the high offices they have filled; the first having been French ambassador at Constantinople, and the other resident of the good Duke Henry at the Court of Rome; so that I do not think I could have given an instance more fit to convince you of there being real and veritable possessions than this of Mademoiselle de Ranfaing.

I do not relate that of the nuns of Loudun, on which such various opinions have been given, the reality of which was doubted at the very time, and is very problematical to this day. Those who are curious to know the history of that affair will find it very well detailed in a book I have already cited, entitled, *Examen et Discussion Critique de l'Histoire des Diables de Loudon, etc.*, par M. de la Ménardaye, à Paris, chez de Bure Aîné, 1749.

CHAPTER 27

Objections against the Obsessions and Possessions of the Demon – Reply to the Objections

Several objections may be raised against the obsessions and possessions of demons; nothing is subject to greater difficulties than this matter, but Providence constantly and uniformly permits the clearest and most certain truths of religion to remain enveloped in some degree of obscurity; that facts the best averred and the most indubitable should be subject to doubts and contradictions; that the most evident miracles should be disputed by some incredulous persons, on account of circumstances, which appear to them doubtful and disputable.

All religion has its lights and shadows; God has permitted it to be so in order that the just may have somewhat to exercise their faith in believing, and the impious and incredulous persist in their wilful impiety and incredulity. The greatest mysteries of Christianity are to the one subjects of scandal, and to the others means of salvation; the one regarding the mystery of the Cross as folly, and the others as the work of sublimest wisdom, and of the most admirable power of God. Pharaoh hardened his heart when he saw the wonders wrought by Moses; but the magicians of Egypt were at last obliged to recognise in them the hand of God. The Hebrews on sight of these wonders take confidence in Moses and Aaron, and yield themselves to their guidance, without fearing the dangers to which they may be exposed.

We have already remarked, that the demon often seems to act against his own interest, and destroy his own empire, by saying that everything which is related of the return of spirits, the obsessions and possessions of the demon, of spells, magic, and sorcery, are only tales wherewith to frighten children; that they all have no existence except in weak and prejudiced minds. How can it serve the demon to maintain this, and destroy the general opinion of nations on all these things? If in all there is only falsehood and illusion, what does he gain by undeceiving people? and if there is any truth in them, why decry his own work, and take away the credit of his subordinates and his own operations?

Jesus Christ in the Gospel refutes those who said that he expelled devils in the name of Beelzebub; he maintains that the accusation is unfounded, because it was incredible that Satan should destroy his own work, and his own empire. The reasoning is doubtless solid and conclusive, above all to the Jews, who thought that Jesus Christ did not differ from other exorcists who expelled demons, unless it was that he commanded the prince of devils, while the others commanded only the subaltern demons. Now, on this supposition, the prince of the demons could not expel his subalterns without destroying his own empire, without decrying himself, and without ruining the reputation of those who only acted by his orders.

It may be objected to this argument, that Jesus Christ supposed, as did the Jews, that the demons whom he expelled really possessed those whom he cured, in whatever manner he might cure them; and consequently that the empire of the demons subsisted, both in Beelzebub the prince of the demons, and in the other demons, who were subordinate to him, and who obeyed his orders; thus his empire was not entirely destroyed, supposing that Jesus Christ expelled them in the name of Beelzebub; that subordination, on the contrary, supposed that power or empire of the prince of the demons, and strengthened it.

But Jesus Christ not only expelled demons by his own authority, without ever making mention of Beelzebub; he expelled them in spite of themselves, and sometimes they loudly complained that he was come to torment them before the time. There was neither collusion between him and them, nor subordination similar to that which might be supposed to exist between Beelzebub and the other demons.

The Lord pursued them, not only in expelling them from bodies, but also in overthrowing their bad maxims, by establishing doctrines and maxims quite contrary to their own; he made war upon every vice, error, and falsehood; he attacked the demon face to face, everywhere, unflinchingly; thus it cannot be said that he spared him, or was in collusion with him. If the devil will sometimes pass off as chimeras and illusions all that is said of apparitions, obsessions and possessions, magic and sorcery; and if he appears so absolutely to overthrow his reign, even so far as to deny the most marked and palpable effects of his own power and presence, and impute them to the weakness of mind of men, and their foolish prejudices; in all this he can only gain advantage for himself: for if he can persuade people of the truth of what he advances, his power will only be more solidly confirmed by it, since it will no longer be attacked, and he will be left to enjoy his conquests in peace, and the ecclesiastical and secular powers interested in repressing the effects of his malice and cruelty will no longer take the trouble to make war upon him, and caution or put the nations on their guard against his stratagems and ambuscades. It will close the mouth of parliaments, and stay the hand of judges and powers; and the simple people will become the sport of the demon, who will not cease continuing to tempt, persecute, corrupt, deceive and cause the perdition of those who shall no longer mistrust his snares and his malice. The world will relapse into the same state as when under paganism, given up to error, to the most shameful passions, and will even deny or doubt those truths which shall be the best attested, and the most necessary to our salvation.

Moses in the Old Testament well foresaw that the evil spirit would set every spring to work, to lead the Israelites into error and unruly conduct; he foresaw that in the midst of the chosen people he would instigate seducers, who would predict to them the hidden future, which predictions would come true and be followed up. He always forbids their listening to any prophet or diviners who wished to mislead them to impiety or idolatry.

Tertullian, speaking of the delusions performed by demons, and the foresight they have of certain events, says, that being spiritual in their nature, they find themselves in a moment in any place they may wish, and announce at a distance what they have seen and heard. All this is attributed to the Divinity, because neither the cause nor the manner is known; often, also, they boast of causing events, which they do but announce; and it is true that often they are themselves the authors of the evils they predict, but never of any good. Sometimes they make use of the knowledge they have derived from the predictions of the prophets respecting the designs of God, and they utter them as coming from themselves. As they are spread abroad in the air, they see in the clouds what must happen, and thus foretell the rain which they were aware of before it had been felt upon earth. As to maladies, if they cure them, it is because they have occasioned them; they prescribe remedies which produce effect, and it is believed that they have cured maladies simply because they have not continued them. *Quia desinunt loedere, curasse credentur.*

The demon can then foresee the future and what is hidden, and discover them by means of his votaries; he can also doubtlessly do wonderful things which surpass the usual and known powers of nature; but it is never done except to deceive us, and lead us into disorder and impiety. And even should he wear the semblance of leading to virtue and practising those things which are praiseworthy and useful to salvation, it would only be to win the confidence of such as would listen to his suggestions, to make them afterward fall into misfortune, and engage them in some sin of presumption or vanity: for as he is a spirit of malice and lies, it little imports to him by what means he surprises us, and establishes his reign among us.

But he is very far from always foreseeing the future, or succeeding always in misleading us; God has set bounds to his malice. He often deceives himself, and often makes use of disguise and perversion, that he may not appear to be ignorant of what he is ignorant of, or he will appear unwilling to do what God will not allow him to do; his power is always bounded, and his knowledge limited. Often, also, he will mislead and deceive through malice, because he is the father of falsehood. He deceives men, and rejoices when he sees them doing wrong; but not to lose his credit amongst those who consult him directly or indirectly, he lays the fault on those who undertake to interpret his words, or the equivocal signs which he has given. For instance, if he is consulted whether to begin an enterprise, or give battle, or set off on a journey, if the thing succeeds, he takes all the glory and merit to himself; if it does not succeed, he imputes it to the men who have not well understood the sense of his oracle, or to the aruspices, who have made mistakes in consulting the entrails of the immolated animals, or the flight of birds, etc.

We must not, then, be surprised to find so many contradictions, doubts, and difficulties, in the matter of apparitions, angels, demons and spirits. Man naturally loves to distinguish himself from the common herd, and rise above the opinions of the people; it is a sort of fashion not to suffer one's self to be drawn along by the torrent, and to desire to sound and examine everything. We know that there is an infinity of prejudices, errors, vulgar opinions, false miracles, illusions and seductions in the world; we know that many things are attributed to the devil which are purely natural, or that a thousand apocryphal stories are related. It is then right to hold one's self on one's guard, in order not to be deceived. It is very important for religion to distinguish between true and false miracles, certain or uncertain events, and works wrought by the hand of God, from those which are the work of the seducing spirit.

In all that he does, the demon mixes up a great many illusions amid some truths, in order that the difficulty of discerning the true from the false may make mankind take the side which pleases them most, and that the incredulous may always have some points to maintain them in their incredulity. Although the apparitions of spirits, angels, and demons, and their operations, may not, perhaps, always be miraculous, nevertheless, as the greater part appear above the common course of nature, many of the persons of whom we have just spoken, without giving themselves the trouble to examine the things, and seek for the causes of them, the authors, and the circumstances, boldly take upon themselves to deny them all. It is the shortest way, but neither the most sensible, nor the most rational; for in what is said on this subject, there are effects which can be reasonably attributed to the almighty power of God alone, who acts immediately, or makes secondary causes act to his glory, for the advancement of religion, and the manifestation of the truth; and other effects there are, which bear visibly the character of illusion, impiety, and seduction, and in which it would seem that instead of the finger of God, we can observe only the marks of the spirit of deceit and falsehood.

CHAPTER 28

Continuation of Objections against Possessions, and some Replies to those Objections

We read in works, published and printed, composed by Catholic authors of our days, that it is proved by reason, that possessions of the demon are naturally impossible, and that it is not true in regard to ourselves and our ideas, that the demon can have any natural power over the corporeal world; that as soon as we admit in the created wills a power to act upon bodies, and to move them, it is impossible to set bounds to it, and that this power is truly infinite.

They maintain that the demon can act upon our souls simply by means of suggestion; that it is impossible the demon should be the physical cause of the least external effect; that all the Scripture tells us of the snares and stratagems of Satan signifies nothing more than the temptations of the flesh and concupiscence; and that to seduce us, the demon requires only mental suggestions. His is a moral, not a physical power; in a word, *that the demon can do neither good nor harm; that his might is nought;* that we do not know if God has given to any other spirit than the soul of man the power to move the body; that on the contrary, we ought to presume that the wisdom of God has willed that pure spirits should have no commerce with the body; they maintain moreover that the pagans never knew what we call bad angels and demons.

All these propositions are certainly contrary to Scripture, to the opinions of the Fathers, and to the tradition of the Catholic Church. But these gentlemen do not trouble themselves about that; they affirm that the sacred writers have often expressed themselves according to the opinions of their time, whether because the necessity of making themselves under-stood forced them to conform to it, or that they themselves had adopted those opinions. There is, say they, more likelihood that several infirmities which the Scripture has ascribed to the demon had simply a natural cause; that in these places the sacred authors have spoken according to vulgar opinions; the error of this language is of no importance.

The prophets of Saul, and Saul himself, were never what are properly termed Prophets; they might be attacked with those (fits) which the pagans call *sacred*. You must be asleep when you read, not to see that the temptation of Eve is only an allegory. It is the same with the permission given by God to Satan to tempt Job. Why wish to explain the whole book of Job literally, and as a true history, since its beginning is only a fiction? It is anything but certain that Jesus Christ was transported by the demon to the highest pinnacle of the temple.

The Fathers were prepossessed on one side by the reigning ideas of the philosophy of Pythagoras and Plato on the influences of mean intelligences, and on the other hand by the language of the holy books, which to conform to popular opinions often ascribed to the demon effects which were purely natural. We must then return to the doctrine of reason to decide on the submission which we ought to pay to the authority of the Scriptures and the Fathers concerning the power of the demons.

The uniform method of the Holy Fathers in the interpretations of the Old Testament is human opinion, whence one can appeal to the tribunal of reason. They go so far as to say that the sacred authors were informed of the metempsychosis, as the author of the Book of Wisdom, 8:19, 20: 'I was an innocent child, and I received a good spirit; and as I was already good, I entered into an uncorrupted body.'

Persons of this temper will certainly not read this work of ours, or, if they do read it, it will be with contempt or pity. I do not think it necessary to refute those paradoxes here; the Bishop of Senez has done it with his usual erudition and zeal, in a long letter printed at Utrecht in 1736. I do not deny that the sacred writers may sometimes have spoken in a popular manner, and in accordance with the prejudice of the people. But it is carrying things too far to reduce the power of the demon to being able to act upon us only by means of suggestion; and it is a presumption unworthy of a philosopher, to decide on the power of spirits over bodies, having no knowledge, either by revelation or by reason, of the extent of the power of angels and demons over matter, and human bodies. We may exceed due measure by granting them excessive power, as well as in not according them enough. But it is of infinite importance to religion to discern justly between what is natural, or supernatural, in the operations of angels and demons, that the simple may not be left in error, nor the wicked triumph over the truth, and make a bad use of their own wit and knowledge, to render doubtful what is certain, and deceiving both themselves and others by ascribing to chance or illusion of the senses, or a vain prepossession of the mind, what is said of the apparitions of angels, demons, and deceased persons; since it is certain that several of these apparitions are quite true, although there may be a great number of others that are very uncertain, and even manifestly false.

I shall therefore make no difficulty in owning that even miracles, at least things that appear such, the prediction of future events, movements of the body which appear beyond the usual powers of nature, to speak and understand foreign languages unknown before, to penetrate the thoughts, discover concealed things, to be raised up, and transported in a moment from one place to another, to announce truths, lead a good life externally, preach Jesus Christ, decry magic and sorcery, make an outward profession of virtue; I readily own that all these things may not prove invincibly that all who perform them are sent by God, or that these operations are real miracles; yet we cannot reasonably suppose the demon to be mixed up in them by God's permission, or that the demons or the angels do not act upon those persons who perform prodigies, and foretell things to come, or who can penetrate the thoughts of the heart, or that God himself does not produce these effects by the immediate action of his justice or his might.

The examples which have been cited, or which may be cited hereafter, will never prove that man can of himself penetrate the sentiments of another, or discover his secret thoughts. The wonders worked by the magicians of Pharaoh were only illusion; they appeared, however, to be true miracles, and passed for such in the eyes of the King of Egypt and all his court. Balaam, the son of Beor, was a true Prophet, although a man whose morals were very corrupt.

Pomponatius writes, that the wife of Francis Maigret, savetier of Mantua, spoke divers languages, and was cured by Calderon, a physician, famous in his time, who gave her a potion of hellebore. Erasmus says also that he had seen an Italian, a native of Spoletta, who spoke German very well, although he had never been in Germany; they gave him a medicine which caused him to eject a quantity of worms, and he was cured so as not to speak German any more.

Le Loyer, in his *Book of Spectres* avows that all those things appear to him much to be doubted. He rather believes Fernel, one of the gravest physicians of his age, who maintains that there is not such power in medicine, and brings forward as an instance the history of a young gentleman, the son of a Knight of the Order, who being seized upon by the demon, could be cured neither by potions, by medicines, or by diet, (*i.e.* fasting,) but who was cured by the conjurations and exorcisms of the Church.

As to the reality of the return of souls, or spirits, and their apparitions, the Sorbonne, the most celebrated school of theology in France, has always believed that the spirits of the defunct returned sometimes, either by the order and power of God, or by his permission. The Sorbonne confessed this in its decisions of the year 1518, and still more positively the 23rd January 1724. *Nos respondemus vestroe petitioni animas defunctorum divinitus, seu divinâ virtute, ordinatione aut permissione interdum ad vivas redire exploratum esse.* Several jurisconsults and several sovereign companies have decreed that the apparition of a deceased person in a house could suffice to break up the lease. We may count it for much, to have proved to certain persons that there is a God whose providence extends over all things past, present, and to come; that there is another life, that there are good and bad spirits, rewards for good works, and punishments after this life for sins; that Jesus Christ has ruined the power of Satan; that he exercised in himself, in his Apostles, and continues to exercise in the ministers of his Church, an absolute empire over the infernal powers; that the devil is now chained; he may bark and threaten, but he can bite only those who approach him, and voluntarily give themselves up to him.

We have seen in these parts a woman who followed a band of mountebanks and jugglers, who stretched out her legs in such an extraordinary manner, and raised up her feet to her head, before and behind, with as much suppleness as if she had had neither nerves nor joints. There was nothing supernatural in all that; she had exercised herself from extreme youth in these movements, and had contracted the habit of performing them.

St Augustine speaks of a soothsayer whom he had known at Carthage, an illiterate man, who could discover the secrets of the heart, and replied to those who consulted him on secret and unknown affairs. He had himself made an experiment on him, and took to witness St Alypius, Licentius, and Trygnius, his interlocutors in his Dialogue against the Academicians. They, like him, had consulted Albicerius, and had admired the certainty of his replies. He gives as an instance, a spoon which had been lost. They told him that someone had lost something; and he instantly, without hesitation, replied that such a thing was lost, that such a one had taken it, and had hid it in such a place, which was found to be quite true.

They sent him a certain quantity of pieces of silver; he who was charged to carry them had taken away some of them. He made the person return them, and perceived the theft before the money had been shown to him. St Augustine was present. A learned and distinguished man, named Flaccianus, wishing to buy a field, consulted the soothsayer, who declared to him the name of the land, which was very extraordinary, and gave him all the details of the affair in question. A young student, wishing to prove Albicerius, begged of him to declare to him what he was thinking of; he told him he was thinking of a verse of Virgil, and, as he then asked him which verse it was, the diviner repeated it instantly, though he had never studied the Latin language.

This Albicerius was a scoundrel, as St Augustine says, who calls him *flagitiosum hominem*. The knowledge which he had of hidden things was not, doubtless, a gift of heaven, any more than the Pythonic spirit which animated that maid in the Acts of the Apostles whom St Paul obliged to keep silence. It was then the work of the evil spirit.

The gift of tongues, the knowledge of the future, and power to divine the thoughts of others, are always adduced, and with reason, as solid proofs of the presence and inspiration of the Holy Spirit; but if the demon can sometimes perform the same things, he does it to mislead and induce sin, or simply to render true prophecies doubtful: but never to lead to truth, the fear and love of God, and the edification of those around. God may allow such corrupt men as Balaam, and such rascals as Albicerius, to have some knowledge of the future, and secret things, and even of the hidden thoughts of men; but he never permits their criminality to remain unrevealed to the end, and so become a stumbling-block for simple or worthy people. The malice of these hypocritical and corrupt men will be made manifest sooner or later by some means; their malice and depravity will be found out, by which it will be judged, either that they are inspired only by the evil spirit, or that the Holy Spirit makes use of their agency to foretell some truth, as he prophesied by Balaam, and by Caïphas. Their morals and their conduct will throw discredit on them, and oblige us to be careful in discerning between their true predictions and their bad example. We have seen hypocrites who died with the reputation of being worthy people, and who at bottom were scoundrels, as, for instance, that curé, the director of the nuns of Louviers, whose possession was so much talked of.

Jesus Christ in the Gospel tells us to be on our guard against wolves in sheep's clothing; and, elsewhere, he tells us that there will be false Christs and false prophets, who will prophesy in his name, and perform wonders capable of deceiving the very elect themselves, were it possible. But he refers us to their works to distinguish them.

To apply all these things to the possessed nuns of Loudun, and to Mademoiselle de Ranfaing, even to that girl whose hypocrisy was unmasked by Mademoiselle Acarie, I appeal to their works, and their conduct both before and after.

God will not allow those who sincerely seek the truth to be deceived.

A juggler will guess which card you have touched, or even simply thought of; but it is known that there is nothing supernatural in that, and that it is done by the combination of the cards according to mathematical rules. We have seen a deaf man who understood what they wished to say to him by simply observing the motion of the lips of those who spoke. There is nothing more miraculous in this than in two persons conversing together by signs upon which they have agreed.

CHAPTER 29

Of Familiar Spirits

If all that is related of spirits which are perceived in houses, in the cavities of mountains, and in mines, is certain, we cannot disavow that they also must be placed in the rank of apparitions of the evil spirit; for although they usually do neither wrong nor violence to anyone, unless they are irritated or receive abusive words; nevertheless we do not read that they lead to the love or fear of God, to prayer, piety, or acts of devotion; it is known, on the contrary, that they show a distaste to those things, so that we shall place them in earnest among the spirits of darkness.

I do not find that the ancient Hebrews knew anything of what we call *esprits follets*, or familiar spirits, which infest houses, or attach themselves to certain persons, to serve them, watch over and warn them, and guard them from danger; such as the demon of Socrates, who warned him to avoid certain misfortunes. Some other examples are also related of persons who said they had similar genii attached to their persons.

The Jews and Christians confess that every one of us has his good angel, who guides him from his early youth. Several of the ancients have thought that we have also our evil angel, who leads us into error. The Psalmist says distinctly, that God has commanded his angels to guide us in all our ways. But this is not what we understand here under the name of *esprits follets*.

The prophets in some places speak of *fauns*, or *hairy men*, or *satyrs*, who have some resemblance to our elves.

Isaiah, speaking of the state to which Babylon shall be reduced after her destruction, says that the ostriches shall make it their dwelling, and that the hairy men, *pilosi*, the satyrs, and goats, shall dance there. And elsewhere the same prophet says, *Occurrent doemonia onocentauris et pilosus clamabit alter ad alterum*, by which clever interpreters understand spectres which appear in the shape of goats. Jeremiah calls them *fauns* — the dragons with the fauns, which feed upon figs. But this is not the place for us to go more fully into the signification of the terms of the original; it suffices for us to show, that in the Scripture, at least in the Vulgate, are found the names of *lamioe, fauns*, and *satyrs*, which have some resemblance to *esprits follets*.

Cassian, who had studied deeply the lives of the fathers of the desert, and who had been much with the hermits or anchorites of Egypt, speaking of divers sorts of demons, mentions some which they commonly called *fauns* or *satyrs*, which the pagans regard as kinds of divinities of the fields or groves, who delighted, not so much in tormenting or doing harm to mankind, as in deceiving and fatiguing them, diverting themselves at their expense, and sporting with their simplicity.

Pliny the younger had a freedman named Marcus, a man of letters, who slept in the same bed with his brother, who was younger than himself. It seemed to him that he saw a person sitting on the same bed, who was cutting off his hair from the crown of his head. When he awoke, he found his head shorn of hair, and his hair thrown on the ground in the middle of the chamber. A little time after, the same thing happened to a youth who slept with several others at a school. This one saw two men dressed in white come in at the window, who cut off his hair as he slept, and then went out by the same window: on awaking, he found his hair scattered about on the floor. To what can these things be attributed, if not to an elf?

Plotinus, a Platonic philosopher, had, it is said, a familiar demon, who obeyed him from the moment he called him, and was superior in his nature to the common genii; he was of the order of gods, and Plotinus paid continual attention to this divine guardian. This it was which led him to undertake a work on the demon which belongs to each of us in particular. He endeavours to explain the difference between the genii which watch over men.

Trithemius, in his Chronicon Hirsauginse, under the year 1130, relates, that in the diocese of Hildesheim, in Saxony, they saw for some time a spirit which they called in German *heidekind*, as if they would say, *rural spirit, heide* signifying vast country, *kind*, child (or boy). He appeared sometimes in one form, sometimes in another; and sometimes without appearing at all, he did several things by which he proved both his presence and his power. He chose sometimes to give very important advice to those in power; and often he has been seen in the bishop's kitchen, helping the cooks and doing sundry jobs.

A young scullion, who had grown familiar with him, having offered him some insults, he warned the head cook of it, who made light of it; or thought nothing about it; but the spirit avenged himself cruelly. This youth having fallen asleep in the kitchen, the spirit stifled him, tore him to pieces, and roasted him. He carried his fury still further against the officers of the kitchen, and the other officers of the prince. The thing went on to such a point, that they were obliged to proceed against him by ecclesiastical censures, and to constrain him by exorcisms to go out of the country.

I think I may put amongst the number of elves the spirits which are seen, they say, in mines and mountain caves. They appear clad like the miners, run here and there, appear in haste as if to work and seek the veins of mineral ore, lay it in heaps, draw it out, turning the wheel of the crane; they seem to be very busy helping the workmen, and at the same time they do nothing at all.

These spirits are not mischievous, unless they are insulted and laughed at; for then they fall into an ill humour, and throw things at those who offend them. One of these genii, who had been addressed in injurious terms by a miner, twisted his neck, and placed his head the hind part before. The miner did not die, but remained all his life with his neck twisted and awry.

George Agricola, who has treated very learnedly on mines, metals, and the manner of extracting them from the bowels of the earth, mentions two or three sorts of spirits which appear in mines. Some are very small, and resemble dwarfs or pygmies; the others are like old men dressed like miners, having their shirts tucked up, and a leathern apron round their loins; others perform, or seem to perform, what they see others do, are very gay, do no harm to anyone, but from all their labours nothing real results.

In other mines are seen dangerous spirits, who ill use the workmen, hunt them away, and sometimes kill them, and thus constrain them to forsake mines which are very rich and abundant. For instance, at Anneberg, in a mine called Crown of Rose, a spirit in the shape of a spirited, snorting horse, killed twelve miners, and obliged those who worked the mine to abandon the undertaking, though it brought them in a great deal.

In another mine, called St Gregory, in Siveberg, there appeared a spirit whose head was covered with a black hood, and he seized a miner, raised him up to a considerable height, then let him fall, and hurt him extremely.

Olaus Magnus says, that in Sweden and other northern countries, they saw formerly familiar spirits, which, under the form of men or women, waited on certain persons. He speaks of certain nymphs dwelling in caverns and in the depths of the forest, who announce things to come; some are good, others bad; they appear and speak to those who consult them. Travellers and shepherds also often see during the night divers phantoms which burn the spot where they appear, so that henceforward neither grass nor verdure are seen there.

He says, that the people of Finland, before their conversion to Christianity, sold the winds to sailors, giving them a string with three knots, and warning them that by untying the first knot they would have a gentle and favourable wind, at the second knot a stronger wind, and at the third knot a violent and dangerous gale. He says moreover, that the Bothnians, striking on an anvil hard blows with a hammer, upon a frog or a serpent of brass, fall down in a swoon, and during this swoon they learn what passes in very distant places.

But all those things have more relation to magic than to familiar spirits; and if what is said about them be true, it must be ascribed to the evil spirit.

The same Olaus Magnus says, that in mines, above all in silver mines, from which great profit may be expected, six sorts of demons may be seen, who under divers forms labour at breaking the rocks, drawing the buckets, and turning the wheels; who sometimes burst into laughter, and play different tricks; all of which are merely to deceive the miners, whom they crush under the rocks, or expose to the most imminent dangers, to make them utter blasphemy, and swear and curse. Several very rich mines have been obliged to be disused through fear of these dangerous spirits.

Notwithstanding all that we have just related, I doubt very much if there are any spirits in mountain caves or in mines. I have interrogated on the subject people of the trade and miners by profession, of whom there is a great number in our mountains, the Vosges, who have assured me, that all which is related on that point is fabulous; that if sometimes they see these elves or grotesque figures, it must be attributed to a heated and prepossessed imagination; or else that the circumstance is so rare, that it ought not to be repeated as something usual or common.

A new *Traveller in the Northern Countries*, printed at Amsterdam in 1708, says, that the people of Iceland are almost all conjurors or sorcerers; that they have familiar demons, whom they call *troles*, who wait upon them as servants, and warn them of the accidents or illnesses which are to happen to them; they awake them to go fishing when the season is favourable, and if they go for that purpose without the advice of these genii, they do not succeed. There are some persons among these people who evoke the dead, and make them appear to those who wish to consult them: they also conjure up the appearance of the absent far from the spot where they dwell.

Father Vadingue relates, after an old manuscript legend, that a lady named Lupa, had had during thirteen years a familiar demon, who served her as a waiting-woman, and led her into many secret irregularities, and induced her to treat her servants with inhumanity. God gave her grace to see her fault, and to do penance for it, by the intercession of St François d'Assise and St Anthony of Padua, to whom she had always felt particular devotion.

Cardan speaks of a bearded demon of Niphus, who gave him lessons of philosophy.

Agrippa had a demon who waited upon him in the shape of a dog. This dog, says Paulus Jovius, seeing his master about to expire, threw himself into the Rhone.

Much is said of certain spirits which are kept confined in rings, that are bought, sold or exchanged. They speak also of a crystal ring, in which the demon represented the objects desired to be seen.

Some also speak highly of those enchanted mirrors, in which children see the face of a robber who is sought for; others will see it in their nails; all which can only be diabolical illusions.

Le Loyer relates, that when he was studying the law at Toulouse, he was lodged near a house where an elf never ceased all the night to draw water from the well, making the pulley creak all the while; at other times he seemed to drag something heavy up the stairs; but he very rarely entered the rooms, and then he made but little noise.

CHAPTER 30

Some other Examples of Elves

On the 25th August 1746, I received a letter from a very worthy man, the curé of the parish of Walsche, a village situated in the mountains of Vosges, in the county of Dabo, or Dasburg, in Lower Alsatia, diocese of Metz. In this letter he tells me, that the 10th June 1740, at eight o'clock in the morning, he being in his kitchen, with his niece and the servant, he saw on a sudden an iron pot that was placed on the ground turn round three or four times, without its being set in motion by anyone. A moment after, a stone, weighing about a pound, was thrown from the next room into the same kitchen, in presence of the same persons, without their seeing the hand which threw it. The next day, at nine o'clock in the morning, some panes of glass were broken, and through these panes were thrown some stones, with what appeared to them supernatural dexterity. The spirit never hurt anybody, and never did anything in the night time, but always during the day. The curé employed the prayers marked out in the ritual to bless his house, and thenceforth the spirit broke no more panes of glass; but he continued to throw stones at the curé's people, without hurting them, however. If they fetched water from the fountain, he threw stones into the bucket; and afterwards he began to serve in the kitchen. One day, as the servant was planting some cabbages in the garden, he pulled them up as fast as she planted them, and laid them in a heap. It was in vain that she stormed, threatened, and swore in the German style; the spirit continued to play his tricks.

One day, when a bed in the garden had been dug and prepared, the spade was found thrust two feet deep into the ground, without any trace being seen of him who had thus stuck it in; but they observed that on the spade was a ribbon, and by the spade were two pieces of two soles, which the girl had locked up the evening before in a little box. Sometimes he took pleasure in displacing the earthenware and pewter, and putting it either all round the kitchen, or in the porch, or even in the cemetery, and always in broad daylight. One day he filled an iron pot with wild herbs, bran, and leaves of trees, and, having put some water in it, carried it to the alley or walk in the garden; another time he suspended it to the pothook, over the fire. The servant having broken two eggs into a little dish for the curé's supper, the spirit broke two more into it in his presence, the maid having merely turned to get some salt. The curé having gone to say mass, on his return found all his earthenware, furniture, linen, bread, milk, and other things, scattered about over the house.

Sometimes the spirit would form circles on the paved floor, at one time with stones, at another with corn or leaves, and in a moment, before the eyes of all present, all was overturned and deranged. Tired with these games, the curé sent for the mayor of the place, and told him he was resolved to quit the parsonage house. Whilst this was passing, the curé's niece came in, and told them that the spirit had torn up the cabbages in the garden, and had put some money in a hole in the ground. They went there, and found things exactly as she had said. They picked up the money, which was what the curé had put away in a place not locked up; and in a moment after they found it anew, with some liards, two by two, scattered about the kitchen.

The agents of the Count de Linange being arrived at Walsche, went to the curé's house, and persuaded him that it was all the effect of a spell; they told him to take two pistols, and fire them off at the place where he might observe there were any movements. The spirit at the same moment threw out of the pocket of one of these officers two pieces of silver; and from that time he was no longer perceived in the house.

The circumstance of two pistols terminating the scenes with which the elf had disturbed the good curé, made him believe that this tormenting imp was no other than a certain bad parishioner, whom the curé had been obliged to send away from his parish, and who to revenge himself had done all that we have related. If that be the case, he had rendered himself invisible, or he had had credit enough to send in his stead a familiar spirit who puzzled the curé for some weeks; for if he were not bodily in this house, what had he to fear from any pistol shot which might have been fired at him? And if he was there bodily, how could he render himself invisible?

I have been told several times that a monk of the Cistercian order had a familiar spirit who attended upon him, arranged his chamber, and prepared everything ready for him when he was coming back from the country. They were so accustomed to this, that they expected him home by these signs, and he always arrived. It is affirmed of another monk of the same order, that he had a familiar spirit, who warned him, not only of what passed in the house, but also of what happened out of it; and one day he was awakened three times, and warned that some monks were quarrelling, and were ready to come to blows; he ran to the spot, and put an end to the dispute.

St Sulpicius Severus relates, that St Martin often had conversations with the Holy Virgin, and other saints, and even with the demons and false gods of paganism; he talked with them, and learned from them many secret things. One day, when a council was being held at Nîmes, where he had not thought proper to be present, but the decisions of which he desired to know, being in a boat with St Sulpicius, but apart from others, as usual with him, an angel appeared, and informed him what had passed in this assembly of bishops. Inquiry was made as to the day and hour when the council was held, and it was found to be at the same hour at which the angel had appeared to Martin.

We have been told several times that a young ecclesiastic, in a seminary at Paris, had a spirit who waited upon him, and arranged his room and his clothes. One day, when the superior was passing by the chamber of this seminarist, he heard him talking with someone; he entered, and asked who he was conversing with. The youth affirmed that there was no one in his room, and, in fact, the superior could neither see nor discover anyone there. Nevertheless, as he had heard their conversation, the young man owned that for some years he had been attended by a familiar spirit, who rendered him every service that a domestic could have done, and had promised him great advantages in the ecclesiastical profession. The superior pressed him to give some proofs of what he said. He ordered the spirit to set a chair for the superior; the spirit obeyed. Information of this was sent to the archbishop, who did not think proper to give it publicity. The young clerk was sent away, and this singular adventure was buried in silence.

Bodin speaks of a person of his acquaintance, who was still living at the time he wrote, which was in 1588. This person had a familiar, who from the age of thirty-seven had given him good advice respecting his conduct, sometimes to correct his faults, sometimes to make him practise virtue, or to assist him; resolving the difficulties which he might find in reading holy books, or giving him good counsel upon his own affairs. He usually rapped at his door at three or four o'clock in the morning to awaken him; and as that person mistrusted all these things, fearing that it might be an evil angel, the spirit showed himself in broad day, striking gently on a glass bowl, and then upon a bench. When he desired to do anything good and useful, the spirit touched his right ear; but if it was anything wrong and dangerous, he touched his left ear; so that from that time nothing occurred to him of which he was not warned beforehand. Sometimes he heard his voice; and one day, when he found his life in imminent danger, he saw his spirit, under the form of a child of extraordinary beauty, who saved him from it.

William, Bishop of Paris, says that he knew a rope-dancer who had a familiar spirit, which played and joked with him, and prevented him from sleeping, throwing something against the wall, dragging off the bed-clothes, or pulling him about when he was in bed. We know by the account of a very sensible person, that it has happened to him in the open country, and in the day time, to feel his cloak and boots pulled at, and his hat thrown down; then he heard the bursts of laughter and the voice of a person deceased and well known to him, who seemed to rejoice at it.

The discovery of things hidden or unknown, which is made in dreams, or otherwise, can hardly be ascribed to anything but to familiar spirits. A man who did not know a word of Greek came to M. de Saumaise, senior, a counsellor of the parliament of Dijon, and showed him these words, which he had heard in the night, as he slept, and which he wrote down in French characters on awaking: '*Apithi ouc osphraine tén sén apsychian.*' He asked him what that meant. M. de Saumaise told him it meant, 'Save yourself; do you not perceive the death with which you are threatened?' Upon this hint, the man removed, and left his house, which fell down the following night.

The same story is related, with a little difference, by another author, who says that the circumstance happened at Paris; that the spirit spoke in Syriac, and that M. de Saumaise being consulted, replied, 'Go out of your house, for it will fall in ruins today, at nine o'clock in the evening.' It is but too much the custom in reciting stories of this kind to add a few circumstances by way of embellishment.

Gassendy, in the Life of M. Peiresch, relates, that M. Peiresch, going one day to Nismes, with one of his friends, named M. Rainier, the latter, having heard Peiresch talking in his sleep in the night, waked him, and asked him what he said. Peiresch answered him, 'I dreamed that, being at Nismes, a jeweller had offered me a medal of Julius Caesar, for which he asked four crowns, and as I was going to count him down his money, you waked me, to my great regret.' They arrived at Nismes, and going about the town, Peiresch recognised the goldsmith whom he had seen in his dream; and on his asking him if he had nothing curious, the goldsmith told him he had a gold medal, or coin, of Julius Caesar. Peiresch asked him how much he esteemed it worth; he replied, four crowns. Peiresch paid them, and was delighted to see his dream so happily accomplished.

Here is a dream much more singular than the preceding, although a little in the same style. A learned man of Dijon, after having wearied himself all day with an important passage in a Greek poet, without being able to comprehend it at all, went to bed thinking of this difficulty. During his sleep, his spirit transported him in spirit to Stockholm, introduced him into the palace of Queen Christina, conducted him into the library, and showed him a small volume, which was precisely what he sought. He opened it, read in it ten or twelve Greek verses, which absolutely cleared up the difficulty which had so long beset him; he awoke, and wrote down the verses he had seen at Stockholm. On the morrow, he wrote to M. Descartes, who was then in Sweden, and begged of him to look in such a place, and in such a division of the library, if the book, of which he sent him the description, were there, and if the Greek verses which he sent him were to be read in it.

M. Descartes replied, that he had found the book in question, and also the verses he had sent were in the place he pointed out; that one of his friends had promised him a copy of that work, and he would send it him by the first opportunity.

We have already said something of the spirit, or familiar spirit of Socrates, which prevented him from doing certain things, but did not lead him to do others. It is asserted that after the defeat of the Athenian army, commanded by Laches, Socrates, flying like the others, with this Athenian general, and being arrived at a spot where several roads met, Socrates would not follow the road taken by the other fugitives, and when they asked him the reason, he replied, because his spirit drew him away from it. The event justified his foresight. All those who had taken the other road were either killed or made prisoners by the enemy's cavalry.

It is doubtful whether the elves, of which so many things are related, are good or bad spirits; for the faith of the Church admits nothing between these two kinds of genii. Every spirit is either good or bad; but as there are in heaven many mansions, as the Gospel says, and as there are among the blessed various degrees of glory, differing from each other, so we may believe that there are in hell various degrees of pain and punishment for the damned and the demons.

But are they not rather magicians, who render themselves invisible, and divert themselves in disquieting the living? Why do they attach themselves to certain spots and certain persons rather than to others? Why do they make themselves perceptible only during a certain time, and that sometimes a short space?

I could willingly conclude that what is said of them is mere fancy and prejudice; but their reality has been so often experienced by the discourse they have held, and the actions they have performed in the presence of many wise and enlightened persons, that I cannot persuade myself that among the great number of stories related of them, there are not at least some of them true.

It may be remarked that these elves never lead one to anything good, to prayer, or piety, to the love of God, or to godly and serious actions. If they do no other harm, they leave hurtful doubts about the punishments of the damned, on the efficacy of prayer and exorcisms; if they hurt not those men or animals which are found on the spot where they may be perceived, it is because God sets bounds to their malice and power. The demon has a thousand ways of deceiving us. All those to whom these genii attach themselves have a horror of them, mistrust and fear them; and it rarely happens that these familiar demons do not lead them to a dangerous end, unless they deliver themselves from them by grave acts of religion and penance.

There is the story of a spirit, 'which,' says he who wrote it to me, 'I no more doubt the truth of, than if I had been a witness of it.' Count Despilliers, the father, being a young man, and captain of cuirassiers, was in winter quarters in Flanders. One of his men came to him one day, to beg that he would change his landlord, saying, that every night there came into his bedroom a spirit, which would not allow him to sleep. The Count Despilliers sent him away, and laughed at his simplicity. Some days after, the same horseman came back and made the same request to him; the only reply of the captain would have been a volley of blows with a stick, had not the soldier avoided them by a prompt flight. At last, he returned a third time to the charge, and protested to his captain that he could bear it no longer, and should be obliged to desert if his lodging was not changed. Despilliers, who knew the soldier to be brave and reasonable, said to him, with an oath, 'I will go this night and sleep with you, and see what is the matter.'

At ten o'clock in the evening the captain repaired to his soldier's lodging, and having laid his pistols ready primed upon the table, he laid down in his clothes, his sword by his side, with his soldier, in a bed without curtains. About midnight he heard something which came into the room, and in a moment turned the bed upside down, covering the captain and the soldier with the mattress and paillasse. Despilliers had great trouble to disengage himself and find again his sword and pistols, and he returned home much confounded. The horse-soldier had a new lodging the very next day, and slept quietly in the house of his new host.

M. Despilliers related this adventure to anyone who would listen to it. He was an intrepid man, who had never known what it was to fall back before danger. He died Field Marshal of the armies of the Emperor Charles VI and governor of the fortress of Ségedin. His son has confirmed this adventure to me within a short time, as having heard it from his father.

The person who writes to me adds: 'I doubt not that spirits sometimes return; but I have found myself in a great many places which it was said they haunted. I have even tried several times to see them, but I have never seen any. I found myself once with more than four thousand persons, who all said they saw the spirit; I was the only one in the assembly who saw nothing.' So writes me a very worthy officer, this year 1745, in the same letter wherein he relates the affair of M. Despilliers.

CHAPTER 31

Spirits that Keep Watch over Treasure

Everybody acknowledges that there is an infinity of riches buried in the earth, or lost under the waters by shipwrecks; they fancy that the demon, whom they look upon as the god of riches, the god Mammon, the Pluto of the Pagans, is the depositary, or at least the guardian, of these treasures. He said to Jesus Christ, when he tempted him in the wilderness, showing to him all the kingdoms of the earth, and their glory: 'All these things will I give thee, if thou wilt fall down and worship me.' We know also, that the ancients very often interred vast treasures in the tombs of the dead; either that the dead might make use of them in the other world, or that their souls might keep guard over them in those gloomy places. Job seems to make allusion to this ancient custom, when he says, 'Would to God I had never been born: I should now sleep with the kings and great ones of the earth, who built themselves solitary places; like unto those who seek for treasure, and are rejoiced when they find a tomb;' doubtless because they hope to find great riches therein.

There were very precious things in the tomb of Cyrus. Semiramis caused to be engraved on her own mausoleum, that it contained great riches. Josephus relates, that Solomon placed great treasures in the tomb of David his father; and that the High Priest Hyrcanus, being besieged in Jerusalem by King Antiochus, took thence three thousand talents. He says, moreover, that years after, Herod the Great having caused this tomb to be searched, took from it large sums. We see several laws against those who violate sepulchres to take out of them the precious things they contain. The Emperor Marcianus forbade that riches should be hidden in tombs. If such things have been placed in the mausoleums of worthy and holy persons, and if they have been discovered through the revelation of the good spirits of persons who died in the faith and grace of God, we cannot conclude from those things, that all hidden treasures are in the power of the demon, and that he alone knows anything of them; the good angels know of them; and the saints may be much more faithful guardians of them than the demons, who usually have no power to enrich, or to deliver from the horrors of poverty, from punishment and death itself, those who yield themselves to them in order to receive some reward from them.

Melancthon relates, that the demon informed a priest where a treasure was hid; the priest, accompanied by one of his friends, went to the spot indicated; they saw there a black dog lying on a chest. The priest, having entered to take out the treasure, was crushed and smothered under the ruins of the cavern.

M. Remy, in his Demonology, speaks of several persons whose causes he had heard in his quality of Lieutenant-General of Lorraine, at the time when that country swarmed with wizards and witches; those amongst them who believed they had received money from the demon, found nothing in their purses but bits of broken pots, coals, or leaves of trees, or other things equally vile and contemptible.

The Reverend Father Abram, a Jesuit, in his manuscript History of the University of Pont à Mousson, reports, that a youth of good family but small fortune, placed himself at first to serve in the army among the valets and serving men; from thence his parents sent him to school, but not liking the subjection which study requires, he quitted the school and returned to his former kind of life. On his way he met a man dressed in a silk coat, but ill-looking, dark, and hideous, who asked him where he was going to, and why he looked so sad; 'I am able to set you at your ease,' said this man to him, 'if you will give yourself to me.'

The young man, believing that he wished to engage him as a servant, asked for time to reflect upon it; but beginning to mistrust the magnificent promises which he made him, he looked at him more narrowly, and having remarked that his left foot was divided like that of an ox, he was seized with affright, made the sign of the cross, and called on the name of Jesus, when the spectre directly disappeared.

Three days after, the same figure appeared to him again, and asked him if he had made up his mind; the young man replied that he did not want a master. The spectre said to him, 'Where are you going?' 'I am going to such a town,' replied he. At that moment the demon threw at his feet a purse which chinked, and which he found filled with thirty or forty Flemish crowns, amongst which were about twelve which appeared to be gold, newly coined, and as if from the stamps of the coiner. In the same purse was a powder, which the spectre said was of a very subtle quality.

At the same time he gave him abominable counsels to satisfy the most shameful passions; and exhorted him to renounce the use of holy water, and the adoration of the Host – which he called in derision that little cake. The boy was horrified at these proposals, and made the sign of the cross on his heart; and at the same time he felt himself thrown roughly down on the ground, where he remained for half an hour, half-dead. Having got up again, he returned home to his mother, did penance, and changed his conduct. The pieces of money which looked like gold and newly coined, having been put in the fire, were found to be only of copper.

I relate this instance, to show that the demon seeks only to deceive and corrupt, even those to whom he makes the most specious promises, and to whom he seems to give great riches.

Some years ago, two monks, both of them well-informed and prudent men, consulted me upon a circumstance which occurred at Orbé, a village of Alsatia, near the Abbey of Pairis. Two men of that place told them, that they had seen come out of the ground a small box or casket, which they supposed was full of money, and having a wish to lay hold of it, it had retreated from them and hidden itself again underground. This happened to them more than once.

Theophanes, a celebrated and grave Greek historiographer, under the year of our era, 408, relates that Cabades, King of Persia, being informed that between the Indian country and Persia there was a castle called Zubdadeyer, which contained a great quantity of gold, silver, and precious stones, resolved to make himself master of it; but these treasures were guarded by demons, who would not permit anyone to approach it. He employed some of the magi and some Jews who were with him, to conjure them and exorcise them; but their efforts were useless. The king bethought himself of the God of the Christians – prayed to him, and sent for the bishop who was at the head of the Christian Church in Persia, and begged of him to use his efforts to obtain for him these treasures, and to expel the demons by whom they were guarded. The prelate offered the holy sacrifice, participated in it, and going to the spot, drove away the demons who were guardians of these riches, and put the king in peaceable possession of the castle.

Relating this story to a man of some rank, he told me, that in the Isle of Malta, two knights having hired a slave, who boasted that he possessed the secret of evoking demons, and forcing them to discover the most hidden secrets, they led him into an old castle, where it was thought that treasures were concealed. The slave performed his evocations, and at last the demon opened a rock whence issued a coffer. The slave would have taken hold of it, but the coffer went back into the rock. This occurred more than once; and the slave, after vain efforts, came and told the knights what had happened to him; but he was so much exhausted, that he had need of some restorative; they gave him refreshment, and when he had returned, they after a while heard a noise. They went into the cave with a light, to see what had happened, and they found the slave lying dead, and all his flesh full of cuts as of a penknife, in form of a cross; he was so covered with them, that there was not room to place a finger where he was not thus marked. The knights carried him to the shore, and threw him into the sea with a great stone hung round his neck. We could name these persons and note the dates, were it necessary.

The same person related to us at that same time, that about ninety years before, an old woman of Malta was warned by a spirit that there was a great deal of treasure in her cellar, belonging to a knight of high consideration, and desired her to give him information of it; she went to his abode, but could not obtain an audience. The following night the same spirit returned, and gave her the same command; and as she refused to obey, he abused her and again sent her on the same errand. The next day she returned to seek this lord, and told the domestics that she would not go away until she had spoken to the master. She related what had happened to her; and the knight resolved to go to her dwelling, accompanied by people with the proper instruments for digging; they dug, and very shortly there sprung up such a quantity of water from the spot where they inserted their pickaxes, that they were obliged to give up the undertaking.

The knight confessed to the Inquisitor what he had done, and received absolution for it; but he was obliged to inscribe the fact we have recounted in the Registers of the Inquisition.

About sixty years after, the canons of the Cathedral of Malta, wishing for a wider space before their church, bought some houses which it was necessary to pull down, and amongst others that which had belonged to that old woman. As they were digging there, they found the treasure, consisting of a good many gold pieces of the value of a ducat, bearing the effigy of the Emperor Justinian the First. The Grand Master of the Order of Malta affirmed that the treasure belonged to him as sovereign of the isle; the canons contested the point. The affair was carried to Rome; the grand master gained his suit, and the gold was brought to him, amounting in value to about sixty thousand ducats; but he gave them up to the cathedral.

Some time afterwards, the knight of whom we have spoken, who was then very aged, remembered what had happened to himself, and asserted that the treasure ought to belong to him; he made them lead him to the spot, recognised the cellar where he had formerly been, and pointed out in the Register of the Inquisition what had been written therein sixty years before. They did not permit him to recover the treasure; but it was a proof that the demon knew of and kept watch over this money. The person who told me this story has in his possession three or four of these gold pieces, having bought them of the canons.

CHAPTER 32

Other Instances of Hidden Treasures, which were Guarded by Good or Bad Spirits

We read in a new work, that a man, Honoré Mirable, having found in a garden near Marseilles a treasure consisting of several Portuguese pieces of gold, from the indication given him by a spectre, which appeared to him at eleven o'clock at night, near the *Bastide*, or country house called *du Paret*, he made the discovery of it in presence of the woman who farmed the land of this *Bastide*, and the farm-servant named Bernard. When he first perceived the treasure buried in the earth, and wrapt up in a bundle of old linen, he was afraid to touch it, for fear it should be poisoned and cause his death. He raised it by means of a hook made of a branch of the almond-tree, and carried it into his room, where he undid it without any witness, and found in it a great deal of gold; to satisfy the wishes of the spirit who had appeared to him, he caused some masses to be said for him. He revealed his good fortune to a countryman of his, named Anquier, who lent him forty livres, and gave him a note by which he acknowledged he owed him twenty thousand livres, and receipted the payment of the forty livres lent; this note bore date the 27th September 1726.

Some time after, Mirable asked Anquier to pay the note. Anquier denied everything. A great lawsuit ensued; informations were taken and perquisitions held in Anquier's house; sentence was given on the 10th September 1727, importing that Anquier should be arrested, and have the question applied to him. An appeal was made to the Parliament of Aix. Anquier's note was declared a forgery. Bernard, who was said to have been present at the discovery of the treasure, was not cited at all; the other witnesses only deposed from hearsay; Magdalen Caillot alone, who was present, acknowledged having seen the packet wrapped round with linen, and had heard a ringing as of pieces of gold or silver, and had seen one of them, a piece about as large as a piece of two liards.

The Parliament of Aix issued its decree the 17th February 1728, by which it ordained that Bernard, farming servant at the *Bastide du Paret*, should be heard; he was heard on different days, and deposed that he had seen neither treasure, nor rags, nor gold pieces. Then came another decree of the 2nd June 1728, which ordered that the Attorney General should proceed by way of ecclesiastical censures on the facts resulting from these proceedings.

The indictment was published, fifty-three witnesses were heard; another sentence of the 18th February 1729, discharged Anquier from the courts and the lawsuit; condemned Mirable to the galleys to perpetuity after having previously undergone the question; and Caillot was to pay a fine of ten francs. Such was the end of this grand lawsuit. If we examine narrowly these stories of spectres who watch over treasures, we shall doubtless find, as here, a great deal of superstition, deception and fancy.

Delrio relates some instances of people who have been put to death, or who have perished miserably as they searched for hidden treasures. In all this we may perceive the spirit of lying and seduction on the part of the demon, bounds set to his power, and his malice arrested by the will of God; the impiety of man, his avarice, his idle curiosity, the confidence which he places in the angel of darkness, by the loss of his wealth, his life, and his soul.

John Wierus, in his work entitled '*De Proestigiis Doemonum,*' printed at Basle in 1577, relates that in his time, 1430, the demon revealed to a certain priest at Nuremberg some treasures hidden in a cavern near the town, and enclosed in a crystal vase. The priest took one of his friends with him as a companion; they began to dig up the ground in the spot designated, and they discovered in a subterranean cavern a kind of chest, near which a black dog was lying; the priest eagerly advanced to seize the treasure, but hardly had he entered the cavern, than it fell in, crushed the priest, and was filled up with earth as before.

The following is extracted from a letter, written from Kirchheim, 1st January 1747, to M. Schopfflein, Professor of History and Eloquence at Strasburg. 'It is now more than a year ago, that M. Cavallari, first musician of my Serene master, and by birth a Venetian, desired to have the ground dug up at Rothenkirchen, a league from hence, and which was formerly a renowned abbey, and was destroyed in the time of the Reformation. The opportunity was afforded him by an apparition, which showed itself more than once at noon-day to the wife of the Censier of Rothenkirchen, and above all, on the 7th May for two succeeding years. She swears, and can make oath, that she has seen a venerable priest in pontifical garments embroidered with gold, who threw before her a great heap of stones; and although she is a Lutheran, and consequently not very credulous in things of that kind, she thinks nevertheless that if she had had the presence of mind to put down a handkerchief or an apron, all the stones would have become money.

'M. Cavallari then asked leave to dig there, which was the more readily granted, because the tithe or tenth part of the treasure is due to the sovereign. He was treated as a visionary, and the matter of treasure was regarded as an unheard-of thing. In the meantime he laughed at the anticipated ridicule, and asked me if I would go halves with him. I did not hesitate a moment to accept this offer; but I was much surprised to find there were some little earthen pots full of gold pieces, all these pieces finer than the ducats of the fourteenth and fifteenth century generally are. I have had for my share 666, found at three different times. There are some of the Archbishops of Mayence, Treves, and Cologne, of the towns of Oppenheim, Baccarat, Bingen, and Coblentz; there are some also of the Palatine Rupert, of Frederic, Burgrave of Nuremberg, some few of Wenceslaus, and one of the Emperor Charles IV, etc.'

This shows that not only the demons, but also the saints, are sometimes guardians of treasure; unless you will say that the devil had taken the shape of the prelate. But what could it avail the demon to give the treasure to these gentlemen, who did not ask him for it, and scarcely troubled themselves about him? I have seen two of these pieces in the hands of M. Schopfflein.

The story we have just related is repeated, with a little difference, in a printed paper, announcing a lottery of pieces found at Rothenkirchen, in the province of Nassau, not far from Donnersberg. They say in this, that the value of these pieces is twelve livres ten sols, French money. The lottery was to be publicly drawn the first of February 1750. Every ticket cost six livres of French money. I repeat these details only to prove the truth of the circumstance.

We may add to the preceding, what is related by Bartholinus in his book on the cause of the contempt of death shown by the ancient Danes, (lib. ii. c. 2.) He relates that the riches concealed in the tombs of the great men of that country were guarded by the shades of those to whom they belonged, and that these shades or these demons spread terror in the souls of those who wished to take away those treasures, either by pouring forth a deluge of water, or by flames which they caused to appear around the monuments which enclosed those bodies and those treasures.

CHAPTER 33

Spectres which Appear, and Predict Things Unknown and to Come

Both in ancient and modern writers, we find an infinite number of stories of spectres. We have not the least doubt that their apparitions are the work of the demon, if they are real. Now, it cannot be denied that there is a great deal of illusion and falsehood in all that is related by them. We shall distinguish two sorts of spectres: those which appear to mankind to hurt or deceive them, or to announce things to come, fortunate or unfortunate as circumstances may occur; the other spectres infest certain houses, of which they have made themselves masters, and where they are seen and heard. We shall treat of the latter in another chapter; and show that the greater number of these spectres and apparitions may be suspected of falsehood.

Pliny the younger, writing to his friend, Sura, on the subject of apparitions, testifies that he is much inclined to believe them true; and the reason he gives, is what happened to Quintus Curtius Rufus, who, having gone into Africa in the train of the quaestor or treasurer for the Romans, walking one day towards evening under a portico, saw a woman of uncommon height and beauty, who told him that she was Africa, and assured him that he would one day return into that same country as proconsul. This promise inspired him with high hopes; and by his intrigues, and help of friends, whom he had bribed, he obtained the quaestorship, and afterwards was praetor, through the favour of the Emperor Tiberius.

This dignity having veiled the obscurity and baseness of his birth, he was sent proconsul to Africa, where he died, after having obtained the honours of the triumph. It is said that, on his return to Africa, the same person who had predicted his future grandeur appeared to him again at the moment of his landing at Carthage.

These predictions, so precise, and so exactly followed up, made Pliny the younger believe that predictions of this kind are never made in vain. This story of Curtius Rufus was written by Tacitus, long enough before Pliny's time, and he might have taken it from Tacitus.

After the fatal death of Caligula, who was massacred in his palace, he was buried half-burnt in his own gardens. The princesses, his sisters, on their return from exile, had his remains burnt with ceremony, and honourably inhumed; but it was averred that before this was done, those who had to watch over the gardens and the palace had every night been disturbed by phantoms and frightful noises.

The following instance is so extraordinary, that I should not repeat it if the account were not attested by more than one writer, and also preserved in the public monuments of a considerable town of Upper Saxony; this town is Hamelin in the principality of Kalenberg, at the confluence of the rivers Hamel and Weser.

In the year 1384, this town was infested by such a prodigious multitude of rats, that they ravaged all the corn which was laid up in the granaries; everything was employed that art and experience could invent to chase them away, and whatever is usually employed against this kind of animals. At that time there came to the town an unknown person, of taller stature than ordinary, dressed in a robe of divers colours, who engaged to deliver them from that scourge, for a certain recompense which was agreed upon.

Then he drew from his sleeve a flute, at the sound of which all the rats came out of their holes and followed him; he led them straight to the river, into which they ran and were drowned. On his return he asked for the promised reward, which was refused him, apparently on account of the facility with which he had exterminated the rats. The next day, which was a fête day, he chose the moment when the elder inhabitants of the burgh were at church, and by means of another flute which he began to play, all the boys in the town above the age of fourteen, to the number of a hundred and thirty, assembled round him: he led them to the neighbouring mountain, named Kopfelberg, under which is a sewer for the town, and where criminals are executed; these boys disappeared and were never seen afterwards.

A young girl, who had followed at a distance, was witness of the matter, and brought the news of it to the town.

They still show a hollow in this mountain, where they say that he made the boys go in. At the corner of this opening is an inscription, which is so old that it cannot now be deciphered; but the story is represented on the panes of the church windows; and it is said, that in the public deeds of this town it is still the custom to put the dates in this manner: *Done in the year – , after the disappearance of our children.*

If this recital is not wholly fabulous, as it seems to be, we can only regard this man as a spectre and an evil spirit, who, by God's permission, punished the bad faith of the burghers in the persons of their children, although innocent of their parents' fault. It might be, that a man could have some natural secret to draw the rats together and precipitate them into the river; but only diabolical malice would cause so many innocent children to perish, out of revenge on their fathers.

Julius Caesar having entered Italy, and wishing to pass the Rubicon, perceived a man of more than ordinary stature, who began to whistle. Several soldiers having run to listen to him, this spectre seized the trumpet of one of them, and began to sound the alarm, and to pass the river. Caesar at that moment, without further deliberation, said, 'Let us go where the presages of the gods and the injustice of our enemies call upon us to advance.'

The Emperor Trajan was extricated from the town of Antioch by a phantom, which made him go out at a window, in the midst of that terrible earthquake which overthrew almost all the town. The philosopher Simonides was warned by a spectre that his house was about to fall; he went out of it directly, and soon after it fell down.

The Emperor Julian, the apostate, told his friends, that at the time when his troops were pressing him to accept the empire, being at Paris, he saw during the night a spectre in the form of a woman, as the spirit of an empire is depicted, who presented herself to remain with him; but she gave him notice that it would be only for a short time. The same emperor related, moreover, that writing in his tent a little before his death, his familiar spirit appeared to him, leaving the tent with a sad and afflicted air. Shortly before the death of the Emperor Constans, the same Julian had a vision in the night, of a luminous phantom, who pronounced and repeated to him, more than once, four Greek verses, importing that when Jupiter should be in the sign of the water-pot, or Aquarius, and Saturn in the 25th degree of the Virgin, Constans would end his life in Asia in a shocking manner.

The same Emperor Julian takes Jupiter to witness that he has often seen Esculapius, who cured him of his sicknesses.

CHAPTER 34

Other Apparitions of Spectres

Plutarch, whose gravity and wisdom are well known, often speaks of spectres and apparitions. He says, for instance, that at the famous battle of Marathon against the Persians, several soldiers saw the phantom of Theseus, who fought for the Greeks against the enemy.

The same Plutarch, in the life of Sylla, says, that that general saw in his sleep the goddess whom the Romans worshipped according to the rites of the Cappadocians, (who were fire-worshippers,) whether it might be Bellona or Minerva, or the moon. This divinity presented herself before Sylla, and put into his hand a kind of thunder-bolt, telling him to launch it against his enemies, whom she named to him one after the other; at the same time that he struck them, he saw them fall and expire at his feet. There is reason to believe that this same goddess was Minerva, to whom, as to Jupiter, Paganism attributes the right to hurl the thunder-bolt; or rather, that it was a demon.

Pausanias, general of the Lacedemonians, having inadvertently killed Cleonice, a daughter of one of the first families of Byzantium, was tormented night and day by the ghost of that maiden, who left him no repose, repeating to him angrily a heroic verse, the sense of which was, *Go before the tribunal of justice, which punishes crimes and awaits thee. Insolence is in the end fatal to mortals*.

Pausanias, always disturbed by this image, which followed him every-where, retired to Heraclea in Elis, where there was a temple served by priests who were magicians, called *Psychagogues*, that is to say, who profess to evoke the souls of the dead. There, Pausanias, after having offered the customary libations and funeral effusions, called upon the spirit of Cleonice, and conjured her to renounce her anger against him. Cleonice at last appeared, and told him that very soon, when he should be arrived at Sparta, he would be freed from his woes, wishing apparently by these mysterious words to indicate that death which awaited him there.

We see there the custom of evocations of the dead distinctly pointed out, and solemnly practised in a temple consecrated to these ceremonies; that demonstrates at least the belief and custom of the Greeks. And if Cleonice really appeared to Pausanias and announced his approaching death, can we deny that the evil spirit, or the spirit of Cleonice, is the author of this prediction, unless indeed it were a trick of the priests, which is likely enough, and as the ambiguous reply given to Pausanias seems to insinuate.

Pausanias the historian writes, that four hundred years after the battle of Marathon, every night a noise was heard there of the neighing of horses, and cries like those of soldiers exciting themselves to combat. Plutarch speaks also of spectres which were seen, and frightful howlings that were heard in some public baths, where they had put to death several citizens of Chaeronea, his native place; they had even been obliged to shut up these baths, which did not prevent those who lived near from continuing to hear great noises, and seeing from time to time spectres.

Dion the philosopher, the disciple of Plato, and general of the Syracusans, being one day seated, towards the evening, very full of thought, in the portico of his house, heard a great noise, then perceived a terrible spectre of a woman of monstrous height, who resembled one of the furies, as they are depicted in tragedies; there was still daylight, and she began to sweep the house. Dion, quite alarmed, sent to beg his friends to come and see him, and stay with him all night; but this woman appeared no more. A short time afterwards, his son threw himself down from the top of the house, and he himself was assassinated by conspirators.

Marcus Brutus, one of the murderers of Julius Caesar, being in his tent during a night which was not very dark, towards the third hour of the night, beheld a monstrous and terrific figure enter. 'Who art thou, a man or a god, and why comest thou here?' The spectre answered, 'I am thine evil spirit. Thou shalt see me at Philippi!' Brutus replied undauntedly, 'I will meet thee there.' And on going out, he went and related the circumstance to Cassius, who being of the sect of Epicurus, and a disbeliever in that kind of apparition, told him that it was mere imagination; that there were no genii or other kind of spirits which could appear unto men, and that even did they appear, they would have neither the human form nor the human voice, and could do nothing to harm us. Although Brutus was a little reassured by this reasoning, still it did not remove all his uneasiness.

But the same Cassius, in the campaign of Philippi, and in the midst of the combat, saw Julius Caesar, whom he had assassinated, who came up to him at full gallop; which frightened him so much, that at last he threw himself upon his own sword. Cassius of Parma, a different person from him of whom we have spoken above, saw an evil spirit, who came into his tent, and declared to him his approaching death.

Drusus, when making war on the Germans (Allemani) during the time of Augustus, desiring to cross the Elbe, in order to penetrate farther into the country, was prevented from so doing by a woman of taller stature than common, who appeared to him and said, 'Drusus, whither wilt thou go? Wilt thou never be satisfied? Thy end is near – go back from hence.' He retraced his steps, and died before he reached the Rhine, which he desired to recross.

St Gregory of Nicea, in the Life of St Gregory Thaumaturgus, says, that during a great plague, which ravaged the city of Neocesarea, spectres were seen in open day, who entered houses, into which they carried certain death.

After the famous sedition which happened at Antioch, in the time of the Emperor Theodosius, they beheld a kind of fury running about the town, with a whip, which she lashed about like a coachman who hastens on his horses.

St Martin, Bishop of Tours, being at Trèves, entered a house, where he found a spectre which frightened him at first. Martin commanded him to leave the body which he possessed: instead of going out (of the place), he entered the body of another man who was in the same dwelling; and throwing himself upon those who were there, began to attack and bite them. Martin threw himself across his way, put his fingers in his mouth, and defied him to bite him. The demoniac retreated, as if a bar of red-hot iron had been placed in his mouth, and at last the demon went out of the body of the possessed, not by the mouth but behind.

John, Bishop of Atria, who lived in the sixth century, in speaking of the great plague which happened under the Emperor Justinian, and which is mentioned by almost all the historians of that time, says, that they saw boats of brass, containing black men without heads, which sailed upon the sea, and went towards the places where the plague was beginning its ravages; that this infection having depopulated a town of Egypt, so that there remained only seven men and a boy ten years of age, these persons, wishing to get away from the town with a great deal of money, fell down dead suddenly.

The boy fled without carrying anything with him, but at the gate of the town he was stopped by a spectre, who dragged him, in spite of his resistance, into the house where the seven dead men were. Some time after, the steward of a rich man having entered therein, to take away some furniture belonging to his master, who had gone to reside in the country, was warned by the same boy to go away – but he died suddenly. The servants who had accompanied the steward ran away, and carried the news of all this to their master.

The same Bishop John relates, that he was at Constantinople during a very great plague, which carried off ten, twelve, fifteen, and sixteen thousand persons a day, so that they reckon that two hundred thousand persons died of this malady – he says, that during this time demons were seen running from house to house, wearing the habits of ecclesiastics or monks, and who caused the death of those whom they met therein.

The death of Carlostadt was accompanied by frightful circumstances, according to the ministers of Basle, his colleagues, who bore witness to it at the time. They relate, that at the last sermon which Carlostadt preached in the temple of Basle, a tall black man came and seated himself near the consul. The preacher perceived him, and appeared disconcerted at it. When he left the pulpit, he asked who that stranger was who had taken his seat next to the chief magistrate; no one had seen him but himself. When he went home, he heard more news of the spectre. The black man had been there, and had caught up by the hair the youngest and most tenderly loved of his children. After he had thus raised the child from the ground, he appeared disposed to throw him down so as to break his head; but he contented himself with ordering the boy to warn his father that in three days he should return, and he must hold himself in readiness. The child having repeated to his father what had been said to him, Carlostadt was terrified. He went to bed in alarm, and in three days he expired. These apparitions of the demons, by Luther's own avowal, were pretty frequent, in the case of the first reformers.

These instances of the apparitions of spectres might be multiplied to infinity; but if we undertook to criticise them, there is hardly one of them very certain, or proof against a serious and profound examination. Here follows one, which I relate on purpose because it has some singular features, and its falsehood has at last been acknowledged.

CHAPTER 35

Examination of the Apparition of a Pretended Spectre

Business having led the Count d'Alais to Marseilles, a most extraordinary adventure happened to him there: he desired Neuré to write to our philosopher (Gassendi), to know what he thought of it; which he did in these words: the Count and Countess being come to Marseilles, saw, as they were lying in bed, a luminous spectre; they were both wide awake. In order to be sure that it was not some illusion, they called their valets de chambre; but no sooner had these appeared with their flambeaux, than the spectre disappeared. They had all the openings and cracks which they found in the chamber stopped up, and then went to bed again; but hardly had the valets de chambre retired, than it appeared again.

Its light was less shining than that of the sun; but it was brighter than that of the moon. Sometimes this spectre was of an angular form, sometimes a circle, and sometimes an oval. It was easy to read a letter by the light it gave; it often changed its place, and sometimes appeared on the Count's bed. It had, as it were, a kind of little buckler, above which were characters imprinted. Nevertheless, nothing could be more agreeable to the sight; so that instead of alarming, it gave pleasure. It appeared every night whilst the Count stayed at Marseilles. This prince, having once cast his hands upon it, to see if it was not something attached to the bed curtain, the spectre disappeared that night, and reappeared the next.

Gassendi being consulted upon this circumstance, replied on the 13th of the same month. He says, in the first place, that he knows not what to think of this vision. He does not deny that this spectre might be sent from God, to tell them something. What renders this idea probable, is the great piety of them both, and that this spectre had nothing frightful in it, but quite the contrary. What deserves our attention still more is this, that if God had sent it, he would have made known why he sent it. God does not jest; and since it cannot be understood what is to be hoped or feared, followed up or avoided, it is clear that this spectre cannot come from him; otherwise his conduct would be less praiseworthy than that of a father, or a prince, or a worthy, or even a prudent man, who being informed of somewhat which greatly concerned those in subjection to them, would not content themselves with warning them enigmatically.

If this spectre is anything natural, nothing is more difficult than to discover it, or even to find any conjecture which may explain it. Although I am well persuaded of my ignorance, I will venture to give my idea. Might it not be advanced, that this light has appeared because the eye of the Count was internally affected, or because it was so externally? The eye may be so internally in two ways. First: if the eye was affected in the same manner as that of the Emperor Tiberius always was when he awoke in the night and opened his eyes; a light proceeded from them, by means of which he could discern objects in the dark by looking fixedly at them. I have known the same thing happen to a lady of rank. Secondly: if his eyes were disposed in a certain manner, as it happens to myself when I awake: if I open my eyes, they perceive rays of light though there has been none. No one can deny, that some flash may dart from our eyes, which represents objects to us – which objects are reflected in our eyes, and leave their traces there. It is known that animals which prowl by night have a piercing sight, to enable them to discern their prey and carry it off; that the animal spirit which is in the eye, and which may be shed from it, is of the nature of fire, and consequently lucid. It may happen that, the eyes being closed during sleep, this spirit heated by the eyelids becomes inflamed, and sets some faculty in motion, as the imagination. For, does it not happen that wood of different kinds, and fish bones, produce some light when their heat is excited by putrefaction; why then may not the heat excited in this confined spirit produce some light? He proves afterwards that imagination alone may do it.

The Count d'Alais having returned to Marseilles, and being lodged in the same apartment, the same spectre appeared to him again. Neuré wrote to Gassendi, that they had observed that this spectre penetrated into the chamber by the wainscot; which obliged Gassendi to write to the count to examine the thing more attentively; and notwithstanding this discovery, he dare not yet decide upon it. He contents himself with encouraging the Count, and telling him, that if this apparition is from God, he will not allow him to remain long in expectation, and will soon make known his will to him; and also, if this vision does not come from him, he will not permit it to continue, and will soon discover that it proceeds from a natural cause. Nothing more is said of this spectre any where.

Three years afterwards, the Countess d'Alais avowed ingenuously to the Count that she herself had caused this farce to be played by one of her women, because she did not like to reside at Marseilles; that her woman was under the bed, and that she from time to time caused a phosphoric light to appear. The Count d'Alais related this himself to M. Puger of Lyons, who told it, about thirty-five years ago, to M. Falconet, a medical doctor of the Royal Academy of Belle-Lettres, from whom I learnt it. Gassendi, when consulted seriously by the count, answered like a man who had no doubt of the truth of this apparition; so true it is, that the greater number of these extraordinary facts require to be very carefully examined, before any opinion can be passed upon them.

CHAPTER 36

Of Spectres which Haunt Houses

There are several kinds of spectres or ghosts, which haunt certain houses, make noises, appear there, and disturb those who live in them: some are sprites, or elves, which divert themselves by troubling the quiet of those who dwell there; others are spectres or ghosts of the dead, who molest the living until they have received sepulture: some of them, as it is said, make the place their purgatory; others show themselves or make themselves heard, because they have been put to death in that place, and ask that their death may be avenged, or that their bodies may be buried. So many stories are related concerning those things, that now they are not cared for, and nobody will believe any of them. In fact, when these pretended apparitions are thoroughly examined into, it is easy to discover their falsehood and illusion.

Now, it is a tenant who wishes to decry the house in which he resides, to hinder others from coming who would like to take his place; then a band of coiners have taken possession of a dwelling, whose interest it is to keep their secret from being found out; or a farmer who desires to retain his farm, and wishes to prevent others from coming to offer more for it; in this place it will be cats or owls, or even rats, which by making a noise frighten the master and domestics, as it happened some years ago at Mosheim, where large rats amused themselves in the night by moving and setting in motion the machines with which the women bruise hemp and flax. An honest man who related it to me, desiring to behold the thing nearer, mounted up to the garret armed with two pistols, with his servant armed in the same manner. After a moment of silence, they saw the rats begin their game; they let fire upon them, killed two, and dispersed the rest. The circumstance was reported in the country and served as an excellent joke.

I am about to relate some of these spectral apparitions upon which the reader will pronounce judgment for himself. Pliny the younger says that there was a very handsome mansion at Athens, which was forsaken on account of a spectre which haunted it. The philosopher Athenodorus, having arrived in the city, and seeing a board which informed the public that this house was to be sold at a very low price, bought it and went to sleep there with his people. As he was busy reading and writing during the night, he heard on a sudden a great noise, as if of chains being dragged along, and perceived at the same time something like a frightful old man loaded with iron chains, who drew near to him. Athenodorus continuing to write, the spectre made him a sign to follow him; the philosopher in his turn made signs to him to wait, and continued to write; at last he took his light and followed the spectre, who conducted him into the court of the house, then sank into the ground and disappeared.

Athenodorus, without being frightened, tore up some of the grass to mark the spot, and on leaving it, went to rest in his room. The next day he informed the magistrates of what had happened; they came to the house and searched the spot he designated, and there found the bones of a human body loaded with chains. They caused him to be properly buried, and the dwelling-house remained quiet.

Lucian relates a very similar story. There was, says he, a house at Corinth, which had belonged to one Eubatides, in the quarter named Cranaüs; a man named Arignotes undertook to pass the night there, without troubling himself about a spectre which was said to haunt it. He furnished himself with certain magic books of the Egyptians to conjure the spectre. Having gone into the house at night with a light, he began to read quietly in the court. The spectre appeared in a little while, taking sometimes the shape of a dog, then that of a bull, and then that of a lion. Arignotes very composedly began to pronounce certain magical invocations, which he read in his books, and by their power forced the spectre into a corner of the court, where he sank into the earth and disappeared.

The next day Arignotes sent for Eubatides, the master of the house, and having had the ground dug up where the phantom had disappeared, they found a skeleton, which they had properly interred, and from that time nothing more was seen or heard.

It is Lucian, that is to say the man in the world the least credulous concerning things of this kind, who makes Arignotes relate this event. In the same passage he says that Democritus, who believed in neither angels, nor demons, nor spirits, having shut himself up in a tomb without the city of Athens, where he was writing and studying, a party of young men, who wanted to frighten him, covered themselves with black garments, as the dead are represented, and having taken hideous disguises, came in the night, shrieking and jumping around the place where he was; he let them do what they liked, and without at all disturbing himself, coolly told them to have done with their jesting.

I know not if the historian who wrote the life of St Germain l'Auxerrois had in his eye the stories we have just related, and if he did not wish to ornament the life of the saint by a recital very much like them. The saint travelling one day through his diocese, was obliged to pass the night with his clerks in a house forsaken long before on account of the spirits which haunted it. The clerk, who read to him during the night, saw on a sudden a spectre which alarmed him at first; but having awakened the holy bishop, the latter commanded the spectre in the name of Jesus Christ to declare to him who he was, and what he wanted. The phantom told him that he and his companion had been guilty of several crimes; that having died and been interred in that house, they disturbed those who lodged there until the burial rites should have been accorded them. St Germain commanded him to point out where their bodies were buried, and the spectre led him thither. The next day he assembled the people in the neighbourhood; they sought amongst the ruins of the building where the brambles had been disturbed, and they found the bones of two men thrown in a heap together, and also loaded with chains; they were buried, prayers were said for them, and they returned no more.

If these men were wretches dead in crime and impenitence, all this can be attributed only to the artifice of the devil, to show the living that the reprobates take pains to procure rest for their bodies by getting them interred, and to their souls by getting them prayed for. But if these two men were Christians who had expiated their crimes by repentance, and who died in communion with the Church, God might permit them to appear, to ask for clerical sepulture, and those prayers which the Church is accustomed to say for the repose of defunct persons, who die while yet some slight fault remains to be expiated.

Here is a fact of the same kind as those which precede, but which is attended by circumstances which may render it more credible. It is related by Antonio Torquemada, in his work entitled *Flores Curiosas*, printed at Salamanca in 1570. He says that a little before his own time, a young man named Vasquez de Ayola, being gone to Bologna with two of his companions to study the law there, and not having found such a lodging in the town as they wished to have, lodged themselves in a large and handsome house, which was abandoned by everybody, because it was haunted by a spectre which frightened away all those who wished to live in it; they laughed at such discourse, and took up their abode there.

At the end of a month, as Ayola was sitting up alone in his chamber, and his companions sleeping quietly in their beds, he heard at a distance a noise as of several chains dragged along upon the ground, and the noise advanced towards him by the great staircase; he recommended himself to God, made the sign of the cross, took a shield and sword, and having his taper in his hand, he saw the door opened by a terrific spectre that was nothing but bones, but loaded with chains. Ayola conjured him, and asked him what he wished for; the phantom signed to him to follow, and he did so; but as he went down the stairs, his light blew out; he went back to light it, and then followed the spirit, which led him along a court where there was a well. Ayola feared that he might throw him into it, and stopped short. The spectre beckoned to him to continue to follow him; they entered the garden, where the phantom disappeared. Ayola tore up some handfuls of grass upon the spot, and returning to the house, related to his companions what had happened. In the morning he gave notice of this circumstance to the Principals of Bologna.

They came to reconnoitre the spot, and had it dug up; they found there a fleshless body, but loaded with chains. They inquired who it could be, but nothing certain could be discovered, and the bones were interred with suitable obsequies, and from that time the house was never disquieted by such visits. Torquemada asserts that in his time there were still living at Bologna and in Spain some who had been witnesses of the fact; and that on his return to his own country, Ayola was invested with a high office, and that his son, before this narration was written, was President in a good city of the kingdom (of Spain).

Plautus, still more ancient than either Lucian or Pliny, composed a comedy entitled *Mostellaria*, or *Monstellaria*, a name derived from 'Monstrum,' or 'Monstellum,' from a monster, a spectre, which was said to appear in a certain house, and which on that account had been deserted. We agree that the foundation of this comedy is only a fable, but we may deduce from it the antiquity of this idea among the Greeks and Romans.

The poet makes this pretended spirit say, that having been assassinated about sixty years before by a perfidious comrade who had taken his money, he had been secretly interred in that house; that the god of Hades would not receive him on the other side of Acheron, as he had died prematurely; for which reason he was obliged to remain in that house of which he had taken possession.

> 'Haec mihi dedita habitatio;
> Nam me Acherontem recipere noluit,
> Quia praematurè vitâ careo.'

The Pagans, who had the simplicity to believe that the Lamiae and evil spirits disquieted those who dwelt in certain houses and certain rooms, and who slept in certain beds, conjured them by magic verses, and pretended to drive them away by fumigations composed of sulphur and other stinking drugs, and certain herbs mixed with sea water. Ovid, speaking of Medea, that celebrated magician, says –

> 'Terque senem flamma, ter aqua, ter sulphure lustrat.'

And elsewhere he adds:

'Adveniat quae lustret anus lectumque locumque,
Deferat et tremula sulphur et ova manu.'

In addition to this they adduce the instance of the Archangel Raphael, who drove away the devil Asmodeus from the chamber of Sarah, by the smell of the liver of a fish which he burnt upon the fire. But the instance of Raphael ought not to be placed along with the superstitious ceremonies of magicians, which were laughed at by the Pagans themselves; if they had any power, it could only be by the operation of the demon with the permission of God; whilst what is told of the Archangel Raphael is certainly the work of a good spirit, sent by God to cure Sarah the daughter of Raguel, who was as much distinguished by her piety as the magicians are degraded by their malice and superstition.

CHAPTER 37

Other Instances of Spectres which Haunt certain Houses

Father Pierre Thyrée, a Jesuit, relates an infinite number of anecdotes of houses haunted by ghosts, spirits, and demons; for instance, that of a tribune named Hesperius, whose house was infested by a demon who tormented the domestics and animals, and who was driven away, says St Augustine, by a good priest of Hippo, who offered therein the divine sacrifice of the body of our Lord.

St Germain, Bishop of Capua, taking a bath in one particular quarter of the town, found there Paschasius, a deacon of the Roman Church, who had been dead some time, and who began to wait upon him, telling him that he underwent his purgatory in that place for having favoured the party of Laurentius the anti-pope, against Pope Symachus.

St Gregory of Nicea, in the life of St Gregory of Neocaesarea, says that a deacon of this holy bishop, having gone into a bath where no one dared go after a certain hour in the evening, because all those who had entered there had been put to death, beheld spectres of all kinds, which threatened him in a thousand ways, but he got rid of them by crossing himself and invoking the name of Jesus.

Alexander ab Alexandro a learned Neapolitan lawyer of the fifteenth century, says that all the world knows that there are a number of houses at

Rome so much out of repute on account of the ghosts which appear in them every night, that nobody dares to inhabit them. Nicholas Tuba, his friend, a man well known for his probity and veracity, who came once with some of his comrades to try if all that was said of those houses was true, would pass the night in one of them with Alexander. As they were together, wide awake, and with plenty of light, they beheld a horrible spectre, which frightened them so much by its terrific voice and the great noise which it made, that they hardly knew what they did, nor what they said; 'and by degrees, as we approached,' says he, 'with the light, the phantom retreated; at last, after having thrown all the house into confusion, it disappeared entirely.'

I might also relate here the spectre noticed by Father Sinson the Jesuit, which he saw, and to which he spoke at Pont-à-Mousson, in the cloister belonging to those fathers; but I shall content myself with the instance which is reported in the *Causes Célèbres*, and which may serve to undeceive those who too lightly give credit to stories of this kind.

At the Château d'Arsillier in Picardy, on certain days of the year, towards November, they saw flames and a horrible smoke proceeding thence. Cries and frightful howlings were heard. The bailiff, or farmer of the château, had got accustomed to this uproar, because he himself caused it. All the village talked of it, and everybody told his own story thereupon. The gentleman to whom the château belonged, mistrusting some contrivance, came there near All Saints' Day with two gentlemen his friends, resolved to pursue the spirit, and fire upon it with a brace of good pistols. A few days after they arrived, they heard a great noise above the room where the owner of the château slept; his two friends went up thither, holding a pistol in one hand and a candle in the other; and a sort of black phantom with horns and a tail presented itself, and began to gambol about before them.

One of them fired off his pistol; the spectre, instead of falling, turns, and skips before him: the gentleman tries to seize it, but the spirit escapes by the back staircase; the gentleman follows it, but loses sight of it, and after several turnings, the spectre throws itself into a granary, and disappears at the moment its pursuer reckoned on seizing and stopping it. A light was brought, and it was remarked that where the spectre had disappeared, there was a trap-door which had been bolted after it entered; they forced open the trap, and found the pretended spirit. He owned all his artifices, and that what had rendered him proof against the pistol shot, was buffalo's hide tightly fitted to his body.

Cardinal de Retz in his memoirs relates very agreeably the alarm which seized himself and those with him, on meeting a company of black Augustine friars, who came to bathe in the river by night, and whom they took for a troop of quite another description.

A physician, in a dissertation which he has given on spirits or ghosts, says that a maid servant in the Rue St Victor, who had gone down into the cellar, came back very much frightened, saying she had seen a spectre standing upright between two barrels. Some persons who were bolder went down, and saw the same thing. It was a dead body, which had fallen from a cart coming from the Hôtel Dieu. It had slid down by the cellar window (or grating), and had remained standing between two casks. All these collective facts, instead of confirming one another, and establishing the reality of those ghosts which appear in certain houses, and keep away those who would willingly dwell in them, are only calculated, on the contrary, to render such stories in general very doubtful; for on what account should those people who have been buried and turned to dust for a long time find themselves able to walk about with their chains? How do they drag them? How do they speak? What do they want? Is it sepulture? Are they not interred? If they are heathens and reprobates, they have nothing to do with prayers. If they are good people, who died in a state of grace, they may require prayers to take them out of purgatory; but can that be said of the spectres spoken of by Pliny and Lucian? Is it the devil, who sports with the simplicity of men? Is it not ascribing to him most excessive power, by making him the author of all these apparitions, which we conceive he cannot cause without the permission of God? And we can still less imagine that God will concur in the deceptions and illusions of the demon. There is then reason to believe that all the apparitions of this kind, and all these stories, are false, and must be absolutely rejected, as more fit to keep up the superstition and idle credulity of the people than to edify and instruct them.

CHAPTER 38

Prodigious Effects of Imagination in those Men or Women who Believe they Hold Intercourse with the Demon

As soon as we admit it as a principle that angels and demons are purely spiritual substances, we must consider, not only as chimerical, but also as impossible, all personal intercourse between a demon and a man, or a woman, and consequently regard as the effect of a depraved or deranged imagination all that is related of demons, whether incubi or succubi, and of the *ephialtes* of which such strange tales are told.

The author of the Book of Enoch, which is cited by the fathers, and regarded as canonical Scripture by some ancient writers, has taken occasion from these words of Moses – 'The children of God, seeing the daughters of men, who were of extraordinary beauty, took them for wives,' and begat the giants of them,' – of setting forth that the angels, smitten with love for the daughters of men, wedded them, and had by them children, which are those giants so famous in antiquity. Some of the ancient fathers have thought that this irregular love of the angels was the cause of their fall, and that till then they had remained in the just and due subordination which they owed to their Creator.

It appears from Josephus, that the Jews of his day seriously believed that the angels were subject to these weaknesses like men. St Justin Martyr thought that the demons were the fruit of this commerce of the angels with the daughters of men.

But these ideas are now almost entirely given up, especially since the belief in the spirituality of angels and demons has been adopted. Commentators and the fathers have generally explained the passage in Genesis which we have quoted as relating to the children of Seth, to whom the Scripture gives the name of *children of God*, to distinguish them from the sons of Cain, who were the fathers of those here called *the daughters of men*. The race of Seth having then formed alliances with the race of Cain, by means of those marriages before alluded to, there proceeded from these unions powerful, violent, and impious men, who drew down upon the earth the terrible effects of God's wrath, which burst forth at the universal deluge.

Thus, then, these marriages between the *children of God* and the *daughters of men* have no relation to the question we are here treating; what we have to examine is – if the demon can have personal commerce with man or woman, and if what is said on that subject can be connected with the apparitions of evil spirits amongst mankind, which is the principal object of this dissertation.

I will give some instances of those persons who have believed that they held such intercourse with the demon. Torquemada relates, in a detailed manner, what happened in his time, and to his knowledge, in the town of Cagliari, in Sardinia, to a young lady, who suffered herself to be corrupted by the demon; and having been arrested by the Inquisition, she suffered the penalty of the flames, in the mad hope that her pretended lover would come and deliver her.

In the same place he speaks of a young girl who was sought in marriage by a gentleman of good family; when the devil assumed the form of this young man, associated with the young lady for several months, made her promises of marriage, and took advantage of her. She was only undeceived when the young lord who sought her in marriage informed her that he was absent from town, and more than fifty leagues off, the day that the promise in question had been given, and that he never had the slightest knowledge of it. The young girl, thus disabused, retired into a convent, and did penance for her double crime.

We read in the life of St Bernard, Abbot of Clairvaux, that a woman of Nantes, in Brittany, saw, or thought she saw the demon every night, even when lying by her husband. She remained six years in this state; at the end of that period, having her disorderly life in horror, she confessed herself to a priest, and by his advice began to perform several acts of piety, as much to obtain pardon for her crime, as to deliver herself from her abominable lover. But when the husband of this woman was informed of the circumstance, he left her, and would never see her again.

This unhappy woman was informed by the devil himself, that St Bernard would soon come to Nantes, but she must mind not to speak to him, for this abbot could by no means assist her; and if she did speak to him, it would be a great misfortune to her; and that from being her lover, he who warned her of it would become her most ardent persecutor.

The saint reassured this woman, and desired her to make the sign of the cross on herself on going to bed, and to place next her in the bed the staff which he gave her. 'If the demon comes,' said he, 'let him do what he can.' The demon came; but, without daring to approach the bed, he threatened the woman greatly, and told her that after the departure of St Bernard he would come again to torment her.

On the following Sunday, St Bernard repaired to the Cathedral Church,

with the Bishop of Nantes and the Bishop of Chartres, and having caused
lighted tapers to be given to all the people, who had assembled in a great
crowd, the saint, after having publicly related the abominable action of the
demon, exorcised and anathematised the evil spirit, and forbade him, by
the authority of Jesus Christ, ever again to approach that woman, or any
other. Everybody extinguished their tapers, and the power of the demon
was annihilated.

This example and the two preceding ones, related in so circumstantial a
manner, might make us believe that there is some reality in what is said of
demons, incubi, and succubi; but if we deeply examine the facts, we shall
find that an imagination strongly possessed, and violent prejudice, may
produce all that we have just repeated.

St Bernard begins by curing the woman's mind, by giving her a stick,
which she was to place by her side in the bed. This staff sufficed for the
first impression; but to dispose her for a complete cure, he exorcises the
demon, and then anathematises him, with all the éclat he possibly could:
the bishops are assembled in the cathedral, the people repair thither in
crowds; the circumstance is recounted in pompous terms; the evil spirit
is threatened; the tapers are extinguished – all of them striking ceremonies: the woman is moved by them, and her imagination is restored to a
healthy tone.

Jerome Cardan relates two singular examples of the power of imagination in this way; he had them from Francis Pico de Mirandola. 'I know,'
says the latter, 'a priest, seventy-five years of age, who lived with a
pretended woman, whom he called Hermeline, with whom he slept,
conversed, and conducted in the streets as if she had been his wife. He
alone saw her, or thought he saw her, so that he was looked upon as a man
who had lost his senses. This priest was named Benedict Beïna. He had
been arrested by the Inquisition, and punished for his crimes; for he
owned that in the sacrifice of the mass he did not pronounce the
sacramental words, that he had given the consecrated wafer to women to
make use of in sorcery, and that he had sucked the blood of children. He
avowed all this while undergoing the question.

Another, named Pineto, held converse with a demon, whom he kept as
his wife, and with whom he had intercourse for more than forty years. This
man was still living in the time of Pico de Mirandola.

Devotion and spirituality, when too contracted and carried to excess,
have also their derangements of imagination. Persons so affected often
believe they see, hear, and feel, what passes only in their brain, and which
takes all its reality from their prejudices and self-love. This is less
mistrusted, because the object of it is holy and pious; but error and excess,
even in matters of devotion, are subject to very great inconveniences, and

it is very important to undeceive all those who give way to this kind of mental derangement.

For instance, we have seen persons eminent for their devotion, who believed they saw the Holy Virgin, St Joseph, the Saviour, and their guardian angel, who spoke to them, conversed with them, touched the wounds of the Lord, and tasted the blood which flowed from his side and his wounds. Others thought they were in company with the Holy Virgin and the Infant Jesus, who spoke to them and conversed with them; in idea, however, and without reality.

In order to cure the two ecclesiastics of whom we have spoken, gentler and perhaps more efficacious means might have been made use of than those employed by the tribunal of the Inquisition. Every day hypochondriacs, or maniacs, with fevered imaginations, diseased brains, or with the viscera too much heated, are cured by simple and natural remedies, either by cooling the blood, and creating a diversion in the humours thereof, or by striking the imagination through some new device, or by giving so much exercise of body and mind to those who are afflicted with such maladies of the brain, that they may have something else to do or to think of, than to nourish such fancies, and strengthen them by reflections daily recurring, and having always the same end and object.

CHAPTER 39

Return and Apparitions of Souls after the Death of the Body, Proved from Scripture

The dogma of the immortality of the soul, and of its existence after its separation from the body which it once animated, being taken for indubitable, and Jesus Christ having invincibly established it against the Sadducees, the return of souls and their apparition to the living, by the command or permission of God, can no longer appear so incredible, nor even so difficult.

It was a known and received truth among the Jews in the time of our Saviour; he assumed it as certain, and never pronounced a word which could give anyone reason to think that he disapproved of, or condemned it; he only warned us that in common apparitions, spirits have neither flesh nor bones, as he had himself after his resurrection. If St Thomas doubted of the reality of the resurrection of his master, and the truth of his appearance, it was because he was aware that those who suppose they see apparitions of spirits are subject to illusion; and that one strongly prepossessed, will often believe he beholds what he does not see, and hears that which he hears not; and even had Jesus Christ appeared to his Apostles, that would not prove that he was resuscitated, since a spirit can appear, while its body is in the tomb and even corrupted or reduced to dust and ashes.

The Apostles doubted not of the possibility of the apparition of spirits: when they saw the Saviour coming towards them, walking upon the waves of the Lake of Gennesareth, they at first believed that it was a phantom.

After St Peter had left the prison by the aid of an angel, and came and knocked at the door of the house where the brethren were assembled, the servant whom they sent to open it, hearing Peter's voice, thought it was his spirit, or an angel who had assumed his form and voice. The wicked rich man, being in the flames of hell, begged of Abraham to send Lazarus to earth, to warn his brothers not to expose themselves to the danger of falling like him in the extreme of misery: he believed, without doubt, that souls could return to earth, make themselves visible, and speak to the living.

In the transfiguration of Jesus Christ, Moses, who had been dead for ages, appeared on Mount Tabor with Elias, conversing with Jesus Christ then transfigured. After the resurrection of the Saviour, several persons, who had long been dead, arose from their graves, went into Jerusalem and appeared unto many.

In the Old Testament, King Saul addresses himself to the witch of Endor, to beg of her to evoke for him the soul of Samuel; that prophet appeared and spoke to Saul. I know that considerable difficulties and objections have been formed, as to this evocation and this apparition of Samuel. But, whether he appeared or not – whether the pythoness did really evoke him, or only deluded Saul with a false appearance – I deduce from it, that Saul and those with him were persuaded that the spirits of the dead could appear to the living, and reveal to them things unknown to men.

St Augustine, in reply to Simplicius, who had proposed to him his difficulties respecting the truth of this apparition, says at first, that it is no more difficult to understand that the demon could evoke Samuel by the help of a witch, than it is to comprehend how that Satan could speak to God, and tempt the holy man Job, and ask permission to tempt the Apostles; or that he could transport Jesus Christ himself to the highest pinnacle of the Temple of Jerusalem.

We may believe also, that God, by a particular dispensation of his will, may have permitted the demon to evoke Samuel, and make him appear before Saul, to announce to him what was to happen to him, not by virtue of magic, not by the power of the demon alone, but solely because God willed it, and ordained it thus to be.

He adds, that it may be advanced that it is not Samuel who appears to Saul, but a phantom, formed by the illusive power of the demon, and by the force of magic; and that the Scripture, in giving the name of Samuel to this phantom, has made use of ordinary language, which gives the name of things themselves, to that which is but their image or representation in painting or in sculpture.

If it should be asked, how this phantom could discover the future, and predict to Saul his approaching death: we may likewise ask, how the demon could know Jesus Christ for God alone, while the Jews knew him not – and the girl possessed with a spirit of divination, spoken of in the Acts of the Apostles, could bear witness to the Apostles, and undertake to become their advocate in rendering good testimony to their mission.

Lastly; St Augustine concludes by saying, that he does not think himself sufficiently enlightened to decide whether the demon can, or cannot, by means of magical enchantments, evoke a soul after the death of the body, so that it may appear and become visible in a corporeal form, which may be recognised, and capable of speaking and revealing the hidden future. And if this potency be not accorded to magic and the demon, we must conclude that all which is related of this apparition of Samuel to Saul, is an illusion and a false apparition made by the demon to deceive men.

In the books of the Maccabees, the High Priest Onias, who had been dead several years before that time, appeared to Judas Maccabaeus, in the attitude of a man whose hands were outspread, and who was praying for the people of the Lord: at the same time the Prophet Jeremiah, long since dead, appeared to the same Maccabaeus; and Onias said to him, 'Behold that holy man, who is the protector and friend of his brethren; it is he who prays continually for the Lord's people, and for the Holy City of Jerusalem.' So saying, he put into the hands of Judas a golden sword, saying to him, 'Receive this sword as a gift from heaven, by means of which you shall destroy the enemies of my people Israel.'

In the same second book of the Maccabees, it is related, that in the thickest of the battle fought by Timotheus, general of the armies of Syria, against Judas Maccabaeus, they saw five men as if descended from heaven, mounted on horses with golden bridles, who were at the head of the army of the Jews, two of them on each side of Judas Maccabaeus, the chief captain of the army of the Lord; they shielded him with their arms, and launched against the enemy such fiery darts and thunder-bolts, that they were blinded and mortally afraid and terrified.

These five armed horsemen, these combatants for Israel, are apparently no other than Mattathias, the father of Judas Maccabaeus, and four of his sons, who were already dead; there yet remained of his seven sons, but Judas Maccabaeus, Jonathan, and Simon. We may also understand it as five angels, who were sent by God to the assistance of the Maccabees. In whatever way we regard it, these are not doubtful apparitions, both on account of the certainly of the book in which they are related, and the testimony of a whole army by which they were seen.

Whence I conclude, that the Hebrews had no doubt that the spirits of the dead could return to earth, that they did return in fact, and that they discovered to the living things beyond our natural knowledge. Moses expressly forbids the Israelites to consult the dead. But these apparitions did not show themselves in solid and material bodies; the Saviour assures us of it when he says, 'Spirits have neither flesh nor bones.' It was often only an aerial figure which struck the senses and the imagination, like the images which we see in sleep, or that we firmly believe we hear and see. The inhabitants of Sodom were struck with a species of blindness, which prevented them from seeing the door of Lot's house, into which the angels had entered. The soldiers who sought for Elisha, were in the same way blinded in some sort, although they spoke to him they were seeking for, who led them into Samaria without their perceiving him. The two disciples who went on Easter-day to Emmaus, in company with Jesus Christ their Master, did not recognise him till the breaking of the bread.

Thus, the apparitions of spirits to mankind are not always in a corporeal form, palpable and real; but God, who ordains or permits them, often causes the persons to whom these apparitions appear, to behold, in a dream or otherwise, those spirits which speak to, warn, or threaten them; who makes them see things as if present, which in reality are not before their eyes, but only in their imagination; which does not prove these visions and warnings not to be sent from God, who, by Himself, or by the ministration of His angels, or by souls disengaged from the body, inspires the minds of men with what He judges proper for them to know, whether in a dream, or by external signs, or by words, or else by certain impressions made on their senses, or in their imagination, in the absence of every external object.

If the apparitions of the souls of the dead were things in nature and of their own choice, there would be few persons who would not come back to visit the things or the persons which have been dear to them during this life. St Augustine says it of his mother, St Monica, who had so tender and constant an affection for him, and who, while she lived, followed him and sought him by sea and land. The bad rich man would not have failed, either, to come in person to his brethren and relations, to inform them of the wretched condition in which he found himself in hell. It is a pure favour of the mercy or the power of God, and which He grants to very few persons, to make their appearance after death; for which reason we should be very much on our guard against all that is said, and all that we find written on the subject in books.

CHAPTER 40

Apparitions of Spirits Proved from History

St Augustine acknowledges that the dead have often appeared to the living, have revealed to them the spot where their body remained unburied, and have shown them that where they wished to be interred. He says, morever, that a noise was often heard in churches where the dead were inhumed, and that dead persons have been seen often to enter the houses wherein they dwelt before their decease.

We read that in the Council of Elvira, which was held about the year 300, it was forbidden to light tapers in the cemeteries, that the souls of the saints might not be disturbed. The night after the death of Julian the Apostate, St Basil had a vision in which he fancied he saw the martyr, St

Mercurius, who received an order from God to go and kill Julian. A little time afterwards the same saint Mercurius returned and cried out – 'Lord, Julian is pierced and wounded to death, as thou commandedst me.' In the morning St Basil announced this news to the people.

St Ignatius, Bishop of Antioch, who suffered martyrdom in 107, appeared to his disciples, embracing them, and standing near them; and as they persevered in praying with still greater fervour, they saw him crowned with glory, as if in perspiration, coming from a great combat, environed with light.

After the death of St Ambrose, which happened on Easter Eve, the same night in which they baptised neophytes, several newly baptised children saw the holy Bishop, and pointed him out to their parents, who could not see him because their eyes were not purified, at least says St Paulinus, a disciple of the saint, and who wrote his life.

He adds, that on the day of his death the saint appeared to several holy persons dwelling in the East, praying with them and giving them the imposition of hands; they wrote to Milan, and it was found, on comparing the dates, that this occurred on the very day he died. These letters were still preserved in the time of Paulinus, who wrote all these things. This holy Bishop was also seen several times after his death praying in the Ambrosian Church at Milan, which he promised during his life that he would often visit. During the siege of Milan, St Ambrose appeared to a man of that same city, and promised that the next day succour would arrive, which happened accordingly. A blind man having learnt in a vision that the bodies of the holy martyrs Sicineus and Alexander would come by sea to Milan, and that Bishop Ambrose was going to meet them, he prayed the same Bishop to restore him to sight, in a dream; Ambrose replied, 'Go to Milan; come and meet my brethren; they will arrive on such a day, and they will restore you to sight.' The blind man went to Milan, where he had never been before, touched the shrine of the holy martyrs, and recovered his eyesight. He himself related the circumstance to Paulinus.

The lives of the Saints are full of apparitions of deceased persons; and if they were collected, large volumes might be filled. St Ambrose, of whom we have just spoken, discovered after a miraculous fashion the bodies of St Gervasius and St Protasius, and those of St Nazairius and St Celsus.

Evodius, Bishop of Upsal in Africa, a great friend of St Augustine, was well persuaded of the reality of apparitions of the dead, from his own experience, and he relates several instances of such things, which happened in his own time; as, that of a good widow to whom a deacon appeared, who had been dead for four years. He was accompanied by several of the servants of God, of both sexes, who were preparing a palace of extraordinary beauty. This widow asked him for whom they were making these preparations; he replied that it was for the youth who died the preceding day. At the same time a venerable old man, who was in the same palace, commanded two young men, arrayed in white, to take the deceased young man out of his grave, and conduct him to this place. As soon as he had left the grave, fresh roses and rose beds sprang up, and the young man appeared to a monk, and told him that God had received him into the number of his elect, and had sent him to fetch his father, who in fact died four days after of slow fever.

Evodius asks himself diverse questions on this recital: If the soul on quitting its mortal body does not retain a certain subtle body, with which it appears, and by means of which it is transported from one spot to another? If the angels, even, have not a certain kind of body; for if they are incorporeal, how can they be counted? And if Samuel appeared to Saul, how could it take place if Samuel had no members? He adds, 'I remember well that Profuturus, Privatus and Servitius, whom I had known in the monastery here, appeared to me, and talked with me after their decease; and what they told me, happened. Was it their soul which appeared to me, or was it some other spirit which assumed their form?' He concludes from this that the soul is not absolutely bodiless, since God alone is incorporeal.

St Augustine, who was consulted on this matter by Evodius, does not think that the soul, after the death of the body, is clothed with any material substantial form; but he confesses that it is very difficult to explain how an infinite number of things are done, which pass in our minds, as well in our sleep as when we are awake, in which we seem to see, feel, and discourse, and do things which it would appear could be done only by the body, although it is certain that nothing bodily occurs. And how can we explain things so unknown, and so far beyond anything that we experience every day, since we cannot explain even what daily experience shows us. Evodius adds, that several persons after their decease have been going and coming in their houses as before, both day and night; and that in churches where the dead were buried, they often heard a noise in the night, as of persons praying aloud.

St Augustine, to whom Evodius writes all this, acknowledges that there is a great distinction to be made between true and false visions, and that he could wish he had some sure means of discerning them correctly. The same saint relates on this occasion a remarkable story, which has much connexion with the matter we are treating upon. A physician named Gennadius, a great friend of St Augustine's, and well known at Carthage for his great talent and his kindness to the poor, doubted whether there was another life. One day he saw, in a dream, a young man who said to him, 'Follow me;' he followed him in spirit, and found himself in a city, where, on his right hand, he heard a most admirable melody; he did not remember what he heard on his left.

Another time he saw the same young man, who said to him, 'Do you know me?' 'Very well,' answered he. 'And whence comes it that you know me?' He related to him what he had showed him in the city whither he had led him. The young man added, 'Was it in a dream, or awake, that you saw all that?' 'In a dream,' he replied. The young man then asked. 'Where is your body now?' 'In my bed,' said he. 'Do you know that now you see nothing with the eyes of your body?' 'I know it,' answered he. 'Well, then, with what eyes do you behold me?' As he hesitated, and knew not what to reply, the young man said to him, 'In the same way that you see and hear me now that your eyes are shut, and your senses asleep; thus after your death you will live, you will see, you will hear, but with eyes of the spirit; so doubt not that there is another life after the present one.'

The great St Anthony, one day when he was wide awake, saw the soul of the hermit, St Ammon, being carried into heaven in the midst of choirs of angels. Now St Ammon died that same day, at five days' journey from thence, in the desert of Nitria. The same St Anthony saw also the soul of St Paul Hermitus ascending to heaven surrounded by choirs of angels and prophets. St Benedict beheld the spirit of St Germain, Bishop of Capua, at the moment of his decease, who was carried into heaven by angels. The same saint saw the soul of his sister, St Scholastica, rising to heaven in the form of a dove. We might multiply such instances without end. They are true apparitions of souls separated from their bodies.

St Sulpicius Severus, being at some distance from the city of Tours, and ignorant of what was passing there, fell one morning into a light slumber; as he slept he beheld St Martin, who appeared to him in a white garment, his countenance shining, his eyes sparkling, his hair of a purple colour; it was, nevertheless, very easy to recognise him by his air and his face. St Martin showed himself to him with a smiling countenance, and holding in his hand the book which St Sulpicius Severus had composed upon his life. Sulpicius threw himself at his feet, embraced his knees, and implored his benediction, which the saint bestowed upon him. All this passed in a vision; and as St Martin rose into the air, Sulpicius Severus saw still in the spirit the priest Clarus, a disciple of the saint, who went the same way and rose towards heaven. At that moment Sulpicius awoke, and a lad who served him, on entering, told him that two monks who were just arrived from Tours, had brought word that St Martin was dead.

The Baron de Coussey, an old and respectable magistrate, has related to me more than once, that being at more than sixty leagues from the town where his mother died, the night she breathed her last, he was awakened by the barking of a dog which laid at the foot of his bed; and at the same moment he perceived the head of his mother environed by a great light, who, entering by the window into his chamber, spoke to him distinctly, and announced to him various things concerning the state of his affairs.

St Chrysostom, in his exile, and the night preceding his death, saw the martyr, St Basilicus, who said to him, 'Courage, brother John; tomorrow we shall be together.' The same thing was foretold to a priest who lived in the same place. St Basilicus said to him, 'Prepare a place for my brother John; for, behold, he is coming.'

The discovery of the body of St Stephen, the first martyr, is very celebrated in the Church; this occurred in the year 415. St Gamaliel, who had been the master of St Paul before his conversion, appeared to a priest named Lucius, who slept in the Baptistery of the Church at Jerusalem, to guard the sacred vases, and told him that his own body and that of St Stephen the proto-martyr were interred at Caphargamala, in the suburb named Dilagabis; that the body of his son named Abibas, and that of Nicodemus, reposed in the same spot. Lucius had the same vision three times following, with an interval of a few days between. John, the Patriarch of Jerusalem, who was then at the Council of Dioscopolis, repaired to the spot, made the discovery and translation of the relics, which were transported to Jerusalem, and a great number of miracles were performed there.

Licinius, being in his tent, thinking of the battle he was to fight on the morrow, saw an Angel, who dictated to him a form of prayer which he made his soldiers learn by heart, and by means of which he gained the victory over the Emperor Maximian.

Mascezel, general of the Roman troops which Stilicho sent into Africa against Gildas, prepared himself for this war, in imitation of Theodosius the Great, by prayer and the intervention of the servants of God. He took with him in his vessel some monks, whose only occupation during the voyage was to pray, fast, and sing psalms. Gildas had an army of seventy thousand men; Mascezel had but five thousand, and did not think he could without rashness attempt to compete with an enemy so powerful, and so far superior in the number of his forces. As he was pondering uneasily on these things, St Ambrose, who died the year before, appeared to him by night, holding a staff in his hand, and struck the ground three times, crying, 'Here, here, here!' Mascezel understood that the saint promised him the victory in that same spot three days after. In fact, the third day he marched upon the enemy, offering peace to the first whom he met; but an ensign having replied to him very arrogantly, he gave him a severe blow with his sword upon his arm, which made his standard swerve; those who were afar off thought that he was yielding, and that he lowered his standard in sign of submission, and they hastened to do the same. Paulinus, who wrote the life of St Ambrose, assures us that he had these particulars from the lips of Mascezel himself; and Orosius heard them from those who had been eyewitnesses of the fact.

The persecutors having inflicted martyrdom on seven Christian virgins, one of them appeared the following night to St Theodosius of Ancyra, and revealed to him the spot where herself and her companions had been thrown into the lake, each one with a stone tied round her neck. As Theodosius and his people were occupied in searching for their bodies, a voice from heaven warned Theodosius to be on his guard against the traitor, meaning to indicate Polycronius, who betrayed Theodosius, and was the occasion of his being arrested and martyred.

St Potamienna, a Christian virgin who suffered martyrdom at Alexandria, appeared after her death to several persons, and was the cause of their conversion to Christianity. She appeared in particular to a soldier named Basilidus, who, as he was conducting her to the place of execution, had protected her from the insults of the populace. This soldier, encouraged by Potamienna, who in a vision placed a garland upon his head, was baptised, and received the crown of martyrdom.

St Gregory Thaumaturgus, Bishop of Neocaesarea in Pontus, being greatly occupied with certain theological difficulties, raised by heretics concerning the mysteries of religion, and having passed great part of the night in studying those matters, saw a venerable old man enter his room, having by his side a lady of august and divine form; he comprehended that these were the Holy Virgin and St John the Evangelist. The Virgin exhorted St John to instruct the Bishop, and dissipate his embarrassment, by explaining clearly to him the mystery of the Trinity, and the Divinity of the Verb or Word. He did so, and St Gregory wrote it down instantly. It is the doctrine which he left to his Church, and which they have to this very day.

CHAPTER 41

More Instances of Apparitions

Peter the Venerable, Abbot of Cluny, relates, that a good priest named Stephen, having received the confession of a lord named Guy, who was mortally wounded in a combat, this lord appeared to him completely armed some time after his death, and begged of him to tell his brother Anselm, to restore an ox which he, Guy, had taken from a peasant, whom he named, and to repair the damage which he had done to a village which did not belong to him, and which he had taxed with undue charges; that he had forgotten to declare these two sins in his last confession, and that he was cruelly tormented for it. 'And as assurance of the truth of what I tell you,' added he, 'when you return home, you will find that you have been robbed of the money you intended for your expenses in going to St Jacques.' The curé, on his return to his house, found his money gone, but could not acquit himself of his commission, because Anselm was absent. A few days after, Guy appeared to him again, and reproached him for having neglected to perform what he had asked of him. The curé excused himself on account of the absence of Anselm; and at length went to him and told him what he was charged to do. Anselm answered him harshly, that he was not obliged to do penance for his brother's sins.

The dead man appeared a third time, and implored the curé to assist him in this extremity; he did so, and restored the value of the ox; but as the rest exceeded his power, he gave alms, and recommended Guy to the worthy people of his acquaintance; and he appeared no more.

Richer, a monk of Senones, speaks of a spirit which returned in his time, in the town of Epinal, about the year 1212, in the house of a burgess named Hugh de la Cour, and who, from Christmas to Midsummer, did a variety of things in that same house, in sight of every body. They could hear him speak, they could see all he did, but nobody could see him. He said, he belonged to Cléxenteine, a village seven leagues from Epinal; and what is also remarkable is, that during the six months he was heard about the house, he did no harm to anyone. One day, Hugh having ordered his domestic to saddle his horse, and the valet being busy about something else, deferred doing it, when the spirit did his work, to the great astonishment of all the household. Another time, when Hugh was absent, the spirit asked Stephen, the son-in-law of Hugh, for a penny, to make an offering of it to St Goëric, the patron saint of Epinal. Stephen presented him with an old denier of Provence; but the spirit refused it, saying, he would have a good denier of Toulouse. Stephen placed on the threshold of the door a Toulousian denier, which disappeared immediately; and the following night, a noise, as of a man who was walking therein, was heard in the Church of St Goëric.

Another time, Hugh having bought some fish to make his family a repast, the spirit transported the fish to the garden which was behind the house, put half of it on a tile, (*scandula,*) and the rest in a mortar, where it was found again. Another time, Hugh desiring to be bled, told his daughter to get ready some bandages. Immediately the spirit went into another room, and fetched a new shirt, which he tore up into several bandages, presented them to the master of the house, and told him to choose the best. Another day, the servant having spread out some linen in the garden to dry, the spirit carried it all up stairs, and folded them more neatly than the cleverest laundress could have done.

A man named Guy de la Torre, who died at Verona in 1306, at the end of eight days spoke to his wife and the neighbours of both sexes, to the prior of the Dominicans, and to the professor of theology, who asked him several question in theology, to which he replied very pertinently. He declared that he was in purgatory for certain unexpiated sins. They asked him how he could possibly speak, not having the organs of the voice; he replied, that souls separated from the body have the faculty of forming for themselves instruments of the air capable of pronouncing words; he added, that the fire of hell acted upon spirits, not by its natural virtue, but by the power of God, of which that fire is the instrument.

Here follows another remarkable instance of an apparition, related by M. d'Aubigné. 'I affirm upon the word of the king the second prodigy, as being one of the three stories which he reiterated to us, his hair standing on end at the time, as we could perceive. This one is, that the queen having gone to bed at an earlier hour than usual, and there being present at her *coucher*, amongst other persons of note, the King of Navarre, the Archbishop of Lyons, the Ladies de Retz, de Lignerolles, and de Sauve, two of whom have since confirmed this conversation. As she was hastening to bid them good night, she threw herself with a start upon her bolster, put her hands before her face, and crying out violently, she called to her assistance those who were present, wishing to show them, at the foot of the bed, the cardinal, (de Lorraine,) who extended his hand towards her; she cried out several times, "M. the Cardinal, I have nothing to do with you." The King of Navarre at the same time sent one of his gentlemen, who brought back word that he had expired at that same moment.'

I take from Sully's Memoirs, which have just been reprinted in better order than they were before, another singular fact, which may be related with these. We still endeavour to find out what can be the nature of that illusion, seen so often and by the eyes of so many persons in the Forest of Fontainebleau; it was a phantom surrounded by a pack of hounds, whose cries were heard, while they might be seen at a distance, but all disappeared if anyone approached.

The note of M. d'Ecluse, editor of these Memoirs, enters into longer details. He observes, that M. de Peréfixe makes mention of this phantom; and he makes him say, with a hoarse voice, one of these three sentences: Do you expect me? or, Do you hear me? or, Amend yourself. 'And they believe,' says he, 'that these were sports of sorcerers, or of the malignant spirit.' The Journal of Henry IV, and the Septenary Chronicle, speak of them also, and even assert that this phenomenon alarmed Henry IV and his courtiers very much. And Peter Matthew says something of it in his *History of France*, tom. ii, p. 68. Bongars speaks of it as others do, and asserts that it was a hunter, who had been killed in this forest in the time of Francis I. But now we hear no more of this spectre, though there is still a road in this forest which retains the name of the *Grand Veneur*, in memory, it is said, of this visionary scene.

A Chronicle of Metz, under the date of the year 1330, relates the apparition of a spirit at Lagni sur Marne, six leagues from Paris. It was a good lady, who after her death spoke to more than twenty people, her father, sister, daughter, and son-in-law, and to her other friends – asking them to have said for her particular masses, as being more efficacious than the common mass. As they feared it might be an evil spirit, they read to it the beginning of the Gospel of St John; and they made it say the *Pater, credo*, and *confiteor*. She said, she had beside her two angels, one bad and one good; and that the good angel revealed to her what she ought to say. They asked her, if they should go and fetch the Holy Sacrament from the altar; she replied, it was with them, for her father, who was present, and several others among them, had received it on Christmas Day, which was the Tuesday before.

Father Taillepied, a Cordelier, and professor of theology at Rouen, who composed a book expressly on the subject of apparitions, which was printed at Rouen in 1600, says, that one of his fraternity with whom he was acquainted, named Brother Gabriel, appeared to several monks of the convent at Nice, and begged of them to satisfy the demand of a shop-keeper at Marseilles, of whom he had taken a coat he had not paid for. On being asked why he made so much noise, he replied, that it was not himself, but a bad spirit who wished to appear instead of him, and prevent him from declaring the cause of his torment.

I have been told by two canons of St Diez, in our neighbourhood, that three months after the death of M. Henri, canon of St Diez, of their brotherhood, the canon to whom the house devolved, going with one of his brethren, at two o'clock in the afternoon, to look at the said house, and see what alterations it might suit him to make in it, they went into the kitchen, and both of them saw in the next room, which was large and very light, a tall ecclesiastic of the same height and figure as the defunct canon, who, turning towards them, looked them in the face for two minutes, then crossed the said room, and went up a little dark staircase which led to the garret.

These two gentlemen, being much frightened, left the house instantly, and related the adventure to some of the brotherhood, who were of opinion that they ought to return and see if there was not someone hidden in the house; they went, they sought, they looked everywhere, without finding anyone.

We read in the History of the Bishops of Mans, that in the time of Bishop Hugh, who lived in 1135, they heard, in the house of Provost Nicholas, a spirit, who alarmed the neighbours and those who lived in the house, by uproar and frightful noises, as if he had thrown enormous stones against the walls, with a force which shook the roof, walls, and ceilings; he transported the dishes and the plates from one place to another, without their seeing the hand which moved them. This spirit lighted a candle, though very far from the fire. Sometimes, when the meat was placed on the table, he would scatter bran, ashes, or soot, to prevent them from touching any of it. Amica, the wife of the Provost Nicholas, having prepared some thread to be made into cloth, the spirit twisted and ravelled it in such a way, that all who saw it could not sufficiently admire the manner in which it was done.

Priests were called in, who sprinkled holy water everywhere, and desired all those who were there to make the sign of the cross. Towards the first and second night, they heard as it were the voice of a young girl, who, with sighs that seemed drawn from the bottom of her heart, said in a lamentable and sobbing voice, that her name was Garnier; and addressing itself to the provost, said, 'Alas! whence do I come? From what distant country, through how many storms, dangers, through snow, cold, fire, and bad weather, have I arrived at this place! I have not received power to harm anyone – but prepare yourselves with the sign of the cross against a band of evil spirits, who are here only to do you harm; have a mass of the Holy Ghost said for me, and a mass for those defunct; and you, my dear sister-in-law, give some clothes to the poor, for me.'

They asked this spirit several questions on things past and to come, to which it replied very pertinently; it explained even the salvation and damnation of several persons; but it would not enter into any argument, nor yet into conference with learned men, who were sent by the Bishop of Mans; this last circumstance is very remarkable, and casts some suspicion on this apparition.

CHAPTER 42

On the Apparitions of Spirits who Imprint their Hands on Clothes or on Wood

Within a short time, a work composed by a Father Prémontré, of the Abbey of Toussaints, in the Black Forest, has been communicated to me. His work is in manuscript, and entitled, 'Umbra Humberti, hoc est historia memorabilis D. Humberti Birkii mirâ post mortem apparitione, per A. G. N.'

This Humbert Birck was a burgess of note, in the town of Oppenheim, and master of a country house called Berenbach; he died in the month of November 1620, a few days before the feast of St Martin. On the Saturday which followed his funeral, they began to hear certain noises in the house where he had lived with his first wife; for at the time of his death he had married again.

The master of this house, suspecting that it was his brother-in-law who haunted it, said to him, 'If you are Humbert, my brother-in-law, strike three times against the wall.' At the same time they heard three strokes only, for ordinarily he struck several times. Sometimes, also, he was heard at the fountain where they went for water, and he frightened all the neighbourhood; he did not always utter articulate sounds, but he would knock repeatedly, make a noise, or a groan, or a shrill whistle, or sounds as a person in lamentation; all this lasted for six months, and then it suddenly ceased. At the end of a year he made himself heard more loudly than ever. The master of the house, and his domestics, the boldest amongst them, at last asked him what he wished for, and in what they could help him? He replied, but in a hoarse low tone, 'Let the curé come here next Saturday with my children.' The curé being indisposed, could not go thither on the appointed day, but he went on the Monday following, accompanied by a good many people.

Humbert received notice of this, and he answered in a very intelligible manner. They asked him if he required any masses to be said? He asked for three. They then wished to know if alms should be given in his name? He said, 'I wish them to give eight measures of corn to the poor, and that my widow may give something to all my children.' He afterwards ordered that what had been badly distributed in his succession, which amounted to about twenty florins, should be set aside. They asked why he infested that house rather than another? He answered, that he was forced to it by conjuration and maledictions. Had he received the sacraments of the Church? 'I received them from the curé, your predecessor.' He was made to say the *Pater* and the *Ave*; he recited them with difficulty, saying, that he was prevented by an evil spirit, who would not let him tell the curé many other things.

The curé, who was named Prémontré, of the abbey of Toussaints, came to the monastery on Tuesday the 12th January 1621, in order to take the opinion of the Superior on this singular affair; they let him have three monks to help him with their counsels. They all repaired to the house wherein Humbert continued his importunity; for nothing that he had requested had as yet been executed. A great number of those who lived near were assembled in the house. The master of it told Humbert to rap against the wall; he knocked very gently: then the master desired him to go and fetch a stone and knock louder; he deferred a little, as if he had been to pick up a stone, and gave a stronger blow upon the wall: the master whispered in his neighbour's ear as softly as he could that he should rap seven times, and directly he rapped seven times. He always showed great respect to the priests, and did not reply to them so boldly as to the laity; and when he was asked why – 'It is,' said he, 'because they have with them the Holy Sacrament.' However, they had it no otherwise than because they had said mass that day. The next day the three masses which he had required were said, and all was disposed for a pilgrimage, which he had specified in the last conversation they had with him; and they promised to give alms for him the first day possible. From that time Humbert haunted them no more.

The same monk, Prémontré, relates that on the 9th September 1625, a man named John Steinlin died at a place called Altheim, in the diocese of Constance. Steinlin was a man in easy circumstances, and a common councilman of his town. Some days after his death he appeared during the night to a tailor, named Simon Bauh, in the form of a man surrounded by a sombre flame, like that of lighted sulphur, going and coming in his own house, but without speaking. Bauh, who was disquieted by this sight, resolved to ask him what he could do to serve him. He found an opportunity to do so, the 17th November in the same year, 1625; for, as he was reposing at night near his stove, a little after eleven o'clock, he beheld this spectre environed by fire like sulphur, who came into his room, going and coming, shutting and opening the windows. The tailor asked him what he desired. He replied, in a hoarse interrupted voice, that he could help very much, if he would; 'But,' added he, 'do not promise me to do so, if you are not resolved to execute your promises.' 'I will execute them, if they are not beyond my power,' replied he.

'I wish, then,' replied the spirit, 'that you would cause a mass to be said, in the chapel of the Virgin at Rotembourg; I made a vow to that intent during my life, and I have not acquitted myself of it. Moreover, you must have two masses said at Altheim, the one of the Defunct and the other of the Virgin; and as I did not always pay my servants exactly, I wish that a quarter of corn should be distributed to the poor.' Simon promised to satisfy him on all these points. The spectre held out his hand, as if to ensure his promise; but Simon, fearing that some harm might happen to himself, tendered him the board which came to hand, and the spectre having touched it, left the print of his hand with the four fingers and thumb, as if fire had been there, and had left a pretty deep impression. After that, he vanished with so much noise that it was heard three houses off.

I related in the first edition of this dissertation on the return of spirits, an adventure which happened at Fontenoy on the Moselle, where it was affirmed that a spirit had in the same manner made the impression of its hand on a handkerchief, and had left the impress of the hand and of the palm, well marked. The handkerchief is in the hands of one Casmer, a constable living at Toul, who received it from his uncle, the curé of Fontenoy; but, on a careful investigation of the thing, it was found that a young blacksmith, who courted a young girl to whom the handkerchief belonged, had forged an iron hand to print it on the handkerchief, and persuade people of the reality of the apparition.

At St Avold, a town of German Lorraine, in the house of the curé, named M. Royer de Monelos, there was something very similar which appears to have been performed by a servant girl, sixteen years of age, who heard and saw, as she said, a woman who made a great noise in the house; but she was the only person who saw and heard her, although others heard also the noise which was made in the house. They saw also the young servant, as it were pushed, dragged, and struck, by the spirit, but never saw it, nor yet heard his voice. This contrivance began on the night of the 31 January 1694, and finished about the end of February the same year. The curé conjured the spirit in German and French. He made no reply to the exorcisms in French but sighs; and as they terminated the German exorcism, saying, 'Let every spirit praise the Lord,' the girl said that the spirit had said, 'And me also;' but she alone heard it.

Some monks of the abbey were requested to come also and exorcise the spirit. They came, and with them some burgesses of note of St Avold; and neither before nor after the exorcisms did they see or hear anything, except that the servant girl seemed to be pushed violently, and the doors were roughly knocked at. By dint of exorcisms they forced the spirit, or rather the servant who alone heard and saw it, to declare that she was neither maid nor wife; that she was called Claire Margaret Henri; that a hundred and fifty years ago she had died at the age of twenty, after having lived servant at the curé of St Avold's first of all for eight years, and that she had died at Guenvillier of grief and regret for having killed her own child. At last, the servant maintaining that she was not a good spirit, she said to her, 'Give me hold of your petticoat (or skirt).' She would do no such thing; at the same time the spirit said to her, 'Look at your petticoat; my mark is upon it.' She looked and saw upon her skirt the five fingers of the hand so distinctly that it did not appear possible for any living creature to have marked them better. This affair lasted about two months, and at this day, at St Avold, as in all the country, they talk of the spirit of St Avold as of a game played by that girl, in concert, doubtless, with some persons who wished to divert themselves by puzzling the good curé with his sisters, and all those who fell into the trap. They printed at Cusson's, at Nancy, in 1718, a relation of this event, which at first gained credence with a number of people, but who were quite undeceived in the end.

I shall add to this story that which is related by Philip Melancthon, whose testimony in this matter ought not to be doubted. He says that his aunt having lost her husband when she was *enceinte* and near her time, she saw one day, towards evening, two persons come into her house; one of them wore the form of her deceased husband, the other that of a tall Franciscan. At first she was frightened, but her husband reassured her, and told her that he had important things to communicate to her; at the same time he begged the Franciscan to pass into the next room, whilst he imparted his wishes to his wife. Then he begged of her to have some masses said for the relief of his soul, and tried to persuade her to give her hand without fear; as she was unwilling to give it, he assured her she would feel no pain. She gave him her hand, and her hand felt no pain when she withdrew it, but was so blackened that it remained discoloured all her life. After that, the husband called in the Franciscan; they went out, and disappeared. Melancthon believes that these were two spectres; he adds, that he knows several similar instances, related by persons worthy of credit.

If these two men were only spectres, having neither flesh nor bones, how could one of them imprint a black colour on the hand of this widow? How could he who appeared to the tailor Bauh imprint his hand on the board which he presented to him? If they were evil genii, why did they ask for masses and order restitutions? Does Satan destroy his own empire, and does he inspire the living with the idea of doing good actions and of fearing the pains with which the sins of the wicked are punished by God?'

But on looking at the affair in another light, may not the demon in this kind of apparition, by which he asks for masses and prayers, intend to foment superstition, by making the living believe that masses and prayers made for them after their death would free them from the pains of hell, even if they died in habitual crime and impenitence? Several instances are cited of rascals who have appeared after their death, asking for prayers like the bad rich man, and to whom prayers and masses can be of no avail, from the unhappy state in which they died. Thus, in all this, Satan seeks to establish his kingdom, and not to destroy it or diminish it.

We shall speak hereafter, in the Dissertation on Vampires, of apparitions of dead persons who have been seen, and acted like living ones in their own bodies.

The same Melancthon relates that a monk came one day and rapped loudly at the door of Luther's dwelling, asking to speak to him; he entered and said, 'I entertain some popish errors upon which I shall be very glad to confer with you.' 'Speak,' said Luther. He at first proposed to him several syllogisms, to which he easily replied; he then proposed others, that were more difficult. Luther, being annoyed, answered him hastily, 'Go, you embarrass me; I have something else to do just now besides answering you.' However, he rose and replied to his arguments. At the same time, having remarked that the pretended monk had hands like the claws of a bird, he said to him, 'Art not thou he of whom it is said, in Genesis, "He who shall be born of woman shall break the head of the serpent?" ' The demon added, 'But *thou* shalt engulf them all.' At these words the confused demon retired angrily and with much fracas; he left the room infested with a very bad smell, which was perceptible for some days.

Luther, who assumes so much the *esprit fort*, and inveighs with so much warmth against private masses wherein they pray for the souls of the defunct, maintains boldly that all the apparitions of spirits which we read in the lives of the saints, and who ask for masses for the repose of their souls, are only illusions of Satan, who appears to deceive the simple, and inspire them with useless confidence in the sacrifice of the mass. Whence he concludes that it is better at once to deny absolutely that there is any purgatory.

He, then, did not deny either apparitions or the operations of the devil; and he maintained that Ecolampadius died under the blows of the devil, whose efforts he could not rebut; and, speaking of himself, he affirms that awaking once with a start in the middle of the night, the devil appeared, to argue against him, when he was seized with mortal terror. The arguments of the demon were so pressing that they left him no repose of mind; the sound of his powerful voice, his overwhelming manner of disputing when the question and the reply were perceived at once, left him no breathing time. He says again that the devil can kill and strangle, and, without doing all that, press a man so home by his arguments that it is enough to kill one; 'As I,' says he, 'have experienced several times.' After such avowals, what can we think of the doctrine of this chief of the innovators?

CHAPTER 43

Opinions of the Jews, Greeks, and Latins, concerning the Dead who are Left Unburied

The ancient Hebrews, as well as the greater number of other nations, were very careful in burying their dead. That appears from all history; we see in the Scripture how much attention the patriarchs paid in that respect to themselves and those belonging to them; we know what praises are bestowed on the holy man Tobit, whose principal devotion consisted in giving sepulture to the dead.

Josephus the historian says, that the Jews refused burial only to those who committed suicide. Moses commanded them to give sepulture the same day and before sunset to any who were executed and hanged on a tree; 'Because,' says he, 'he who is hung upon the tree is accursed of God, you will take care not to pollute the land which the Lord your God has given you.' That was practised in regard to our Saviour, who was taken down from the cross the same day that he had been crucified, and a few hours after his death.

Homer, speaking of the inhumanity of Achilles, who dragged the body of Hector after his car, says that he dishonoured and outraged the earth by this barbarous conduct. The Rabbis write, that the soul is not received into heaven until the gross body is interred, and entirely consumed. They believe, moreover, that after death the souls of the wicked are clothed with a kind of covering, with which they accustom themselves to suffer the torments which are their due; and that the souls of the just are invested with a resplendent body and a luminous garment, with which they accustom themselves to the glory which awaits them.

Origen acknowledges that Plato, in his Dialogue of the Soul, advances that the images and shades of the dead appeared sometimes near their tombs. Origen concludes from that, that those shades and those images must be produced by some cause; and that cause, according to him, can only be, that the soul of the dead is invested with a subtle body like that of light, on which they are borne as in a car, where they appear to the living. Celsus maintained that the apparitions of Jesus Christ after his resurrection were only the effects of an imagination smitten and prepossessed, which formed to itself the object of its illusions according to its wishes. Origen refutes this solidly by the recital of the evangelists, of the appearance of our Saviour to Thomas, who would not believe it was truly our Saviour until he had seen and touched his wounds; it was not, then, purely the effect of his imagination.

The same Origen, and Theophylact after him, assert that the Jews and Pagans believe that the soul remained for some time near the body it had formerly animated; and that it is to destroy that futile opinion that Jesus Christ, when he would resuscitate Lazarus, cries with a loud voice, 'Lazarus, come forth;' as if he would call from a distance the soul of this man who had been dead three days.

Tertullian places the angels in the category of extension, in which he places God himself, and maintains that the soul is corporeal. Origen believes also that the soul is material, and has a form; an opinion which he may have taken from Plato. Arnobius, Lactantius, St Hilary, several of the ancient fathers, and some theologians, have been of the same opinion; and Grotius is displeased with those who have absolutely spiritualised the angels, demons, and souls separated from the body.

The Jews of our days believe that after the body of a man is interred, his spirit goes and comes, and departs from the spot where it is destined to visit his body, and to know what passes around him; that it is wandering during a whole year after the death of the body, and that it was during that year of delay that the Pythoness of Endor evoked the soul of Samuel, after which time the evocation would have had no power over his spirit.

The Pagans thought much in the same manner upon it. Lucan introduces Pompey, who consults a witch, and commands her to evoke the soul of a dead man to reveal to him what success he would meet with in his war against Caesar; the poet makes this woman say, 'Shade, obey my spells, for I evoke not a soul from gloomy Tartarus, but one which hath gone down thither a little while since, and which is still at the gate of hell.'

The Egyptians believed that when the spirit of an animal is separated from its body by violence, it does not go to a distance, but remains near it. It is the same with the soul of a man who has died a violent death; it remains near the body – nothing can make it go away; it is retained there by sympathy; several have been seen sighing near their bodies which were interred. The magicians abuse their power over such in their incantations;

they force them to obey, when they are masters of the dead body, or even of part of it. Frequent experience taught them that there is a secret virtue in the body, which draws towards it the spirit which has once inhabited it; wherefore those who wish to receive or become the receptacles of the spirits of such animals as know the future, eat the principal parts of them, as the hearts of cows, moles, or hawks. The spirit of these creatures enters into them at the moment they eat this food, and makes them give out oracles like divinities.

The Egyptians believed that when the spirit of a beast is delivered from its body, it is rational and predicts the future, gives oracles, and is capable of all that the soul of man can do when disengaged from the body – for which reason they abstained from eating the flesh of animals, and worshipped the gods in the form of beasts.

At Rome and at Metz there were colleges of priests consecrated to the service of the manes, lares, images, shades, spectres, Erebus, Avernus or hell, under the protection of the god Sylvanus; which demonstrates that the Latins and the Gauls recognised the return of souls and their apparition, and considered them as divinities to whom sacrifices should be offered to appease them and prevent them from doing harm. Nicander confirms the same thing, when he says that the Celts or the Gauls watched near the tombs of their great men, to derive from them knowledge concerning the future.

The ancient northern nations were fully persuaded that the spectres which sometimes appear are no other than the souls of persons lately deceased, and in their country they knew no remedy so proper to put a stop to this kind of apparition, as to cut off the head of the dead person, or to impale him, or pierce him through the body with a stake, or to burn it, as is now practised at this day in Hungary and Moravia with regard to vampires.

The Greeks, who had derived their religion and theology from the Egyptians and Orientals, and the Latins, who took it from the Greeks, believed that the souls of the dead sometimes appeared to the living; that the necromancers evoked them, and thus obtained answers concerning the future, and instructions relating to the time present. Homer, the greatest theologian, and perhaps the most curious of the Grecian writers, relates several apparitions, both of gods and heroes, and of men after their death.

In the Odyssey Ulysses goes to consult the diviner Tyresias; and this sorcerer having prepared a grave full of blood to evoke the manes, Ulysses draws his sword, and prevents them from coming to drink this blood, for which they appear to thirst, and of which they would not permit them to taste before they had replied to what was asked of them; they (the Greeks and Latins) believed also that souls were not at rest, and that they wandered around their corpses, so long as they remained uninhumed. When they gave burial to a body, they called that *animam condere*, to cover the soul, put it under the earth, and shelter it. They called it with a loud voice, and offered it libations of milk and blood. They also called that ceremony, hiding the shades, sending them with their body under ground.

The sybil, speaking to Aeneas, shows him the manes or shades wandering on the banks of the Acheron; and tells him that they are souls of persons who have not received sepulture, and who wander about for a hundred years.

The philosopher Sallust, speaks of the apparitions of the dead around their tombs in dark bodies; he tries to prove thereby the dogma of the metempsychosis.

Here is a singular instance of a dead man, who refuses the rite of burial, acknowledging himself unworthy of it. Agathias relates, that some Pagan philosophers, not being able to relish the dogma of the unity of a God, resolved to go from Constantinople to the court of Chosroes, King of Persia, who was spoken of as a humane prince, and one who loved learning. Simplicius of Silicia, Eulamius the Phrygian, Protanus the Lydian, Hermenes and Philogenes of Phoeonicia, and Isidorus of Gaza, repaired then to the court of Chosroes, and were well received there; but they soon perceived that that country was much more corrupt than Greece, and they resolved to return to Constantinople, where Justinian then reigned.

As they were on their way, they found an unburied corpse, took pity on it, and had it put in the ground by their own servants. The following night this man appeared to one of them, and told him not to inter him, who was not worthy of receiving sepulture; for the earth abhorred one who had defiled his own mother. The next day they found the same corpse cast out of the ground, and they comprehended that it was defiled by incest, which rendered it unworthy of the honour of receiving burial, although such crimes were known in Persia, and did not excite the same horror there as in other countries.

The Greeks and Latins believed, that the souls of the dead came and tasted what was presented on their tombs, especially honey and wine; that the demons loved the smoke and odour of sacrifices, melody, the blood of victims, commerce with women; that they were attached for a time to certain spots or to certain edifices, which they haunted, and where they appeared; that souls separated from their terrestrial body, retained after death a subtle one, flexible, aerial, which preserved the form of that they once had animated during their life; that they haunted those who had done them wrong and whom they hated. Thus Virgil describes Dido, in a rage, threatening to haunt the perfidious Aeneas.

When the spirit of Patroclus appeared to Achilles, it had his voice, his shape, his eyes, his garments, but not his palpable body. When Ulysses went down to the infernal regions, he saw there the divine Hercules, that is to say, says Homer, his likeness; for he himself is with the immortal gods, seated at their feast. Aeneas recognised his wife Creüsa, who appeared to him in her usual form, only taller and more majestic.

We might cite a quantity of passages from the ancient poets, even from the fathers of the Church, who believed that spirits often appeared to the living. Tertullian believes that the soul is corporeal, and that it has a certain figure. He appeals to the experience of those to whom the ghosts of dead persons have appeared, and who have seen them sensibly, corporeally, and palpably, although of an aerial colour and consistency. He defines the soul, a breath sent from God, immortal, and having body and form. Speaking of the fictions of the poets, who have asserted that souls were not at rest while their bodies remain uninterred, he says, all this is invented only to inspire the living with that care which they ought to take for the burial of the dead and to take away from the relations of the dead the sight of an object which would only uselessly augment their grief, if they kept it too long in their houses; *ut instantiâ funeris et honor corporum servetur et moeror affectuum temperetur.*

St Irenaeus teaches, as a doctrine received from the Lord, that souls not only subsist after the death of the body – without however passing from one body into another, as those will have it who admit the metempsychosis – but that they retain the form and remain near this body, as faithful guardians of it, and remember nought of what they have done or not done in this life. These fathers believed, then, in the return of souls, their apparition, and their attachment to their body; but we do not adopt their opinion on the corporeality of souls; we are persuaded that they can appear with God's permission, independently of all matter and of any corporeal substance which may belong to them.

As to the opinion, of the soul being in a state of unrest while its body is not interred, that it remains for some time near the tomb of the body, and appears there in a bodily form; those are opinions which have no solid foundation, either in Scripture, or in the traditions of the Church, which teach us that directly after death the soul is presented before the judgment-seat of God, and is there destined to the place that its good or bad actions have deserved.

CHAPTER 44

Examination of what is Required or Revealed to the Living by the Dead who Return to Earth

The apparitions which are seen are those of good angels, or of demons, or the spirits of the dead, or of living persons to others still living.

Good angels usually bring only good news, and announce nothing but what is fortunate; or if they do announce any future misfortunes, it is to persuade men to prevent them, or turn them aside by repentance, or to profit by the evils which God sends them by exercising their patience, and showing submission to his orders.

Bad angels generally foretell only misfortune; wars, the effect of the wrath of God on nations; and often even they execute the evils, and direct the wars and public calamities which desolate kingdoms, provinces, cities and families. The spectres whose appearance to Brutus, Cassius, and Julian the Apostate we have related, are only bearers of the fatal orders of the wrath of God. If they sometimes promise any prosperity to those to whom they appear, it is only for the present time, never for eternity, nor for the glory of God, nor for the eternal salvation of those to whom they speak. It only extends to a temporal fortune, always of short duration, and very often deceitful.

The souls of the defunct, if these be Christians, ask very often that the sacrifice of the body and blood of Christ should be offered, according to the observation of St Gregory the Great; and, as experience shows, there is hardly any apparition of a Christian that does not ask for masses, pilgrimages, restitutions, or that alms should be distributed, or that they would satisfy those to whom the deceased died indebted. They also often give salutary advice, for the salvation or correction of the morals, or good regulation of families. They reveal the state in which certain persons find themselves in the other world, in order to relieve their pain, or to put the living on their guard, that the like misfortune may not befall them. They talk of hell, paradise, purgatory, angels, demons, of the supreme Judge, of the rigour of His judgments, of the goodness He exercises towards the just, and the rewards with which He crowns their good works.

But we must greatly mistrust those apparitions which ask for masses, pilgrimages and restitution. St Paul warns us that the demon often transforms himself into an angel of light; and St John warns us to distrust the 'depths of Satan,' his illusions, and deceitful appearances. That spirit of malice and falsehood is found among the true prophets, to put into the mouth of the false prophets falsehood and error. He makes a wrong use of the text of the Scriptures, of the most sacred ceremonies, even of the sacraments and prayers of the church, to seduce the simple, and win their confidence, to share as much as in him lies the glory which is due to the Almighty alone, and to appropriate it to himself. How many false miracles has he not wrought? How many times has he foretold future events? What cures has he not operated? How many holy actions has he not counselled? How many enterprises, praiseworthy in appearance, has he not inspired, in order to draw the faithful into his snare?

Bodin, in his Demonology, cites more than one instance of demons who have requested prayers, and have even placed themselves in the posture of persons praying over a grave, to point out that the dead person wanted prayers. Sometimes it will be the demon in the shape of a wretch dead in crime, who will come and ask for masses, to show that his soul is in purgatory, and has need of prayers, although it may be certain that he finally died impenitent, and that prayers are useless for his salvation. All this is only a stratagem of the demon, who seeks to inspire the wicked with foolish and dangerous confidence in their being saved, notwithstanding their criminal life and their impenitence; and that they can obtain salvation by means of a few prayers, and a few alms, which shall be made after their death; not regarding that these good works can be useful only to those who died in a state of grace, although stained by some venial fault, since the Scripture informs us that nothing impure will enter the kingdom of heaven.

It is believed that the reprobate can sometimes return to earth by permission, as persons dead in idolatry, and consequently in sin, and excluded from the kingdom of God, have been seen to come to life again, be converted, and receive baptism. St Martin was as yet only the simple abbot of his monastery of Ligugé, when, in his absence, a catechumen who had placed himself under his discipline to be instructed in the truths of the Christian religion, died without having been baptised. He had been three days deceased when the saint arrived. He sent everybody away, prayed over the dead man, resuscitated him, and administered to him the baptismal rite.

This catechumen related that he had been led before the tribunal of the Supreme Judge, who had condemned him to descend into the darkness with an infinity of other persons condemned like himself; but that two angels having represented to the Judge that it was this man for whom St Martin interceded, God commanded the two angels to bring him back to earth, and restore him to Martin. This is an instance which proves what I have just said, that the reprobate can return to life, do penance, and receive baptism.

But as to what some have affirmed of the salvation of Falconila, procured by St Thecla, of that of Trajan, saved by the prayers of St Gregory, Pope, and of some others who died heathens, this is all entirely contrary to the faith of the church and to the Holy Scripture, which teach us that without faith it is impossible to please God, and that he who believes not and has not received baptism, is already judged and condemned. Thus, the opinions of those who accord salvation to Plato, Aristotle, Seneca, etc., because it may appear to them that they lived in a praiseworthy manner, according to the rules of a merely human and philosophical morality, must be considered as rash, erroneous, false, and dangerous.

Philip, Chancellor of the Church of Paris, maintained that it was permitted to one man to hold a plurality of benefices. Being on his death bed, he was visited by William, Bishop of Paris, who died in 1248. This prelate urged the chancellor to give up all his benefices save one only; he refused, saying that he wished to try if the holding a plurality of livings was so wrong as it was said to be; and in this disposition of mind he died in 1237.

Some days after his decease, Bishop William, or Guillaume, praying by night, after matins, in his cathedral, beheld before him the hideous and frightful figure of a man. He made the sign of the cross, and said to him, 'If you are sent by God, speak.' He spoke, and said: 'I am that wretched chancellor, and have been condemned to eternal punishment.' The bishop having asked him the cause, he replied, 'I am condemned, first, for not having distributed the superfluity of my benefices; secondly, for having maintained that it was allowable to hold several at once; thirdly, for having remained for several days in the guilt of incontinence.'

This story was often preached by Bishop William to his clerks. It is related by the Bishop Albertus Magnus, who was a contemporary, in his book on the sacraments; by William Durand, Bishop of Mande, in his book *De Modo celebrandi Concilia*; and in Thomas de Cantimpré, in his work *Des Abeilles*. He believed, then, that God sometimes permitted the reprobate to appear to the living.

Here is an instance of the apparition of a man and woman who were in a state of reprobation. The Prince of Ratzivil, in his Journey to Jerusalem, relates that when in Egypt he bought two mummies, had them packed up, and secretly as possible conveyed on board his vessel, so that only himself and his two servants were aware of it; the Turks making a great difficulty of allowing mummies to be carried away, because they fancy that the Christians make use of them for magical operations. When they were at sea there arose at sundry times such a violent tempest that the pilot despaired of saving the vessel. A good Polish priest, of the suite of the Prince de

Ratzivil, recited the prayers suitable to the circumstance; but he was tormented, he said, by two hideous black spectres, a man and a woman, who were one on each side of him, and threatened to take away his life. It was thought at first that terror disturbed his mind.

A calm coming on, he appeared tranquil; but very soon, the storm beginning again, he was more tormented than before, and was only delivered from these haunting spectres when the two mummies, which he had not seen, were thrown into the sea, and neither himself nor the pilot knew of their being in the ship.

I will not deny the fact, which is related by a prince incapable of desiring to impose on anyone. But how many reflections may we make on this event! Were they the souls of these two pagans, or two demons who assumed their form? What interest could the demon have in not permitting these bodies to come under the power of the Christians?

CHAPTER 45

Apparitions of Men still Alive, to other Living Men, Absent and very Distant from each other

We find in all history, both sacred and profane, ancient and modern, an infinite number of examples of the apparition of persons alive to other living persons. The prophet Ezekiel says of himself, 'I was seated in my house, in the midst of the elders of my people, when on a sudden a hand, which came from a figure shining like fire, seized me by the hair; and the spirit transported me between heaven and earth, and took me to Jerusalem, where he placed me near the inner gate, which looks towards the north, where I saw the idol of jealousy' (apparently Adonis), 'and I there remarked the majesty of the Lord, as I had seen it in the field; he showed me the idol of jealousy, to which the Israelites burned incense; and the angel of the Lord said to me: "Thou seest the abominations which the children of Israel commit, in turning away from my sanctuary; thou shalt see still greater."

'And having pierced the wall of the temple, I saw figures of reptiles and animals, the abominations and idols of the house of Israel, and seventy men of the elders of Israel, who were standing before these figures, each one bearing a censer in his hand; after that the angel said to me, "Thou shalt see yet something yet more abominable" and he showed me women who were mourning for Adonis. Lastly, having introduced me into the inner court of the temple, I saw twenty men between the vestibule and the altar, who turned their back upon the temple of the Lord, and stood with their face to the east, and paid adoration to the rising sun.'

Here we may remark two things; first, that Ezekiel is transported from Chaldaea to Jerusalem through the air between heaven and earth by the hand of an angel; which proves the possibility of transporting a living man through the air to a very great distance from the place where he was.

The second is, the vision or apparition of those prevaricators who commit even within the temple the greatest abominations, the most contrary to the majesty of God, the sanctity of the spot, and the law of the Lord. After all these things the same angel brings back Ezekiel into Chaldaea; but it was not until after God had showed him the vengeance He intended to exercise upon the Israelites.

It will, perhaps, be said, that all this passed only in a vision; that Ezekiel thought that he was transported to Jerusalem and afterwards brought back again to Babylon; and that what he saw in the temple, he saw only by revelation. I reply, that the text of this prophet indicates a real removal, and that he was transported by the hair of his head between heaven and earth. He was brought back from Jerusalem in the same way.

I do not deny that the thing might have passed in a vision, and that Ezekiel might have seen in spirit what was passing in the temple of Jerusalem. But I shall still deduce from it a consequence which is favourable to my design, that is, the possibility of a living man being carried through the air to a very great distance from the place he was in, or at least that a living man can imagine strongly that he is being carried from one place to another, although this transportation may be only imaginary and in a dream or vision, as they pretend it happens in the transportation of sorcerers to the witches' sabbath.

In short, there are true appearances of the living, to others who are also alive. How is this done? The thing is not difficult to explain in following the recital of the prophet, who is transferred from Chaldaea into Judea in his own body by the ministration of angels; but the apparitions related in St Augustine and in other authors are not of the same kind: the two persons who see and converse with each other go not from their places; and the one who appears knows nothing of what is passing in regard to him to whom he appears, and to whom he explains several things of which he did not even think at that moment.

In the third book of Kings, Obadiah, steward of king Ahab, having met the prophet Elijah, who had for some time kept himself concealed, tells him that King Ahab had him sought for everywhere, and that not having been able to discover him anywhere, had gone himself to seek him out. Elijah desires him to go and tell the king that Elijah had appeared; but Obadiah replied, 'See to what you expose me; for if I go and announce to Ahab that I have spoken to you, the spirit of God will transport you into some unknown place, and the king, not finding you, will put me to death.'

There again is an instance which proves the possibility of the transportation of a living man to a very distant spot. The same prophet, being on Mount Carmel, was seized by the Spirit of God, which transported him thence to Jezreel in very little time, not through the air, but by making him walk and run with a promptitude that was quite extraordinary.

In the Gospel, Elias appeared with Moses on Mount Tabor, at the Transfiguration of the Saviour. Moses had long been dead; but the Church believes that Elijah (or Elias) is still living. In the Acts of the Apostles, Ananias appeared to St Paul, and put his hands on him in a vision before he arrived at his house in Damascus.

Two men of the court of the Emperor Valens, wishing to discover by the aid of magical secrets who would succeed that emperor, caused a table of laurel-wood to be made into a tripod, on which they placed a basin made of divers metals. On the border of this basin were engraved, at some distance from each other, the twenty-four letters of the Greek alphabet. A magician with certain ceremonies approached the basin, and holding in his hand a ring suspended by a thread, suffered it at intervals to fall upon the letters of the alphabet whilst they were rapidly turning the table; the ring falling on the different letters formed obscure and enigmatical verses like those pronounced by the oracle of Delphi.

At last they asked what was the name of him who should succeed to the Emperor Valens? The ring touched the four letters $\Theta\, \partial\, \sqrt{}\, \Delta$ which they interpreted of Theodosius, the second secretary of the Emperor Valens. Theodosius was arrested, interrogated, convicted, and put to death; and with him all the culprits or accomplices in this operation; search was made for all the books of magic, and a great number were burnt. The great Theodosius, of whom they thought not at all, and who was at a great distance from the Court, was the person designated by these letters. In 379, he was declared Augustus by the Emperor Gratian, and in coming to Constantinople in 380, he had a dream, in which it seemed to him that Melitus, Bishop of Antioch, whom he had never seen, and knew only by reputation, invested him with the imperial mantle and placed the diadem on his head.

They were then assembling the Eastern bishops to hold the Council of Constantinople. Theodosius begged that Melitus might not be pointed out to him, saying that he should recognise him by the signs he had seen in his dream. In fact he distinguished him amongst all the other bishops, embraced him, kissed his hands, and looked upon him ever after as his father. This was a distinct apparition of a living man.

St Augustine relates, that a certain man saw, in the night, before he slept, a philosopher who was known to him, enter his house, and who explained to him some of Plato's opinions which he would not explain to him before. This apparition of the Platonist was merely fantastic; for the person to whom he had appeared having asked him why he would not explain to him at his house what he had come to explain to him when at home, the philosopher replied, 'I did not do so, but I dreamt I did so.' Here, then, are two persons both alive, one of whom, in his sleep and dreaming, speaks to another who is wide awake, and sees him only in imagination.

The same St Augustine acknowledges in the presence of his people that he has appeared to two persons who had never seen him, and knew him only by reputation, and that he advised them to come to Hippo, to be there cured by the merit of the martyr St Stephen: they came there, and recovered their health.

Evodius teaching rhetoric at Carthage, and finding himself puzzled concerning the sense of a passage in the books of the Rhetoric of Cicero, which he was to explain the next day to his scholars, was much disquieted when he went to bed, and could hardly get to sleep. During his sleep he fancied he saw St Augustine, who was then at Milan, a great way from Carthage, who was not thinking of him at all, and was apparently sleeping very quietly in his bed at Milan, who came to him and explained the passage in question. St Augustine avows that he does not know how it happens; but in whatever way it may occur, it is very possible for us to see in a dream a dead person as we see a living one, without either one or the other knowing how, when, or where, these images are formed in our mind. It is also possible that a dead man may appear to the living without being aware of it, and discover to them secret and hidden things, the result of which reveals their truth and reality. When a living man appears in a dream to another man, we do not say that his body or his spirit have appeared, but simply that such a one has appeared to him. Why can we not say that the dead appear without body and without soul, but simply that their form presents itself to the mind and imagination of the living person?

St Augustine, in the book which he has composed on the care which we ought to take of the dead, says, that a holy monk, named John, appeared to a pious woman, who ardently desired to see him. The saintly doctor reasons a great deal on this apparition – whether this solitary foresaw what would happen to him; if he went in spirit to this woman; if it is his angel or his spirit in his bodily form which appeared to her in her sleep, as we behold in our dreams absent persons who are known to us. We should be able to speak to the monk himself, to know from himself how that occurred, if by the power of God, or by his permission; for there is little appearance that he did it by any natural power.

It is said that St Simeon Stylites appeared to his disciple St Daniel, who had undertaken the journey to Jerusalem, where he would have to suffer much for Jesus Christ's sake. St Benedict had promised to comply with the request of some architects, who had begged him to come and show them how he wished them to build a certain monastery; the saint did not go to them bodily, but he went thither in spirit, and gave them the plan and design of the house which they were to construct. These men did not comprehend that it was what he had promised them, and came to him again to ask what were his intentions relative to this edifice: he said to them, 'I have explained it to you in a dream; you can follow the plan which you have seen.'

The Caesar Bardas, who had so mightily contributed to the deposition of St Ignatius, patriarch of Constantinople, had a vision, which he thus related to Philothes his friend. I thought I was that night going in procession to the high church with the Emperor Michael. When we had entered and were near the ambe, there appeared two eunuchs of the chamber, with a cruel and ferocious mien, one of whom, having bound the emperor, dragged him out of the choir on the right side; the other dragged me in the same manner to the left. Then I saw on a sudden an old man seated on the throne of the sanctuary. He resembled the image of St Peter, and two terrific men were standing near him, who looked like provosts. I beheld, at the knees of St Peter, St Ignatius weeping, and crying aloud – "You have the keys of the kingdom of heaven; if you know the injustice which has been done me, console my afflicted old age."

'St Peter replied, "Point out the man who has used you ill." Ignatius, turning round, pointed to me, saying, "That is he who has done me most wrong." St Peter made a sign to the one at his right, and placing in his hand a short sword, he said to him aloud, "Take Bardas, the enemy of God, and cut him in pieces before the vestibule." As they were leading me to death, I saw that he said to the emperor, holding up his hand in a threatening manner, "Wait, unnatural son!" after which I saw them cut me absolutely in pieces.'

This took place in 866. The year following, in the month of April, the emperor having set out to attack the Isle of Crete, was made so suspicious of Bardas, that he resolved to get rid of him. He accompanied the Emperor Michael in this expedition. Bardas, seeing the murderers enter the emperor's tent, sword in hand, threw himself at his feet to ask his pardon; but they dragged him out, cut him in pieces, and in derision carried some of his members about at the end of a pike. This happened the 29th April, 867.

Roger, Count of Calabria and Sicily, besieging the town of Capua, one named Sergius, a Greek by birth, to whom he had given the command of 200 men, having suffered himself to be bribed, formed the design of betraying him, and of delivering the army of the count to the Prince of Capua, during the night. It was on the 1st March that he was to execute his intention. St Bruno, who then dwelt in the Desert of Squilantia, appeared to Count Roger, and told him to fly to arms promptly, if he would not be oppressed by his enemies. The count starts from his sleep, commands his people to mount their horses and see what is going on in the camp. They met the men belonging to Sergius, with the Prince of Capua, who having perceived them retired promptly into the town; those of Count Roger took 162 of them, from whom they learned all the secret of the treason. Roger went, on the 29th July following, to Squilantia, and having related to Bruno what had happened to him, the saint said to him, 'It was not I who warned you, it was the angel of God, who is near princes in time of war.' Thus Count Roger relates the affair himself, in a privilege granted to St Bruno.

A monk named Fidus, a disciple of St Euthymius, a celebrated abbot in Palestine, having been sent by Martyrius, the patriarch of Jerusalem, on an important mission concerning the affairs of the Church, embarked at Joppa, and was shipwrecked the following night; he supported himself above water for some time by clinging to a piece of wood, which he found by chance. Then he invoked the help of St Euthymius, who appeared to him walking on the sea, and who said to him, 'Know that this voyage is not pleasing to God, and will be of no utility to the mother of the Churches, that is to say, to Jerusalem. Return to him who sent you, and tell him from me not to be uneasy at the separation of the schismatics – union will take place ere long; for you, you must go to my laurel grove, and you must build there a monastery.'

Having said this, he enveloped Fidus in his mantle, and Fidus found himself immediately at Jerusalem, and in his house, without knowing how he came there; he related it all to the Patriarch Martyrius, who remembered the prediction of St Euthymius, concerning the building in the laurel grove a monastery.

Queen Margaret, in her memoirs, asserts that God protects the great in a particular manner, and that he lets them know, either in dreams or otherwise, what is to happen to them. 'As Queen Catherine de Medicis, my mother,' says she, 'who the night before that unhappy day dreamt she saw the king, Henry II, my father, wounded in the eye, as it really happened; when she awoke she several times implored the king not to tilt that day.

'The same queen being dangerously ill at Metz, and having around her bed the king, Charles IX, my sister and brother of Lorraine, and many ladies and princesses, she cried out as if she had seen the battle of Jarnac fought: "See how they fly! my son has the victory! Do you see the Prince of Condé dead in that hedge?" All those who were present fancied she was dreaming; but the night after, M. de Losse brought her the news. "I knew it well," said she; "did I not behold it the day before yesterday?" '

The Duchess Philippa of Gueldres, wife of the Duke of Lorraine, René II, being a nun at St Claire du Pont-à-Mousson, saw, during her orisons, the unfortunate battle of Pavia. She cried out suddenly, 'Ah! my sisters, my dear sisters, for the love of God, say your prayers; my son de Lambesc is dead, and the king (Francis I) my cousin is made prisoner.' Some days after, news of this famous event, which happened the day on which the duchess had seen it, was received at Nancy. Certainly, neither the young Prince de Lambesc, nor the king, Francis I, had any knowledge of this revelation, and they took no part in it. It was, then, neither their spirit nor their phantoms which appeared to the princess: it was apparently their angel, or God himself, who by his power struck her imagination, and represented to her what was passing at that moment.

Mezeray affirms, that he had often heard people of quality relate, that the duke Charles the III of Lorraine, who was at Paris when King Henry II was wounded with the splinter of a lance, of which he died, told the circumstance often, of a lady who lodged in his hotel, having seen in a dream, very distinctly, that the king had been struck and brought to the ground by a blow from a lance.

To these instances of the apparition of living persons to other living persons in their sleep, we may add an infinite number of other instances of apparitions of angels and holy personages, or even of dead persons, to the living when asleep, to give them instructions, warn them of dangers which menace them, inspire them with salutary counsel relative to their salvation, or to give them aid; thick volumes might be composed on such matters. I shall content myself with relating here some examples of those apparitions drawn from profane authors.

Xerxes, King of Persia, when deliberating in council whether he should carry the war into Greece, was strongly dissuaded from it by Artabanes, his paternal uncle. Xerxes took offence at this liberty, and uttered some very disobliging words to him. The following night he reflected seriously on the arguments of Artabanes, and changed his resolution. When he was asleep, he saw in a dream a man of extraordinary size and beauty, who said to him, 'You have then renounced your intention of making war on the Greeks, although you have already given orders to the Persian chiefs to assemble your army. You have not done well to change your resolve, even should no one be of your opinion. Go forward; believe me: follow your first design.' Having said this, the vision disappeared. The next day he again assembled his council, and, without speaking of his dream, he testified his regret for what he said in his rage the preceding day to his uncle Artabanes, and declared that he had renounced his design of making war upon the Greeks. Those who composed the council, transported with joy, prostrated themselves before him, and congratulated him upon it.

The following night he had a second time the same vision, and the same phantom said to him, 'Son of Darius, thou hast then abandoned thy design of declaring war against the Greeks, regardless of what I said to thee. Know that if thou dost not instantly undertake this expedition, thou wilt soon be reduced to a situation as low as that in which thou now findest thyself is elevated.' The king directly rose from his bed, and sent in all haste for Artabanes, to whom he related the two dreams which he had had two nights consecutively. He added, 'I pray you to put on my royal ornaments, sit down on my throne, and then lie down in my bed. If the phantom which appeared to me appears to you also, I shall believe that the thing is ordained by the decrees of the gods, and I shall yield to their commands.'

Artabanes would in vain have excused himself from putting on the royal ornaments, sitting on the king's throne, and lying down in his bed, alleging that all those things would be useless if the gods had resolved to let him know their will; that it would even be more likely to exasperate the gods, as if he desired to deceive them by external appearances. As for the rest, dreams in themselves deserve no attention, and usually they are only the consequences and representations of what is most strongly in the mind when awake.

Xerxes did not yield to his arguments, and Artabanes did what the king desired, persuaded that if the same thing should occur more than once, it would be a proof of the will of the gods, of the reality of the vision, and the truth of the dream. He then laid down in the king's bed, and the same phantom appeared to him, and said, 'It is you, then, who prevent Xerxes from executing his resolve, and accomplishing what is decreed by fate. I have already declared to the king what he has to fear if he disobeys my orders.' At the same time it appeared to Artabanes that the spectre would burn his eyes with a red-hot iron. He directly sprang from the couch, and related to Xerxes what had appeared to him and what had been said to him, adding, 'I now absolutely change my opinion, since it pleases the gods that we should make war, and that the Greeks be threatened with great misfortunes; give your orders and dispose every thing for this war,' – which was executed immediately.

The terrible consequences of this war, which was so fatal to Persia, and at last caused the overthrow of that famous monarchy, leads us to judge that this apparition, if a true one, was announced by an evil spirit, hostile to that monarchy, sent by God to dispose things for events predicted by the prophets, and the succession of great empires predestined by the decrees of the Almighty.

Cicero remarks that two Arcadians, who were travelling together, arrived at Megara, a city of Greece, situated between Athens and Corinth. One of them, who could claim hospitality in the town, was lodged at a friend's, and the other at an inn. After supper, he who was at a friend's house retired to rest. In his sleep it seemed to him that the man whom he had left at the inn appeared to him, and implored his help, because the innkeeper wanted to kill him. He arose directly, much alarmed at this dream, but having reassured himself, and fallen asleep again, the other again appeared to him, and told him that since he had not had the kindness to aid him, at least he must not leave his death unpunished; that the innkeeper, after having killed him, had hidden his body in a wagon, and covered it over with dung, and that he must not fail to be the next morning at the opening of the city gate, before the wagon went forth. Struck with this new dream, he went early in the morning to the city gate, saw the wagon, and asked the driver what he had got under the manure. The carter took flight directly, the body was extricated from the wagon, and the innkeeper arrested and punished.

Cicero relates also some other instances of similar apparitions which occurred in sleep; one is of Sophocles, the other of Simonides. The former saw Hercules in a dream, who told him the name of a robber who had taken a golden patera from his temple. Sophocles neglected this notice, as an effect of disturbed sleep; but Hercules appeared to him a second time, and repeated to him the same thing, which induced Sophocles to denounce the robber, who was convicted by the Areopagus, and from that time the temple was dedicated to Hercules the Revealer.

The dream or apparition of Simonides was more useful to himself personally. He was on the point of embarking, when he found on the shore the corpse of an unknown person, as yet without sepulture. Simonides had him interred, from humanity. The next night the dead man appeared to Simonides, and, through gratitude, counselled him not to embark in the vessel then riding in the harbour, because he would be shipwrecked if he did. Simonides believed him, and a few days after, he heard of the wreck of the vessel in which he was to have embarked.

John Pico de la Mirandola assures us in his treatise, *De Auro*, that a man, who was not rich, finding himself reduced to the last extremity, and without any resources either to pay his debts or procure nourishment for a numerous family in a time of scarcity, overcome with grief and uneasiness, fell asleep. At the same time one of the blessed appeared to him in a dream, taught him by some enigmatical words the means of making gold, and pointed out to him at the same moment the water he must make use of to succeed in it. On his awaking, he took some of that water, and made gold of it, in small quantity, indeed, but enough to maintain his family. He made some twice with iron and three times with orpiment. 'He has convinced me by my own eyes,' says Pico de la Mirandola, 'that the means of making gold artificially is not a falsehood, but a true art.'

Here is another sort of apparition of one living man to another, which is so much the more singular, because it proves at once the might of spells, and that a magician can render himself invisible to several persons, while he discovers himself to one man alone. The fact is taken from the Treatise on Superstitions, of the reverend father Le Brun, and is characterised by all which can render it incontestible. On Friday, the first day of May 1705, about five o'clock in the evening, Denis Misanger de la Richardière, eighteen years of age, was attacked with an extraordinary malady, which began by a sort of lethargy. They gave him every assistance that medicine and surgery could afford. He fell afterwards into a kind of furor or convulsion, and they were obliged to hold him, and have five or six persons to keep watch over him, for fear that he should throw himself out of the windows, or break his head against the wall. The emetic which they gave him made him throw up a quantity of bile, and for four or five days he remained pretty quiet.

At the end of the month of May, they sent him into the country, to take the air; and some other circumstances occurred, so unusual, that they judged he must be bewitched. And what confirmed this conjecture was, that he never had any fever, and retained all his strength, notwithstanding all the pains and violent remedies which he had been made to take. They asked him if he had not had some dispute with a shepherd, or some other person suspected of sorcery or malpractices.

He declared that on the 18th April preceding, when he was going through the village of Noysi on horseback for a ride, his horse stopped short in the midst of the Rue Feret, opposite the chapel, and he could not make him go forward, though he touched him several times with the spur. There was a shepherd standing leaning against the chapel, with his crook in his hand, and two black dogs at his side. This man said to him, 'Sir, I advise you to return home, for your horse will not go forward.' The young La Richardière, continuing to spur his horse, said to the shepherd, 'I do not understand what you say.' The shepherd replied, in a low tone, 'I will make you understand.' In effect, the young man was obliged to get down from his horse, and lead it back by the bridle to his father's dwelling in the same village. Then the shepherd cast a spell upon him, which was to take effect on the 1st May, as was afterwards known.

During this malady, they caused several masses to be said in different places, especially at St Maur des Fossés, at St Amable, and at St Esprit.

Young La Richardière was present at some of these masses which were said at St Maur; but he declared that he should not be cured till Friday, the 26th June, on his return from St Maur. On entering his chamber, the key of which he had in his pocket, he found there that shepherd, seated in his armchair, with his crook, and his two black dogs. He was the only person who saw him; none other in the house could perceive him. He said even that this man was called Damis, although he did not remember that anyone had before this revealed his name to him. He beheld him all that day, and all the succeeding night. Towards six o'clock in the evening, as he felt his usual sufferings, he fell on the ground, exclaiming that the shepherd was upon him, and crushing him; at the same time he drew his knife, and aimed five blows at the shepherd's face, of which he retained the marks. The invalid told those who were watching over him that he was going to be very faint at five different times, and begged of them to help him, and move him violently. The thing happened as he had predicted.

On Friday, the 26th June, M. de la Richardière, having gone to the mass at St Maur, asserted that he should be cured on that day. After mass, the priest put the stole upon his head, and recited the Gospel of St John, during which prayer the young man saw St Maur standing, and the unhappy shepherd at his left, with his face bleeding from the five knife-wounds which he had given him. At that moment the youth cried out, unintentionally, 'A miracle! a miracle!' and asserted that he was cured, as in fact he was.

On the 29th June, the same M. de la Richardiére returned to Noysi, and amused himself with shooting. As he was shooting in the vineyards, the shepherd presented himself before him; he hit him on the head with the butt-end of his gun. The shepherd cried out, 'Sir, you are killing me!' and fled. The next day this man presented himself again before him, and asked his pardon, saying, 'I am called Damis; it was I who cast a spell over you which was to have lasted a year. By the aid of masses and prayers which have been said for you, you have been cured at the end of eight weeks. But the charm has fallen back upon myself, and I can be cured of it only by a miracle. I implore you then to pray for me.'

During all these reports, the *maré chausée* had set off in pursuit of the shepherd; but he escaped them, having killed his two dogs and thrown away his crook. On Sunday, the 13th September, he came to M. de la Richardière, and related to him his adventure; that after having passed twenty years without approaching the sacraments, God had given him grace to confess himself at Troyes; and that after divers delays he had been admitted to the Holy Communion. Eight days after, M. de la Richardière received a letter from a woman who said she was a relation of the shepherd's, informing him of his death, and begging him to cause a requiem mass to be said for him, which was done.

How many difficulties may we make about this story! How could this wretched shepherd cast the spell without touching the person? How could he introduce himself into young M. de la Richardière's chamber without either opening or forcing the door? How could he render himself visible to him alone, whilst none other beheld him? Can one doubt of his corporeal presence, since he received five cuts from a knife in his face, of which he afterwards bore the marks, when, by the merit of the holy mass and the intercession of the saints, the spell was taken off? How could St Maur appear to him in his Benedictine habit, having the wizard on his left hand? If the circumstance is certain, as it appears, who shall explain the manner in which all passed or took place?

CHAPTER 46

Arguments Concerning Apparitions

After having spoken at some length upon apparitions, and after having established the truth of them, as far as it has been possible for us to do so, from the authority of the Scripture, from examples, and by arguments, we must now exercise our judgment on the causes, means, and reasons for these apparitions, and reply to the objections which may be made to destroy the reality of them, or at least to raise doubts on the subject.

We have supposed that apparitions were the work of angels, demons, or souls of the defunct; we do not talk of the appearance of God himself; His will, His operations, His power, are above our reach; we acknowledge that He can do all that He wills to do, that His will is all-powerful, and that He places Himself, when He chooses, above the laws which He has made. As to the apparitions of the living, to others, also living, they are of a different nature from what we propose to examine in this place; we shall not fail to speak of them hereafter.

Whatever system we may follow on the nature of angels, or demons, or souls separated from the body; whether we consider them as purely spiritual substances, as the Christian Church at this day holds; whether we give them an aerial body, subtle, and invisible, as many have taught; it appears almost as difficult to render palpable, perceptible, and thick, a subtle and aerial body, as it is to condense the air, and make it seem like a solid and perceptible body; as, when the angels appeared to Abraham and Lot, the Angel Raphael to Tobias, whom he conducted into Mesopotamia;

or when the Demon appeared to Jesus Christ, and led him to a high
mountain, and on the pinnacle of the Temple at Jerusalem; or when Moses
appeared with Elias on Mount Tabor: for those apparitions are certain
from Scripture.

If you will say that these apparitions were seen only in the imagination
and mind of those who saw, or believed they saw, angels, demons, or souls
separated from the body, as it happens every day in our sleep, and
sometimes when awake, if we are strongly occupied with certain objects, or
struck with certain things which we desire ardently, or fear exceedingly – as
when Ajax, thinking he saw Ulysses and Agamemnon, or Menelaus, threw
himself upon some animals, which he killed, thinking he was killing those
two men his enemies, and whom he was dying with the desire to wreak his
vengeance upon – on this supposition, the apparition will not be less
difficult to explain. There was neither prepossession nor disturbed imagination, nor any preceding emotion, which led Abraham to figure to himself
that he saw three persons, to whom he gave hospitality, to whom he spoke,
who promised him the birth of a son, of which he was scarcely thinking at
that time. The three Apostles who saw Moses conversing with Jesus Christ
on Mount Tabor, were not prepared for that appearance; there was no
emotion of fear, love, revenge, ambition, or any other passion which struck
their imagination, to dispose them to see Moses; as neither was there in
Abraham, when he perceived the three angels who appeared to him.

Often in our sleep we see, or we believe we see, what has struck our
attention very much when awake; sometimes we represent to ourselves in
sleep things of which we have never thought, which even are repugnant to
us, and which present themselves to our mind in spite of ourselves. None
bethink themselves of seeking the causes of these kinds of representations;
they are attributed to chance, or to some disposition of the humours of the
blood or of the brain, or even of the way in which the body is placed in bed;
but nothing like that is applicable to the apparitions of angels, demons, or
spirits, when these apparitions are accompanied and followed by converse,
predictions, and real effects preceded and predicted by those which
appear.

If we have recourse to a pretended fascination of the eyes or the other
senses, which sometimes make us believe that we see and hear what we do
not, or that we neither see nor hear what is passing before our eyes, or
which strikes our ears; as when the soldiers sent to arrest Elisha spoke to
him and saw him before they recognised him, or when the inhabitants of
Sodom could not discover Lot's door, although it was before their eyes, or
when the disciples of Emmaus knew not that it was Jesus Christ who
accompanied them and expounded the Scriptures; they opened their eyes
and knew him *only by the breaking of bread.*

That fascination of the senses which makes us believe that we see what we do not see, or that suspension of the exercise and natural functions of our senses which prevents us from seeing and recognising what is passing before our eyes, is all of it hardly less miraculous than to condense the air, or rarefy it, or give solidity and consistence to what is purely spiritual and disengaged from matter.

From all this it follows that no apparition can take place without a sort of miracle, and without a concurrence, both extraordinary and supernatural, of the power of God who commands, or causes, or permits an angel, or a demon, or a disembodied soul, to appear, act, speak, walk, and perform other functions which belong only to an organised body.

I shall be told that it is useless to recur to the miraculous and the supernatural, if we have acknowledged in spiritual substances a natural power of showing themselves, whether by condensing the air, or by producing a massive and palpable body, or in raising up some dead body, to which these spirits give life and motion for a certain time.

I own it all; but I dare maintain that that is not possible either to angel or demon, nor to any spiritual substance whatsoever. The soul can produce in herself thoughts, will, and wishes; she can give her impulsion to the movements of her body, and repress its sallies and agitations; but how does she do that? Philosophy can hardly explain it, but by saying that by virtue of the union between herself and the body, God, by an effect of His wisdom, has given her power to act upon the humours, its organs, and impress them with certain movements; but there is reason to believe that the soul performs all that only as an occasional cause, and that it is God as the first, necessary, immediate and essential cause, which produces all the movements of the body that are made in a natural way.

Neither angel nor demon has more privilege in this respect over matter than the soul of man has over its own body. They can neither modify matter, change it, nor impress it with action and motion, save by the power of God, and with His concurrence both necessary and immediate: our knowledge does not permit us to judge otherwise; there is no physical proportion between the spirit and the body; those two substances cannot act mutually and immediately one upon the other; they can act only occasionally, by determining the first cause, in virtue of the laws which wisdom has judged it proper to prescribe to herself for the reciprocal action of the creatures upon each other, to give them being, to preserve it, and perpetuate movement in the mass of matter which composes the universe, in Himself giving life to spiritual substances, and permitting them with His concurrence, as the First Cause, to act, the body on the soul, and the soul on the body, one on the other, as secondary causes.

Porphyry, when consulted by Anebo, an Egyptian priest, if those who foretell the future and perform prodigies have more powerful souls, or whether they receive power from some strange spirit, replies, that according to appearance all those things are done by means of certain evil spirits that are naturally knavish, and take all sorts of shapes, and do everything that one sees happen, whether good or evil; but that in the end they never lead men to what is truly good.

St Augustine, who cites this passage of Porphyry, lays much stress on his testimony, and says that every extraordinary thing which is done by certain tones of the voice, by figures or phantoms, is usually the work of the demon, who sports with the credulity and blindness of men; that everything marvellous which is transacted in nature, and has no relation to the worship of the true God, ought to pass for an illusion of the devil. The most ancient Fathers of the Church, Minutius Felix, Arnobius, St Cyprian, attribute equally all these kinds of extraordinary effects to the evil spirit.

Tertullian had no doubt that the apparitions which are produced by magic, and by the evocation of souls, which, forced by enchantments, come out, say they, from the depth of hell (or Hades), are but pure illusions of the demon, who causes to appear to those present a fantastical form, which fascinates the eyes of those who think they see what they see not; 'which is not more difficult for the demon,' says he, 'than to seduce and blind the souls which he leads into sin. Pharaoh thought he saw real serpents produced by his magicians: it was mere illusion. The truth of Moses devoured the falsehood of these impostors.'

Is it more easy to cause the fascination of the eyes of Pharaoh and his servants than to produce serpents, and can it be done without God's concurring thereto? And how can we reconcile this concurrence with the wisdom, independence, and truth of God? Has the devil in this respect a greater power than an angel and a disembodied soul? And if once we open the door to this fascination, everything which appears supernatural and miraculous will become uncertain and doubtful. It will be said that the wonders related in the Old and New Testament are in this respect, in regard both to those who were witnesses of them, and those to whom they happened, only illusions and fascinations: and whither may not these premises lead? It leads us to doubt everything, to deny everything; to believe that God, in concert with the devil, leads us into error, and fascinates our eyes and other senses, to make us believe that we see, hear, and know, what is neither present to our eyes, nor known to our mind, nor supported by our reasoning powers, since by that the principles of reasoning are overthrown.

We must, then, have recourse to the solid and unshaken principles of religion, which teach us –

1 That angels, demons, and souls disembodied, are pure spirit, free from all matter.

2 That it is only by the order or permission of God that spiritual substances can appear to men, and seem to them to be true and tangible bodies, in which and by which they perform what they are seen to do.

3 That to make these bodies appear, and make them act, speak, walk, eat, etc., they must produce tangible bodies, either by condensing the air, or substituting other terrestrial, solid bodies, capable of performing the functions we speak of.

4 That the way in which this production and apparition of a perceptible body is achieved, is absolutely unknown to us; that we have no proof that spiritual substances have a natural power of producing this kind of change when it pleases them, and that they cannot produce them independently of God.

5 That although there may be often a great deal of illusion, prepossession, and imagination in what is related of the operations and apparitions of angels, demons, and disembodied souls, there is still some reality in many of these things, and we cannot reasonably doubt of them all, and still less deny them all.

6 That there are apparitions which bear about them the character and proof of truth, from the quality of him who relates them; from the circumstances which accompany them; from the events following those apparitions that announce things to come; which perform things impossible to the natural strength of man, and too much in opposition to the interest of the demon, and his malicious and deceitful character, for us to be able to suspect him to be the author or contriver of them. In short, these apparitions are certified by the belief, the prayers, and the practice of the Church, which recognises them, and supposes their reality.

7 That although what appears miraculous is not so always, we must at least usually perceive in it *some* illusion and operation of the demon; consequently, that the demon can, with the permission of God, do many things which surpass our knowledge, and the natural power which we suppose him to have.

8 That those who wish to explain them by fascination of the eyes and other senses, do not resolve the difficulty, and throw themselves into still greater embarrassment than those who admit simply that apparitions appear by the order or the permission of God.

CHAPTER 47

Objections against Apparitions, and Replies
to those Objections

The greatest objection that can be raised against the apparitions of angels, demons, and disembodied souls, takes its rise in the nature of these substances, which, being purely spiritual, cannot appear with evident, solid, and palpable bodies, nor perform those functions which belong only to matter, and living or animated bodies.

For, either spiritual substances are united to the bodies which appear, or not. If they are not united to them, how can they move them, and cause them to act, walk, speak, reason, and eat? If they are united to them, then they form but one individual; and how can they separate themselves from them, after being united to them? Do they take them and leave them at will, as we lay aside a habit or a mask? That would be to suppose that they are at liberty to appear or disappear, which is not the case, since all apparitions are solely by the order or permission of God. Are those bodies which appear, only instruments which the angels, demons, or souls, make use of to affright, warn, chastise, or instruct the person or persons to whom they appear? This is, in fact, the most rational thing that can be said concerning these apparitions; the exorcisms of the Church fall directly on the agent and cause of these apparitions, and not on the phantom which appears, nor on the first author, which is God, who orders and permits it.

Another objection, both very common and very striking, is that which is drawn from the multitude of false stories and ridiculous reports which are spread amongst the people, of the apparitions of spirits, demons, and elves, of possessions and obsessions.

It must be owned that, out of a hundred of these pretended appearances, hardly two will be found to be true. The ancients are not more to be credited on that point than the moderns, since they were, at least, equally credulous as people are in our own age, or rather they were more credulous than we are at this day.

I grant, that the foolish credulity of the people, and the love of everything that seems marvellous and extraordinary, have produced an infinite number of false histories on the subject we are now treating of. There are here two dangers to avoid: a too great credulity, and an excessive difficulty in believing what is above the ordinary course of nature; as likewise, we must not conclude what is general from what is particular, or make a general case of a particular one, nor say that all is false because some stories are so; also, we must not assert that such a particular history is a mere invention, because there are many stories of this latter kind. It is allowable to examine, prove, and select; we must never form our judgment, but with knowledge of the case; a story may be false in many of its circumstances as related, but true in its foundation.

The history of the deluge, and that of the passage across the Red Sea, are certain in themselves, and in the simple and natural recital given of them by Moses. The profane historians, and some Hebrew writers, and even Christians, have added some embellishment which must militate against the story in itself. Josephus, the historian, has much embellished the history of Moses; Christian authors have added much to that of Josephus; the Mahometans have altered several points of the sacred history of the Old and New Testament. Must we, on this account, consider these histories as problematical? The life of St Gregory Thaumaturgus is full of miracles, as are also those of St Martin and St Bernard; St Augustine relates several miraculous cures worked by the relics of St Stephen. Many extraordinary things are related in the life of St Ambrose. Why not give faith to them after the testimony of these great men, and that of their disciples, who had lived with them, and had been witnesses of a good part of what they relate?

It is not permitted us to dispute the truth of the apparitions noted in the Old and New Testament; but we may be permitted to explain them. For instance, it is said that the Lord appeared to Abraham in the valley of Mamre; that he entered Abraham's tent, and that he promised him the birth of a son; also, it is allowed, that he received three angels, who went from thence to Sodom. St Paul notices it expressly in his Epistle to the Hebrews; *angelis hospitio receptis*. It is also said, that the Lord appeared unto Moses, and gave him the law; and St Stephen, in the Acts, informs us, that it was an angel who spoke to him from the burning bush, and on Mount Horeb; and St Paul, writing to the Galatians, says, that the law was given by angels.

Sometimes, the name of angel of the Lord is taken for a prophet, a man filled with his Spirit, and deputed by him. It is certain, that the Hebrew *malae* and the Greek *angelos*, bear the same signification as our *envoy*. For instance, at the beginning of the Book of Judges, it is said, that there came an angel of the Lord from Gilgal to the place of tears, (or Bochim,) and that he there reproved the Israelites for their infidelity and ingratitude. The ablest commentators think, that this *angel of the Lord* is no other than Phineas, or the then high priest, or rather a prophet, sent expressly to the people assembled at Gilgal.

In the Scripture, the prophets are sometimes styled angels of the Lord. 'Here is what saith the envoy of the Lord, amongst the envoys of the Lord,' says Haggai, speaking of himself.

The prophet Malachi, the last of the lesser prophets, says, that 'The Lord will send his angel, who will prepare the way before his face.' This angel is St John the Baptist, who prepares the way for Jesus Christ, who is himself styled the Angel of the Lord – 'And soon the Lord whom ye demand, and the so much desired Angel of the Lord, will come into his temple.' This same Saviour is designated by Moses under the name of a prophet: 'The Lord will raise up in the midst of your nation, a prophet like myself.' The name of angel is given to the prophet Nathan, who reproved David for his sin. I do not pretend, by these testimonies, to deny that the angels have often appeared to men; but I infer from them, that sometimes these angels were only prophets or other persons, raised up and sent by God to His people.

As to apparitions of the demon, it is well to observe, that in Scripture the greater part of public calamities and maladies are attributed to evil spirits; for example, it is said, that Satan inspired David with the idea of numbering his people; but in another place it is simply said, that the anger of the Lord was inflamed against Israel, and led David to cause his subjects to be numbered. There are several other passages in the Holy Books, where they relate what the demon said and what he did, in a popular manner, by the figure termed prosopopoeia; for instance, the conversation between Satan and the first woman, and the discourse which the demon holds in company with the good angels before the Lord, when he talks to him of Job, and obtains permission to tempt and afflict him. In the New Testament, it appears that the Jews attributed to the malice of the demon and to his possession almost all the maladies with which they were afflicted. In St Luke, the woman who was bent and could not raise herself up, and had suffered this for eighteen years, 'had,' says the evangelist, 'a spirit of infirmity;' and Jesus Christ, after having healed her, says, 'that Satan held her bound for eighteen years;' and in another place it is said, that a lunatic or epileptic person was possessed by the demon. It is clear from what is said by St Matthew and St Luke, that he was attacked by epilepsy. The Saviour cured him of this evil malady, and by that means took from the demon the opportunity of tormenting him still more; as David, by dissipating with the sound of his harp the sombre melancholy of Saul, delivered him from the evil spirit, who abused the power of those inclinations which he found in him, to awaken his jealousy against David. All this means, that we often ascribe to the demon things of which he is not guilty, and that we must not lightly adopt all the prejudices of the people, nor take literally all that is related of the works of Satan.

CHAPTER 48

Some other Objections and Replies

In order to combat the apparitions of angels, demons, and disembodied souls, we still bring forward the effects of a prepossessed fancy, struck with an idea, and of a weak and timid mind, which imagine they see and hear what subsists only in idea; we advert to the inventions of the malignant spirits, who like to make sport of and to delude us; we call to our assistance the artifices of the charlatans, who do so many things which pass for supernatural in the eyes of the ignorant. Philosophers, by means of certain glasses, and what are called magic lanterns, by optical secrets, sympathetic powders, by their phosphorus, and lately by means of the electrical machine, show us an infinite number of things which the simpletons take for magic, because they know not how they are produced.

Eyes that are diseased, do not see things as others see them, or else behold them differently. A drunken man will see objects double; to one who has the jaundice, they will appear yellow; in the obscurity, people fancy they see a spectre, when they see only the trunk of a tree.

A mountebank will appear to eat a sword; another will vomit coals or pebbles; one will drink wine and send it out again at his forehead; another will cut off his companion's head, and put it on again. You will think you see a chicken dragging a beam. The mountebank will swallow fire and vomit it forth, he will draw blood from fruit, he will send from his mouth strings of iron nails, he will put a sword on his stomach and press it strongly, and instead of running into him, it will bend back to the hilt; another will run a sword through his body without wounding himself; you will sometimes see a child without a head, then a head without a child, and all of them alive. That appears very wonderful; nevertheless, if it were known how all those things are done, people would only laugh, and be surprised that they could wonder at and admire such things.

What has not been said for and against the divining rod of Jacques Aimar? Scripture proves to us the antiquity of divination by the divining rod, in the instance of Nebuchadnezzar, and in what is said of the prophet Hosea. Fable speaks of the wonders wrought by the golden rod of Mercury. The Gauls and Germans also used the rod for divination; and there is reason to believe that often God permitted that the rods should make known by their movements what was to happen; for that reason they were consulted. Every body knows the secret of Circe's wand, which changed men into beasts. I do not compare it with the rod of Moses, by means of which God worked so many miracles in Egypt; but we may compare it with those of the magicians of Pharaoh, which produced so many marvellous effects.

Albertus Magnus relates, that there had been seen in Germany two brothers, one of whom passing near a door securely locked, and presenting his left side, would cause it to open of itself; the other brother had the same virtue in the right side. St Augustine says, that there are men who move their two ears one after another, or both together, without moving their heads; others, without moving it also, make all the skin of their head with the hair thereon come down over their forehead, and put it back as it was before; some imitate so perfectly the voices of animals, that it is almost impossible not to mistake them. We have seen men speak from the hollow of the stomach, and make themselves heard as if speaking from a distance, although they were close by. Others swallow an incredible quantity of different things, and by tightening their stomachs ever so little, throw up whole, as from a bag, whatever they please. Last year, in Alsatia, there was seen and heard a German who played on two French horns at once, and gave airs in two parts, the first and the second, at the same time. Who can explain to us the secret of intermitting fevers, of the flux and reflux of the sea, and the cause of many effects which are certainly all natural?

Galen relates, that a physician named Theophilus, having fallen ill, fancied that he saw near his bed a great number of musicians, whose noise split his head, and augmented his illness. He cried out incessantly for them to send those people away. Having recovered his health, and good sense, he perfectly well remembered all that had been said to him, but he could not get those players on musical instruments out of his head, and he affirmed that they tired him to death.

In 1629, Desbordes, valet-de-chambre of Charles IV , Duke of Lorraine, was accused of having hastened the death of the Princess Christina of Salms, wife of Duke Francis II, and mother of the Duke Charles IV , and of having inflicted maladies on different persons, which maladies the doctors attributed to evil spells. Charles IV had conceived violent suspicions against Desbordes, since one day when in a hunting party this valet-de-chambre had served a grand dinner to the Duke and his company, without any other preparation than having to open a box with three shelves; and to wind up the wonders, he had ordered three robbers, who were dead and hung to a gibbet, to come down from it, and come and make their bow to the Duke, and then to go back and resume their place at the gallows. It was said, moreover, that on another occasion he had commanded the person-ages in a piece of tapestry to detach themselves from it, and to come and present themselves in the middle of the room.

Charles IV was not very credulous; nevertheless, he allowed Desbordes to be tried. He was, it is said, convicted of magic, and condemned to the flames; but I have since been assured that he made his escape, and some years after, on presenting himself before the Duke, and clearing himself, he demanded the restitution of his property, which had been confiscated; but he recovered only a very small part of it. Since the adventure of Desbordes, the partisans of Charles IV wished to cast a doubt on the validity of the baptism of the Duchess Nichola, his wife, because she had been baptised by Lavallée, Chantre de St George, a friend of Desbordes, and like him convicted of several crimes, which drew upon him similar condemnation. From a doubt of the baptism of the duchess, they wished to infer the invalidity of her marriage with Charles, which was then the grand business of Charles IV.

Father Delrio, a Jesuit, says that the magician called Trois-Echelles, by his enchantments, detached in the presence of King Charles IX the rings or links of a collar of the Order of the King, worn by some knights who were at a great distance from him; he made them come into his hand, and after that replaced them, without the collar appearing deranged.

John Faust Cudlingen, a German, was requested, in a company of gay people, to perform in their presence some tricks of his trade; he promised to show them a vine loaded with grapes, ripe and ready to gather. They thought, as it was then the month of December, he could not execute his promise. He strongly recommended them not to stir from their places, and not to lift up their hands to cut the grapes, unless by his express order. The vine appeared directly, covered with leaves and loaded with grapes, to the great astonishment of all present; everyone took up his knife, awaiting the order of Cudlingen to cut some grapes; but after having kept them for some time in that expectation, he suddenly caused the vine and the grapes to disappear; then everyone found himself armed with his knife, and holding his neighbour's nose with one hand, so that if they had cut off a bunch without the order of Cudlingen, they would have cut off one another's noses.

We have seen in these parts a horse which appeared gifted with wit and discernment, and to understand what his master said. All the secret consisted in the horse's having been taught to observe certain motions of his master; and from these motions he was led to do certain things to which he was accustomed, and to go to certain persons, which he would never have done, but for the sign or motion which he saw his master make.

A hundred other similar facts might be cited, which might pass for magical operations, if we did not know that they are simple contrivances and tricks of art, performed by persons well exercised in such things. It may be that sometimes people have ascribed to magic and the evil spirit operations like those we have just related, and that what have been taken for the spirits of deceased persons, were often arranged on purpose by young people to frighten passers-by. They will cover themselves with white or black, and show themselves in a cemetery in the posture of persons requesting prayers; after that they will be the first to exclaim that they have seen a spirit: at other times it will be pickpockets, or young men, who will hide their amorous intrigues, or their thefts and knavish tricks, under this disguise.

Sometimes a widow, or heirs, from interested motives, will publicly declare that the deceased husband appears in his house, and is in torment; that he has asked or commanded such and such things, or such and such restitutions. I own that this may happen, and does happen sometimes; but it does not follow that spirits never return. The return of souls is infinitely more rare than the common people believe; I say the same of pretended magical operations and apparitions of the demon.

It is remarked that the greater the ignorance which prevails in a country, the more superstition reigns there; and that the spirit of darkness there exercises greater power, in proportion as the nations are plunged in irregularity, and into deeper moral darkness. Louis Vivez testifies, that in the newly-discovered countries in America, nothing is more common than to see spirits which appear at noonday, not only in the country, but in towns and villages, speaking, commanding, sometimes even striking men. Olaüs Magnus, Archbishop of Upsal, who has written on the antiquities of the northern nations, observes, that in Sweden, Norway, Finland, Finmark, and Lapland, they frequently see spectres or spirits, which do many wonderful things; that there are even some amongst them who serve as domestics to men, and take the horses and other cattle to pasture.

The Laplanders even at this day, as well those who have remained in idolatry as those who have embraced Christianity, believe the apparition of the manes or ghosts, and offer them a kind of sacrifice. I believe that prepossession, and the prejudices of childhood, have much more to do with this belief than reason and experience. In effect, among the Tartars, where barbarism and ignorance reign as much as in any country in the world, they talk neither of spirits nor of apparitions, no more than among the Mahometans, although they admit the apparitions of angels made to Abraham and the patriarchs, and that of the Archangel Gabriel to Mahomet himself.

The Abyssinians, a very rude and ignorant people, believe neither in sorcerers, nor spells, nor magicians; they say that it is giving too much power to the demon, and by that they fall into the error of the Manichaeans, who admit two Principles, the one of good, which is God, and the other of evil, which is the devil. The Minister Becker, in his work entitled *The Enchanted World*, (*Le Monde Enchanté*) laughs at apparitions of spirits and evil angels, and ridicules all that is said of the effects of magic: he maintains that to believe in magic is contrary to Scripture and religion.

But whence comes it, then, that the Scriptures forbid us to consult magicians, and that they make mention of Simon the magician, of Elymas, another magician, and of the works of Satan? What will become of the apparitions of angels, so well noted in the Old and New Testaments? What will become of the apparitions of Onias to Judas Maccabeus, and of the devil to Jesus Christ himself, after his fast of forty days? What will be said of the apparition of Moses at the Transfiguration of the Saviour; and an infinity of other appearances made to all kinds of persons, and related by wise, grave, and enlightened authors? Are the apparitions of devils and spirits more difficult to explain and conceive than those of angels, which we cannot rationally dispute without overthrowing the entire Scriptures, and practices and belief of the Churches?

Does not the Apostle tell us, that the angel of darkness transforms himself into an angel of light? Is not the absolute renunciation of all belief in apparitions assaulting Christianity in its most sacred authority, in the belief of another life, of a Church still subsisting in another world, of rewards for good actions, and of punishments for bad ones; the utility of prayers for the dead, and the efficacy of exorcisms? We must then in these matters keep the medium between excessive credulity and extreme incredulity; we must be prudent, moderate and enlightened; we must, according to the advice of St Paul, test everything, examine everything, yield only to evidence and known truth.

CHAPTER 49

The Secrets of Physics and Chemistry Taken for Supernatural things

It is possible to allege against my reasoning the secrets of physics and chemistry, which produce an infinity of wonderful effects, and appear beyond the power of natural agency. We have the composition of a phosphorus, with which they write; the characters do not appear by daylight, but in the dark we see them shine; with this phosphorus figures can be traced which would surprise and even alarm during the night, as has been done more than once, apparently to cause maliciously useless fright. *La poudre ardente* is another phosphorus, which, provided it is exposed to the air, sheds a light both by night and by day. How many people have been frightened by those little worms which are found in certain kinds of rotten wood, and which give a brilliant flame by night.

We have the daily experience of an infinite number of things, all of them natural, which appear above the ordinary course of nature, but which have nothing miraculous in them, and ought not to be attributed to angels or demons; for instance, teeth and noses taken from other persons, and applied to those who have lost similar parts; of this we find many instances in authors. These teeth and noses fall off directly the person from whom they were taken dies, however great the distance between these two persons may be.

The presentiments experienced by certain persons of what happens to their relations and friends, and even of their own death, are not at all miraculous. There are many instances of persons who are in the habit of feeling these presentiments, and who in the night, even when asleep, will say that such a thing has happened, or is about to happen; that such messengers are coming, and will announce to them such and such things.

There are dogs that have the sense of smelling so keen, that they scent from a good distance the approach of any person who has done them good or harm. This has been proved many times, and can only proceed from the diversity of organs in those animals, some of which have the scent much keener than others, and upon which the spirits which exhale from other bodies act more quickly and at a greater distance than in others. Certain persons have such an acute sense of hearing, that they can hear what is whispered even in another chamber, of which the door is well closed. They cite as an example of this, a certain Marie Bucaille, to whom it was thought that her guardian angel discovered what was said at a great distance from her.

Others have the smell so keen that they distinguish by the odour all the men and animals they have ever seen, and scent their approach a long way off. Blind persons pretty often possess this faculty as well as that of discerning the colour of different stuffs by the touch, from horsehair to playing-cards.

Others discern by the taste everything that composes a ragoût, better than the most expert cook could do. Others possess so piercing a sight that at the first glance they can distinguish the most confused and distant objects, and remark the least change which takes place in them.

There are both men and women who, without intending to hurt, do a great deal of harm to children, and all the tender and delicate animals which they look at attentively, or which they touch. This happens particularly in hot countries; and many examples might be cited of it; from which arises what both ancients and moderns call fascination (or the evil eye); hence the precautions which were taken against these effects by amulets and preservatives which were suspended to children's necks.

There have been known to be men from whose eyes there proceeded such venomous spirits that they did harm to every body or thing they looked at, even to the breasts of nurses, which they caused to dry up – to plants, flowers, the leaves of trees, which were seen to wither and fall off. They dare not enter any place till they had warned the people beforehand to send away the children and nurses, newborn animals, and, generally speaking, everything which they could infect by their breath or their looks.

We should laugh, and with reason, at those, who, to explain all these singular effects, should have recourse to charms, spells, to the operations of demons, or of good angels. The evaporation of corpuscles, or atoms, or the insensible perspiration of the bodies which produce all these effects, suffices to account for it. We have recourse neither to miracles, nor to superior causes, above all when these effects are produced at once, and at a short distance; but when the distance is great, the exhalation of the spirits, or essence, and of insensible corpuscles, does not equally satisfy us any more than when we meet with things and effects which go beyond the known force of nature, such as foretelling future events, speaking unknown languages, i.e. languages unknown to the speaker, to be in such ecstasy that the person is beyond earthly feeling, to rise up from the ground, and remain so a long time.

The chemists demonstrate that the palingenesis, or a sort of restoration or resurrection of animals, insects, and plants, is possible and natural.

When the ashes of a plant are placed in a phial, these ashes rise, and arrange themselves as much as they can in the form which was first impressed on them by the Author of Nature.

Father Schol, a Jesuit, affirms that he has often seen a rose which was made to arise from its ashes every time they wished to see it done, by means of a little heat.

The secret of a mineral water has been found by means of which a dead plant which has its root can be made green again, and brought to the same state as if it were growing in the ground. Digby asserts that he has drawn from dead animals, which were beaten and bruised in a mortar, the representation of these animals, or other animals of the same species.

Duchesne, a famous chemist, relates that a physician of Cracow preserved in phials the ashes of almost every kind of plant, so that when anyone from curiosity desired to see, for instance, a rose in these phials, he took that in which the ashes of the rose-bush were preserved, and placing it over a lighted candle, as soon as it felt a little warmth, they saw the ashes stir and rise like a little dark cloud, and, after some movements, they represented a rose as beautiful and fresh as if newly gathered from the rose-tree.

Gaffard assures us that M. de Cleves, a celebrated chemist, showed everyday plants drawn from their own ashes. David Vanderbroch affirms that the blood of animals contains the idea of their species, as well as their seed; he relates on this subject the experiment of M. Borelli, who asserts, that the human blood, when warm, is still full of its spirits or sulphurs, acid and volatile, and that being excited in cemeteries, and in places where great battles are fought, by some heat in the ground, the phantoms or ideas of the persons who are there interred are seen to rise; that we should see them as well by day as by night, were it not for the excess of light which prevents us even from seeing the stars. He adds, that by this means we might behold the idea, and represent by a lawful and natural necromancy the figure or phantom of all the great men of antiquity, our friends and our ancestors, provided we possess their ashes.

These are the most plausible objections intended to destroy or obviate all that is said of the apparitions of spirits. Whence some conclude that these are either very natural phenomena and exhalations produced by the heat of the earth imbued with blood and the volatile spirit of the dead, above all, those dead by violence; or that they are the consequences of a stricken and prepossessed fancy, or simply illusions of the mind, or sports of persons who like to divert themselves by the panics into which they terrify others; or, lastly, movements produced naturally by men, rats, monkeys, and other animals; for it is true that the oftener we examine into what have been taken for apparitions, the more satisfied must we be that nothing is found real, extraordinary, or supernatural; but to conclude from hence that all the apparitions and operations attributed to angels, spirits or souls, and demons, are chimerical, is carrying things to excess; it is to conclude that we mistake always, because we mistake often.

CHAPTER 50

Conclusions of the Treatise of Apparitions

After having made this exposition of my opinion concerning the apparitions of angels, demons, souls of the dead, and even of one living person to another, and having spoken of magic, of oracles, of obsessions and possessions of the demon; of sprites and familiar spirits; of sorcerers and witches; of spectres which predict the future; of those which haunt houses – after having stated the objections which are made against apparitions, and having replied to them in as weighty a manner as I possibly could, I think I may conclude that although this matter labours still under very great difficulties, as much respecting the foundation of the thing – I mean as regards the truth and reality of apparitions in general – as for the way in which they are made, still we cannot reasonably disallow that there may be true apparitions of all the kinds of which we have spoken, and that there may be also a great number very disputable, and some others which are manifestly the work of knavery, of maliciousness, of the art of charlatans, and flexibility of those who play sleight of hand tricks.

I acknowledge, moreover, that imagination, prepossession, simplicity, superstition, excess of credulity, and weakness of mind have given rise to many stories which are related; that ignorance of pure philosophy has caused to be taken for miraculous effects, and unlawful magic, what is the simple effect of natural magic, or the secrets of a philosophy hidden from the ignorant and common herd of men. Moreover, I confess that I see insurmountable difficulties in explaining the manner or properties of apparitions, whether we admit with several ancients that angels, demons and disembodied souls have a sort of subtle transparent body of the nature of air, whether we believe them purely spiritual and disengaged from all matter, visible, gross, or subtle.

I lay down as a principle that to explain the philosophy of apparitions, and to give on this subject any certain rules, we should –

1   Know perfectly the nature of spirits, angels and souls, and demons. We should know whether souls by nature are so spiritualised that they have no longer any relation to matter; or if they have, again, any alliance with an aerial, subtle, invisible body, which they still govern after death; or whether they exert any power over the body they once animated, to impel it to certain movements, as the soul which animates us gives to our bodies such impulsions as she thinks proper; or whether the soul, as occasional or secondary cause, determines simply by its will, the first cause which is God, to put in motion the machine which it once animated.

2   If after death the soul still retains that power over its own body, or over others; for instance, over the air and other elements.

3   If angels and demons have respectively the same power over sublunary bodies – for instance, to thicken air, inflame it, produce in it clouds and storms; to make phantoms appear in it; to spoil or preserve fruits and crops; to cause animals to perish, produce maladies, excite tempests and shipwrecks at sea; or even to fascinate the eyes and deceive the other senses.

4   If they can do all these things naturally, and by their own virtue, as often as they think proper; or if there must be a particular order, or at least permission from God, for them to do what we have just said.

5   And, lastly, we should know exactly what power is possessed by these substances which we suppose to be purely spiritual, and how far the power of the angels, demons, and souls separated from their gross bodies, extends, in regard to the apparitions, operations and movements attributed to them. For whilst we are ignorant of the power which the Creator has given or left to disembodied souls, or to demons, we can in no way define what is miraculous, or prescribe the just bound to which may extend, or within which may be limited, the natural operations of spirits, angels and demons.

If we accord the demon the faculty of fascinating our eyes when it pleases him, or of disposing the air so as to form the appearance of a phantom, or phenomenon; or of restoring movement to a body which is dead but not entirely corrupted; or of disturbing the living by ill dreams, or terrific representations – we should no longer wonder at many things which astonish us at present, nor regard as miracles certain cures and certain apparitions, if they are only the natural effects of the power of souls, angels and demons.

If a man invested with his body produced such effects of himself, we should say with reason that they are supernatural operations, because they exceed the known ordinary and natural power of the living man; but if a man held commerce with a spirit, an angel, or a demon, whom by virtue of some compact, explicit or implicit, he commanded to perform certain things which would be above his natural powers, but not beyond the powers of the spirit whom he commanded, would the effect resulting from it be miraculous or supernatural? No, without doubt, supposing that the spirit which produced the result did nothing that was above his natural powers and faculties.

But would it be a miracle if a man had anything to do with an angel or a demon, and that he should make an explicit and implicit compact with them, to oblige them on certain conditions, and with certain ceremonies, to produce effects which would appear externally, and in our minds, to be beyond the power of man? For instance, in the operations of certain magicians who boast of having an explicit compact with the devil, and who by this means raise tempests, or go with extraordinary haste when they walk, or cause the death of animals, and to men incurable maladies; or who enchant arms; or in other operations, as in the use of the divining rod, and in certain remedies against the maladies of men and horses, which having no natural proportion to these maladies do not fail to cure them, although those who use these remedies protest that they have never thought of contracting any alliance with the devil.

To reply to this question, the difficulty always recurs to know if there is between living and mortal man a proportion or natural relation, which renders him capable of contracting an alliance with the angel or the demon, by virtue of which these spirits obey him, and exert, under his empire, by virtue of the preceding compact, a power which is natural to them; for if there is nothing beyond the ordinary force of nature, either on the side of man, or on that of angels and demons, there is nothing miraculous in one or the other; neither is there in God's permitting secondary causes to act according to their natural faculties, of which He is nevertheless always the principle, and the absolute master, to limit, stop, suspend, extend, or augment them, according to His good pleasure.

But as we know not, and it seems even impossible that we should know by the light of reason, the nature and extent of the power of angels, demons, and disembodied souls, it seems that it would be rash to decide in this matter, as we derive consequences from causes by their effects, or effects by causes. For instance, to say that souls, demons, and angels have sometimes appeared to men – *then* they have naturally the faculty of returning and appearing, is a bold and rash proposition. For it is very possible that angels and demons appear only by the particular will of God, and not in consequence of his general will, and by virtue of his natural and physical concurrence with his creatures.

In the first case, these apparitions are miraculous, as being above the natural power of the agents in question; in the second case, there is nothing supernatural in them except the permission (which God rarely grants) to souls to return, to angels and demons to appear, and to produce the effects of which we have spoken.

According to these principles we may advance without temerity –

1   That angels and demons have often appeared unto men, that souls separated from the body have often returned, and that both the one and the other may do the same thing again.

2   That the manner of these apparitions, and of these returns to earth, is perfectly unknown, nor given up by God to the discussions and researches of mankind.

3   That there is some likelihood that these kinds of apparitions are not absolutely miraculous on the part of the good and evil angels, but that God allows them sometimes to take place, for reasons the knowledge of which is reserved to himself alone.

4   That no certain rule on this point can be given, nor any demonstrative argument formed, for want of knowing perfectly the nature and extent of the power of the spiritual beings in question.

5   That we should reason upon those apparitions which appear in dreams otherwise than upon those which appear when we are awake; differently also upon apparitions wearing solid bodies, speaking, walking, eating, and drinking, and those which seem like a shade, or a nebulous and aerial body.

6   Thus it would be rash to lay down principles, and raise uniform arguments, on all these things in common, every species of apparition demanding its own particular explanation.

CHAPTER 51

Way of Explaining Apparitions

There have been real apparitions in dreams; as for instance, that of the angel, who told St Joseph to carry the infant Jesus into Egypt because King Herod wished to put him to death. There are two things appertaining to this apparition worthy of note: the first is, the impression made on the mind of St Joseph that an angel appeared to him; the second is, the prediction or revelation of the ill will of Herod. Both these are above the ordinary powers of our nature, but we know not if they be above the power of angels: it is certain that it could not have been done except by the will and command of God.

There have been apparitions of a spirit, or of an angel and a demon, which show themselves clothed in an apparent body, and only as a shadow or a phantom, as that of the angel who showed himself to Manoah the father of Samson, and vanished with the smoke of the sacrifice; and of him who extricated St Peter from prison, and disappeared in the same way after having conducted him the length of a street. The bodies which these angels assumed, and which we suppose to have been only apparent and aerial, present great difficulties; for either those bodies were their own, or they were assumed or borrowed.

If those forms were their own, and we suppose, with several ancient and some new writers, that angels, demons, and even human souls have a kind of subtle, transparent, and aerial body, the difficulty lies in knowing how they can condense the transparent body, and render it visible when it was before invisible; for if it were always and naturally evident to the senses and visible, there would be another kind of continual miracle to render it invisible, and hide it from our sight; and if of its nature it is invisible, what might can render it visible? On whatever side we regard this object it seems equally miraculous, whether to make evident to the senses that which is purely spiritual, or to render invisible that which in its nature is palpable and corporeal.

The ancient fathers of the Church, who gave to angels subtle bodies of an airy nature, explained, according to their principles, more easily the predictions made by the demons, and the wonderful operations which they cause in the air, in the elements, in our bodies, and which are far beyond what the ablest and the most learned men can know, predict, and perform. They likewise conceived more easily that evil angels can cause maladies, render the air impure and contagious, that they inspire the wicked with wrong thoughts and unjust desires, that they can penetrate our thoughts and our wishes, that they foresee tempests and changes in the air, and derangements of the seasons; all which can be explained with much more facility on the hypothesis that demons have bodies composed of very fine and subtle air.

St Augustine had written that they could also discover what is passing in our mind, and at the bottom of our heart, not only by our words, but also by certain signs and movements, which escape from the most circumspect; but reflecting on what he had advanced in this passage, he retracted, and owned that he had spoken too affirmatively upon a subject but little known, and that the manner in which the evil angels penetrate our thoughts is a very hidden thing, and very difficult for men to discover and explain; thus he preferred suspending his judgment upon it, and remaining in doubt.

CHAPTER 52

The Difficulty of Explaining the Manner in which Apparitions Make their Appearance, whatever System may be Proposed on the Subject

The difficulty is much greater, if we suppose that these spirits are absolutely disengaged from any kind of matter; for how can they assemble about them a certain quantity of matter, clothe themselves with it, give it a human form, which can be discerned, is capable of acting, speaking, conversing, eating and drinking, as did the angels who appeared to Abraham, and the one who appeared to the young Tobias, and conducted him to Ragés? Is all that accomplished by the natural power of these spirits? Has God bestowed on them this power in creating them, and has He engaged Himself, by virtue of His natural laws, and by a consequence of His acting intimately and essentially on the creature, in His quality of Creator, to impress on occasion, at the will of these spirits, certain motions in the air, and in the bodies which they would move, condense, and cause to act, in the same manner proportionally that He has willed by virtue of the union of the soul with a living body, that that soul should impress on that body motions proportioned to its own will, although, naturally, there is no natural proportion between matter and spirit, and, according to the laws of physics, the one cannot act upon the other, unless the First Cause, the Creator, has chosen to subject Himself to create this movement and to produce these effects at the will of man, movements which without that would pass for superhuman, (supernatural.)

Or shall we say with some modern philosophers, that although we may have ideas of matter and thought, perhaps we shall never be capable of knowing whether a being purely material thinks or not, because it is impossible for us to discover by the contemplative powers of our own minds without revelation, whether God has not given to some collections of matter, disposed as He thinks proper, the power to perceive and to think, or whether He has joined and united to the matter thus arranged, an immaterial substance which thinks? Now in relation to our notions, it is not less easy for us to conceive that God can add to our idea of matter the faculty of thinking, since we know not in what thought consists, and to what species of substance that Almighty Being has judged proper to grant this faculty, which could exist in no created being except by virtue of the goodness and the will of the Creator.

This system certainly embraces great absurdities, and greater to my mind than those it would fain avoid. We conceive clearly that matter is divisible, and capable of motion; but we do not conceive that it is capable of thought, nor that thought can consist of a certain configuration or a certain motion of matter. And even could thought depend on an arrangement, or on a certain subtlety, or on a certain motion of matter, as soon as that arrangement should be disturbed, or the motion interrupted, or this heap of subtle matter dispersed, thought would cease to be produced, and consequently that which constitutes man, or the reasoning animal, would no longer subsist; thus all the economy of our religion, all our hopes of a future life, all our fears of eternal punishment would vanish; even the principles of our philosophy would be overthrown.

God forbid that we should wish to set bounds to the almighty power of God; but that all-powerful Being having given us as a rule of our knowledge the clearness of the ideas which we form of everything, and not being permitted to affirm that which we know but indistinctly, it follows that we ought not to assert that thought can be attributed to matter. If the thing were known to us through revelation, and taught by the authority of the Scriptures, then we might impose silence on human reason, and make captive our judgment in obedience to faith; but it is owned that the thing is not at all revealed; neither is it demonstrated, either by its cause, or by its effects. It must, then, be considered as a simple system, invented to do away certain difficulties which result from the opinion opposed to it.

If the difficulty of explaining how the soul acts upon our bodies appears so great, how can we comprehend that the soul itself should be material and extended? In the latter case will it act upon itself, and give itself the impulsion to think, or will this movement or impulsion be thought itself, or will it produce thought? Will this thinking matter think on always, or only at times; and when it has ceased to think, who will make it think anew? Will it be God, will it be itself? Can so simple an agent as the soul act upon itself, and reproduce itself in some sort by thinking, after it has ceased to think?

My reader will say that I leave him here embarrassed, and that instead of giving him any light on the subject of the apparition of spirits, I cast doubt and uncertainty on the subject. I own it; but I better like to doubt prudently, than to affirm that which I know not. And if I hold by what my religion teaches me concerning the nature of souls, angels, and demons, I shall say that being purely spiritual, it is impossible that they should appear clothed with a body except through a miracle; always supposing that God has not created them *naturally* capable of these operations, with subordination to His sovereignly powerful will, which but rarely allows them to use this faculty of showing themselves corporeally to mortals.

If sometimes angels have eaten, spoken, acted, walked, like men, it was not from any need they had to drink or eat to sustain themselves and to be able to live, but to execute the designs of God, whose will it was that they should appear to men acting, drinking, and eating, as the Angel Raphael observes – 'When I was staying with you, I was there by the will of God; I seemed to you to eat and drink, but for my part I make use of an invisible nourishment which is unknown to men.'

It is true that we know not what may be the food of angels who are substances which are purely spiritual, nor what became of that food which Raphael and the angels that Abraham entertained in his tent, took, or seemed to take, in the company of men. But there are so many other things in nature which are unknown and incomprehensible to us, that we may very well console ourselves for not knowing how it is that the apparitions of angels, demons, and disembodied souls are made to appear.

The Phantom World
VOLUME TWO

Dissertation on those Persons who Return to Earth
Bodily, the Excommunicated, the Oupires or
Vampires, Vroucolacas, etc.

Author's Preface to the second volume

Every age, every nation, every country, has its prejudices, its maladies, its customs, its inclinations, which characterise it, and which pass away, and succeed one to another; often, that which has appeared admirable at one time, becomes pitiful and ridiculous at another. We have seen that in some ages the attention of all was turned towards a certain kind of devotion, of studies, and of exercises. It is known that, for more than one century, the prevailing taste of Europe was the journey to Jerusalem. Kings, princes, nobles, bishops, ecclesiastics, monks, all pressed thither in crowds. The pilgrimages to Rome were formerly very frequent and very famous. All this is now fallen away. We have seen provinces overrun with flagellants, and now none of them remain, except in the brotherhoods of penitents, which are still found in several parts.

We have seen in more recent times, jumpers and dancers, who, every moment, jumped and danced in the streets, squares, or market places, and even in the churches. The convulsionaries of our own days seem to have revived them; posterity will be surprised at them, as we laugh at them now. Towards the end of the sixteenth and at the beginning of the seventeenth century, nothing was talked of in Lorraine but wizards and witches. For a long time we have heard nothing of them. When the philosophy of M. Descartes appeared, what a vogue it had! The ancient philosophy was despised; nothing was talked of but experiments in physics, new systems, new discoveries. Newton appears; all minds turn to him. The system of Law, bank notes, the rage of the Rue Quinquampoix, what movements did they not cause in the kingdom! A sort of convulsion had seized on the French. In this age, a new scene presents itself to our eyes, and has done for about sixty years in Hungary, Moravia, Silesia, and Poland; men, it is said, who have been dead for several months, come back to earth, talk, walk, infest villages, ill use both men and beasts, suck the blood of their near relations, destroy their health, and finally cause their death; so that people can only save themselves from their dangerous visits and their hauntings, by exhuming them, impaling them, cutting off their heads, tearing out their hearts, or burning them. These are called by the name of oupires or vampires, that is to say, leeches; and such particulars are related of them, so singular, so detailed, and attended by such probable circumstances, and such judicial information, that one can hardly refuse to credit the belief which is held in those countries, that they come out of their tombs, and produce those effects which are proclaimed of them.

Antiquity certainly neither saw nor knew anything like it. Let us read through the histories of the Hebrews, the Egyptians, the Greeks, and the Latins; nothing approaching to it will be met with.

It is true that we remark in history, though rarely, that certain persons after having been some time in their tombs and considered as dead, have returned to life. We shall see even that the ancients believed that magic could cause death, and evoke the souls of the dead. Several passages are cited, which prove that at certain times they fancied that sorcerers sucked the blood of men and children, and caused their death. In the twelfth century also, in England and Denmark, some resuscitations similar to those of Hungary were seen. But in no history do we read anything similar, so common, or so decided, as what is related to us of the vampires of Poland, Hungary, and Moravia.

Christian antiquity furnishes some instances of excommunicated persons, who have visibly come out of their tombs and left the churches, when the deacon commanded the excommunicated, and those who did not partake of the communion, to retire. For several centuries nothing like this has been seen, although it is known that the bodies of several excommunicated persons, who died while under sentence of excommunication and censure of the Church, have been buried in churches.

The belief of the modern Greeks, who will have it that the bodies of the excommunicated do not decay in their tombs or graves, is an opinion which has no foundation, either in antiquity, in good theology, or even in history. This idea seems to have been invented by the modern Greek schismatics, only to authorise and confirm them in their separation from the Church of Rome. Christian antiquity believed, on the contrary, that the incorruptibility of a body was rather a probable mark of the sanctity of the person, and a proof of the particular protection of God, extended to a body which during its lifetime had been the temple of the Holy Spirit, and of one who had retained, in justice and innocence, the mark of Christianity.

The vroucolacas of Greece and the Archipelago are revisitors of a new kind. We can hardly persuade ourselves that a nation so witty as the Greeks, could fall into so extraordinary an opinion. Ignorance or prejudice must be extreme among them, since neither an ecclesiastic nor any other writer has undertaken to undeceive them.

The fancy of those who believe that the dead eat in their graves, with a noise similar to that made by hogs, is so ridiculous, that it does not deserve to be seriously refuted. I undertake to treat here on the matter of the vampires of Hungary, Moravia, Silesia, and Poland, at the risk of being criticised, however I may discuss it; those who believe them to be true, will accuse me of rashness and presumption, for having raised a doubt on the subject, or even of having denied their existence and reality; others will blame me for having employed my time in discussing this matter, which is considered as frivolous and useless by many sensible people. Whatever may be thought of it, I shall be satisfied with myself for having sounded a question which appeared to me important in a religious point of view. For, if the return of vampires is real, it is of import to defend it, and prove it; and if it is illusory, it is of consequence to the interests of religion to undeceive those who believe in its truth, and destroy an error which may produce dangerous effects.

CHAPTER 1

The Resurrection of a Dead Person is the Work of God Only

After having treated in a separate dissertation on the matter of the apparitions of angels, demons, and disembodied souls, the connexion of the subject invites me to speak also of the ghosts and excommunicated persons, whom, it is said, the earth rejects from her bosom; of the vampires of Hungary, Silesia, Bohemia, Moravia, and Poland; and of the vroucolacas of Greece. I shall report first, what has been said and written of them; then I shall deduce some consequences, and bring forward the reasons or arguments that may be adduced for, and against, their existence and reality.

The revenants of Hungary, or vampires, which form the principal object of this dissertation, are men who have been dead a considerable time, sometimes more, sometimes less; who leave their tombs, and come and disturb the living, sucking their blood, appearing to them, making a noise at their doors and in their houses, and lastly, often causing their death. They are named vampires, or oupires, which signifies, they say, in Slavonic, a leech. The only way to be delivered from their haunting, is to disinter them, cut off their head, impale them, burn them, or pierce their heart.

Several systems have been propounded to explain the return and apparition of the vampires. Some persons have denied and rejected them as chimerical, and as an effect of the prepossession and ignorance of the people of these countries, where they are said to return.

Others have thought that these people were not really dead, but that they had been interred alive, and returned naturally out of their tombs.

Others believe that these people are truly dead, but that God, by a particular permission or command, permits or commands them to come back to earth, and resume for a time their own body; for when they are exhumed, their bodies are found entire, their blood red and fluid, and their limbs supple and pliable.

Others maintain that it is the demon who causes these revenants to appear, and by their means does all the harm he can both to men and animals.

In the supposition that vampires veritably resuscitate, we may raise an infinity of difficulties on the subject. How is this resurrection accomplished? Is it by the strength of the revenant, by the return of his soul into his body? Is it an angel, is it a demon who reanimates it? Is it by the order, or by the permission of God that he resuscitates? Is this resurrection voluntary on his part, and by his own choice? Is it for a long time, like that of the persons who were restored to life by Jesus Christ? Or that of persons resuscitated by the Prophets and Apostles? Or is it only momentary, and for a few days and a few hours, like the resurrection operated by St Stanislaus upon the lord who had sold him a field; or that spoken of in the life of St Macarius of Egypt, and of St Spiridion, who made the dead to speak, simply to bear testimony to the truth, and then left them to sleep in peace, awaiting the Last, the Judgement Day.

First, I lay it down as an undoubted principle, that the resurrection of a person really dead is effected by the power of God alone. No man can either resuscitate himself, or restore another man to life, without a visible miracle.

Jesus Christ resuscitated himself, as he had promised he would; he did it by his own power; he did it with circumstances which were all miraculous. If he had returned to life as soon as he was taken down from the cross, it might have been thought that he was not quite dead, that there was yet in him some remains of life, that he might have been revived by warming him, or by giving him cordials and something capable of bringing him back to his senses.

But he revives only on the third day. He had, as it were, been killed after his apparent death, by the opening made in his side with a lance, which pierced him to the heart, and would have put him to death, if he had not then been beyond receiving it.

When he resuscitated Lazarus, he waited until he had been four days in the tomb, and began to show corruption; which is the most certain mark that a man is really deceased, without a hope of returning to life, except by supernatural means.

The resurrection which Job so firmly expected; and that of the man who came to life on touching the body of the Prophet Elisha in his tomb; that of the child of the widow of Shunem, whom the same Elisha restored to life; that army of skeletons, whose resurrection was predicted by Ezekiel, and which in spirit he saw accomplished before his eyes, as a type and pledge of the return of the Hebrews from their captivity at Babylon; in short, all the resurrections related in the sacred books of the Old and New Testament, are manifestly miraculous effects, and attributed solely to the almighty power of God. Neither angels, nor demons, nor men, the holiest and most favoured of God, could by their own power restore to life a person really dead. They can do it by the power of God alone, who when he thinks proper so to do, is free to grant this favour to their prayers and intercession.

CHAPTER 2

On the Revival of Persons who were not Really Dead

The resuscitation of some persons who were believed to be dead, and who were not so, but simply asleep, or in a lethargy; and of those who were supposed to be dead, having been drowned, and who came to life again through the care taken of them, or by medical skill, must not pass for real resuscitations; they were not dead, or were so only in appearance.

We intend to speak in this place of another order of resuscitated persons, who had been buried sometimes for several months, or even several years; who ought to have been suffocated in their graves, had they been interred alive, and in whom are still found signs of life: the blood in a liquid state, the flesh entire, the complexion fine and florid, the limbs flexible and pliable. Those persons, who return either by night or by day, disturb the living, suck their blood, kill them, appear in their clothes, in their families, sit down to table, and do a thousand other things; then return to their graves without anyone seeing how they re-enter them. This is a kind of momentary resurrection, or revival; for whereas the other dead persons spoken of in Scripture have lived, drank, eaten and conversed with other men after their return to life, as Lazarus, the brother of Mary and Martha, and the son of the widow of Shunem, resuscitated by Elisha; these appear during a certain time, in certain places, in certain circumstances; and come no more as soon as they have been impaled, or burned, or have had their heads cut off.

If this last order of resuscitated persons were not really dead, there is nothing wonderful in their revisiting the world, except the manner in which it is done, and the circumstances by which that return is accompanied. Do these revenants simply awaken from their sleep, or do they recover themselves like those who fall down in syncope, in fainting fits, or in swoons, and who at the end of a certain time come naturally to themselves when the blood and animal spirits have resumed their natural course and motion.

But how can they come out of their graves without opening the earth, and how re-enter them again without its appearing? Have we ever seen lethargies, or swoons, or syncopes last whole years together? If people insist on these resurrections being real ones, did we ever see dead persons resuscitate themselves, and by their own power?

If they are not resuscitated by themselves, is it by the power of God that they have left their graves? What proof is there that God has anything to do with it? What is the object of these resurrections? Is it to show forth the works of God in these vampires? What glory does the Divinity derive from them? If it is not God who drags them from their graves, is it an angel? Is it a demon? Is it their own spirit? Can the soul when separated from the body re-enter it when it will, and give it new life, were it but for a quarter of an hour? Can an angel or a demon restore a dead man to life? Undoubtedly not, without the order, or at least the permission of God. This question of the natural power of angels and demons over human bodies has been examined in another place, and we have shown that neither revelation nor reason throws any certain light on the subject.

CHAPTER 3

Revival of a Man who had been Interred for Three Years, and was Resuscitated by St Stanislaus

All the lives of the saints are full of resurrections of the dead; thick volumes might be composed on the subject.

These resurrections have a manifest relation to the matter which we are here treating of, since it treats of persons who are dead, or held to be so, who appear bodily and animated to the living, and who live on after their return to life. I shall content myself with relating the history of St Stanislaus, Bishop of Cracow, who restored to life a man that had been dead for three years, attended by such singular circumstances, and in so public a manner, that the thing is beyond the severest criticism. If it is really true, it must be regarded as one of the most unheard of miracles which are related in history. They assert that the life of this saint was written either at the time of martyrdom, or a short time afterwards, by different well-informed authors; for the martyrdom of the saint, and, above all, the restoration to life of the dead man of whom we are about to speak, were seen and known by an infinite number of persons, by all the court of

King Boleslaus. And this event having taken place in Poland, where vampires are frequently met with even in our days, it concerns, for that reason, more particularly the subject we are treating.

The bishop, St Stanislaus, having bought of a gentleman, named Pierre, an estate situated on the banks of the Vistula, in the territory of Lublin, for the profit of his church at Cracow, gave the price of it to the seller, in the presence of witnesses, and with the solemnities requisite in that country, but without written deeds, for they then wrote but seldom in Poland on the occasion of sales of this kind; they contented themselves with having witnesses. Stanislaus took possession of this estate by the king's authority, and his church enjoyed it peaceably for about three years.

In the interim, Pierre, who had sold it, happened to die. The King of Poland, Boleslaus, who had conceived an implacable hatred against the holy bishop, because he had freely reproved him for his excesses, seeking occasion to cause him trouble, excited against him the three sons of Pierre, and his heirs, and told them to claim the estate which their father had sold, on pretence of its not having been paid for. He promised to support their demand, and to cause it to be restored to them. Thus these three gentlemen had the bishop cited to appear before the king, who was then at Solech, occupied in rendering justice under some tents in the country, according to the ancient custom of the land, in the general assembly of the nation. The bishop was cited before the king, and maintained that he had bought and paid for the estate in question. The day was beginning to close, and the bishop ran great risk of being condemned by the king and his counsellors. Suddenly, as if inspired by the Divine Spirit, he promised the king to bring him in three days Pierre, of whom he had bought it, and the condition was accepted mockingly, as a thing impossible to be executed.

The holy bishop repairs to Pictravin, remains in prayer, and keeps fast with his household for three days; on the third day he goes in his pontifical robes, accompanied by his clergy and a multitude of people, causes the gravestone to be raised, and makes them dig until they found the corpse of the defunct all fleshless and corrupted. The saint commands him to come forth and bear witness to the truth before the king's tribunal. He rises; they cover him with a cloak; the saint takes him by the hand, and leads him alive to the feet of the king. No one had the boldness to interrogate him; but he addressed the assembly, and declared that he had in good faith sold the estate to the prelate, and that he had received the value of it; after which he severely reprimanded his sons, who had so maliciously accused the holy bishop.

Stanislaus asked Pierre if he wished to remain alive to do penance. He thanked him, and said he would not anew expose himself to the danger of sinning. Stanislaus reconducted him to his tomb, and being arrived there, he again fell asleep in the Lord. It may be supposed that such a scene had an infinite number of witnesses, and that all Poland was quickly informed of it. The king was only the more irritated against the saint. He some time after killed him with his own hand, as he was coming from the altar, and had his body cut into seventy-two parts, that they might never more be collected together in order to pay them the worship which was due to them as the body of a martyr for the truth and for pastoral liberty.

We now come to that which is the principal subject of these researches, the vampires, or revenants, of Hungary, Moravia, and similar ones, which appear only for a little time in their natural bodies.

CHAPTER 4

Can a Man who is Really Dead Appear in his own Body?

If what is related of vampires were certainly true, the question here proposed would be frivolous and useless; they would reply to us directly: In Hungary, Moravia, and Poland, persons who were dead and interred a long time, have been seen to return, to appear, and torment men and animals, suck their blood, and cause their death.

These persons come back to earth in their own bodies; people see them, know them, exhume them, try them, impale them, cut off their heads, burn them. It is then not only possible, but very true and very real, that they appear in their own bodies.

It might be added in support of this belief, that the Scriptures themselves give instances of these apparitions: for example, at the Transfiguration of our Saviour, Elias and Moses appeared on Mount Tabor there conversing with Jesus Christ. We know that Elias is still alive. I do not cite him as an instance; but in regard to Moses, his death is not doubtful; and yet he appeared bodily talking with Jesus Christ. The dead who came out of their graves at the Resurrection of the Saviour, and who appeared to many persons in Jerusalem, had been in their sepulchres for several years; there was no doubt of their being dead; and nevertheless they appeared and bore testimony to the Resurrection of the Saviour.

When Jeremiah appeared to Judas Maccabaeus, and placed in his hand a golden sword, saying to him, 'Receive this sword as a gift from God, with which you will vanquish the enemies of my people of Israel;' it was apparently this prophet in his own person who appeared to him and made him that present, since by his mien he was recognised as the prophet Jeremiah.

I do not speak of those persons who were really restored to life by a miracle, as the son of the widow of Shunem resuscitated by Elijah; nor of the dead man who, on touching the coffin of the same prophet, rose upon his feet, and revived; nor of Lazarus, to whom Jesus Christ restored life in a way so miraculous and striking. Those persons lived, drank, ate, and conversed with mankind, after, as before their death and resurrection.

It is not of such persons that we now speak. I speak, for instance, of Pierre resuscitated by Stanislaus for a few hours; of those persons of whom I made mention in the treatise on the Apparitions of Spirits, who appeared, spoke, and revealed hidden things, and whose resurrection was but momentary, and only to manifest the power of God, in order to bear witness to truth and innocence, or to maintain the credit of the Church against obstinate heretics, as we read in various instances.

St Martin, being newly made Archbishop of Tours, conceived some suspicions against an altar which the bishops his predecessors had erected to a pretended martyr, of whom they knew neither the name nor the history, and of whom none of the priests or ministers of the chapel could give any certain account. He abstained for some time from going to this spot, which was not far from the city; but one day he repaired thither, accompanied by a few monks, and having prayed, he besought God to let him know who it was that was interred there. He then perceived on his left a hideous and dirty-looking apparition; and having commanded it to tell him who he was, the spectre declared his name, and confessed to him that he was a robber, who had been put to death for his crimes and acts of violence, and that he had nothing in common with the martyrs. Those who were present heard distinctly what he said, but saw no one. St Martin had the tomb overthrown, and cured the ignorant people of their superstitions.

The philosopher Celsus, writing against the Christians, maintained that the apparitions of Jesus Christ to his Apostles were not real, but that they were simply shadowy forms which appeared. Origen, retorting his reasoning, tells him, that the pagans give an account of various apparitions of Aesculapius and Apollo, to which they attribute the power of predicting future events. If these appearances are admitted to be real, because they are well attested, why not receive as true those of Jesus Christ, which are related by ocular witnesses, and believed by millions of persons?

He afterwards relates this history. Aristeus, who belonged to one of the first families of Proconnesus, having one day entered a shop, died there suddenly. The shopkeeper having locked the door, ran directly to inform the relations of the deceased; but as the report was instantly spread in the town, a man of Cyzica, who came from Astacia, affirmed that it could not be, because he had met Aristeus on the road from Cyzica, and had spoken to him, which he loudly maintained before all the people of Proconnesus.

Thereupon the relations arrived at the shop, with all the necessary apparatus for carrying away the body; but when they entered the house, they could not find Aristeus there, either dead or alive. Seven years after he showed himself in the very town of Proconnesus; made there those verses which are termed Arimaspean, and then disappeared for the second time. Such is the story related of him in those places.

Three hundred and forty years after that event, the same Aristeus showed himself in Metapontus, in Italy, and commanded the Metapontines to build an altar to Apollo, and afterwards to erect a statue in honour of Aristeus of Proconnesus, adding that they were the only people of Italy whom Apollo had honoured with his presence; as for himself who spoke to them, he had accompanied that god in the form of a crow; and having thus spoken, he disappeared.

The Metapontines sent to consult the oracle of Delphi concerning this apparition; the Delphic oracle told them to follow the counsel which Aristeus had given them, and it would be well for them; in fact, they did erect a statue to Apollo, which was still to be seen there in the time of Herodotus; and at the same time, another statue to Aristeus, which stood in a small plantation of laurels, in the midst of the public square of Metapontus. Celsus made no difficulty of believing all this on the word of Herodotus, though he refused credence to what the Christians taught of the miracles wrought by Jesus Christ, related in the Gospel and sealed with the blood of martyrs. Origen adds, What could providence have designed in performing for this Proconnesian the miracles we have just mentioned? What benefit could mankind derive from them? Whereas, what the Christians relate of Jesus Christ serves to confirm a doctrine which is beneficial to the human race. We must, then, either reject this story of Aristeus as fabulous, or ascribe all that is told of it to the work of the evil spirit.

CHAPTER 5

Revival or Apparition of a Girl who had been Dead some Months

Phlegon, freedman of the Emperor Hadrian, in the fragment of the book which he wrote on wonderful things, says, that at Tralla, in Asia, a certain man named Machates, an innkeeper, was acquainted with a girl named Philinium, the daughter of Demostratus and Chariton. This girl being dead, and placed in her grave, continued to come every night for six months to see her gallant. One day she was recognised by her nurse, when sitting by Machates. The nurse ran to give notice of this to Chariton, the girl's mother, who after making many difficulties, came at last to the inn; but as it was very late, and everybody gone to bed, she could not satisfy her curiosity. However, she recognised her daughter's clothes, and thought she recognised the girl herself with Machates. She returned the next morning, but having missed her way, she no longer found her daughter, who had already withdrawn. Machates related everything to her; how, since a certain time, she had come to him every night; and in proof of what he said, he opened his casket and showed her the gold ring which Philinium had given him, and the band with which she covered her bosom, and which she had left with him the preceding night.

Chariton, who could no longer doubt the truth of the circumstance, now gave way to cries and tears; but as they promised to inform her the following night, when Philinium should return, she went away home. In the evening the girl came back as usual, and Machates sent directly to let her father and mother know, for he began to fear that some other girl might have taken Philinium's clothes from the sepulchre, in order to deceive him by the illusion.

Demostratus and Chariton, on arriving, recognised their daughter and ran to embrace her; but she cried out, 'Oh, father and mother, why have you grudged me my happiness, by preventing me from remaining three days longer with this innkeeper without injury to anyone? For I did not come here without permission from the gods, that is to say, from the demon, since we cannot attribute to God, or to a good spirit, a thing like this. Your curiosity will cost you dear.' At the same time she fell down stiff and dead, and extended on the bed.

Phlegon, who had some command in the town, stayed the crowd and prevented a tumult. The next day, the people being assembled at the theatre, they agreed to go and inspect the vault in which Philinium, who had died six months before, had been laid. They found there the corpses of her family arranged in their places, but they found not the body of Philinium. There was only an iron ring which Machates had given her, with a gilded cup, which she had also received from him. Afterwards they went back to the dwelling of Machates, where the body of the girl remained lying on the ground.

They consulted a diviner, who said that she must be interred beyond the limits of the town; they must appease the Furies and the terrestrial Mercury, make solemn funeral ceremonies to the god Manes, and sacrifice to Jupiter, to Mercury, and to Mars. Phlegon adds, speaking to him to whom he was writing: 'If you think proper to inform the emperor of it, write to me, that I may send you some of those persons who were eyewitnesses of all these things.'

Here is a fact circumstantially related, and accompanied with all the marks which can make it pass for true. Nevertheless, how numerous are the difficulties it presents! Was this young girl really dead, or only sleeping? Was her resurrection effected by her own strength and will, or was it a demon who restored her to life? It appears that it cannot be doubted that it was her own body; all the circumstances noted in the recital of Phlegon persuade us of it. If she was not dead, and all she did was merely a game and a play which she performed to satisfy her passion for Machates, there is nothing in all this recital very incredible. We know what illicit love is capable of, and how far it may lead anyone who is devoured by a violent passion.

The same Phlegon says, that a Syrian soldier of the army of Antiochus, after having been killed at Thermopylae, appeared in open day in the Roman camp, where he spoke to several persons.

Haralde, or Harappe, a Dane, who caused himself to be buried at the entrance of his kitchen, appeared after his death, and was wounded by one Olaüs Pa, who left the iron of his lance in the wound. This Dane, then, appeared bodily. Was it his soul which moved his body, or a demon which made use of this corpse to disturb and frighten the living? Did he do this by his own strength, or by the permission of God? And what glory to God, what advantage to men, could accrue from these apparitions? Shall we deny all these facts, related in so circumstantial a manner by enlightened authors, who have no interest in deceiving us, nor any wish to do so?

St Augustine relates that during his abode at Milan, a young man had a suit instituted against him by a person who repeated his demand for a debt already paid by the young man's father, but the receipt for which could not be found. The ghost of the father appeared to the son, and informed him where the receipt was which occasioned him so much trouble.

St Macarius, the Egyptian, made a dead man speak who had been interred some time, in order to discover a deposit which he had received and hidden unknown to his wife. The dead man declared that the money was placed at the foot of his bed.

The same St Macarius, not being able to refute in any other way a heretic Eunomian, according to some, or Hieracitus, according to others, said to him, 'Let us go to the grave of a dead man, and ask him to inform us of the truth which you will not agree to.'

The heretic dared not present himself at the grave, but St Macarius went thither accompanied by a multitude of persons. He interrogated the dead, who replied from the depth of the tomb, that if the heretic had appeared in the crowd he should have arisen to convince him, and to bear testimony to the truth. St Macarius commanded him to fall asleep again in the Lord, till the time when Jesus Christ should awaken him in his place at the end of the world.

The ancients, who have related the same fact, vary in some of the circumstances, as is usual enough when these things are related only from memory.

St Spiridion, Bishop of Trinitontis, in Egypt, had a daughter named Irene, who lived in virginity till her death. After her decease a person came to Spiridion and asked him for a deposit which he had confided to Irene unknown to her father. They sought in every part of the house, but could find nothing. At last Spiridion went to his daughter's tomb, and, calling her by her name, asked her where the deposit was. She declared the same, and Spiridion restored it.

A holy abbot named Erricles resuscitated for a moment a man who had been killed, and of whose death they accused a monk who was perfectly innocent. The dead man did justice to the accused, and the Abbot Erricles said to him, 'Sleep in peace, till the Lord shall come at the last day to resuscitate you to all eternity.'

All these momentary resurrections may serve to explain how the revenants of Hungary come out of their graves, then return to them, after having caused themselves to be seen and felt for some time. But the difficulty will always be to know, first, if the thing be true; second, if they can resuscitate themselves; and, third, if they are really dead, or only asleep. In what way soever we regard this circumstance, it always appears equally impossible and incredible.

CHAPTER 6

A Woman Taken Alive from her Grave

We read in a new work, a story which has some connexion with this subject. A shopkeeper of the Rue St Honoré at Paris had promised his daughter to one of his friends, a shopkeeper like himself, residing also in the same street. A financier having presented himself as a husband for this young girl, was accepted instead of the young man to whom she had been promised. The marriage was accomplished, and the young bride falling ill, was looked upon as dead, enshrouded and interred. The first lover having an idea that she had fallen into a lethargy or a trance, had her taken out of the ground during the night; they brought her to herself and he espoused her. They crossed the channel, and lived quietly in England for some years. At the end of ten years they returned to Paris, where the first husband having recognised his wife in a public walk, claimed her in a court of justice; and this was the subject of a great lawsuit.

The wife and her second husband defended themselves on the ground, that death had broken the bonds of the first marriage. The first husband was even accused of having caused his wife to be too precipitately interred. The lovers foreseeing that they might be nonsuited, again withdrew to a foreign land, where they ended their days. This circumstance is so singular, that our readers will have some difficulty in giving credence to it. I only give it as it is told. It is for those who advance the fact, to guarantee and prove it.

Who can say, that in the story of Phlegon, the young Philinium was not thus placed in the vault without being dead, and that every night she came to see her lover Machates? This was much easier for her, than would have been the return of the Parisian woman, who had been enshrouded, buried, and remained covered with earth, and enveloped in linen, during a considerable time.

The other example related in the same work, is of a girl, who fell into a trance and was regarded as dead, and became enceinte during this interval, without knowing the author of her pregnancy. It was a monk, who having made himself known, asserted that his vows should be annulled, he having been forced into the sacred profession. A great lawsuit ensued upon it, of which the documents are preserved to this day. The monk obtained a dispensation from his vows, and married the young girl.

This instance may be adduced with that of Philinium, and the young woman of the Rue St Honoré. It is possible that these persons might not be dead, and consequently not restored to life.

CHAPTER 7

The Revenants or Vampires of Moravia

I have been told by the late Monsieur de Vassimont, counsellor of the Chamber of the Counts of Bar, that having been sent into Moravia by his late Royal Highness Leopold, first Duke of Lorraine, for the affairs of the Prince Charles his brother, Bishop of Olmutz and Osnaburgh, he was informed by public report, that it was common enough in that country to see men who had died some time before, present themselves in a party, and sit down to table with persons of their acquaintance without saying anything; but that nodding to one of the party, he would infallibly die some days afterwards. This fact was confirmed by several persons, and amongst others by an old curé, who said he had seen more than one instance of it.

The bishops and priests of the country consulted Rome on so extraordinary a fact; but they received no answer, because, apparently, all those things were regarded there as simple visions, or popular fancies. They afterwards bethought themselves of taking up the corpses of those who came back in that way, of burning them, or of destroying them in some other manner. Thus they delivered themselves from the importunity of these spectres, which are now much less frequently seen than before. So said that good priest.

These apparitions have given rise to a little work, entitled, *Magia Posthuma*, printed at Olmutz, in 1706, composed by Charles Ferdinand de Schertz, dedicated to Prince Charles of Lorraine, Bishop of Olmutz and Osnaburgh. The author relates, that in a certain village, a woman being just dead, who had taken all her sacraments, she was buried in the usual way in the cemetery. Four days after her decease, the inhabitants of this village heard a great noise and extraordinary uproar, and saw a spectre, which appeared sometimes in the shape of a dog, sometimes in the form of a man, not to one person only, but to several, and caused them great pain, grasping their throats, and compressing their stomachs, so as to suffocate them. It bruised almost the whole body, and reduced them to extreme weakness, so that they became pale, lean and attenuated.

The spectre attacked even animals, and some cows were found debili-
tated and half-dead. Sometimes it tied them together by their tails. These
animals gave sufficient evidence by their bellowing of the pain they
suffered. The horses seemed overcome with fatigue, perspired profusely,
principally on the back; were heated, out of breath, covered with foam, as
after a long and rough journey. These calamities lasted several months.

The author whom I have mentioned examines the affair in a lawyer-like
way, and reasons much on the fact and the law. He asks, if, supposing that
these disturbances, these noises and vexations, proceeded from that
person who is suspected of causing them, they can burn her, as is done to
other ghosts who do harm to the living. He relates several instances of
similar apparitions, and of the evils which ensued; as of a shepherd of the
village of Blow, near the town of Kadam, in Bohemia, who appeared during
some time, and called certain persons, who never failed to die within eight
days after. The peasants of Blow took up the body of this shepherd, and
fixed it in the ground with a stake which they drove through it.

This man when in that condition derided them for what they made him
suffer, and told them they were very good to give him thus a stick to defend
himself from the dogs. The same night he got up again, and by his presence
alarmed several persons, and strangled more amongst them than he had
hitherto done. Afterwards, they delivered him into the hands of the
executioner, who put him in a cart to carry him beyond the village and
there burn him. This corpse howled like a madman, and moved his feet
and hands as if alive. And when they again pierced him through with
stakes he uttered very loud cries, and a great quantity of bright vermilion
blood flowed from him. At last he was consumed, and this execution put
an end to the appearance and hauntings of this spectre.

The same has been practised in other places, where similar ghosts have
been seen; and when they have been taken out of the ground they have
appeared red, with their limbs supple and pliable, without worms or
decay; but not without great stench. The author cites divers other writers,
who attest what he says of these spectres, which still appear, he says, very
often in the mountains of Silesia and Moravia. They are seen by night and
by day; the things which once belonged to them are seen to move
themselves and change their place without being touched by anyone. The
only remedy for these apparitions is to cut off the heads and burn the
bodies of those who come back to haunt their old abodes.

At any rate they do not proceed to this without a form of justicial law.
They call for and hear the witnesses; they examine the arguments; they
look at the exhumed bodies, to see if they can find any of the usual marks
which lead them to conjecture that they are the parties who molest the
living, as the mobility and suppleness of the limbs, the fluidity of the

blood, and the flesh remaining uncorrupted. If all these marks are found, then these bodies are given up to the executioner, who burns them. It sometimes happens that the spectres appear again for three or four days after the execution. Sometimes the interment of the bodies of suspicious persons is deferred for six or seven weeks. When they do not decay, and their limbs remain as supple and pliable as when they were alive, then they burn them. It is affirmed as certain that the clothes of these persons move without anyone living touching them; and within a short time, continues our author, a spectre was seen at Olmutz, which threw stones, and gave great trouble to the inhabitants.

CHAPTER 8

Dead Persons in Hungary who Suck the Blood of the Living

About fifteen years ago, a soldier who was billeted at the house of a Haidamaque peasant, on the frontiers of Hungary, as he was one day sitting at table near his host, the master of the house saw a person he did not know come in and sit down to table also with them. The master of the house was strangely frightened at this, as were the rest of the company. The soldier knew not what to think of it, being ignorant of the matter in question. But the master of the house being dead the very next day, the soldier inquired what it meant. They told him that it was the body of the father of his host, who had been dead and buried for ten years, which had thus come to sit down next to him, and had announced and caused his death.

The soldier informed the regiment of it in the first place, and the regiment gave notice of it to the general officers, who commissioned the Count de Cabreras, captain of the regiment of Alandetti infantry, to make information concerning this circumstance. Having gone to the place, with some other officers, a surgeon and an auditor, they heard the depositions of all the people belonging to the house, who attested unanimously that the ghost was the father of the master of the house, and that all the soldier had said and reported was the exact truth, which was confirmed by all the inhabitants of the village.

In consequence of this, the corpse of this spectre was exhumed, and found to be like that of a man who has just expired, and his blood like that of a living man. The Count de Cabreras had his head cut off, and caused him to be laid again in his tomb. He also took information concerning other similar ghosts; amongst others, of a man dead more than thirty years, who had come back three times to his house at mealtime. The first time he had sucked the blood from the neck of his own brother, the second time from one of his sons, and the third from one of the servants in the house; and all three died of it instantly and on the spot. Upon this deposition the commissary had this man taken out of his grave, and finding that, like the first, his blood was in a fluid state, like that of a living person, he ordered them to run a large nail into his temple, and then to lay him again in the grave.

He caused a third to be burnt, who had been buried more than sixteen years, and had sucked the blood and caused the death of two of his sons. The commissary having made his report to the general officers, was deputed to the court of the emperor, who commanded that some officers, both of war and justice, some physicians and surgeons, and some learned men, should be sent to examine the causes of these extraordinary events. The person who related these particulars to us had heard them from the Count de Cabreras, at Fribourg in Brigau, in 1730.

CHAPTER 9

Account of a Vampire, taken from the Jewish Letters (Lettres Juives); Letter 137

We find another instance in the *Lettres Juives*, new edition, 1738, Letter 137.

> We have just had in this part of Hungary a scene of vampirism, which is duly attested by two officers of the tribunal of Belgrade, who went down to the places specified; and by an officer of the emperor's troops at Graditz, who was an ocular witness of the proceedings.
>
> In the beginning of September there died in the village of Kisilova, three leagues from Graditz, an old man who was sixty-two years of age. Three days after he had been buried, he appeared in the night to his son, and asked him for something to eat; the son having given him

something, he ate and disappeared. The next day the son recounted to his neighbours what had happened. That night the father did not appear, but the following night he showed himself, and asked for something to eat. They know not whether the son gave him anything, or not; but the next day he was found dead in his bed. On the same day, five or six persons fell suddenly ill in the village, and died one after the other in a few days.

The officer, or bailiff of the place, when informed of what had happened, sent an account of it to the tribunal of Belgrade, which despatched to the village two of these officers and an executioner, to examine into this affair. The imperial officer from whom we have this account repaired thither from Graditz, to be witness of a circumstance which he had so often heard spoken of.

They opened the graves of those who had been dead six weeks. When they came to that of the old man, they found him with his eyes open, having a fine colour, with natural respiration, nevertheless motionless as the dead; whence they concluded that he was most evidently a vampire. The executioner drove a stake into his heart; they then raised a pile and reduced the corpse to ashes. No mark of vampirism was found either on the corpse of the son, or on the others.

Thanks be to God, we are by no means credulous. We avow that all the light which science can throw on this fact discovers none of the causes of it. Nevertheless, we cannot refuse to believe that to be true which is juridically attested, and by persons of probity. We will here give a copy of what happened in 1732, and which is inserted in the *Glaneur*, No. XVIII.

CHAPTER 10

Other Instances of Ghosts – continuation of the Gleaner

In a certain canton of Hungary, named in Latin *Oppida Heidanum*, beyond the Tibisk, *vulgo* Teiss, that is to say, between that river which waters the fortunate territory of Tokay and Transylvania, the people known by the name of *Heyducqs* believe that certain dead persons, whom they call vampires, suck all the blood from the living, so that these become visibly attenuated, whilst the corpses, like leeches, fill themselves with blood in such abundance that it is seen to come from them by the conduits, and even oozing through the pores. This opinion has just been confirmed by several facts which cannot be doubted, from the rank of the witnesses who have certified them. We will here relate some of the most remarkable.

About five years ago, a certain Heyducq, inhabitant of Madreiga, named Arnald Paul, was crushed to death by the fall of a wagonload of hay. Thirty days after his death four persons died suddenly, and in the same manner in which, according to the tradition of the country, those die who are molested by vampires. They then remembered that this Arnald Paul had often related that in the environs of Cassovia, and on the frontiers of Turkish Servia, he had often been tormented by a Turkish vampire; for they believe also that those who have been passive vampires during life become active ones after their death, that is to say, that those who have been sucked, suck also in their turn; but that he had found means to cure himself by eating earth from the grave of the vampire, and smearing himself with his blood; a precaution which, however, did not prevent him from becoming so after his death, since, on being exhumed forty days after his interment, they found on his corpse all the indications of an arch-vampire. His body was red, his hair, nails, and beard had all grown again, and his veins were replete with fluid blood, which flowed from all parts of his body upon the winding-sheet which encompassed him. The Hadnagi, or bailli of the village, in whose presence the exhumation took place, and who was skilled in vampirism, had, according to custom, a very sharp stake driven into the heart of the defunct Arnald Paul, and which pierced his body through and through, which made him, as they say, utter a frightful shriek, as if he had been alive: that done, they cut off his head, and burnt the whole body. After that they performed the same on the corpses of the four other persons who died of vampirism, fearing that they in their turn might cause the death of others.

All these performances, however, could not prevent the recommencement of similar fatal prodigies towards the end of last year, (1732) that is to say, five years after, when several inhabitants of the same village perished miserably. In the space of three months seventeen persons of different sexes and different ages died of vampirism; some without being ill, and others after languishing two or three days. It is reported, amongst other things, that a girl named Stanoska, daughter of the Heyducq Jotiützo, who went to bed in perfect health, awoke in the middle of the night all in a tremble, uttering terrible shrieks, and saying that the son of the Heyducq Millo, who had been dead nine weeks, had nearly strangled her in her sleep. She fell into a languid state from that moment, and at the end of three days she died. What this girl had said of Millo's son made him known at once for a vampire: he was exhumed, and found to be such. The principal people of the place, with the doctors and surgeons, examined how vampirism could have sprung up again after the precautions they had taken some years before.

They discovered at last, after much search, that the defunct Arnald Paul had killed not only the four persons of whom we have spoken, but also several oxen, of which the new vampires had eaten, and amongst others the son of Millo. Upon these indications they resolved to disinter all those who had died within a certain time. Amongst forty, seventeen were found with all the most evident signs of vampirism; so they transfixed their hearts and cut off their heads also, and then cast their ashes into the river.

All the informations and executions we have just mentioned were made juridically, in proper form, and attested by several officers who were garrisoned in the country, by the chief surgeons of the regiments, and by the principal inhabitants of the place. The verbal process of it was sent towards the end of last January to the Imperial Council of War at Vienna, which had established a military commission to examine into the truth of all these circumstances.

Such was the declaration of the Hadnagi Barriarar and the ancient Heyducqs, and it was signed by Battuer, first lieutenant of the regiment of Alexander of Wurtemburg, Clickstenger, surgeon-in-chief of the regiment of Frustemburch, three other surgeons of the company, and Guoichitz, captain at Stallach.

CHAPTER 11

Arguments of the Author of the Lettres Juives, *on the Subject of these Pretended Ghosts*

There are two different ways of effacing the opinion concerning these pretended ghosts, and showing the impossibility of the effects which are made to be produced by corpses entirely deprived of sensation. The first is, to explain by physical causes all the prodigies of vampirism; the second is, to deny totally the truth of these stories; and the latter means, without doubt, is the surest and the wisest. But as there are persons to whom the authority of a certificate given by people in a certain place appears a plain demonstration of the reality of the most absurd story, before I show how little they ought to rely on the formalities of the law in matters which relate solely to philosophy, I will for a moment suppose that several persons do really die of the disease which they term vampirism.

I lay down at first this principle, that it may be that there are corpses which, although interred some days, shed fluid blood through the pores of their body. I add moreover, that it is very easy for certain people to fancy themselves sucked by vampires, and that the fear caused by that fancy should make a revolution in their frame sufficiently violent to deprive them of life. Being occupied all day with the terror inspired by these pretended ghosts or revenants, is it very extraordinary, that during their sleep the idea of these phantoms should present itself to their imagination, and cause them such violent terror, that some of them die of it instantaneously, and others a short time afterwards? How many instances have we not seen of people who expired with fright in a moment; and has not joy itself sometimes produced an equally fatal effect?

I have seen in the Leipsic journals an account of a little work entitled, *Philosophicoeet Christianoe Cogitationes de Vampiriis,* à Joanne Christophoro Herenbergio; (*Philosophical and Christian Thoughts upon Vampires*, by John Christopher Herenberg) at Gerolferliste, in 1733, in 8vo. The author names a large number of writers who have already discussed this matter; he speaks, en passant, of a spectre which appeared to him at noonday. He maintains that the vampires do not cause the death of the living, and that all that is said about them ought to be attributed only to the troubled fancy of the invalids; he proves by divers experiments that the imagination is capable of causing very great derangements in the body and its humours; he shows that in Slavonia they impaled murderers, and drove a stake through the heart of the culprit; that they used the same chastisement for vampires, supposing them to be the authors of the death of those whose blood they were said to suck. He gives some examples of this punishment exercised upon them, the one in the year 1337, and the other in 1347. He speaks of the opinion of those who believe that the dead eat in their tombs; a sentiment of which he endeavours to prove the antiquity by the authority of Tertullian, at the beginning of his book on the Resurrection, and by that of St Augustine, Bk viii, ch. 27, on the City of God, and in Sermon xv on the Saints.

Such are nearly the contents of the work of M. Herenberg on vampires. The passage of Tertullian which he cites, proves very well that the pagans offered food to their dead, even to those whose bodies had been burned, believing that their spirits regaled themselves with it: *Defunctis et quidem impensissimo studio, pro moribus eorum pro temporibus esculentorum, ut quos sentire quicquam negant escam desiderare proesumant.* This concerns only the pagans.

But St Augustine, in several places, speaks of the custom of the Christians, above all those of Africa, of carrying to the tombs meats and wine, which they placed upon them as a repast of devotion, and to which the poor were invited, in whose favour these offerings were principally instituted. This practice is founded on the passage of the book of Tobit: 'Place your bread and wine on the sepulchre of the just, and be careful not to eat or drink of it with sinners.' St Monica, the mother of St Augustine, having desired to do at Milan what she had been accustomed to do in Africa, St Ambrose, Bishop of Milan, testified that he did not approve of this practice, which was unknown in his Church. The holy woman restrained herself to carrying thither a basket full of fruits and wine, of which she partook very soberly with the women who accompanied her, leaving the rest for the poor. St Augustine remarks, in the same passage, that some intemperate Christians abused these offerings by drinking wine to excess: *Ne ulla occasio se ingurgitandi daretur ebriosis.*

St Augustine, however, by his preaching and remonstrances, did so much good, that he entirely uprooted this custom, which was common throughout the African Church, and the abuse of which was too general. In his books on the City of God, he avows that this usage is neither general nor approved in the Church, and that those who practise it content themselves with offering this food upon the tombs of the martyrs, in order that through their merits these offerings should be sanctified; after which they carry them away, and make use of them for their own nourishment and that of the poor: *Quicumque suas epulas eò deferant, quod quidem à melioribus Christianis non fit, et in plerisque terrarum nulla talis est consuetudo; tamen quicumque id faciunt, quas cùm apposuerint, orant, et auferunt, ut vescantur vel ex eis etiam indigentibus largiantur.* It appears, from two sermons which have been attributed to St Augustine, that in former times this custom had crept in at Rome, but did not long subsist there, and was blamed and condemned.

Now, if it were true that the dead could eat in their tombs, and that they had a wish or occasion to eat, as is believed by those of whom Tertullian speaks, and as it appears may be inferred from the custom of carrying fruit and wine to be placed on the graves of martyrs and other Christians, I have good proof, that in certain places they spread near the bodies of the dead, whether buried in the cemeteries or the churches, meat, wine, and other liquors. I have in my study several vases of clay and glass, and even plates, where may be seen small bones of pig and fowls, all found deep underground in the church of the Abbey of St Mansuy, near the town of Toul.

It has been remarked to me that these vestiges found in the ground were plunged in virgin earth which had never been disturbed, and near certain vases or urns filled with ashes, and containing some small bones which the flames could not consume; and as it is known that the Christians did not burn their dead, and that these vases we are speaking of are placed beneath the disturbed earth, in which the graves of Christians are found, it has been inferred, with much semblance of probability, that these vases, with the food and beverage buried near them, were intended, not for Christians, but for heathens. The latter, then, at least, believed that the dead ate in the other life. There is no doubt that the ancient Gauls were persuaded of this; they are often represented on their tombs with bottles in their hands, and baskets, or drinking vessels and goblets; they carried with them even the contracts and bonds for what was due to them, to have it paid to them in Hades. *Negotiorum ratio, etiam exactio crediti deferebatur ad inferos.*

Now, if they believed that the dead ate in their tombs, that they could return to earth, visit, console, instruct, or disturb the living, and predict to them their approaching death, the return of vampires is neither impossible nor incredible in the opinion of these ancients.

But as all that is said of dead men who eat in their graves and out of their graves is chimerical, and beyond all likelihood, and the thing is even impossible and incredible, whatever may be the number and quality of those who have believed it, or appeared to believe it, I shall always say, that the return to earth of the vampires is unmaintainable and impracticable.

CHAPTER 12

Continuation of the Argument of the Dutch Gleaner, *or* Glaneur Hollandais

On examining the narrative of the death of the pretended martyrs of vampirism, I discover the symptoms of an epidemical fanaticism; and I see clearly that the impression made upon them by fear is the true cause of their death. A girl named Stanoska, say they, daughter of the Heyducq Sovitzo, who went to bed in perfect health, awoke in the middle of the night, all trembling, and shrieking dreadfully, saying that the son of the Heyducq Millo, who had been dead for nine weeks, had nearly strangled her in her sleep. From that moment she fell into a languishing state, and at the end of three days died.

For anyone who has eyes, however little philosophical they may be, must not this recital alone clearly show him that this pretended vampirism is merely the result of a stricken imagination? A girl awakes and says that someone wanted to strangle her, and whose blood nevertheless has not been sucked, since her cries have prevented the vampire from making his repast. She apparently was not so served afterwards either, since, doubtlessly, they did not leave her by herself during the other nights; and if the vampire had wished to molest her, her moans would have warned those of it who were present. Nevertheless, she dies three days afterwards. Her fright and depression, her sadness and languor, evidently show how strongly her imagination had been affected.

Those persons who find themselves in cities afflicted with the plague, know by experience how many people lose their lives through fear. As soon as a man finds himself attacked with the least illness, he fancies that he is seized with the epidemic disease, which idea occasions him so great a sensation, that it is almost impossible for the system to resist such a revolution. The Chevalier de Maifin assured me, when I was at Paris, that being at Marseilles during the contagion which prevailed in that city, he had seen a woman die of the fear she felt at a slight illness of her servant, whom she believed attacked with the pestilence. This woman's daughter was sick and near dying.

Other persons who were in the same house went to bed, sent for a doctor, and assured him they had the plague. The doctor, on arriving, visited the servant, and the other patients, and none of them had the epidemic disorder. He tried to calm their minds, and ordered them to rise, and live in their usual way; but his care was useless as regarded the mistress of the family, who died in two days of the fright alone.

Reflect upon the second narrative of the death of a passive vampire, and you will see most evident proofs of the terrible effects of fear and prejudice. (See the preceding Chapter.) This man, three days after he was buried, appears in the night to his son, asks for something to eat, eats, and disappears. On the morrow, the son relates to his neighbours what had happened to him. That night the father does not appear; but the following night they find the son dead in his bed. Who cannot perceive in these words the surest marks of prepossession and fear? The first time these act upon the imagination of the pretended victim of vampirism they do not produce their entire effect, and only dispose his mind to be more vividly struck by them; that also does not fail to happen, and to produce the effect which would naturally follow.

Notice well that the dead man did not return on the night of the day that his son communicated his dream to his friends, because, according to all appearances, these sat up with him, and prevented him from yielding to his fear.

I now come to those corpses full of fluid blood, and whose beard, hair and nails had grown again. One may dispute three parts of these prodigies, and be very complaisant if we admit the truth of a few of them. All philosophers know well enough how much the people, and even certain historians, enlarge upon things which appear but a little extraordinary. Nevertheless, it is not impossible to explain their cause physically.

Experience teaches us that there are certain kinds of earth which will preserve dead bodies perfectly fresh. The reasons of this have been often explained, without my giving myself the trouble to make a particular recital of them. There is at Toulouse a vault in a church belonging to some monks, where the bodies remain so entirely perfect that there are some which have been there nearly two centuries, and appear still living.

They have been ranged in an upright posture against the wall, and are clothed in the dress they usually wore. What is very remarkable is, that the bodies which are placed on the other side of this same vault become in two or three days the food of worms.

As to the growth of the nails, the hair and the beard, it is often perceived in many corpses. While there yet remains a great deal of moisture in the body, it is not surprising that during some time we see some augmentation in those parts which do not demand a vital spirit.

The fluid blood flowing through the canals of the body seems to form a greater difficulty; but physical reasons may be given for this. It might very well happen that the heat of the sun warming the nitrous and sulphureous particles which are found in those earths that are proper for preserving the body, those particles having incorporated themselves in the newly interred corpses, ferment, decoagulate, and melt the curdled blood, render it liquid, and give it the power of flowing by degrees through all the channels.

This opinion appears so much the more probable from its being confirmed by an experiment. If you boil in a glass or earthen vessel one part of chyle, or milk, mixed with two parts of cream of tartar, the liquor will turn from white to red, because the tartaric salt will have rarified and entirely dissolved the most oily part of the milk, and converted it into a kind of blood. That which is formed in the vessels of the body is a little redder, but it is not thicker; it is, then, not impossible that the heat may cause a fermentation which produces nearly the same effects as this experiment. And this will be found easier, if we consider that the juices of the flesh and bones resemble chyle very much, and that the fat and marrow are the most oily parts of the chyle. Now all these particles in fermenting must, by the rule of the experiment, be changed into a kind of blood. Thus, besides that which has been decoagulated and melted, the pretended vampires shed also that blood which must be formed from the melting of the fat and marrow.

CHAPTER 13

Narration Extracted from the Mercure Galent of 1693 and 1694, concerning Ghosts

The public memorials of the years 1693 and 1694 speak of *oupires*, vampires or ghosts, which are seen in Poland, and above all in Russia. They make their appearance from noon to midnight, and come and suck the blood of living men or animals in such abundance that sometimes it flows from them at the nose, and principally at the ears, and sometimes the corpse swims in its own blood oozed out in its coffin. It is said that the vampire has a sort of hunger, which makes him eat the linen which envelops him. This reviving being, or *oupire*, comes out of his grave, or a demon in his likeness, goes by night to embrace and hug violently his near relations or his friends, and sucks their blood so much as to weaken and attenuate them, and at last cause their death. This persecution does not stop at one single person; it extends to the last person of the family, if the course be not interrupted by cutting off the head or opening the heart of the ghost, whose corpse is found in his coffin, yielding, flexible, swollen, and rubicund, although he may have been dead some time. There proceeds from his body a great quantity of blood, which some mix up with flour to make bread of; and that bread eaten in the usual manner protects them from being tormented by the spirit, which returns no more.

CHAPTER 14

Conjectures of the Glaneur de Hollande, (Dutch Gleaner) *in 1733, No.* IX

The *Dutch Gleaner*, who is by no means credulous, supposes the truth of these facts as certain, having no good reason for disputing them, and reasons upon them in a way which shows he thinks lightly of the matter; he asserts that the people, amongst whom vampires are seen, are very ignorant and very credulous, so that the apparitions we are speaking of are only the effects of a prejudiced fancy. The whole is occasioned and augmented by the bad nourishment of these people, who, the greater part of their time, eat only bread made of oats, roots, and the bark of trees – aliments which can only engender gross blood, which is consequently much disposed to corruption, and produces dark and bad ideas in the imagination.

He compares this disease to the bite of a mad dog, which communicates its venom to the person who is bitten; thus, those who are infected by vampirism communicate this dangerous poison to those with whom they associate. Thence the wakefulness, dreams, and pretended apparitions of vampires.

He conjectures that this poison is nothing else than a worm, which feeds upon the purest substance of man, constantly gnaws his heart, makes the body die away, and does not forsake it even in the depth of the grave. It is certain that the bodies of those who have been poisoned, or who die of contagion, do not become stiff after their death, because the blood does not congeal in the veins; on the contrary, it rarifies and bubbles much the same as in vampires, whose beard, hair and nails grow, whose skin is rosy, who appear to have grown fat, on account of the blood which swells and abounds in them everywhere.

As to the cry uttered by the vampires when the stake is driven through their heart, nothing is more natural; the air which is there confined, and thus expelled with violence, necessarily produces that noise in passing through the throat. Dead bodies often do as much without being touched. He concludes that it is only an imagination that is deranged by melancholy or superstition, which can fancy that the malady we have just spoken of can be produced by vampire corpses, which come and suck away, even to the last drop, all the blood in their body.

A little before he says, that in 1732 they discovered again some vampires in Hungary, Moravia, and Turkish Serbia; that this phenomenon is too well averred for it to be doubted; that several German physicians have composed pretty thick volumes in Latin and German on this matter; that the Germanic Academies and Universities still resound with the names of Arnold Paul, of Stanoska, daughter of Sovitzo, and of the Heyducq Millo, all famous vampires of the quarter of Médreiga, in Hungary.

Here is a letter which has been written to one of my friends, to be communicated to me; it is on the subject of the ghosts of Hungary; the writer thinks very differently from the Gleaner on the subject of vampires.

In reply to the questions of the Abbé dom Calmet, concerning vampires, the undersigned has the honour to assure him that nothing is more true or more certain than what he will doubtless have read about it in the deeds or attestations which have been made public, and printed in all the Gazettes in Europe. But amongst all these public attestations which have appeared, the Abbé must fix his attention as a true and notorious fact on that of the deputation from Belgrade, ordered by his late Majesty Charles VI, of glorious memory, and executed by His Serene Highness the late Duke Charles Alexander of Wirtemberg, then viceroy or governor of the kingdom of Serbia; but I cannot at present cite the year or the day, for want of papers which I have not now by me.

That prince sent off a deputation from Belgrade, half consisting of military officers and half of civil, with the auditor-general of the kingdom, to go to a village where a famous vampire, several years deceased, was making great havoc amongst his kin; for note well, that it is only in their family and amongst their own relations that these bloodsuckers delight in destroying our species. This deputation was composed of persons well known for their morality and even their information, of irreproachable character, and there were even some learned men amongst the two orders; they were put to the oath, and accompanied by a lieutenant of the grenadiers of the regiment of Prince Alexander of Wirtemberg, and by twenty-four grenadiers of the said regiment.

All that were most respectable, and the Duke himself, who was then at Belgrade, joined this deputation, in order to be eyewitnesses of the veracious proof about to be made.

When they arrived at the place, they found that in the space of a fortnight the vampire, uncle of five persons, nephews and nieces, had already dispatched three of them and one of his own brothers. He had begun with his fifth victim, the beautiful young daughter of his niece, and had already sucked her twice, when a stop was put to this sad tragedy by the following operations.

They repaired with the deputed commissaries to a village not far from Belgrade, and that publicly, at nightfall, and went to the vampire's grave. The gentleman could not tell me the time when those who had died had been sucked, nor the particulars of the subject. The persons whose blood had been sucked found themselves in a pitiable state of languor, weakness, and lassitude, so violent is the torment. He had been interred three years, and they saw on his grave a light resembling that of a lamp, but not so bright.

They opened the grave, and found there a man as whole and apparently as sound as any of us who were present; his hair, and the hairs on his body, the nails, teeth, and eyes as firmly fast as they now are in ourselves who exist, and his heart palpitating.

'Next they proceeded to draw him out of his grave, the body in truth not being flexible, but wanting neither flesh nor bone. Then they pierced his heart with a sort of round, pointed, iron lance; there came out a whitish and fluid matter mixed with blood, but the blood prevailing more than the matter, and all without any bad smell. After that they cut off his head with a hatchet, like what is used in England at executions; there came out also a matter and blood like what I have just described, but more abundantly in proportion to what had flowed from the heart.

And after all this they threw him back again into his grave, with quick-lime to consume him promptly; and thenceforth his niece, who had been twice sucked, grew better. At the place where these persons are sucked a very blue spot is formed; the part whence the blood is drawn is not determinate, sometimes it is in one place and sometimes in another. It is a notorious fact, attested by the most authentic documents, and passed or executed in sight of more than 1,300 persons, all worthy of belief.

But I reserve, to satisfy more fully the curiosity of the learned Abbé dom Calmet, the pleasure of detailing to him more at length what I have seen with my own eyes on this subject, and will give it to the Chevalier de St Urbain to send to him; too glad in that, as in everything else, to find an occasion of proving to him that no one is with such perfect veneration and respect his very humble, and very obedient servant, L. de Beloz, ci-devant Captain in the regiment of His Serene Highness the late Prince Alexander of Wirtemberg, and his Aide-de-Camp, and at this time first Captain of grenadiers in the regiment of Monsieur the Baron Trenck.

CHAPTER 15

Another Letter on Ghosts

In order to omit nothing which can throw light on this matter, I shall insert here the letter of a very honest man, who is well informed respecting ghosts. This letter was written to a relation.

> You wish, my dear cousin, to be exactly informed of what takes place in Hungary, concerning ghosts who cause the death of many people in that country. I can write to you learnedly upon it, for I have been several years in those quarters, and I am naturally curious. I have heard in my lifetime an infinite number of stories, true, or pretended to be such, concerning spirits and sorceries, but out of a thousand I have hardly believed a single one. We cannot be too circumspect on this point, from the danger of being duped. Nevertheless, there are certain facts so well attested that one cannot help believing them. As to the ghosts of Hungary, the thing takes place in this manner: A person finds himself attacked with languor, loses his appetite, grows visibly thinner, and, at the end of eight or ten days, sometimes a fortnight, dies, without fever, or any other symptom than thinness and drying up of the blood.
>
> They say in that country that it is a ghost which attaches itself to such a person and sucks his blood. Of those who are attacked by this malady the greater part think they see a white spectre, which follows them everywhere as the shadow follows the body. When we were quartered among the Walachians, in the ban of Temeswar, two horsemen of the company in which I was cornet died of this malady, and several others, who also were attacked by it, would have died in the same manner, if a corporal of our company had not put a stop to the disorder, by employing the remedy used by the people of the country in such case. It is very remarkable, and although infallible, I never read it in any ritual. This is it:
>
>> They choose a boy young enough to be certain that he is innocent of any impurity; they place him on an unmutilated horse, which has never stumbled, and is absolutely black. They make him ride about the cemetery and pass over all the graves; that over which the animal

refuses to pass, in spite of repeated blows from a switch that is delivered to his rider, is reputed to be filled by a vampire. They open this grave, and find therein a corpse as fat and handsome as if he were a man happily and quietly sleeping. They cut the throat of this corpse with the stroke of a spade, and there flows forth the finest vermilion blood in a great quantity. One might swear that it was a healthy living man whose throat they were cutting. That done, they fill up the grave, and we may reckon that the malady will cease, and that all those who had been attacked by it will recover their strength by degrees, like people recovering from a long illness, and who have been greatly extenuated. That happened precisely to our horsemen who had been seized with it. I was then commandant of the company, my captain and my lieutenant being absent. I was piqued at that corporal's having made the experiment without me, and I had all the trouble in the world to resist the inclination I felt to give him a severe caning – a merchandise which is very cheap in the emperor's troops. I would have given the world to be present at this operation; but I was obliged to make myself contented as it was.

A relation of this same officer has written me word, the 17th October 1746, that his brother, who has served during twenty years in Hungary, and has very curiously examined into everything which is said there concerning ghosts, acknowledges that the people of that country are more credulous and more superstitious than other nations, and they attribute the maladies which happen to them to spells. That as soon as they suspect a dead person of having sent them this illness, they inform the magistrate of it, who, on the deposition of some witnesses, causes the dead body to be exhumed. They cut off the head with a spade, and if a drop of blood comes from it, they conclude that it is the blood which he has sucked from the sick person. But the person who writes to me appears very far from believing what is thought of these things in that country.

At Warsaw, a priest having ordered a saddler to make him a bridle for his horse, died before the bridle was made, and as he was one of those whom they call vampires in Poland, he came out of his grave dressed as the ecclesiastics usually are when inhumed, took his horse from the stable, mounted it, and went in the sight of all Warsaw to the saddler's shop, where at first he found only the saddler's wife, who was frightened, and called her husband; he came, and the priest having asked for his bridle, he replied, 'But you are dead, M. Curé.' To which he answered, 'I am going to show you I am not;' and at the same time struck him so hard that the poor saddler died a few days after, and the priest returned to his grave.

The steward of Count Simon Labienski, starost of Posnania, being dead, the Countess Dowager de Labienski wished, from gratitude for his services, to have him inhumed in the vault of the lords of that family. This was done; and some time after, the sexton, who had the care of the vault, perceived that there was some derangement in the place, and gave notice of it to the Countess, who desired, according to the received custom in Poland, that the steward's head might be cut off, which was done in the presence of several persons, and amongst others of the Sieur Jouvinski, a Polish officer, and governor of the young Count Simon Labienski, who saw that when the sexton took this corpse out of his tomb to cut off his head, he ground his teeth, and the blood came from him as fluidly as that of a person who died a violent death, which caused the hair of all those who were present to stand on end; and they dipped a white pocket handker-chief in the blood of this corpse, and made all the family drink some of the blood, that they might not be tormented.

<h2 style="text-align:center">CHAPTER 16</h2>

<h1 style="text-align:center">*Pretended Vestiges of Vampirism in Antiquity*</h1>

Some learned men have thought they discovered some vestiges of vampirism in the remotest antiquity; but all that they say of it does not come near what is related of the vampires. The lamiae, the strigae, the sorcerers whom they accused of sucking the blood of living persons, and of thus causing their death, the magicians who were said to cause the death of newborn children by charms and malignant spells, are nothing less than what we understand by the name of vampires; even were it to be owned that these lamiae and strigae have really existed, which we do not believe can ever be well proved.

I own that these terms are found in the versions of Holy Scripture. For instance, Isaiah, describing the condition to which Babylon was to be reduced after her ruin, says that she shall become the abode of satyrs, lamiae, and strigae (in Hebrew, *lilith*). This last term, according to the Hebrews, signifies the same thing as the Greeks express by *strix* and *lamioe*, which are sorceresses or magicians, who seek to put to death new-born children. Whence it comes that the Jews are accustomed to write in the four corners of the chamber of a woman just delivered, 'Adam, Eve, begone from hence *lilith*.'

The ancient Greeks knew these dangerous sorceresses by the name of *lamioe*, and they believed that they devoured children, or sucked away all their blood till they died.

The Seventy, in Isaiah, translate the Hebrew *lilith* by *lamia*. Euripides and the Scholiast of Aristophanes also make mention of it as a deadly monster, the enemy of mortals. Ovid, speaking of the strigae, describes them as dangerous birds, which fly by night, and seek for infants, to devour them and nourish themselves with their blood.

These prejudices had taken such deep root in the minds of the barbarous people, that they put to death persons suspected of being strigae, or sorceresses, and of eating people alive. Charlemagne, in his Capitularies, which he composed for his new subjects, the Saxons, condemns to death those who shall believe that a man or a woman are sorcerers (striges esse) and eat living men. He condemns in the same manner those who shall have them burnt, or give their flesh to be eaten, or shall eat of it themselves.

Wherein it may be remarked, first of all, that they believed there were people who ate men alive; that they killed and burnt them; that sometimes their flesh was eaten, as we have seen that in Russia they eat bread kneaded with the blood of vampires; and that formerly their corpses were exposed to wild beasts, as is still done in countries where these ghosts are found, after having impaled them, or cut off their head.

The laws of the Lombards, in the same way, forbid that the servant of another person should be put to death as a witch, *strix*, or *masca*. This last word, *masca*, whence *mask*, has the same signification as the Latin *larva*, a spirit, a phantom, a spectre.

We may class in the number of ghosts the one spoken of in the Chronicle of Sigebert, in the year 858.

Theodore de Gaza had a little farm in Campania, which he had cultivated by a labourer. As he was busy digging up the ground, he discovered a round vase, in which were the ashes of a dead man; directly, a spectre appeared to him, who commanded him to put this vase back again in the ground, with what it contained, or if he did not do so he would kill his eldest son. The labourer gave no heed to these threats, and in a few days his eldest son was found dead in his bed. A little time after, the same spectre appeared to him again, reiterating the same order, and threatening to kill his second son. The labourer gave notice of all this to his master, Theodore de Gaza, who came himself to his farm, and had everything put back into its place. This spectre was apparently a demon, or the spirit of a pagan interred in that spot.

Michael Glycas relates that the emperor Basilius, having lost his beloved son, obtained by means of a black monk of Santabaren, power to behold his said son, who had died a little while before; he saw him and held him embraced a pretty long time, until he vanished away in his arms. It was, then, only a phantom which appeared in his son's form.

In the diocese of Mayence, there was a spirit that year which made itself manifest first of all by throwing stones; striking against the walls of a house, as if with strong blows of a mallet; then talking, and revealing unknown things – the authors of certain thefts, and other things fit to spread the spirit of discord among the neighbours. At last he directed his fury against one person in particular, whom he liked to persecute and render odious to all the neighbourhood, proclaiming that he it was who excited the wrath of God against all the village. He pursued him in every place, without giving him the least moment of relaxation. He burnt all his harvest collected in his house, and set fire to all the places he entered.

The priests exorcised, said their prayers, dashed holy water about. The spirit threw stones at them, and wounded several persons. After the priests had withdrawn, they heard him bemoaning himself, and saying that he had hidden himself under the hood of a priest, whom he named, and accused of having seduced the daughter of a lawyer of the place. He continued these troublesome hauntings for three years, and did not leave off till he had burnt all the houses in the village.

Here follows an instance which bears connexion with what is related of the ghosts of Hungary, who come to announce the death of their near relations. Evodius, Bishop of Upsala, in Africa, writes to St Augustine, in 415, that a young man whom he had with him, as a writer, or secretary, and who led a life of rare innocence and purity, having just died at the age of twenty-two, a virtuous widow saw in a dream a certain deacon who, with other servants of God, of both sexes, were ornamenting a palace which seemed to shine as if it were of silver. She asked who they were preparing it for, and they told her it was for a young man who died the day before. She afterwards beheld in the same palace an old man, clad in white, who commanded two persons to take this young man out of his tomb and lead him to heaven.

In the same house where this young man died, an aged man, half-asleep, saw a man with a branch of laurel in his hand, upon which something was written.

Three days after the death of the young man, his father, who was a priest, named Armenius, having retired to a monastery, to console himself with the saintly old man, Theasus, Bishop of Manblosa, the deceased son appeared to a monk of this monastery, and told him that God had received him among the blessed, and that he had sent him to fetch his father. In effect, four days after, his father had a slight degree of fever, but it was so slight that the physician assured him there was nothing to fear. He nevertheless took to his bed, and at the same time, as he was yet speaking, he expired.

It was not of fright that he died, for it does not appear that he knew anything of what the monk had seen in his dream.

The same bishop, Evodius, relates that several persons had been seen after their death to go and come in their houses as during their lifetime, either in the night, or even in open day. 'They say also,' adds Evodius, 'that in the places where bodies are interred, and especially in the churches, they often hear a noise at a certain hour of the night, like persons praying aloud. I remember,' continues Evodius, 'having heard it said by several, and, amongst others, by a holy priest, who was witness to these apparitions, that they had seen coming out of the baptistry a great number of these spirits, with shining bodies of light, and had afterwards heard them pray in the middle of the church.' The same Evodius says, moreover, that Profuturus, Privus and Servilius, who had lived very piously in the monastery, had talked with himself since their death, and what they had told him had come to pass.

St Augustine, after having related what Evodius said, acknowledges that a great distinction is to be made between true and false visions, and testifies that he could wish to have some sure means of justly discerning between them.

But who shall give us the knowledge necessary for such discerning, so difficult and yet so requisite, since we have not even any certain and demonstrative marks by which to discern infallibly between true and false miracles, or to distinguish the works of the Almighty from the illusions of the angel of darkness?

CHAPTER 17

Of Ghosts in the Northern Countries

Thomas Bartholin, the son, in his treatise entitled, 'Of the Causes of the Contempt of Death felt by the Ancient Danes while yet Gentiles,' remarks, that a certain Hordus, an Icelander, saw spectres with his bodily eyes, fought against them, and resisted them. These people thoroughly believed, that the spirits of the dead came back with their bodies, which they afterwards forsook and returned to their graves. Bartholinus relates in particular, that a man named Asmond, son of Alfus, having had himself buried alive in the same sepulchre with his friend Asvitus, and having had victuals brought there, was taken out from thence some time after covered with blood, in consequence of a combat he had been obliged to maintain against Asvitus, who had haunted him and cruelly assaulted him.

He reports after that what the poets teach concerning the evocation of spirits by the power of magic, and of their return into bodies which are not decayed, although a long time dead. He shows that the Jews have believed the same – that the souls came back from time to time to revisit their dead bodies during the first year after their decease. He demonstrates that the ancient Northern nations were persuaded that persons recently deceased often made their bodily appearance; and he relates some examples of it: he adds, that they attacked these dangerous spectres, which haunted and maltreated all who had any fields in the neighbourhood of their tombs; that they cut off the head of a man named Gretter, who also returned to earth. At other times they thrust a stake through the body, and thus fixed them to the ground.

Nam ferro secui mox caput ejus,
Perfodique nocens stipite corpus.

Formerly they took the corpse from the tomb and reduced it to ashes; they did thus towards a spectre named Gardus, which they believed the author of all the fatal apparitions that had appeared during the winter.

CHAPTER 18

Ghosts in England

William of Malmsbury says, that in England they believed that the wicked came back to earth after their death, and were brought back in their own bodies by the devil, who governed them and caused them to act; *Nequam hominis cadaver post mortem daemone agente discurrere.*

William of Newbridge, who flourished after the middle of the twelfth century, relates, that in his time was seen in England, in the county of Buckingham, a man who appeared bodily, as when alive, three succeeding nights to his wife, and after that to his nearest relatives. They only defended themselves from his frightful visits, by watching and making a noise when they perceived him coming. He even showed himself to a few persons in the day time. Upon that, the Bishop of Lincoln assembled his council, who told him that similar things had often happened in England, and that the only known remedy against this evil was to burn the body of the ghost. The bishop was averse to this opinion, which appeared cruel to him: he first of all wrote a schedule of absolution, which was placed on the body of the defunct, which was found in the same state as if he had been buried that very day; and from that time they heard no more of him.

The author of this narrative adds, that this sort of apparition would appear incredible, if several instances had not occurred in his time, and if they did not know several persons who believed in them.

The same Newbridge says, in the following chapter, that a man who had been interred at Berwick, came out of his grave every night, and caused great confusion in all the neighbourhood. It was even said that he had boasted that he should not cease to disturb the living till they had reduced him to ashes. Then they selected ten bold and vigorous young men, who took him up out of the ground, cut his body to pieces, and placed it on a pile, whereon it was burned to ashes; but beforehand, someone amongst them having said that he could not be consumed by fire until they had torn out his heart, his side was pierced with a stake, and when they had taken out his heart through the opening, they set fire to the pile; he was consumed by the flames, and appeared no more.

The pagans also believed that the bodies of the dead rested not, neither were they safe from magical evocations, so long as they remained unconsumed by fire, or undecayed underground.

> Tali tua membra sepulchro,
> Talibus exuram Stygio cum carmine Sylvis
> Ut nullos cantata Magos exaudiat umbra;

said an enchantress, in Lucan, to a spirit she evoked.

CHAPTER 19

Ghosts in Peru

The instance we are about to relate occurred in Peru, in the country of the Ititans. A girl named Catherine died, at the age of sixteen, an unhappy death, and she had been guilty of several sacrilegious actions. Her body immediately after her decease was so putrid, that they were obliged to put it out of the dwelling in the open air, to escape from the bad smell which exhaled from it. At the same time, they heard as it were dogs howling; and a horse, which before then was very gentle, began to rear, to prance, strike the ground with its feet, and break its bonds; a young man who was in bed, was pulled out of bed violently by the arm; a servant maid received a kick on the shoulder, of which she bore the marks for several days. All that happened before the body of Catherine was inhumed. Some time afterwards, several inhabitants of the place saw a great quantity of tiles and bricks thrown down with a great noise in the house where she died. The servant of the house was dragged about by the foot, without anyone appearing to touch her, and that in the presence of her mistress and ten or twelve other women.

The same servant, on entering a room to fetch some clothes, perceived Catherine, who rose up to seize hold of an earthen pot; the girl ran away directly, but the spectre took the vase, dashed it against the wall, and broke it into a thousand pieces. The mistress, who ran thither on hearing the noise, saw that a quantity of bricks were thrown against the wall. The next day, an image of the crucifix fixed against the wall was all on a sudden torn from its place in the presence of them all, and broken into three pieces.

CHAPTER 20

Ghosts in Lapland

Vestiges of these ghosts are still found in Lapland, where it is said they see a great number of spectres, who appear among those people, speak to them, and eat with them, without their being able to get rid of them; and as they are persuaded that these are the manes or shades of their relations who thus disturb them, they have no means of guarding against their intrusions more efficacious than to inter the bodies of their nearest relatives under the hearthstone, in order, apparently, that there they may be sooner consumed. In general they believe that the manes, or spirits, which come out of bodies, or corpses, are usually malevolent till they have re-entered other bodies. They pay some respect to the spectres, or demons, which they believe roam about rocks, mountains, lakes, and rivers, much as in former times the Romans paid honour to the fauns, the gods of the woods, the nymphs, and the tritons.

Andrew Alciat says, that he was consulted concerning certain women whom the Inquisition had caused to be burnt as witches for having occasioned the death of some children by their spells, and for having threatened the mothers of other children to kill these also; and in fact they did die the following night of disorders unknown to the physicians. Here we see again those strigae, or witches, who delight in destroying children.

But all this relates to our subject very indirectly. The vampires of which we are discoursing are very different from all those just mentioned.

CHAPTER 21

Reappearance of a Man who had been Dead for some Months

Peter the Venerable, Abbot of Clugni, relates the conversation which he had, in the presence of the Bishops of Oleron and of Osma, in Spain, together with several monks, with an old monk named Pierre d'Englebert, who, after having lived a long time in his day in high reputation for valour and honour, had withdrawn from the world after the death of his wife, and entered the order of Clugni. Peter the Venerable having come to see him, Pierre d'Englebert related to him, that one day, when in his bed and wide awake, he saw in his chamber, whilst the moon shone very brightly, a man named Sancho, whom he had several years before sent at his own expense to the assistance of Alphonso, King of Arragon, who was making war on Castile. Sancho had returned safe and sound from this expedition, but some time after he fell sick and died in his house.

Four months after his death Sancho showed himself to Pierre d'Englebert, as we have said. Sancho was naked, with the exception of a rag for mere decency round him. He began to uncover the burning wood, as if to warm himself, or that he might be more distinguishable. Peter asked him who he was. 'I am,' replied he, in a broken and hoarse voice, 'Sancho, your servant.' 'And what do you come here for?' 'I am going,' said he, 'into Castile, with a number of others, in order to expiate the harm we did during the last war, on the same spot where it was committed: for my own part, I pillaged the ornaments of a church, and for that I am condemned to take this journey. You can assist me very much by your good works; and Madame, your spouse, who owes me yet eight sols for the remainder of my salary, will oblige me infinitely if she will bestow them on the poor in my name.' Peter then asked him news of one Pierre de Fais, his friend, who had been dead a short time. Sancho told him he was saved.

'And Bernier, our fellow citizen, what is become of him?' 'He is damned,' said he, 'for having badly performed his office of judge, and for having troubled and plundered the widow and the innocent.'

Peter added, 'Could you tell me any news of Alphonso, King of Arragon, who died a few years ago?'

Then another spectre, that Peter had not before seen, and which he now observed distinctly by the light of the moon, seated in the recess of the window, said to him – 'Do not ask him for news of King Alphonso; he has not been with us long enough to know anything about him. I, who have been dead five years, can give you news of him. Alphonso was with us for some time, but the monks of Clugni extricated him from thence. I know not where he is now.' Then, addressing himself to his companion, Sancho, 'Come,' said he, 'let us follow our companions; it is time to set off.' Sancho reiterated his entreaties to Peter, his lord, and went out of the house.

Peter waked his wife who was lying by him, and who had neither seen nor heard anything of all this dialogue, and asked her the question – 'Do not you owe something to Sancho, that domestic who was in our service, and died a little while ago?' She answered, 'I owe him still eight sols.' From this Peter had no more doubt of the truth of what Sancho had said to him, gave these eight sols to the poor, adding a large sum of his own, and caused masses and prayers to be said for the soul of the defunct. Peter was then in the world and married; but when he related this to Peter the Venerable, he was a monk of Clugni.

St Augustine relates, that Sylla, on arriving at Tarentum, offered there sacrifices to the gods, that is to say, to the demons; and having observed on the upper part of the liver of the victim, a sort of crown of gold, the aruspice assured him that this crown was the presage of a certain victory, and told him to eat alone that liver whereon he had seen the crown.

Almost at the same moment a servitor of Lucius Pontius came to him and said, 'Sylla, I am come from the goddess Bellona. The victory is yours; and as a proof of my prediction, I announce to you that, ere long, the Capitol will be reduced to ashes.' At the same time this man left the camp in great haste, and on the morrow he returned with still more eagerness, and affirmed that the Capitol had been burnt, which was found to be true.

St Augustine had no doubt but that the demon who had caused the crown of gold to appear on the liver of the victim, had inspired this diviner, and that the same bad spirit, having foreseen the conflagration of the Capitol, had announced it after the event by that same man.

The same holy doctor relates, after Julius Obsequens in his Book of Prodigies, that in the open country of Campania, where some time after the Roman armies fought with such animosity during the civil war, they heard at first loud noises like soldiers fighting; and afterwards several persons affirmed that they had seen for some days two armies, who joined battle; after which they remarked in the same part as it were vestiges of the combatants, and the marks of horses' feet, as if the combat had really taken place there. St Augustine doubts not that all this was the work of the devil, who wished to reassure mankind against the horrors of civil warfare, by making them believe that their gods being at war amongst themselves, mankind need not be more moderate, nor more touched by the evils which war brings with it.

The abbot of Ursperg, in his Chronicle, year 1123, says that in the territory of Worms they saw during many days a multitude of armed men, on foot and on horseback, going and coming with great noise, like people who are going to a solemn assembly. Every day they marched, towards the hour of noon, to a mountain, which appeared to be their place of rendezvous. Someone in the neighbourhood, bolder than the rest, having guarded himself with the sign of the cross, approached one of these armed men, conjuring him in the name of God to declare the meaning of this army, and their design. The soldier or phantom replied – 'We are not what you imagine; we are neither vain phantoms, nor true soldiers; we are the spirits of those who were killed on this spot a long time ago. The arms and horses which you behold are the instruments of our punishment, as they were of our sins. We are all on fire, though you can see nothing about us which appears inflamed.' It is said that they remarked in this company the Count Emico, who had been killed a few years before, and who declared that he might be extricated from that state by alms and prayers.

Trithemius, in his *Annales Hirsauginses*, year 1013, asserts that there was seen in broad day, on a certain day in the year, an army of cavalry and infantry, which came down from a mountain and ranged themselves on a neighbouring plain. They were spoken to and conjured to speak, and they declared themselves to be the spirits of those who a few years before had been killed, with arms in their hands, in that same spot.

The same Trithemius relates elsewhere the apparition of the Count of Spanheim, deceased a little while before, who appeared in the fields with his pack of hounds. This count spoke to his curé, and asked his prayers.

Vipert, Archdeacon of the Church of Toul, contemporary author of the Life of the holy Pope Leo IX who died 1059, relates that some years before the death of this holy pope, an infinite multitude of persons, habited in white, was seen to pass by the town of Narni, advancing from the eastern side. This troop defiled from the morning until three in the afternoon, but towards evening it notably diminished. At this sight all the population of the town of Narni mounted upon the walls, fearing they might be hostile troops, and saw them defile with extreme surprise.

One burgher, more resolute than the others, went out of the town, and having observed in the crowd a man of his acquaintance, called to him by name, and asked him the meaning of this multitude of travellers: he replied, 'We are spirits, which not having yet expiated all our sins, and not being as yet sufficiently pure to enter the Kingdom of Heaven, are going into holy places in a spirit of repentance; we are now coming from visiting the tomb of St Martin, and we are going straight to Notre-Dame de Farse.' The man was so frightened at this vision, that he was ill for a twelvemonth – it was he who recounted the circumstance to Pope Leo IX. All the town of Narni was witness to this procession, which took place in broad day.

The night preceding the battle which was fought in Egypt between Mark Antony and Caesar, whilst all the city of Alexandria was in extreme uneasiness in expectation of this action, they saw in the city what appeared a multitude of people, who shouted and howled like bacchanals; and they heard a confused sound of instruments in honour of Bacchus, as Mark Antony was accustomed to celebrate this kind of festival. This troop, after having run through the greater part of the town, went out of it by the gate leading to the enemy, and disappeared.

That is all which has come to my knowledge concerning the vampires and ghosts of Hungary, Moravia, Silesia, and Poland, and of the other ghosts of France and Germany. We will explain our opinion after this on the reality, and other circumstances of these sorts of revived and resuscitated beings. Here follows another species which is not less marvellous; I mean the excommunicated, who leave the church and their graves with their bodies, and do not re-enter till after the sacrifice is completed.

CHAPTER 22

Excommunicated Persons, who Go out of the Churches

St Gregory the Great relates that St Benedict having threatened to excommunicate two nuns, these nuns died in that state. Some time after, their nurse saw them go out of the church, as soon as the deacon had cried out, 'Let all those who do not receive the communion withdraw.' The nurse having informed St Benedict of the circumstance, that saint sent an oblation, or consecrated bread, in order that it might be offered for them in token of reconciliation; and from that time the two nuns remained in quiet in their sepulchres.

St Augustine says that the names of martyrs were recited in the diptychs, not to pray for them; and the names of the virgin nuns deceased, to pray for them. 'Perhibet praeclarissimum testimonium ecclesiastica auctoritas, in quâ fidelibus notum est, quo loco martyres et quo defunctae sanctimoniales ad altaris sacramenta recitantur.' It was then, perhaps, when they were named at the altar, that they left the church. But St Gregory says expressly, that it was when the deacon cried aloud, 'Let those who do not receive the communion retire.'

The same St Gregory relates that a young priest of the same St Benedict, having gone out of his monastery without leave, and without receiving the benediction of the abbot, died in his disobedience and was interred in consecrated ground. The next day they found his body out of the grave; the relations gave notice of it to St Benedict, who gave them a consecrated wafer, and told them to place it with proper respect on the breast of the young priest; it was placed there, and the earth no more rejected him from her bosom.

This usage, or rather this abuse, of placing the holy wafer in the grave with the dead, is very singular; but it was not unknown to antiquity. The author of the Life of St Basil the Great, given under the name of St Amphilochus, says that that saint reserved the third part of a consecrated wafer to be interred with him; he received it, and expired while it was yet in his mouth; but some councils had already condemned this practice, and others have since then proscribed it, as contrary to the institution of Jesus Christ.

Still they did not omit in a few places putting holy wafers in the tombs or graves of some persons who were remarkable for their sanctity, as in the tomb of St Othmar, abbot of St Gal, wherein were found under his head several round leaves, which were indubitably believed to be the Host.

In the Life of St Cuthbert, bishop of Lindisfarn, we read that a quantity of consecrated wafers were found on his breast. Amalarius cites of the Venerable Bede, that a holy wafer was placed on the breast of this saint before he was inhumed; 'oblata super Sanctum pectus positâ.' This particularity is not noted in Bede's History, but in the second Life of St Cuthbert. Amalarius remarks that this custom proceeds doubtless from the Church of Rome, which had communicated it to the English; and the Reverend Father Menard maintains that it is not this practice which is condemned by the above mentioned Councils, but that of giving the communion to the dead by insinuating the holy wafer into their mouths. However it may be regarding this practice, we know that Cardinal Humbert, in his reply to the objections of the patriarch Michael Cerularius, reproves the Greeks for burying the Host, when there remained any of it after the communion of the faithful.

CHAPTER 23

Some other Instances of Excommunicated Persons being Cast out of Consecrated Ground

We see again in history several other examples of the dead bodies of excommunicated persons being cast out of consecrated earth; for instance, in the life of St Gothard, bishop of Hidesheim, it is related that this saint having excommunicated certain persons for their rebellion and their sins, they did not cease, in spite of his excommunications, to enter the church, and remain there though forbidden by the saint; whilst even the dead, who had been interred there years since, and had been placed there without their sentence of excommunication being removed, obeyed him, arose from their tombs, and left the church. After mass, the saint, addressing himself to these rebels, reproached them for their hardness of heart, and told them, those dead people would rise against them in the day of judgment. At the same time, going out of the church, he gave absolution to the excommunicated dead, and allowed them to re-enter it, and repose in their graves as before. The Life of St Gothard was written by one of his disciples, a canon of his cathedral; and this saint died on the 4th May 938.

In the second Council held at Limoges, in 1031, at which a great many bishops, abbots, priests, and deacons, were present, they reported the instances which we have just cited from St Benedict, to show the respect in which sentences of excommunication, pronounced by ecclesiastical superiors, were held. Then the Bishop of Cahors, who was present, related a circumstance which had happened to him a short time before. A cavalier of my diocese, having been killed in excommunication, I would not accede to the prayers of his friends, who implored to grant him absolution; I desired to make an example of him, in order to inspire others with fear. But he was interred by soldiers or gentlemen (*milites*), without my permission, without the presence of the priests, in a church dedicated to St Peter. The next morning, his body was found out of the ground, and thrown naked far from the spot; his grave remaining entire, and without any sign of having been touched. The soldiers or gentlemen (*milites*) who had interred him, having opened the grave, found in it only the linen in which he had been wrapped; they buried him again, and covered him with an enormous quantity of earth and stones. The next day they found the corpse outside the tomb, without its appearing that anyone had worked at it. The same thing happened five times; at last they buried him as they could, at a distance from the cemetery, in unconsecrated ground; which filled the neighbouring seigneurs with so much terror, that they all came to me to make their peace. This is a fact, invested with everything which can render it incontestible.

CHAPTER 24

An Instance of an Excommunicated Martyr being Cast out of the Earth

We read in the *menées* of the Greeks, on the 15th October, that a monk of the Desert of Sheti, having been excommunicated by him who had the care of his conduct, for some act of disobedience, he left the desert, and came to Alexandria, where he was arrested by the governor of the city, despoiled of his conventual habit, and ardently solicited to sacrifice to false gods. The solitary resisted nobly, and was tormented in various ways, until at last they cut off his head, and threw his body outside of the city, to be devoured by dogs. The Christians took it away in the night, and having embalmed it and enveloped it in fine linen, they interred it in the church as a martyr, in an honourable place; but during the holy sacrifice, the deacon having cried aloud, as usual, that the catechumens and those who did not take the communion were to withdraw, they suddenly beheld the martyr's tomb open of itself, and his body retire into the vestibule of the church; after the mass, it returned to its sepulchre.

A pious person having prayed for three days, learnt by the voice of an angel, that this monk had incurred excommunication for having disobeyed his superior, and that he would remain bound until that same superior had given him absolution. Then they went to the desert directly, and brought the saintly old man, who caused the coffin of the martyr to be opened, and absolved him, after which he remained in peace in his tomb.

This instance appears to me rather suspicious. 1. In the time that the Desert of Sheti was peopled with solitary monks, there were no longer any persecutors at Alexandria. They troubled no one there, neither concerning the profession of Christianity, nor the religious profession – they would sooner have persecuted the idolators and pagans. The Christian religion was then dominant and respected throughout all Egypt, above all, in Alexandria. 2. The monks of Sheti were rather hermits than cenobites, and a monk had no authority there to excommunicate his brother. 3. It does not appear that the monk in question had deserved excommunication, at least major excommunication, which deprives the faithful of the entry of the church, and the participation of the holy mysteries. The bearing of the Greek text is simply, that he remained obedient for some time to his spiritual father, but that having afterwards fallen into disobedience, he withdrew from the hands of the old man without any legitimate cause, and went away to Alexandria. All that deserves doubtlessly even major excommunication, if this monk had quitted his profession and retired from the monastery to lead a secular life; but at that time the monks were not, as now, bound by vows of stability and obedience to their regular superiors, who had not a right to excommunicate them with grand excommunication. We will speak of this again by and by.

CHAPTER 25

A Man Rejected from the Church for having Refused to pay Tithes

John Brompton, Abbot of Sornat in England, says that we may read in very old histories that St Augustine, the Apostle of England, wishing to persuade a gentleman to pay the tithes, God permitted that this saint, having said before all the people, before the commencement of the mass, that no excommunicated person should assist at the holy sacrifice, they saw a man who had been interred for a hundred and fifty years leave the church.

After mass St Augustine, preceded by the cross, went to ask this dead man why he went out? The dead man replied that it was because he had died in a state of excommunication. The saint asked him, where was the sepulchre of the priest who had pronounced against him the sentence of excommunication? They went thither; St Augustine commanded him to rise; he came to life, and avowed that he had excommunicated the man for his crimes, and particularly for his obstinacy in refusing to pay tithes; then, by order of St Augustine, he gave him absolution, and the dead man returned to his tomb. The priest entreated the saint to permit him also to return to his sepulchre, which was granted him. This story appears to me still more suspicious than the preceding one. In the time of St Augustine, the Apostle of England, there was no obligation as yet to pay tithes on pain of excommunication, and much less a hundred and fifty years before that time – above all, in England.

CHAPTER 26

Instances of Persons who have shown Signs of Life after their Death, and who have drawn back from Respect, to make room or give place to some who were more worthy than themselves

Tertullian relates an instance to which he had been witness – *de meo didici*. A woman who belonged to the church, to which she had been given as a slave, died in the prime of life, after being once married only, and that for a short time, was brought to the church. Before putting her in the ground, the priest, offering the sacrifice, and raising his hands in prayer, this woman, who had her hands extended at her side, raised them at the same time, and put them together as a supplicant; then, when the peace was given, she replaced herself in her former position.

Tertullian adds, that another body, dead, and buried in a cemetery, withdrew on one side to give place to another corpse which they were about to inter near it. He relates these instances as a sequel to what was said by Plato and Democritus, that souls remained some time near the dead bodies they had inhabited, which they preserved sometimes from corruption, and often caused their hair, beard, and nails to grow in their graves. Tertullian does not approve of the opinion of these – he even refutes them pretty well; but he owns that the instances I have just spoken of are favourable enough to that opinion, which is also that of the Hebrews, as we have before seen.

It is said that after the death of the celebrated Abelard, who was interred at the Monastery of the Paraclete, the Abbess Heloisa, his spouse, being also deceased, and having requested to be buried in the same grave, at her approach Abelard extended his arms and received her into his bosom: *elevatis brachiis illam recepit, et ita eam amplexatus brachia sua strinxit.* This circumstance is certainly neither proved nor probable; the Chronicle whence it is extracted had probably taken it from some popular rumour.

The author of the Life of St John the Almoner, which was written immediately after his death by Leontius, bishop of Naples, a town of the Isle of Cyprus, relates that St John the Almoner being dead at Amatunta, in the same island, his body was placed between that of two bishops, who drew back on each side respectfully, to make room for him, in sight of all present; *non unus, neque decem, neque centum viderunt, sed omnis turba, quae convenit ad ejus sepulturam*, says the author cited. Metaphrastes, who had read the life of the saint in Greek, repeats the same fact.

Evagrius de Pont says, that a holy hermit, named Thomas, and surnamed Salus, because he counterfeited madness, dying in the hospital of Daphné, near the City of Antioch, was buried in the strangers' cemetery, but every day he was found out of the ground at a distance from the other dead bodies, which he avoided. The inhabitants of the place informed Ephraim, Bishop of Antioch, of this, and he had him solemnly carried into the city and honourably buried in the cemetery, and from that time the people of Antioch keep the feast of his translation.

John Mosch reports the same story, only he says that it was some women who were buried near Thomas Salus, who left their graves through respect for the saint.

The Hebrews ridiculously believe that the Jews who are buried without Judea will roll underground at the last day, to repair to the Promised Land, as they cannot come to life again elsewhere than in Judea.

The Persians recognise also a transporting angel, whose care it is to assign to dead bodies the place and rank due to their merits: if a worthy man is buried in an infidel country, the transporting angel leads him underground to a spot near one of the faithful, while he casts into the sewer the body of any infidel interred in holy ground. Other Mahometans have the same notion; they believe that the transporting angel placed the body of Noah, and afterwards that of Ali, in the grave of Adam. I relate these fantastical ideas only to show their absurdity. As to the other stories related in this same chapter, they must not be accepted without examination, for they require confirmation.

CHAPTER 27

Of Persons who Perform a Pilgrimage
after their Death

A scholar of the town of Saint Pons, near Narbonne, having died in a state
of excommunication, appeared to one of his friends, and begged of him to
go to the city of Rhodes, and ask the Bishop to grant him absolution. He set
off in snowy weather; the spirit, who accompanied him without being seen
by him, showed him the road and cleared away the snow. On arriving at
Rhodes, he asked and obtained for his friend the required absolution,
when the spirit reconducted him to Saint Pons, gave him thanks for this
service, and took leave, promising to testify to him his gratitude.

Here follows a letter written to me on the 5th April 1745, and which
somewhat relates to what we have just seen. 'Something has occurred here
within the last few days, relatively to your Dissertation upon Ghosts,
which I think I ought to inform you of. A man of Letrage, a village a few
miles from Remiremont, lost his wife at the beginning of February last, and
married again the week before Lent. At eleven o'clock in the evening of his
wedding-day, his wife appeared and spoke to his new spouse; the result of
the conversation was to oblige the bride to perform seven pilgrimages for
the defunct. From that day, and always at the same hour, the defunct
appeared, and spoke in presence of the curé of the place and several other
persons; on the 15th March, at the moment that the bride was preparing to
repair to St Nicholas, she had a visit from the defunct, who told her to
make haste, and not to be alarmed at any pain or trouble which she might
undergo on her journey.

'This woman with her husband and her brother and sister-in-law, set off
on their way, not expecting that the dead wife would be of the party; but
she never left them until they were at the door of the Church of St
Nicholas. These good people, when they were arrived at two leagues'
distance from St Nicholas, were obliged to put up at a little inn called the
Barracks. There the wife found herself so ill, that the two men were obliged
to carry her to the burgh of St Nicholas. Directly she was under the church
porch, she walked easily, and felt no more pain. This fact has been
reported to me by the sacristan and the four persons. The last thing that
the defunct said to the bride was, that she should neither speak to nor

appear to her again until half the pilgrimages should be accomplished. The simple and natural manner in which these good people related this fact to us, makes me believe that it is certain.'

It is not said that this young woman had incurred excommunication, but apparently she was bound by a vow or promise which she had made, to accomplish these pilgrimages, which she imposed upon the other young wife who succeeded her. Also, we see that she did not enter the church of St Nicholas; she only accompanied the pilgrims to the church door.

We may here add the instance of that crowd of pilgrims, who, in the time of Pope Leo IX passed at the foot of the wall of Narne, as I have before related, and who performed their purgatory by going from pilgrimage to pilgrimage.

CHAPTER 28

Argument concerning the Excommunicated who Quit Churches

All that we have just reported concerning the bodies of persons who had been excommunicated leaving their tombs during mass, and returning into them after the service, deserves particular attention.

It seems that a thing which passed before the eyes of a whole population in broad day, and in the midst of the most redoubtable mysteries, can be neither denied nor disputed. Nevertheless, it may be asked, how these bodies came out? Were they whole, or in a state of decay? Naked, or clad in their own dress, or in the linen and bandages which had enveloped them in the tomb? Where also did they go?

The cause of their forthcoming is well noted; it was the major excommunication. This penalty is decreed only to mortal sin. Those persons had, then, died in the career of deadly sin, and were consequently condemned and in hell; for if there is nought in question but a minor excommunication, why should they go out of the Church after death with such terrible and extraordinary circumstances, since that ecclesiastical excommunication does not deprive one absolutely of communion with the faithful, or of entrance to Church?

If it be said that the crime was remitted, but not the penalty of excommunication, and that these persons remained excluded from the

Church communion until after their absolution, given by the ecclesiastical judge, we ask if a dead man can be absolved and be restored to communion with the church, unless there are unequivocal proofs of his repentance and conversion preceding his death.

Moreover, the persons just cited as instances do not appear to have been released from crime or guilt, as might be supposed. The texts which we have cited sufficiently note that they died in their guilt and sins; and what St Gregory the Great says in the part of his Dialogues there quoted, replying to his interlocutor, Peter, supposes that these nuns had died without doing penance.

Besides, it is a constant rule of the Church that we cannot communicate or have communion with a dead man, whom we have not had any communication with during his life-time. 'Quibus viventibus non communicavimus, mortuis, communicare non possumus,' says pope St Leo. At any rate, it is allowed that an excommunicated person who has given signs of sincere repentance, although there may not have been time for him to confess himself, can be reconciled to the Church and receive ecclesiastical sepulture after his death. But in general, before receiving absolution from sin, they must have been absolved from the censures and excommunication, if such have been incurred: 'Absolutio ab excommunicatione debet paecedere absolutionem à peccatis; quia quamdiu aliquis est excommunicatus, non potest recipere aliquod Ecclesiae Sacramentum,' says St Thomas.

Following this decision, it would have been necessary to absolve these persons from their excommunication, before they could receive absolution from the guilt of their sins. Here, on the contrary, they are supposed to be absolved from their sins as to their criminality, in order to be able to receive absolution from the censures of the Church.

I do not see how these difficulties can be resolved.

1. How can you absolve the dead? 2. How can you absolve him from excommunication, before he has received absolution from sin? 3. How can he be absolved without asking for absolution, or its appearing that he hath requested it? 4. How can people be absolved who died in mortal sin, and without doing penance? 5. Why do these excommunicated persons return to their tombs after mass? 6. If they dared not stay in the church during the mass, where were they?

It appears certain that the nuns and the young monk spoken of by St Gregory, died in their sins, and without having received absolution from them. St Benedict, probably, was not a priest, and had not absolved them as regards their guilt.

It may be said that the excommunication spoken of by St Gregory was not major, and in that case the holy abbot could absolve them; but would this minor and regular excommunication deserve that they should quit the church in so miraculous and public a manner? The persons excommunicated by St Gothard, and the gentleman mentioned at the Council of Limoges, in 1031, had died unrepentant, and under sentence of excommunication; consequently in mortal sin; and yet they are granted peace and absolution after their death, at the simple entreaty of their friends.

The young solitary spoken of in the *Acta Sanctorum* of the Greeks, who after having quitted his cell through incontinency and disobedience, had incurred excommunication, could he receive the crown of martyrdom in that state? And if he had received it, was he not at the same time reconciled to the church? Did he not wash away his fault with his blood? And if his excommunication was only regular and minor, would he deserve after his martyrdom to be excluded from the presence of the holy mysteries?

I see no other way of explaining these facts, if they are as they are related, than by saying that the story has not preserved the circumstances which might have deserved the absolution of these persons, and we must presume that the saints – above all, the bishops who absolved them – knew the rules of the Church, and did nothing in the matter but what was right and conformable to the canons.

But it results from all that we have just said, that as the bodies of the wicked withdraw from the company of the holy through a principle of veneration and a feeling of their own unworthiness, so also the bodies of the holy separate themselves from the wicked, from opposite motives, that they may not appear to have any connexion with them, even after death, or to approve of their bad life. In short, if what is just related be true, the righteous and the saints feel deference for one another, and honour each other ever in the other world; which is probable enough.

We are about to see some instances which seem to render equivocal and uncertain, as a proof of sanctity, the uncorrupted state of the body of a just man, since it is maintained that the bodies of the excommunicated do not rot in the earth until the sentence of excommunication pronounced against them be taken off.

CHAPTER 29

Do the Excommunicated Rot in the Ground?

It is a very ancient opinion that the bodies of the excommunicated do not decompose; it appears in the Life of St Libentius, archbishop of Bremen, who died on the 4th January 1013. That holy prelate having excommunicated some pirates, one of them died, and was buried in Norway; at the end of seventy years they found his body entire and without decay, nor did it fall to dust until after absolution received from Archbishop Alvaridius.

The modern Greeks, to authorise their schism, and to prove that the gift of miracles, and the power of binding and unbinding, subsists in their church even more visibly and more certainly than in the Latin and Roman Church, maintain that amongst themselves the bodies of those who are excommunicated do not decay, but become swollen extraordinarily, like drums, and can neither be corrupted nor reduced to ashes till after they have received absolution from their bishops or their priests. They relate divers instances of these kinds of dead bodies, found uncorrupted in their graves, and which are afterwards reduced to ashes as soon as the excommunication is taken off. They do not deny, however, that the uncorrupted state of a body is sometimes a mark of sanctity, but they require that a body thus preserved should exhale a good smell, be white or reddish, and not black, offensive and swollen.

It is affirmed that persons who have been struck dead by lightning do not decay, and for that reason the ancients neither burnt them nor buried them. That is the opinion of the physician Zachias; but Paré, after Comines, thinks that the reason they are not subject to corruption is because they are as it were embalmed by the sulphur of the thunderbolt, which serves them instead of salt.

In 1727 they discovered in the vault of an hospital near Quebec the unimpaired corpses of five nuns, who had been dead for more than twenty years, and these corpses, though covered with quicklime, still contained blood.

CHAPTER 30

Instances to Demonstrate that the Excommunicated do not Decay, and that they Appear to the Living

The Greeks relate that under the Patriarch of Constantinople Manuel, or Maximus, who lived in the fifteenth century, the Turkish Emperor of Constantinople wished to know the truth of what the Greeks asserted concerning the uncorrupted state of those who died under sentence of excommunication. The Patriarch caused the tomb of a woman to be opened; she had had a criminal connexion with an Archbishop of Constantinople; her body was whole, black, and much swollen. The Turks shut it up in a coffin, sealed with the Emperor's seal; the Patriarch said his prayer, gave absolution to the dead woman, and at the end of three days the coffin or box being opened they found the body fallen to dust.

I see no miracle in this; everybody knows that bodies which are sometimes found quite whole in their tombs fall to dust as soon as they are exposed to the air. I except those which have been well embalmed, as the mummies of Egypt, and bodies which are buried in extremely dry spots, or in an earth replete with nitre and salt, which dissipate in a short time all the moisture there may be in the dead bodies, either of men or animals; but I do not understand that the Archbishop of Constantinople could validly absolve after death a person who died in deadly sin and bound by excommunication. They believe also that the bodies of these excommunicated persons often appear to the living, whether by day or by night, speaking to them, calling them, and molesting them. Leon Allatius enters into long details on this subject; he says that in the Isle of Chio the inhabitants do not answer to the first voice that calls them, for fear that it should be a spirit or ghost; but if they are called twice, it is not a Vroucolaca, which is the name they give those spectres. If anyone answers to them at the first sound, the spectre disappears; but he who has spoken to it, infallibly dies.

There is no other way of guarding against these bad genii than by taking up the corpse of the person who has appeared, and burning it after certain prayers have been recited over it; then the body is reduced to ashes, and appears no more. They have then no doubt that these are the bodies of criminal and malevolent men, which come out of their graves and cause the death of those who see and reply to them; or that it is the demon, who makes use of their bodies to frighten mortals, and cause their death.

They know of no means more certain to deliver themselves from being infested by these dangerous apparitions, than to burn and hack to pieces these bodies, which served as instruments of malice, or to tear out their hearts, or to let them putrefy before they are buried, or to cut off their heads, or to pierce their temples with a large nail.

CHAPTER 31

Instance of the Reappearances of the Excommunicated

Ricaut, in the history he has given us of the present state of the Greek Church, acknowledges, that this opinion, that the bodies of excommunicated persons do not decay, is general, not only among the Greeks of the present day, but also among the Turks. He relates a fact which he heard from a Candiote caloyer [Greek monk], who had affirmed the thing to him on oath; his name was Sophronius, and he was well known and highly respected at Smyrna. A man who died in the Isle of Milo, had been excommunicated for some fault which he had committed in the Morea, and he was interred without any funeral ceremony in a spot apart, and not in consecrated ground. His relations and friends were deeply moved to see him in this plight; and the inhabitants of the isle were every night alarmed by baneful apparitions, which they attributed to this unfortunate man.

They opened his grave, and found his body quite entire, with the veins swollen with blood. After having deliberated upon it, the caloyers were of opinion that they should dismember the body, hack it to pieces, and boil it in wine; for it is thus they treat the bodies of revenants.

But the relations of the dead man, by dint of entreaties, succeeded in deferring this execution, and in the mean time sent in all haste to Constantinople, to obtain the absolution of the young man from the patriarch. Meanwhile, the body was placed in the church, and every day prayers were offered up for the repose of his soul. One day when the caloyer Sophronius, above mentioned, was performing divine service, all on a sudden a great noise was heard in the coffin; they opened it, and found his body decayed as if he had been dead seven years. They observed the moment when the noise was heard, and it was found to be precisely at that hour that his absolution had been signed by the patriarch.

M. le Chevalier Ricaut, from whom we have this narrative, was neither a Greek, nor a Roman Catholic, but a staunch Anglican; he remarks on this occasion, that the Greeks believe that an evil spirit enters the bodies of the excommunicated, and preserves them from putrefaction, by animating them, and causing them to act, nearly as the soul animates and inspires the body.

They imagine moreover, that these corpses eat during the night, walk about, digest what they have eaten, and really nourish themselves – that some have been found who were of a rosy hue, and had their veins still fully replete with the quantity of blood; and although they had been dead forty days, have ejected, when opened, a stream of blood as bubbling and fresh as that of a young man of sanguine temperament would be; and this belief so generally prevails, that everyone relates facts circumstantially concerning it.

Father Theophilus Reynaud, who has written a particular treatise on this subject, maintains that this return of the dead is an indubitable fact, and that there are very certain proofs and experience of the same; but that to pretend that those ghosts who come to disturb the living, are always those of excommunicated persons, and that it is a privilege of the schismatic Greek Church, to preserve from decay those who incurred excommunication, and have died under censure of their Church, is an untenable assumption; since it is certain that the bodies of the excommunicated decay like others, and there are some which have died in communion with the Church, whether the Greek or the Latin, who remain uncorrupted. Such are found even among the Pagans, and amongst animals, of which the dead bodies are sometimes found in an uncorrupted state, both in the ground, and in the ruins of old buildings.

CHAPTER 32

Vroucolaca Exhumed in Presence of
Monsieur de Tournefort

Monsieur Pitton de Tournefort relates the manner in which they exhumed a pretended vroucolaca, in the Isle of Micon, where he was on the 1st January 1701. These are his own words:

We saw a very different scene, (in the same Isle of Micon,) on the occasion of one of those dead people, whom they believe to return to earth after their interment. This one, whose history we shall relate, was a peasant of Micon, naturally sullen and quarrelsome; which is a circumstance to be remarked relatively to such subjects: he was killed in the country, no one knows when, or by whom. Two days after he had been inhumed in a chapel in the town, it was rumoured that he was seen by night walking very fast; that he came into the house, overturning the furniture, extinguishing the lamps, throwing his arms round persons from behind, and playing a thousand sly tricks.

At first, people only laughed at it; but the affair began to be serious, when the most respectable people in the place began to complain: the priests even owned the fact, and doubtless they had their reasons. People did not fail to have masses said; nevertheless, the peasant continued to lead the same life without correcting himself. After several assemblies of the principal men of the city, with priests and monks, it was concluded that they must, according to some ancient ceremonial, await the expiration of nine days after burial.

On the tenth day a mass was said in the chapel where the corpse lay, in order to expel the demon which they believed to have inclosed himself therein. This body was taken up after mass, and they began to set about tearing out his heart; the butcher of the town, who was old, and very awkward, began by opening the belly instead of the breast; he felt for a long time in the entrails without finding what he sought. At last someone told him that he must pierce the diaphragm; then the heart was torn out, to the admiration of all present. The corpse however gave out such a bad smell, that they were obliged to burn incense; but the vapour, mixed with the exhalations of that carrion, only augmented the stink, and began to heat the brain of these poor people.

Their imagination, struck with the spectacle, was full of visions; someone thought proper to say that a thick smoke came from this body. We dared not say that it was the vapour of the incense. They only exclaimed 'Vroucolacas,' in the chapel, and in the square before it. (This is the name which they give to these pretended revenants.) The rumour spread and was bellowed in the street, and the noise seemed likely to shake the vaulted roof of the chapel. Several present affirmed that the blood of this wretched man was quite vermilion; the butcher swore that the body was still quite warm; whence it was concluded that the dead man was very wrong not to be quite dead, or, to express myself better, to suffer himself to be reanimated by the devil. This is precisely the idea of a vroucolaca; and they made this name resound in an astonishing manner. At this time there entered a crowd of people, who protested aloud that they clearly perceived this body was not stiff when they brought it from the country to the church to bury it, and that consequently it was a true vroucolaca; this was the chorus.

I have no doubt that they would have maintained it did not stink, if we had not been present; so stupified were these poor people with the circumstance, and infatuated with the idea of the return of the dead. For ourselves, who got next to the corpse in order to make our observations exactly, we were ready to die from the offensive odour which proceeded from it. When they asked us what we thought of this dead man, we replied that we believed him thoroughly dead; but as we wished to cure, or at least not to irritate their stricken fancy, we represented to them that it was not surprising if the butcher had perceived some heat in searching amidst entrails which were decaying; neither was it extraordinary that some vapour had proceeded from them; since such will issue from a dunghill that is stirred up; as for this pretended red blood, it still might be seen on the butcher's hands that it was only a very foetid mud.

After all these arguments, they bethought themselves of going to the marine, and burning the heart of the dead man, who in spite of this execution was less docile, and made more noise than before. They accused him of beating people by night, of breaking open the doors and even terraces, of breaking windows, tearing clothes, and emptying jugs and bottles. He was a very thirsty dead man; I believe he only spared the consul's house, where I was lodged. In the mean time I never saw anything so pitiable as the state of this island.

Everybody seemed to have lost their senses. The most sensible people appeared as frenzied as the others; it was a veritable brain fever, as dangerous as any mania or madness. Whole families were seen to forsake their houses, and coming from the ends of the town, bring their flock beds to the market-place to pass the night there. Everyone complained of some new insult: you heard nothing but lamentations at nightfall; and the most sensible people went into the country.

Amidst such a general prepossession we made up our minds to say nothing; we should not only have been considered as absurd, but as infidels. How can you convince a whole people of error? Those who believed in their own minds that we had our doubts of the truth of the fact, came and reproached us for our incredulity, and pretended to prove that there were such things as vroucolacas, by some authority which they derived from Father Richard, a Jesuit missionary. It is Latin, said they, and consequently you ought to believe it. We should have done no good by denying this consequence. They every morning entertained us with the comedy of a faithful recital of all the new follies which had been committed by this bird of night; he was even accused of having committed the most abominable sins.

The citizens who were most zealous for the public good believed that they had missed the most essential point of the ceremony. They said that the mass ought not to be celebrated until after the heart of this wretched man had been torn out; they affirmed that with that precaution they could not have failed to surprise the devil, and doubtless he would have taken care not to come back again; instead of which, had they begun by saying mass, he would have had, said they, plenty of time to take flight, and to return afterwards at his leisure.

After all these arguments they found themselves in the same embarrassment as the first day it began; they assembled night and morning, they reasoned upon it, made processions which lasted three days and three nights, they obliged the priests to fast; they were seen running about in the houses with the asperser or sprinkling brush in their hands, sprinkling holy water and washing the doors with it; they even filled the mouth of that poor vroucolaca with holy water. We so often told the administration of the town that in all Christendom people would not fail in such a case to watch by night, to observe all that was going forward in the town, that at last they arrested some vagabonds, who assuredly had a share in all these disturbances. Apparently they were not the principal authors of them, or they were too soon set at liberty; for two days after, to make themselves amends for the fast they had kept in prison, they began again to empty the stone bottles of wine belonging to those persons who were silly enough to forsake their houses at night. Thus, then, they were again obliged to have recourse to prayers.

One day, as certain orisons were being recited, after having stuck I know not how many naked swords upon the grave of this corpse, which was disinterred three or four times a day according to the caprice of the first comer, an Albanian, who chanced to be at Mico accidentally, bethought himself of saying in a sententious tone, that it was very ridiculous to make use of the swords of Christians in such a case. Do you not see, blind as ye are, said he, that the hilt of these swords, forming a cross with the handle, prevents the devil from coming out of that body? Why do you not rather make use of the sabres of the Turks? The advice of this clever man was of no use; the vroucolaca did not appear more tractable, and everybody was in a strange consternation: they no longer knew to which saint to pay their vows; when, with one voice, as if the signal word had been given, they began to shout in all parts of the town that they had waited too long; that the vroucolaca ought to be burnt altogether; that after that, they would defy the devil to return and ensconce himself there; that it would be better to have recourse to that extremity than to let the island be deserted. In fact, there were whole families who were packing up with the intention of retiring to Sira or Tina.

So they carried the vroucolaca, by order of the administration, to the point of the Island of St George, where they had prepared a great pile made up with a mixture of tow, for fear that wood, however dry it might be, would not burn quickly enough by itself. The remains of this unfortunate corpse were thrown upon it and consumed in a very little time; it was on the first day of January, 1701. We saw this fire as we returned from Delos: it might be called a real *feu de joie*; since then, there have been no more complaints against the vroucolaca. They contented themselves with saying that the devil had been properly caught that time, and they made up a song to turn him into ridicule.

Throughout the Archipelago, people are persuaded that it is only the Greeks of the Greek Church whose corpses are reanimated by the devil. The inhabitants of the Isle of Santorin have great apprehensions of these bugbears; those of Maco, after their visions were dissipated, felt an equal fear of being punished by the Turks and by the Bishop of Tina. None of the papas would be present at St George when this body was burned, lest the bishop should exact a sum of money for having disinterred and burned the dead body without his permission. As for the Turks, it is certain that at their first visit they did not fail to make the community of Maco pay the price of the blood of this poor devil, who in every way became the abomination and horror of his country. After this, must we not own that the Greeks of today are not great Greeks, and that there is only ignorance and superstition among them?

So says Monsieur de Tournefort.

Has the Demon Power to Cause anyone to Die, and then to Restore the Dead to Life?

Supposing the principle which we established as indubitable at the commencement of this dissertation – that God alone is the sovereign arbitrator of life and death; that He alone can give life to men, and restore it to them after He has taken it from them – the question that we here propose appears unseasonable and absolutely frivolous, since it concerns a supposition notoriously impossible.

Nevertheless, as some learned men have believed that the demon has power to restore life, and to preserve from corruption, for a time, certain bodies which he makes use of to delude mankind and frighten them, as it happens with the ghosts of Hungary, we shall treat of it in this place, and relate a remarkable instance furnished by Monsieur Nicholas Remy, procureur-general of Lorraine, and which occurred in his own time; that is to say, in 1581, at Dalhem, a village situated between the Mozelle and the Sare. A goatherd of his village, named Pierron, a married man and father of a boy, conceived a violent passion for a girl of the village. One day, when his thoughts were occupied with this young girl, she appeared to him in the fields, or the demon in her likeness. Pierron declared his love to her; she promised to reply to it on condition that he would give himself up to her, and obey her in all things. Pierron consented to this, and consummated his abominable passion with this spectre. Some time afterwards, Abrahel, which was the name assumed by the demon, asked of him as a pledge of his love, that he would sacrifice to her his only son, and gave him an apple for this boy to eat, who, on tasting it, fell down dead. The father and mother, in despair at this fatal and to both unexpected accident, uttered lamentations, and were inconsolable.

Abrahel appeared again to the goatherd, and promised to restore the child to life, if the father would ask this favour of him by paying him the kind of adoration due only to God. The peasant knelt down, worshipped Abrahel, and immediately the boy began to revive. He opened his eyes; they warmed him, chafed his limbs, and at last he began to walk and to speak. He was the same as before, only thinner, paler, and more languid; his eyes heavy and sunken, his movements slower and less free, his mind duller and more stupid. At the end of a year, the demon that had animated him quitted him with a great noise; the youth fell backwards, and his body, which was foetid and stank insupportably, was dragged with a hook out of his father's house, and buried in a field without any ceremony.

This event was reported at Nancy, and examined into by the magistrates, who informed themselves exactly of the circumstance, heard the witnesses, and found that the thing was such as has been related. For the rest, the story does not say how the peasant was punished, nor whether he was so at all. Perhaps his crime with the demon could not be proved; to that there was probably no witness. In regard to the death of his son, it was difficult to prove that he was the cause of it.

Procopius, in his secret history of the Emperor Justinian, seriously asserts, that he is persuaded, as well as several other persons, that that emperor was a demon incarnate. He says the same thing of the Empress Theodora his wife. Josephus, the Jewish historian, says that the souls of the wicked enter the bodies of the possessed, whom they torment, and cause to act and speak.

We see by St Chrysostom that in his time many Christians believed that the spirits of persons who died a violent death were changed into demons, and that the magicians made use of the spirit of a child they had killed for their magical operations, and to discover the future. St Philastrius places among heretics those persons who believed that the souls of worthless men were changed into demons.

According to the system of these authors, the demon might have entered into the body of the child of the shepherd Pierron, moved it and maintained it in a kind of life whilst his body was uncorrupted and the organs underanged; it was not the soul of the boy which animated it, but the demon which replaced his spirit.

Philo believed that as there are good and bad angels, there are also good and bad souls or spirits, and that the souls which descend into the bodies bring to them their own good or bad qualities.

We see by the Gospel that the Jews of the time of our Saviour believed that one man could be animated by several souls. Herod imagined that the spirit of John the Baptist, whom he had beheaded, had entered into Jesus Christ, and worked miracles in him. Others fancied that Jesus Christ was animated by the spirit of Elias, or of Jeremiah, or some other of the ancient prophets.

Examination of the Opinion which Concludes that the Demon can Restore Motion to a Dead Body

We cannot approve these opinions of Jews which we have just shown. They are contrary to our holy religion, and to the dogmas of our schools. But we believe that the spirit which once inspired Elijah, for instance, rested on Elisha his disciple; and that the Holy Spirit which inspired the first animated the second also, and even St John the Baptist, who, according to the words of Jesus Christ, came in the power of Elijah to prepare a highway for the Messiah. Thus, in the prayers of the Church, we pray to God to fill His faithful servants with the spirit of the saints, and to inspire them with a love for that which they loved, and a detestation of that which they hated.

That the demon, and even a good angel by the permission or commission of God, can take away the life of a man, appears indubitable. The angel which appeared to Zipporah, as Moses was returning from Midian to Egypt, and threatened to slay his two sons because they were not circumcised; as well as the one who slew the first-born of the Egyptians, and the one who is termed in Scripture *the Destroying Angel*, and who slew the Hebrew murmurers in the wilderness; and the angel who was near slaying Balaam and his ass; the angel who killed the soldiers of Sennacherib, he who smote the first seven husbands of Sara, the daughter of Raguel; and, finally, the one with whom the Psalmist menaces his enemies, all are instances in proof of this.

Does not St Paul, speaking to the Corinthians of those who took the Communion unworthily, say that the demon occasioned them dangerous maladies, of which many died? Will it be believed that those whom the same Apostle delivered over to Satan suffered nothing bodily; and that Judas, having received from the Son of God a bit of bread dipped in the dish, and Satan having entered into him, that bad spirit did not disturb his reason, his imagination, and his heart, until at last he led him to destroy himself, and to hang himself in despair?

We may believe that all these angels were evil angels, although it cannot be denied that God employs sometimes the good angels also to exercise his vengeance against the wicked, as well as to chastise, correct, and punish those to whom God desires to be merciful; as He sends His Prophets to announce good and bad tidings, to threaten punishment, and excite to repentance.

But nowhere do we read that either the good or the evil angels have of their own authority alone either given life to any person or restored it. This power is reserved to God alone. The demon, according to the Gospel, in the last days, and before the last Judgment, will perform, either by his own power or that of Antichrist and his subordinates, such wonders as would, were it possible, lead the elect themselves into error. From the time of Jesus Christ and his Apostles, Satan raised up false Christs and false Apostles, who performed many seeming miracles, and even resuscitated the dead. At least, it was maintained that they had resuscitated some: St Clement of Alexandria and Hegesippus make mention of a few resurrections operated by Simon the magician; it is also said that Apollonius of Thyana brought to life a girl they were carrying to be buried. If we may believe Apuleius, Asclepiades, meeting a funeral convoy, resuscitated the body they were carrying to the pile. It is asserted that Aesculapius restored to life Hippolytus, the son of Theseus; also Glaucus, the son of Minos, and Campanes, killed at the assault of Thebes, and Admetus, King of Phera in Thessaly. Elian attests that the same Aesculapius joined on again the head of a woman to her corpse, and restored her to life.

But if we possessed the certainty of all these events which we have just cited – I mean to say, were they attested by ocular witnesses, well-informed and disinterested, which is not the case – we ought to know the circumstances attending these events, and then we should be better able to dispute or assent to them.

For there is every appearance that the dead people resuscitated by Aesculapius were only persons who were dangerously ill, and restored to health by that skilful physician. The girl revived by Apollonius of Thyana was not really dead; even those who were carrying her to the funeral pile had their doubts if she were deceased. What is said of Simon the magician is anything but certain; and even if that impostor by his magical secrets could have performed some wonders on dead persons, it should be imputed to his delusions and to some artifice, which may have substituted living bodies or phantoms for the dead bodies which he boasted of having recalled to life. In a word, we hold it as indubitable that it is God only who can impart life to a person really dead, either by power proceeding immediately from himself, or by means of angels or of demons, who perform his behests.

I own that the instance of that boy of Dalhem is perplexing. Whether it was the spirit of the child that returned into his body to animate it anew, or the demon who replaced his soul, the puzzle appears to me the same; in all this circumstance we behold only the work of the evil spirit. God does not seem to have had any share in it. Now, if the demon can take the place of a spirit in a body newly dead, or if he can make the soul by which it was animated before death return into it, we can no longer dispute his power to restore a kind of life to a dead person; which would be a terrible temptation for us, who might be led to believe that the demon has a power which religion does not permit us to think that God shares with any created being.

I would then say, supposing the truth of the fact, of which I see no room to doubt, that God, to punish the abominable crime of the father, and to give an example of His just vengeance to mankind, permitted the demon to do on this occasion what he perhaps had never done, nor ever will again – to possess a body, and serve it in some sort as a soul, and give it action and motion whilst he could retain the body without its being too much corrupted.

And this example applies admirably to the ghosts of Hungary and Moravia, whom the demon will move and animate – will cause to appear and disturb the living, so far as to occasion their death. I say all this under the supposition that what is said of the vampires is true; for if it all be false and fabulous, it is losing time to seek the means of explaining it.

For the rest, several of the ancients, as Tertullian and Lactantius, believed that the demons were the only authors of all the magicians do when they evoke the souls of the dead. They cause borrowed bodies or phantoms to appear, say they, and fascinate the eyes of those present, to make them believe that to be real which is only seeming.

CHAPTER 35

Instances of Phantoms which have Appeared to be Alive, and have Given many Signs of Life

Le Loyer, in his book upon spectres, maintains, that the demon can cause the possessed to make extraordinary and involuntary movements. He can then, if allowed by God, give motion to a dead and insensible man.

He relates the instance of Polycrites, a magistrate of Aetolia, who appeared to the people of Locri nine or ten months after his death, and told them to show him his child, which being born monstrous, they wished to burn with its mother. The Locrians, in spite of the remonstrance of the spectre of Polycrites, persisting in their determination, Polycrites took his child, tore it to pieces and devoured it, leaving only the head, while the people could neither send him away nor prevent him; after that, he disappeared. The Aetolians were desirous of sending to consult the Delphian oracle, but the head of the child began to speak, and foretold the misfortunes which were to happen to their country and to his own mother.

After the battle between King Antiochus and the Romans, an officer named Buptages, left dead on the field of battle, with twelve mortal wounds, rose up suddenly, and began to threaten the Romans with the evils which were to happen to them through the foreign nations who were to destroy the Roman empire. He pointed out, in particular, that armies would come from Asia and desolate Europe, which may designate the irruption of the Turks upon the domains of the Roman empire.

After that, Buptages climbed up an oak tree, and foretold that he was about to be devoured by a wolf, which happened. After the wolf had devoured the body, the head again spoke to the Romans, and forbade them to bury him. All that appears very incredible, and was not accomplished in fact. It was not the people of Asia, but those of the North, who overthrew the Roman empire.

In the war of Augustus against Sextus Pompey, son of the great Pompey, a soldier of Augustus, named Gabinius, had his head cut off by order of young Pompey, so that it only held on to the neck by a narrow strip of flesh. Towards evening they heard Gabinius lamenting; they ran to him, and he said that he had returned from hell to reveal very important things to Pompey. Pompey did not think proper to go to him, but he sent one of his men, to whom Gabinius declared that the gods on high had decreed the happy destiny of Pompey, and that he would succeed in all his designs. Directly Gabinius had thus spoken, he fell down dead and stiff. This pretended prediction was falsified by the facts. Pompey was vanquished, and Caesar gained all the advantage in this war.

A certain female juggler had died, but a magician of the band put a charm under her armpits, which gave her power to move; but another wizard having looked at her, cried out that it was only vile carrion, and immediately she fell down dead, and appeared what she was in fact.

Nicole Aubri, a native of Vervins, being possessed by several devils, one of these devils, named Baltazo, took from the gibbet the body of a man who had been hanged near the plain of Arlon, and in this body went to the husband of Nicole Aubri, promising to deliver his wife from her possession if he would let him pass the night with her. The husband consulted the schoolmaster, who practised exorcising, and who told him on no account to grant what was asked of him. The husband and Baltazo having entered the church, the woman who was possessed called him by his name, and immediately this Baltazo disappeared. The schoolmaster conjuring the possessed, Beelzebub, one of the demons, revealed what Baltazo had done, and that if the husband had granted what he asked, he would have flown away with Nicole Aubri, both body and soul.

Le Loyer again relates four other instances of persons whom the demon had seemed to restore to life, to satisfy the brutal passion of two lovers.

CHAPTER 36

Devoting to Death, a Practice among the Pagans

The ancient heathens, both Greeks and Romans, attributed to magic and to the demon the power of occasioning the destruction of any person by a manner of devoting them to death, which consisted in forming a waxen image as much as possible like the person whose life they wished to take. They devoted him or her to death by their magical secrets; then they burned the waxen statue, and as that by degrees was consumed, so the doomed person became languid and at last died. Theocritus makes a woman transported with love speak thus: she invokes the image of the shepherd, and prays that the heart of Daphnis, her beloved, may melt like the image of wax which represents him.

Horace brings forward two enchantresses who evoke the shades, to make them announce the future. First of all, the witches tear a sheep with their teeth, shedding the blood into a grave, in order to bring those spirits from whom they expect an answer; then they place next to themselves two statues, one of wax, the other of wool; the latter is the largest, and mistress of the other. The waxen image is at its feet, as a suppliant, and awaiting only death. After divers magical ceremonies, the waxen image was inflamed and consumed.

He speaks of this again elsewhere; and after having with a mocking laugh made his complaints to the enchantress Canidia, saying that he is ready to make her honourable reparation, he owns that he feels all the effects of her too powerful art, as he himself has experienced it to give motion to waxen figures, and bring down the moon from the sky.

Virgil also speaks of these diabolical operations, and these waxen images, devoted by magic art.

There is reason to believe that these poets only repeat these things to show the absurdity of the pretended secrets of magic, and the vain and impotent ceremonies of sorcerers.

But it cannot be denied that, idle as all these practices may be, they have been used in ancient times; that many have put faith in them, and foolishly dreaded those attempts.

Lucian relates the effects of the magic of a certain Hyperborean, who, having formed a Cupid with clay, infused life into it, and sent it to fetch a girl named Chryseïs, with whom a young man had fallen in love. The little Cupid brought her, and on the morrow, at dawn of day, the moon, which the magician had brought down from the sky, returned thither. Hecate, whom he had evoked from the bottom of hell, fled away, and all the rest of this scene disappeared. Lucian, with great reason, ridicules all this, and observes that these magicians, who boast of having so much power, ordinarily exercise it only upon contemptible people, and are such themselves.

The oldest instances of this dooming are those which are set down in Scripture, in the Old Testament. God commands Moses to devote to anathema the Canaanites of the kingdom of Arad. He devotes also to anathema all the nations of the land of Canaan. Balac, king of Moab, sends to the diviner, Balaam, to engage him to curse and devote the people of Israel. 'Come,' says he to him, by his messenger, 'and curse me Israel; for I know that those whom you have cursed and doomed to destruction shall be cursed, and he whom you have blessed shall be crowned with blessings.'

We have in history instances of these devotings and maledictions, and evocations of the tutelary gods of cities by magic art. The ancients kept very secret the proper names of towns, for fear that if they came to the knowledge of the enemy, they might make use of them in their invocations, which to their mind had no might unless the proper name of the town was expressed. The usual names of Rome, Tyre, and Carthage, were not their true and secret names. Rome, for instance, was called Valentia, a name known to very few persons, and Valerius Soranus was severely punished for having revealed it.

Macrobius has preserved for us the formula of a solemn devoting or dooming of a city, and of imprecations against her, by devoting her to some hurtful and dangerous demon. We find in the heathen poets a great number of these invocations and magical doomings, to inspire a dangerous passion, or to occasion maladies. It is surprising that these superstitious and abominable practices should have gained entrance among Christians, and have been dreaded by persons who ought to have known their vanity and impoteney.

Tacitus relates, that at the death of Germanicus, who was said to have been poisoned by Piso and Plautina, there were found in the ground and in the walls bones of human bodies, doomings, and charms, or magic verses, with the name of Germanicus engraved upon thin plates of lead steeped in corrupted blood, half-burnt ashes, and other charms, by virtue of which it was believed that spirits could be evoked.

CHAPTER 37

Instances of Devoting or Dooming amongst Christians

Hector Boethius, in his History of Scotland, relates, that Duffus, king of that country, falling ill of a disorder unknown to the physicians, was consumed by a slow fever, passed his nights without sleep, and insensibly wasted away; his body melted in perspiration every night; he became weak, languid, and in a dying state, without, however, his pulse undergoing any alteration. Everything was done to relieve him, but uselessly. His life was despaired of, and those about him began to suspect some evil spell. In the meantime, the people of Moray, a county of Scotland, mutinied, supposing that the king must soon sink under his malady.

It was whispered abroad that the king had been bewitched by some witches who lived at Forres, a little town in the north of Scotland. People were sent there to arrest them, and they were surprised in their dwellings, where one of them was basting an image of King Duffus, made of wax, turning on a wooden spit before a large fire, before which she was reciting certain magical prayers; and she affirmed, that as the figure melted, the king would lose his strength, and at last he would die, when the figure should be entirely melted. These women declared that they had been hired to perform these evil spells by the principal men of the county of Moray, who only awaited the king's decease to burst into open revolt.

These witches were immediately arrested and burnt at the stake. The king was much better, and in a few days he perfectly recovered his health. This account is found also in the History of Scotland by Buchanan, who says he heard it from his elders.

He makes the King Duffus live in 960, and he who has added notes to the text of these historians says, that this custom of melting waxen images by magic art, to occasion the death of certain persons, was not unknown to the Romans, as appears from Virgil and Ovid; and of this we have related a sufficient number of instances. But it must be owned, that all which is related concerning it is very doubtful; not that wizards and witches have not been found, who have attempted to cause the death of persons of high rank by these means, and who attributed the effect to the demon; but there is little appearance that they ever succeeded in it. If magicians possessed the secret of thus occasioning the death of anyone they pleased, where is the prince, prelate, or lord who would be safe? If they could thus roast them slowly to death, why not kill them at once, by throwing the waxen image in the fire? Who can have given such power to the devil? Is it the Almighty, to satisfy the revenge of an insignificant woman, or the jealousy of lovers of either sex?

M. de St André, physician to the king, in his Letters on Witchcraft, would explain the effects of these devotings, supposing them to be true, by the evaporation of animal spirits, which, proceeding from the bodies of the wizards or witches, and uniting with the atoms which fall from the wax, and the atoms of the fire, which render them still more pungent, should fly towards the person they desire to bewitch, and cause in him or her sensations of heat or pain, more or less violent according to the action of the fire. But I do not think that this clever man finds many to approve of his idea. The shortest way, in my opinion, would be, to deny the effects of these charms; for if these effects are real, they are inexplicable by physics, and can only be attributed to the devil.

We read in the History of the Archbishops of Treves, that Eberard, Archbishop of that Church, who died in 1067, having threatened to send away the Jews from his city, if they did not embrace Christianity, these unhappy people, being reduced to despair, suborned an ecclesiastic, who for money baptised for them, by the name of the bishop, a waxen image, to which they tied wicks or wax tapers, and lighted them on Holy Saturday (Easter Eve), as the prelate was going solemnly to administer the baptismal rite.

Whilst he was occupied in this holy function, the statue being half-consumed, Eberard felt himself extremely ill; he was led into the vestry, where he soon after expired.

The Pope John XXII in 1317, complained, in public letters, that some scoundrels had attempted his life by similar operations; and he appeared persuaded of their power, and that he had been preserved from death only by the particular protection of God. "We inform you," says he, "that some traitors have conspired against us, and against some of our brothers the cardinals, and have prepared beverages and images to take away our life, which they have sought to do on every occasion; but God has always preserved us." The letter is dated the 27th July.

From the 27th February, the Pope had issued a commission to inform against these poisoners; his letter is addressed to Bartholomew, Bishop of

Fréjus, who had succeeded the Pope in that see, and to Peter Tessier, doctor *en decret*, afterwards cardinal. The Pope says therein, in substance – "We have heard that John de Limoges, Jacques de Crabançon, Jean d'Arrant, physician, and some others, have applied themselves, through a damnable curiosity, to necromancy and other magical arts, on which they have books; that they have often made use of mirrors, and images consecrated in their manner; that placing themselves within circles, they have often invoked the evil spirits to occasion the death of men by the might of their enchantments, or by sending maladies which abridge their days. Sometimes they have enclosed demons in mirrors, or circles, or rings, to interrogate them, not only on the past, but on the future, and make predictions. They pretend to have made many experiments in these matters, and fearlessly assert, that they can not only by means of certain beverages, or certain meats, but by simple words, abridge or prolong life, and cure all sorts of diseases."

The Pope gave a similar commission, 22nd April 1317, to the Bishop of Riès, to the same Pierre Tessier, to Pierre Després, and two others, to inquire into the conspiracy formed against him and against the cardinals; and in this commission he says: "They have prepared beverages to poison us, and not having been able conveniently to make us take them, they have had waxen images made, with our names, to attack our lives, by pricking these images with magical enchantments, and invocations of demons; but God has preserved us, and caused three of these images to fall into our hands."

We see a description of similar charms in a letter, written three years after, to the Inquisitor of Carcassone, by William de Godin, Cardinal-Bishop of Sabina, in which he says: "The Pope commands you to enquire and proceed against those who sacrifice to demons, worship them, or pay them homage, by giving them for a token a written paper, or something else, to bind the demon, or to work some charm by invoking him; who, abusing the sacrament of baptism, baptise images of wax, or of other matters with invocation of demons; who abuse the eucharist, or consecrated wafer, or other sacraments, by exercising their evil spells. You will proceed against them with the prelates, as you do in matters of heresy; for the Pope gives you the power to do so." The letter is dated from Avignon, the 22nd August 1320.

At the trial of Enguerrand de Marigni, they brought forward a wizard whom they had surprised making waxen images, representing King Louis le Hutin and Charles de Valois, and meaning to kill them by pricking or melting these images.

It is related also, that Cosmo Rugieri, a Florentine, a great atheist and pretended magician, had a secret chamber, where he shut himself up alone, and pricked with a needle a wax image representing the king, after having loaded it with maledictions and devoted it to destruction by horrible enchantments, hoping thus to cause the prince to languish away and die.

Whether these conjurations, these waxen images, these magical words, may have produced their effects or not, it proves at any rate the opinion that was entertained on the subject – the ill will of the wizards, and the fear in which they were held. Although their enchantments and imprecations might not be followed by any effect, it is apparently thought that experience on that point made them dreaded, whether with reason or not.

The general ignorance of physics made people at that time take many things to be supernatural, which were simply the effects of natural causes; and as it is certain, as our faith teaches us, that God has often permitted demons to deceive mankind by prodigies, and do them injury by extraordinary means, it was supposed, without examining into the matter, that there was an art of magic, and sure rules for discovering certain secrets, or causing certain evils by means of demons – as if God had not always been the Supreme Master, to permit or to hinder them; or as if He would have ratified the compacts made with evil spirits.

But on examining closely this pretended magic, we have found nothing but poisonings, attended by superstition and imposture. All that we have just related of the effects of magic, enchantments, and witchcraft, which were pretended to cause such terrible effects on the bodies and the possessions of mankind; and all that is recounted of doomings, evocations, and magic figures, which, being consumed by fire, occasioned the death of those who were destined or enchanted – relates but very imperfectly to the affair of vampires, which we are treating of in this volume; unless it may be said that those ghosts are raised and evoked by magic art, and that the persons who fancy themselves strangled and finally stricken with death by vampires, only suffer these miseries through the malice of the demon, who makes their deceased parents or relations appear to them, and produces all these effects upon them; or simply strikes the imagination of the persons to whom it happens, and makes them believe that it is their deceased relations, who come to torment and kill them; although in all this it is only an imagination strongly affected, which acts upon them.

We may also connect with the history of ghosts what is related of certain persons who have promised each other to return after their death, and to reveal what passes in the other world, and the state in which they find themselves.

CHAPTER 38

Instances of Persons who have Promised to Give each Other News of the other World after their Death

The story of the Marquis de Rambouillet, who appeared after his death to the Marquis de Précy, is very celebrated. These two lords, conversing on the subject of the other world, like people who were not very strongly persuaded of the truth of all that is said upon it, promised each other that the first of the two who died should bring the news of it to the other. The Marquis de Rambouillet set off for Flanders, where the war was then carried on; and the Marquis de Précy remained at Paris, detained by a low fever. Six weeks after, in broad day, he heard someone undraw his bed-curtains, and turning to see who it was, he perceived the Marquis de Rambouillet, in buff-leather jacket and boots. He sprang from his bed to embrace his friend; but Rambouillet, stepping back a few paces, told him that he was come to keep his word as he had promised – that all that was said of the next life was very certain – that he must change his conduct, and in the first action wherein he was engaged he would lose his life.

Précy again attempted to embrace his friend, but he embraced only empty air. Then Rambouillet, seeing that his friend was incredulous as to what he said, showed him where he had received the wound in his side, whence the blood still seemed to flow. Précy soon after received, by the post, confirmation of the death of the Marquis de Rambouillet; and being himself some time after, during the civil wars, at the Battle of the Faubourg of St Antoine, he was there killed.

Peter the Venerable, Abbot of Clugni, relates a very similar story. A gentleman named Humbert, son of a lord named Guichard de Belioc, in the diocese of Mâçon, having declared war against the other principal men in his neighbourhood, a gentleman, named Geoffrey d'Iden, received in the mêlée a wound, of which he died immediately.

About two months afterwards, this same Geoffrey appeared to a gentle-man named Milo d'Ansa, and begged him to tell Humbert de Belioc, in whose service he had lost his life, that he was tormented for having assisted him in an unjust war, and for not having expiated his sins by penance before he died; that he begged him to have compassion on him, and on his own father, Guichard, who had left him great wealth, of which he made a bad use, and of which a part had been badly acquired. That in truth Guichard, the father of Humbert, had embraced a religious life at Clugni; but that he had not had time to satisfy the justice of God, for the sins of his past life; that he conjured him to have mass performed for him and for his father, to give alms, and to employ the prayers of good people, to procure them both a prompt deliverance from the pains they endured. He added, 'Tell him, that if he will not mind what you say, I shall be obliged to go to him myself, and announce to him what I have just told you.'

Milo d'Ansa acquitted himself faithfully of his commission; Humbert was frightened at it, but it did not make him better. Still, fearing that Guichard, his father, or Geoffrey d'Iden, might come and disturb him, above all during the night, he dare not remain alone, and would always have one of his people by him.

One morning then, as he was lying awake in his bed, he beheld in his presence Geoffrey, armed as in a day of battle, who showed him the mortal wound he had received, and which appeared yet quite fresh. He reproached him keenly for his want of pity towards his own father, who was groaning in torment. Take care, added he, that God does not treat you rigorously, and refuse to you that mercy which you refuse to us; and above all, take care not to execute your intention of going to the wars with Count Amadeus. If you go, you will there lose both life and property.

He said, and Humbert was about to reply, when the Squire Vichard de Maracy, Humbert's counsellor, arrived from mass, and immediately the dead man disappeared. From that moment, Humbert endeavoured seriously to relieve his father Geoffrey, and resolved to take a journey to Jerusalem to expiate his sins. Peter the Venerable had been well informed of all the details of this story, which occurred in the year he went into Spain, and made a great noise in the country.

The Cardinal Baronius, a very grave and respectable man, says, that he had heard from several very sensible persons, who had often heard it preached to the people, and in particular from Michael Mercati Protho, notary of the Holy See, a man of acknowledged probity and well informed, particularly in the Platonic philosophy, to which he applied himself unweariedly with Marsilius Ficin, his friend, as zealous as himself for the doctrine of Plato.

One day, these two great philosophers were conversing on the immortality of the soul, and if it remained and existed after the death of the body. After having had much discourse on this matter, they promised each other, and shook hands upon it, that the first of them who quitted this world should come and tell the other somewhat of the state of the other life.

Having thus separated, it happened some time afterwards, that the same Michael Mercati, being wide awake and studying, one morning very early, the same philosophical matters, heard on a sudden a noise like a horseman who was coming hastily to his door, and at the same time he heard the voice of his friend Marsilius Ficin, who cried out to him, 'Michael, Michael, nothing is more true than what is said of the other life.' At the same, Michael opened his window, and saw Marsilius mounted on a white horse, who was galloping away. Michael cried out to him to stop, but he continued his course till Michael could no longer see him.

Marsilius Ficin was at that time dwelling at Florence, and died there at the same hour that he had appeared and spoken to his friend. The latter wrote directly to Florence, to inquire into the truth of the circumstance; and they replied to him, that Marsilius had died at the same moment that Michael had heard his voice and the noise of his horse at his door. Ever after that adventure, Michael Mercati, although very regular in his conduct before then, became quite an altered man, and lived in so exemplary a manner, that he became a perfect model of Christian life. We find a great many such instances in Henry More, and in Joshua Glanville, in his work entitled *Saduceeism Combated.*

Here is one taken from the Life of B. Joseph de Lionisse, a missionary Capuchin. One day when he was conversing with his companion on the duties of religion, and the fidelity which God requires of those who have consecrated themselves to them, of the reward reserved for those who are perfectly religious, and the severe justice which he exercises against unfaithful servants, Brother Joseph said to him, 'Let us promise each other mutually, that the one who dies first will appear to the other, if God allows him so to do, to inform him of what passes in the other world, and the condition in which he finds himself.' 'I am willing,' replied the holy companion, 'I give you my word upon it.' 'And I pledge you mine,' replied Brother Joseph.

Some days after this, the pious companion was attacked by a malady which brought him to the tomb. Brother Joseph felt this the more sensibly, because he knew better than the others all the virtues of this holy monk. He had no doubt of the fulfilment of their agreement, or that the deceased would appear to him, when he least thought of it, to acquit himself of his promise.

In effect, one day when Brother Joseph had retired to his room, in the afternoon, he saw a young Capuchin enter horribly haggard, with a pale thin face, who saluted him with a feeble, trembling voice. As, at the sight of this spectre, Joseph appeared a little disturbed, 'Don't be alarmed,' it said to him; 'I am come here as permitted by God, to fulfil my promise, and to tell you that I have the happiness to be amongst the elect through the mercy of the Lord. But learn that it is even more difficult to be saved than is thought in this world; that God, whose wisdom can penetrate the most secret folds of the heart, weighs exactly the actions which we have done during life, the thoughts, wishes, and motives, which we propose to ourselves in acting; and as much as He is inexorable in regard to sinners, so much is He good, indulgent, and rich in mercy, towards those just souls who have served Him in this life.' At these words the phantom disappeared.

Here follows an instance of a spirit which comes after death to visit his friend without having made an agreement with him to do so. Peter Garmate, Bishop of Cracow, was translated to the archbishopric of Gnesnes, in 1548, and obtained a dispensation from Paul III to retain still his bishopric of Cracow. This prelate, after having led a very irregular life during his youth, began, towards the end of his life, to perform many charitable actions, feeding every day a hundred poor, to whom he sent food from his own table. And when he travelled, he was followed by two wagons, loaded with coats and shirts, which he distributed amongst the poor according as they needed them.

One day, when he was preparing to go to church, towards evening, (it being the eve of a festival,) and he was alone in his closet, he suddenly beheld before him a gentleman named Curosius, who had been dead some time, with whom he had formerly been too intimately associated in evil doing.

The Archbishop Garmate was at first affrighted, but the defunct reassured him, and told him that he was of the number of the blessed. 'What!' said the prelate to him, 'after such a life as you led! For you know the excesses which both you and myself committed in our youth.' 'I know it,' replied the defunct; 'but this is what saved me. One day, when in Germany, I found myself with a man who uttered blasphemous discourse, most injurious to the Holy Virgin. I was irritated at it, and gave him a blow – we drew our swords, I killed him; and for fear of being arrested and punished as a homicide, I took flight, without reflecting much on the action I had committed. But at the hour of death, I found myself most terribly disturbed by remorse for my past life, and I only expected certain destruction; when the Holy Virgin came to my aid, and made such powerful intercession for me with her Son, that she obtained for me the pardon of my sins; and I have the happiness to enjoy beatitude. For yourself, who have only six months to live, I am sent to warn you, that in consideration of your alms, and your charity to the poor, God will show you mercy, and expects you to do penance. Profit while it is time, and expiate your past sins.' After having said this, he disappeared; and the archbishop, bursting into tears, began to live in so Christian a manner, that he was the edification of all who knew him. He related the circumstance to his most intimate friends, and died in 1545, after having directed the Church of Gnesnes for about five years.

The daughter of Dumoulin, a celebrated lawyer, having been inhumanly massacred in her dwelling, appeared by night to her husband, who was wide awake, and declared to him the names of those who had killed herself and her children, conjuring him to revenge her death.

CHAPTER 39

Extract from the Political Works of M. l'Abbe de St Pierre

I was told lately at Valogne, that a good priest of the town, who teaches the children to read, had had an apparition in broad day ten or twelve years ago. As that had made a great deal of noise at first, on account of his reputation for probity and sincerity, I had the curiosity to hear him relate his adventure himself. A lady, one of my relations, who was acquainted with him, sent to invite him to dine with her yesterday, the 7th January 1708; and as on the one hand I showed a desire to learn the thing from himself, and on the other it was a kind of honourable distinction to have had by daylight an apparition of one of his comrades, he related it before dinner without requiring to be pressed, and in a very naive manner.

'In 1695,' said M. Bezuel to us, 'being a schoolboy of about fifteen years of age, I became acquainted with the two children of M. Abaquene, attorney, schoolboys like myself. The eldest was of my own age, the second was eighteen months younger; he was named Desfontaines; we took all our walks and all our parties of pleasure together, and whether it was that Desfontaines had more affection for me, or that he was more gay, obliging, and clever than his brother, I loved him the best.

'In 1696, we were walking both of us in the cloister of the Capuchins. He told me that he had lately read a story of two friends who had promised each other that the first of them who died should come and bring news of his condition to the one still living; that the one who died came back to earth, and told his friend surprising things. Upon that, Desfontaines told me that he had a favour to ask of me; that he begged me to grant it instantly: it was to make him a similar promise, and on his part he would do the same. I told him that I would not. For several months he talked to me of it, often and seriously; I always resisted his wish. At last, towards the month of August 1696, as he was to leave to go and study at Caen, he pressed me so much with tears in his eyes, that I consented to it. He drew out at that moment two little papers which he had ready written: one was signed with his blood, in which he promised me that in case of his death he would come and bring me news of his condition; in the other, I promised him the same thing. I pricked my finger; a drop of blood came, with which I signed my name. He was delighted to have my billet, and embracing me, he thanked me a thousand times.

'Some time after, he set off with his tutor. Our separation caused us much grief, but we wrote to each other now and then, and it was but six weeks since I had had a letter from him, when what I am going to relate to you happened to me.

'The 31st July 1697, one Thursday – I shall remember it all my life – the late M. Sortoville, with whom I lodged, and who had been very kind to me, begged of me to go to a meadow near the Cordeliers, and help his people, who were making hay, and to make haste. I had not been there a quarter of an hour, when, about half past two, I all of a sudden felt giddy and weak. In vain I leant upon my hay fork; I was obliged to place myself on a little hay, where I was nearly half an hour recovering my senses. That passed off; but as nothing of the kind had ever occurred to me before, I was surprised at it, and I feared it might be the commencement of an illness. Neverthe- less, it did not make much impression upon me during the remainder of the day. It is true, I did not sleep that night so well as usual.

'The next day, at the same hour, as I was conducting to the meadow M. de St Simon, the grandson of M. de Sortoville, who was then ten years old, I felt myself seized on the way with a similar faintness, and I sat down on a stone in the shade. That passed off, and we continued our way; nothing more happened to me that day, and at night I had hardly any sleep.

'At last, on the morrow, the second day of August, being in the loft where they laid up the hay they brought from the meadow, I was taken with a similar giddiness and a similar faintness, but still more violent than the other. I fainted away completely; one of the men perceived it. I have been told that I was asked what was the matter with me, and that I replied, "I have seen what I should never have believed;" but I have no recollection of either the question or the answer. That however accords with what I do remember to have seen just then; as it were someone naked to the middle, but whom, however, I did not recognise. They helped me down from the ladder. The faintness seized me again. my head swam as I was between two rounds of the ladder, and again I fainted. They took me down and placed me on a beam which served for a seat in the large square of the Capuchins. I sat down on it, and then I no longer saw M. de Sortoville nor his domestics, although present; but perceiving Desfontaines near the foot of the ladder, who made me a sign to come to him, I moved on my seat as if to make room for him; and those who saw me and whom I did not see, although my eyes were open, remarked this movement.

'As he did not come, I rose to go to him. He advanced towards me, took my left arm with his right arm, and led me about thirty paces from thence into a retired street, holding me still under the arm. The domestics, supposing that my giddiness had passed off, and that I had purposely retired, went everyone to their work, except a little servant who went and told M. de Sortoville that I was talking all alone. M. de Sortoville thought I was tipsy; he drew near, and heard me ask some questions, and make some answers, which he has told me since.

'I was there nearly three-quarters of an hour, conversing with Desfontaines. "I promised you,'" said he to me, "that if I died before you I would come and tell you of it. I was drowned the day before yesterday in the river of Caen, at nearly this same hour. I was out walking with such and such a one. It was very warm, and we had a wish to bathe; a faintness seized me in the water, and I fell to the bottom. The Abbé de Menil-Jean, my comrade, dived to bring me up. I seized hold of his foot; but whether he was afraid it might be a salmon, because I held him so fast, or that he wished to remount promptly to the surface of the water, he shook his leg so roughly, that he gave me a violent kick on the breast, which sent me to the bottom of the river, which is there very deep."

'Desfontaines related to me afterwards all that had occurred to them in their walk, and the subjects they had conversed upon. It was in vain for me to ask him questions – whether he was saved, whether he was damned, if he was in purgatory, if I was in a state of grace, and if I should soon follow him; he continued to discourse as if he had not heard me, and as if he would not hear me.

'I approached him several times to embrace him, but it seemed to me that I embraced nothing, and yet I felt very sensibly that he held me tightly by the arm, and that when I tried to turn away my head that I might not see him, because I could not look at him without feeling afflicted, he shook my arm as if to oblige me to look at and listen to him.

'He always appeared to me taller than I had seen him, and taller even than he was at the time of his death, although he had grown during the eighteen months in which we had not met. I beheld him always naked to the middle of his body, his head uncovered, with his fine fair hair, and a white scroll twisted in his hair over his forehead, on which there was some writing, but I could only make out the word *in*, etc.

'It was his usual tone of voice. He appeared to me neither gay nor sad, but in a calm and tranquil state. He begged of me, when his brother returned, to tell him certain things to say to his father and mother. He begged me to say the Seven Psalms which had been given him as a penance the preceding

Sunday, which he had not yet recited; again he recommended me to speak to his brother, and then he bade me adieu, saying, as he left me, *Jusques, jusques,* (*till, till,*) which was the usual term he made use of when at the end of our walk we bade each other goodbye, to go home.

'He told me that at the time he was drowned, his brother, who was writing a translation, regretted having let him go without accompanying him, fearing some accident. He described to me so well where he was drowned, and the tree in the avenue of Louvigni on which he had written a few words, that two years afterwards, being there with the late Chevalier de Gotol, one of those who were with him at the time he was drowned, I pointed out to him the very spot; and by counting the trees in a particular direction which Desfontaines had specified to me, I went straight up to the tree, and I found his writing. He (the Chevalier) told me also that the article of the Seven Psalms was true, and that on coming from confession they had told each other their penance; and since then his brother has told me that it was quite true that at that hour he was writing his exercise, and he reproached himself for not having accompanied his brother. As nearly a month passed by without my being able to do what Desfontaines had told me in regard to his brother, he appeared to me again twice before dinner at a country house whither I had gone to dine a league from hence. I was very faint. I told them not to mind me, that it was nothing, and that I should soon recover myself; and I went to a corner of the garden. Desfontaines having appeared to me, reproached me for not having yet spoken to his brother, and again conversed with me for a quarter of an hour without answering any of my questions.

'As I was going in the morning to Notre-Dame de la Victoire, he appeared to me again, but for a shorter time, and pressed me always to speak to his brother, and left me, saying still, *Jusques, Jusques*, and without choosing to reply to my questions.

'It is a remarkable thing that I always felt a pain in that part of my arm which he had held me by the first time, until I had spoken to his brother. I was three days without being able to sleep, from the astonishment and agitation I felt. At the end of the first conversation, I told M. de Varonville, my neighbour and schoolfellow, that Desfontaines had been drowned; that he himself had just appeared to me and told me so. He went away and ran to the parents' house to know if it was true; they had just received the news, but by a mistake he understood that it was the eldest. He assured me that he had read the letter of Desfontaines, and he believed it; but I maintained always that it could not be, and that Desfontaines himself had appeared to me. He returned, came back, and told me in tears that it was but too true.

'Nothing has occurred to me since, and there is my adventure just as it happened. It has been related in various ways; but I have recounted it only as I have just told it to you. The Chevalier de Gotol told me that

Desfontaines had appeared also to M. de Menil-Jean; but I am not acquainted with him; he lives twenty leagues from hence near Argentan, and I can say no more about it.'

This is a very singular and circumstantial narrative, related by M. l'Abbé de St Pierre, who is by no means credulous, and sets his whole mind and all his philosophy to explain the most extraordinary events by physical reasonings, by the concurrence of atoms, corpuscles, insensible evaporation of spirit, and perspiration. But this is so far-fetched, and does such palpable violence to the subjects and the attending circumstances, that the most credulous would not yield to such arguments. It is surprising that these gentlemen, who pique themselves on strength of mind, and so haughtily reject everything that appears supernatural, can so easily admit philosophical systems much more incredible than even the facts they oppose. They raise doubts which are often very ill-founded, and attack them upon principles still more uncertain. That may be called refuting one difficulty by another, and resolving a doubt by principles still more doubtful.

But, it will be said, whence comes it that so many other persons who had engaged themselves to come and bring news of the immortality of the soul, after their death, have not come back. Seneca speaks of a Stoic philosopher, named Julius Canus, who, having been condemned to death by Julius Caesar, said aloud that he was about to learn the truth of that question on which they were divided; to wit, whether the soul was immortal or not. And we do not read that he revisited this world. La Motte de Vayer had agreed with his friend Baranzan the Barnabite, that the first of the two who died should warn the other of the state in which he found himself. Baranzan died, and returned not.

Because the dead sometimes return to earth, it would be imprudent to conclude that they always do so. And it would be equally wrong reasoning to say that they never do return, because having promised to revisit this world they have not done so. For in that case we should imagine that it is in the power of spirits to return and make their appearance when they will, and if they will; but it seems indubitable that, on the contrary, it is not in their power, and that it is only by the express permission of God that disembodied spirits sometimes appear to the living.

We see, in the history of the bad rich man, that God would not grant him the favour which he asked, to send to earth one of those who were in Hades. Similar reasons, derived from the hardness of heart or the incredulity of mortals, may have prevented, in the same manner, the return of Julius Canus or of Baranzan. The return of spirits and their apparition is neither a natural thing nor dependent on the choice of those who are dead. It is a supernatural effect, and allied to the miraculous.

St Augustine says on this subject, that if the dead interest themselves in what concerns the living, St Monica, his mother, who loved him so tenderly, and went with him by sea and land everywhere during her life, would not have failed to visit him every night, and come to console him in his troubles; for we must not suppose that she was become less compassionate since she became one of the blest: *absit ut facta sit vitâ feliciore crudelis.*

The return of spirits, their apparition, the execution of the promises which certain persons have made each other, to come and tell their friends what passes in the other world, is not in their own power. All this is in the hands of God.

CHAPTER 40

Divers Systems for Explaining the Return of Spirits

The affair of ghosts having made so much noise in the world as it has done, it is not surprising that a diversity of systems should have been formed upon it, and that so many schemes should have been proposed to explain their return to earth and their operations.

Some have thought that it was a momentary resurrection, caused by the soul of the defunct, which re-entered his body, or by the demon, who re-animated him, and caused him to act for a while, whilst his blood retained its consistency and fluidity, and his organic functions were not entirely corrupted and deranged.

Others, struck with the consequence of such principles, and the arguments which might be deduced from them, chose rather to suppose that these vampires were not really dead; that they still retained certain seeds of life, and that their spirits could from time to time reanimate and bring them out of their tombs, to make their appearance amongst men, take refreshment, and renew the nourishing juices and animal spirits by sucking the blood of their near kindred.

There has lately been printed a dissertation on the uncertainty of the signs of death, and the abuse of hasty interments, by M. Jacques Benigne Vinslow, Doctor, Regent of the Faculty at Paris, translated, with a commentary, by Jacques Jean Bruhier, physician, at Paris, 1742, in 8vo. This work may serve to explain how persons who have been believed to be dead, and have been buried as such, have nevertheless been found alive a considerable time after their funeral obsequies had been performed. This will perhaps render vampirism less incredible.

M. Vinslow, Doctor, and Regent of the Medical Faculty at Paris, maintained, in the month of April 1740, a thesis, in which he asks if the experiments of surgery are fitter than all others to discover the signs of uncertain death. He therein maintained that there are many occurrences in which the signs of death are very doubtful; and he adduces several instances of persons believed to be dead, and interred as such, who nevertheless were afterwards found to be alive.

M. Bruhier MD has translated this thesis into French, and has made some learned additions to it, which serve to strengthen the opinion of M. Vinslow. The work is very interesting, from the matter it treats upon, and very agreeable to read, from the manner in which it is written. I am about to make some extracts from it, which may be useful to my subject. I shall adhere principally to the most certain and singular facts; for to relate them all, we must transcribe the whole work.

It is known that John Duns, surnamed Scot, or the Subtle Doctor, had the misfortune to be interred alive at Cologne, and that when his tomb was opened some time afterwards, it was found that he had gnawed his arm. The same thing is related of the emperor Zeno, who made himself heard from the depth of his tomb by repeated cries to those who were watching over him. Lancisi, a celebrated physician of the pope Clement XI relates, that at Rome he was witness to a person of distinction being still alive when he wrote, who resumed sense and motion whilst they were chanting his funeral service at church.

Pierre Zacchias, another celebrated physician of Rome, says, that in the hospital of the Saint Esprit, a young man, who was attacked with the plague, fell into so complete a state of syncope, that he was believed to be really dead. Whilst they were carrying his corpse, along with a great many others, on the other side of the Tiber, the young man gave signs of life. He was brought back to the hospital and cured. Two days after, he fell into a similar syncope, and that time he was reputed to be dead beyond recovery. He was placed amongst others intended for burial, came to himself a second time, and was yet living when Zacchias wrote.

It is related, that a man named William Foxley, when forty years of age, falling asleep on the 27th April 1546, remained plunged in sleep for fourteen days and fourteen nights, without any preceding malady. He could not persuade himself that he had slept more than one night, and was convinced of his long sleep only by being shown a building begun some days before this drowsy attack, and which he beheld completed on his awaking. It is said that in the time of Pope Gregory II a scholar of Lubec slept for seven years consecutively. Lilius Giraldus relates that a peasant slept through the whole autumn and winter.

CHAPTER 41

Various Instances of Persons being Buried Alive

Plutarch relates, that a man who fell from a great height, having pitched upon his neck, was believed to be dead, without there being the appearance of any hurt. As they were carrying him to be buried, the day after, he all at once recovered his strength and his senses. Asclepiades, meeting a great funeral train of a person they were taking to be interred, obtained permission to look at and to touch the dead man; he found some signs of life in him, and by means of proper remedies he immediately recalled him to life, and restored him in sound health to his parents and relations.

There are several instances of persons who after being interred came to themselves, and lived a long time in perfect health. They relate in particular, that a woman of Orleans was buried in a cemetery, with a ring on her finger, which they had not been able to draw off when she was placed in her coffin. The following night, a domestic, attracted by the hope of gain, broke open the coffin, and as he could not tear the ring off her finger, was about to cut her finger off, when she uttered a loud shriek. The servant fled. The woman disengaged herself as she could from her winding sheet, returned home, and survived her husband.

M. Bernard, a principal surgeon at Paris, attests that, being with his father at the parish of Réal, they took from the tombs, living and breathing, a monk of the order of St Francis, who had been shut up in it three or four days, and who had gnawed his hands around the bands which confined them. But he died almost the moment that he was in the air.

Several persons have made mention of that wife of a counseller of Cologne, who having been interred with a valuable ring on her finger, in 1571, the gravedigger opened the grave the succeeding night to steal the ring. But the good lady caught hold of him, and forced him to take her out of the coffin. He, however, disengaged himself from her hands, and fled. The resuscitated lady went and rapped at the door of her house. At first they thought it was a phantom, and left her a long time at the door, waiting anxiously to be let in; but at last they opened it for her. They warmed her, and she recovered her health perfectly, and had after that three sons, who all belonged to the Church. This event is exhibited on her sepulchre in a picture, or painting, in which the story is represented, and moreover written in German verses.

It is added, that the lady, in order to convince those of the house that it was herself, told the footman who came to the door that the horses had gone up to the hay loft, which was true; and there are still to be seen at the windows of the *grenier* of that house, horses' heads, carved in wood, as a sign of the truth of the matter.

François de Civile, a Norman gentleman, was the captain of a hundred men in the city of Rouen, when it was besieged by Charles IX, and he was then six-and-twenty. He was mortally wounded at the end of an assault; and having fallen into the moat, some pioneers placed him in a grave with some other bodies, and covered them over with a little earth. He remained there from eleven in the morning till half-past six in the evening, when his servant went to disinter him. This domestic, having remarked some signs of life, put him in a bed, where he remained for five days and nights, without speaking, or giving any other sign of feeling, but as burning hot with fever as he had been cold in the grave. The city having been taken by storm, the servants of an officer of the victorious army, who was to lodge in the house wherein was Civile, threw the latter upon a paillasse in a back room, whence the enemies tossed him out of the window upon a dunghill, where he remained for more than seventy-two hours in his shirt. At the end of that time one of his relations, surprised to find him still alive, sent him to a league's distance from Rouen, where he was attended to, and at last was perfectly cured. During a great plague, which attacked the city of Dijon, in 1558, a lady, named Nicole Lentillet, being reputed dead of the epidemic, was thrown into a great pit, wherein they buried the dead. The day after her interment, in the morning, she came to herself again, and made vain efforts to get out; but her weakness, and the weight of the other bodies with which she was covered, prevented her doing so. She remained in this horrible situation for four days, when the burial men drew her out, and carried her back to her house, where she perfectly recovered her health.

A young lady of Augsburg, having fallen into a swoon, or trance, her body was placed under a deep vault, without being covered with earth; but the entrance to this subterranean vault was closely walled up. Some years after that time, someone of the same family died. The vault was opened, and the body of the young lady was found at the very entrance, without any fingers to her right hand, which she had devoured in despair.

On the 25th July 1688, there died at Metz a hairdresser's boy, of an apoplectic fit, in the evening, after supper.

On the 28th of the same month, he was heard to moan again several times. They took him out of his grave, and he was attended by doctors and surgeons. The physician maintained, after he had been opened, that the young man had not been dead two hours. This is extracted from the manuscript of a bourgeois of Metz, who was contemporary with him.

CHAPTER 42

Instances of Drowned Persons Recovering their Health

Here follow some instances of drowned persons who came to themselves several days after they were believed to be dead. Peclin relates the story of a gardener of Troninghalm, in Sweden, who was still alive, and sixty-five years of age, when the author wrote. This man being on the ice to assist another man who had fallen into the water, the ice broke under him, and he sunk under water to the depth of eight ells, his feet sticking in the mud: he remained sixteen hours before they drew him out of the water. In this condition, he lost all sense, except that he thought he heard the bells ringing at Stockholm. He felt the water, which entered his body, not by his mouth, but his ears. After having sought for him during sixteen hours, they caught hold of his head with a hook, and drew him out of the water; they placed him between sheets, put him near the fire, rubbed him, shook him, and at last brought him to himself. The king and chancellor would see him and hear his story, and gave him a pension.

A woman of the same country, after having been three days in the water, was also revived by the same means as the gardener. Another person named Janas, having drowned himself at seventeen years of age, was taken out of the water seven weeks after; they warmed him, and brought him back to life.

Mr d'Egly, of the Royal Academy of Inscriptions and Belles Lettres, at Paris, relates, that a Swiss, an expert diver, having plunged down into one of the hollows in the bed of the river, where he hoped to find fine fish, remained there about nine hours; they drew him out of the water, after having hurt him in several places with their hooks. M. d'Egly, seeing that the water bubbled strongly from his mouth, maintained that he was not dead. They made him throw up as much water as he could for three quarters of an hour, wrapped him up in hot linen, put him to bed, bled him, and saved him.

Some have been recovered after being seven weeks in the water, others after a less time; for instance, Gocellin, a nephew of the Archbishop of Cologne, having fallen into the Rhine, remained under water for fifteen hours before they could find him again; at the end of that time, they carried him to the tomb of St Suitbert, and he recovered his health.

The same St Suitbert resuscitated also another young man who had been drowned several hours. But the author who relates these miracles is of no great authority.

Several instances are related of drowned persons who have remained under water for several days, and at last recovered and enjoyed good health. In the second part of the Dissertation on the Uncertainty of the Signs of Death, by M. Bruhier, cases are mentioned of persons who have been under water forty-eight hours, others during three days, and during eight days. He adds to this the example of the insect chrysalis, which passes all the winter without giving any signs of life, and the aquatic insects which remain all the winter motionless in the mud; which also happens to the frogs and toads; ants even, against the common opinion, are during the winter in a death-like state, which ceases only on the return of spring. Swallows, in the northern countries, bury themselves in heaps, in the lakes and ponds, in rivers even, in the sea, in the sand, in the holes of walls, and the hollows of trees, or at the bottom of caverns; whilst other kinds of swallows cross the sea to find warmer and more temperate climes.

What has just been said of swallows being found at the bottom of lakes, ponds, and rivers, is commonly remarked in Silesia, Poland, Bohemia, and Moravia. Sometimes even storks are fished up as if dead, having their beaks fixed in the flesh of one another; many of these have been seen in the environs of Geneva, and even in the environs of Metz, in the year 1467.

To these may be added quails and herons. Sparrows and cuckoos have been found during the winter in hollow trees, torpid and without the least appearance of life, which being warmed recovered themselves and took flight. We know that hedgehogs, marmots, sloths, and serpents, live underground without breathing, and the circulation of the blood is very feeble in them during all the winter. It is even said that bears sleep during almost all that period.

CHAPTER 43

Instances of Women who have been Believed to be Dead, and who have come to Life again

Very clever physicians assert, that in cases of the suffocation of the uterus, a woman may live thirty days without breathing. I know that a very excellent woman was six-and-thirty hours without giving any sign of life. Everybody thought she was dead, and they wanted to enshroud her, but her husband always opposed it. At the end of thirty-six hours she came to herself, and has lived a long time since then. She told them that she heard very well all that was said about her, and knew that they wanted to lay her out; but her torpor was such that she could not surmount it, and she should have let them do whatever they pleased without the least resistance.

This applies to what St Augustine says of the priest Pretextatus, who in his trances and swoons heard, as if from afar off, what was said, and nevertheless would have let himself be burned, and his flesh cut, without opposing it or feeling it.

Corneille le Bruyn, in his Voyages, relates, that he saw at Damietta, in Egypt, a Turk whom they called the Dead Child, because when his mother was with child with him, she fell ill, and as they believed she was dead, they buried her pretty quickly, according to the custom of the country, where they let the dead remain but a very short time unburied, above all during the plague. She was put into a vault which this Turk had for the sepulture of his family.

Towards evening, some hours after the interment of this woman, it entered the mind of the Turk her husband, that the child she bore might still be alive; he then had the vault opened, and found that his wife had delivered herself, and that his child was alive, but the mother was dead. Some people said that the child had been heard to cry, and that it was on receiving intimation of this that the father had the tomb opened. This man, surnamed the Dead Child, was still living in 1677. Le Bruyn thinks that the woman was dead when her child was born; but being dead, it would not have been possible for her to bring him into the world. It must be remembered, that in Egypt, where this happened, the women have an extraordinary facility of delivery, as both ancients and moderns bear witness, and that this woman was simply shut up in a vault, without being covered with earth.

A woman at Strasburg, who was with child, being reputed to be dead, was buried in a subterranean vault; at the end of some time, this vault having been opened for another body to be placed in it, the woman was found out of the coffin lying on the ground, and having between her hands a child, of which she had delivered herself, and whose arm she held in her mouth, as if she would fain eat it.

Another woman, a Spaniard, the wife of Francisco Aravallos of Suasso, being dead, or believed to be so, in the last months of her pregnancy, was put in the ground; her husband, whom they had sent for from the country, whither he had gone on business, would see his wife at the church, and had her exhumed: hardly had they opened the coffin, when they heard the cry of a child, who was making efforts to leave the bosom of its mother.

He was taken away alive, and lived a long time, being known by the name of the Child of the Earth; and since then he was lieutenant-general of the town of Xéréz, on the frontier of Spain. These instances might be multiplied to infinity, of persons buried alive, and of others who have recovered as they were being carried to the grave, and others who have been taken out of it by fortuitous circumstances. Upon this subject you may consult the new work of Messrs Vinslow and Bruhier, and those authors who have expressly treated on this subject. These gentlemen derive from thence a very wise and very judicious conclusion, which is, that people should never be buried without the absolute certainty of their being dead, above all in times of pestilence, and in certain maladies in which those who are suffering under them lose on a sudden both sense and motion.

CHAPTER 44

Can these Instances be Applied to the Hungarian Ghosts?

Some advantage of these instances and these arguments may be derived in favour of vampirism, by saying that the ghosts of Hungary, Moravia, and Poland are not really dead; that they continue to live in their graves, although without motion and without respiration; the blood which is found in them being fine and red, the flexibility of their limbs, the cries which they utter when their heart is pierced or their head being cut off, all prove that they still exist.

That is not the principal difficulty which arrests my judgment; it is, to know how they come out of their graves without any appearance of the earth having been removed, and how they have replaced it as it was; how they appear dressed in their clothes, go and come, and eat. If it is so, why do they return to their graves? Why do they not remain amongst the living? Why do they suck the blood of their relations? Why do they haunt and fatigue persons who ought to be dear to them, and who have done nothing to offend them? If all this is only imagination on the part of those who are molested, whence comes it that these vampires are found in their graves in an uncorrupted state, full of blood, supple, and pliable; that their feet are found to be in a muddy condition the day after they have run about and frightened the neighbours, and that nothing similar is remarked in the other corpses interred at the same time and in the same cemetery? Whence does it happen that they neither come back nor infest the place any more when they are burned or impaled? Would it be, again, the imagination of the living and their prejudices which reassure them after these executions? Whence comes it that these scenes recur so frequently in those countries, that the people are not cured of their prejudices, and daily experience, instead of destroying, only augments and strengthens them?

CHAPTER 45

Dead Persons who Chew in their Graves like Hogs, and Devour their own Flesh

It is an opinion widely spread in Germany, that certain dead persons masticate in their graves, and devour whatever may be close to them; that they are even heard to eat like pigs, with a certain low cry, and as if growling and grunting.

A German author, named Michael Rauff, has composed a work, entitled *De Masticatione Mortuorum in Tumulis* – 'Of the Dead who masticate in their Graves.' He sets it down as a proved and sure thing, that there are certain dead persons who have devoured the linen and everything that was within reach of their mouth, and even their own flesh, in their graves. He remarks, that in some parts of Germany, to prevent the dead from masticating, they place a lump of earth under their chin in the coffin; elsewhere they place a little piece of money and a stone in their mouth; elsewhere they tie a handkerchief tightly round their throat. The author cites some German writers who make mention of this ridiculous custom; he quotes several others who speak of dead people that have devoured their own flesh in their sepulchre. This work was printed at Leipsic in 1728. It speaks of an author named Philip Rehrius, who printed in 1679 a treatise with the same title – *De Masticatione Mortuorum*.

He might have added to it the circumstance of Henry Count of Salm, who, being supposed to be dead, was interred alive; they heard during the night, in the church of the Abbey of Haute-Seille, where he was buried, loud cries; and the next day, on his tomb being opened, they found him turned upon his face, whilst in fact he had been buried lying upon his back.

Some years ago, at Bar-le-Duc, a man was buried in the cemetery, and a noise was heard in his grave; the next day they disinterred him, and found that he had gnawed the flesh of his arms; and this we learned from ocular witnesses. This man had drunk brandy, and had been buried as dead. Rauff speaks of a woman of Bohemia, who, in 1355, had eaten in her grave half her shroud. In the time of Luther, a man who was dead and buried, and a woman the same, gnawed their own entrails. Another dead man in Moravia ate the linen clothes of a woman who was buried next to him.

All this is very possible, but that those who are really dead move their jaws, and amuse themselves with masticating whatever may be near them, is a childish fancy – like what the ancient Romans said of their *Manducus*, which was a grotesque figure of a man with an enormous mouth, and teeth proportioned thereto, which they caused to move by springs, and grind his teeth together, as if this lifeless figure had wanted to eat. They frightened children with them, and threatened them with the Manducus.

Some remains of this old custom may be seen in certain processions, where they carry a sort of serpent, which at intervals opens and shuts a vast jaw, armed with teeth, into which they throw cakes, as if to gorge it, or satisfy its appetite.

CHAPTER 46

Singular Instance of a Hungarian Ghost

The most remarkable instance cited by Rauff is that of one Peter Plogojovitz, who had been buried ten weeks in a village of Hungary, called Kisolova. This man appeared by night to some of the inhabitants of the village while they were asleep, and grasped their throat so tightly that in four-and-twenty hours it caused their death. Nine persons, young and old, perished thus in the course of eight days.

The widow of the same Plogojovitz declared that her husband since his death had come and asked her for his shoes, which frightened her so much that she left Kisolova to retire to some other spot.

From these circumstances the inhabitants of the village determined upon disinterring the body of Plogojovitz and burning it, to deliver themselves from these visitations. They applied to the Emperor's officer, who commanded in the territory of Gradiska in Hungary, and even to the curé of the same place, for permission to exhume the body of Peter Plogojovitz. The officer and the curé made much demur in granting it, but the peasants declared that if they were refused permission to disinter the body of this man, whom they had no doubt was a true vampire, (for so they called these revived corpses,) they should be obliged to forsake the village, and go where they could.

The Emperor's officer, who wrote this account, seeing he could hinder them neither by threats nor promises, went with the curé of Gradiska to the village of Kisolova, and having caused Peter Plogojovitz to be exhumed, they found that his body exhaled no bad smell; that he looked as when alive, except the tip of the nose; that his hair and beard had grown, and instead of his nails which had fallen off, new ones had come; that under his cuticle, which appeared whitish, there was a new skin, which looked healthy, and of a natural colour; his feet and hands were as whole as could be desired in a living man. They remarked also in his mouth some fresh blood, which these people believed that this vampire had sucked from the men whose death he had occasioned.

The Emperor's officer and the curé having diligently examined all these things, and the people who were present feeling their indignation awakened anew, and being more fully persuaded that he was the true cause of the death of their compatriots, ran directly for a sharp pointed stake, which they thrust into his breast, whence there issued a quantity of fresh and crimson blood, and also from the nose and mouth. After this the peasants placed the body on a pile of wood, and saw it reduced to ashes.

M. Rauff, from whom we have these particulars, cites several authors who have written on the same subject, and have related instances of dead people who have eaten in their tombs. He cites particularly Gabril Rzaczincki in his history of the *Natural Curiosities of the Kingdom of Poland*, printed at Sandomir in 1721.

CHAPTER 47

Reasonings on this Matter

Those authors have reasoned a great deal on these events. 1. Some have believed them to be miraculous. 2. Others have looked upon them simply as the effect of a heated imagination, or a sort of prepossession. 3. Others again have believed that there was nothing in them all but what was very simple and very natural, these persons not being dead, but acting naturally upon other bodies. 4. Others have asserted that it was the work of the devil himself; amongst these, some have advanced the opinion that there were certain benign demons, differing from those who are malevolent and hostile to mankind, to which benign demons they have attributed playful and harmless operations, in contradistinction to those bad demons who inspire the minds of men with crime and sin, ill use them, kill them, and occasion them an infinity of evils. But what greater evils can one have to fear from veritable demons and the most malignant spirits, than those which the ghouls of Hungary inflict on the persons whose blood they suck, and thus cause to die? 5. Others will have it that it is not the dead who eat their own flesh or clothes, but serpents, rats, moles, ferrets, or other voracious animals, or even what the peasants call *striges*, which are birds that devour animals and men, and suck their blood. Some have said that these instances are principally remarked in women, and, above all, in a time of pestilence; but there are instances of ghouls of both sexes, and principally of men; although those who die of plague, poison, hydrophobia, drunkenness, and any epidemic malady, are more apt to return, apparently because their blood coagulates with more difficulty; and sometimes some are buried who are not quite dead, on account of the danger there is in leaving them long without sepulture, from fear of the infection they would cause.

It is added, that these vampires are known only to certain countries, as Hungary, Moravia, and Silesia, where those maladies are more common, and where the people, being badly fed, are subject to certain disorders occasioned by the climate and the food, and augmented by prejudice, fancy, and fright, which are capable of producing or of increasing the most dangerous maladies, as daily experience proves too well. As to what some have asserted, that the dead have been heard to eat and chew like pigs in their graves, it is manifestly fabulous, and such an idea can have its foundation only in ridiculous prepossessions of the mind.

CHAPTER 48

Are the Vampires or Revenants Really Dead?

The opinion of those who hold that all that is related of vampires is the effect of imagination, fascination, or of that disorder which the Greeks term *phrenesis* or *coribantism*, and who pretend by that means to explain all the phenomena of vampirism, will never persuade us that these maladies of the brain can produce such real effects as those we have just recounted. It is impossible that on a sudden, several persons should believe they see a thing which is not there, and that they should die in so short a time of a disorder purely imaginary. And who has revealed to them that such a vampire is undecayed in his grave, that he is full of blood, that he in some measure lives there after his death? Is there not to be found in the nation one sensible man who is exempt from this fancy, or who has soared above the effects of this fascination, these sympathies and antipathies – this natural magic? And besides, who can explain to us clearly and distinctly what these grand terms signify, and the manner of these operations so occult and so mysterious? It is trying to explain a thing which is obscure and doubtful, by another still more uncertain and incomprehensible.

If these persons believe nothing of all that is related of the apparition, the return, and the actions of vampires, they lose their time very uselessly in proposing systems and forming arguments to explain what exists only in the imagination of certain prejudiced persons struck with an absurd idea; but, if all that is related, or at least a part, is true, these systems and these arguments will not easily satisfy those minds which desire proofs far more weighty.

Let us see, then, if the system which asserts that these vampires are not really dead is well founded. It is certain that death consists in the separation of the soul from the body, and that neither the one nor the other perishes, nor is annihilated by death; that the soul is immortal, and that the body, destitute of its soul, still remains entire, and becomes only in part corrupt, sometimes in a few days, and sometimes in a longer space of time; sometimes even it remains uncorrupted during many years or even ages, either by reason of a good constitution, as in Hector and Alexander the Great, whose bodies remained several years undecayed; or by means of the art of embalming; or lastly, owing to the nature of the earth in which they are interred, which has the power of drying up the radical humidity and the principles of corruption. I do not stop to prove all these things, which besides are very well known.

Sometimes the body, without being dead and forsaken by its reasonable soul, remains as if dead and motionless, or at least with so slow a motion and such feeble respiration, that it is almost imperceptible, as it happens in faintings, swoons, in certain disorders very common amongst women, in trances – as we remarked in the case of Pretextatus, priest of Calamis; we have also reported more than one instance of persons considered dead, and buried as such; I may add that of the Abbé Salin, prior of St Christopher, who being in his coffin, and about to be interred, was resuscitated by some of his friends, who made him swallow a glass of champagne.

Several instances of the same kind are related. In the 'Causes Célèbres,' they make mention of a girl who became *enceinte* during a long swoon; we have already noticed this. Pliny cites a great number of instances of persons who have been thought dead, and who have come to life again, and lived for a long time. He mentions a young man, who having fallen asleep in a cavern, remained there forty years without waking. Our historians speak of the seven sleepers, who slept for fifty years, from the year of Christ 253 to 403. It is said that the philosopher Epimenides slept in a cavern during fifty-seven years, or according to others, forty-seven, or only forty years; for the ancients do not agree concerning the number of years; they even affirm, that this philosopher had the power to detach his soul from his body, and recall it when he pleased. The same thing is related of Aristaeus of Proconnesus. I am willing to allow that this is fabulous; but we cannot gainsay the truth of several other stories of persons who have come to life again, after having appeared dead for three, four, five, six, and seven days. Pliny acknowledges that there are several instances of dead people who have appeared after they were interred; but he will not mention them more particularly, because, he says, he relates only natural things and not prodigies – 'Post sepulturam quoque visorum exempla sunt, nisi quod naturae opera non prodigia sectamur.' We believe that Enoch and Elijah are still living. Several have thought that St John the Evangelist was not dead, but that he is still alive in his tomb.

Plato and St Clement of Alexandria relate, that the son of Zoroaster was resuscitated twelve days after his (supposed) death, and when his body had been laid upon the funeral pyre. Phlegon says, that a Syrian soldier in the army of Antiochus, after having been killed at Thermopylae, appeared in open day in the Roman camp, and spoke to several. And Plutarch relates, that a man named Thespesius, who had fallen from the roof of a house, came to himself the third day after he died (or seemed to die) of his fall.

St Paul, writing to the Corinthians, seems to suppose that sometimes the soul transported itself without the body, to repair to the spot where it is in mind or thought; for instance, he says that he has been transported to the third heaven; but he adds, that he knows not whether in the body, or only in spirit – 'Sive in corpora, sive extra corpus, nescio, Deus scit.' We have already cited St Augustine, who mentions a priest of Calamis, named Pretextatus, who, at the sound of the voices of some persons who lamented their sins, fell into such an ecstasy of delight, that he no longer breathed or felt anything; and they might have cut and burnt his flesh without his perceiving it; his soul was absent, or really so occupied with these lamentations, that he was insensible to pain. In swoons and syncope, the soul no longer performs her ordinary functions. She is nevertheless in the body, and continues to animate it, but she perceives not her own action.

A curé of the diocese of Constance, named Bayer, writes me word that in 1728, having been appointed to the cure of Rutheim, he was disturbed a month afterwards by a spectre, or an evil spirit, in the form of a peasant, badly made, and ill-dressed, very ill-looking, and stinking insupportably, who came and knocked at the door in an insolent manner, and having entered his study told him that he had been sent by an official of the

Prince of Constance, his bishop, upon a certain commission, which was found to be absolutely false. He then asked for something to eat, and they placed before him meat, bread, and wine. He took up the meat with both hands, and devoured it bones and all, saying, 'See how I eat both flesh and bone – do the same.' Then he took up the wine-cup, and swallowed it at a draught, asking for another, which he drank off in the same fashion. After that he withdrew, without bidding the curé goodbye; and the servant who showed him to the door having asked his name, he replied, 'I was born at Rutsingen, and my name is George Raulin,' which was false. As he was going down stairs he said to the curé in German, in a menacing tone, 'I will show you who I am.'

He passed all the rest of the day in the village, showing himself to everybody. Towards midnight he returned to the curé's door, crying out three times in a terrible voice, 'Monsieur Bayer!' and adding, 'I will let you know who I am.' In fact, during three years he returned every day towards four o'clock in the afternoon, and every night till dawn of day. He appeared in different forms, sometimes like a water-dog, sometimes as a lion, or some other terrible animal; sometimes in the shape of a man, or a girl, when the curé was at table, or in bed, enticing him to licentiousness. Sometimes he made an uproar in the house, like a cooper putting hoops on his casks; then again you might have thought he wanted to throw the house down by the noise he made in it. To have witnesses to all this, the curé often sent for the beadle and other personages of the village to bear testimony to it. The spectre emitted, wherever he showed himself, an insupportable stench.

At last the curé had recourse to exorcisms, but they produced no effect. And as they despaired almost of being delivered from these vexations, he was advised, at the end of the third year, to provide himself with a holy branch on Palm Sunday, and also with a sword sprinkled with holy water, and to make use of it against the spectre. He did so once or twice, and from that time he was no more molested. This is attested by a Capuchin monk, witness of the greater part of these things, the 29th August 1749.

I will not guarantee the truth of all these circumstances; the judicious reader will make what induction he pleases from them. If they are true, here is a real ghost, who eats, drinks, and speaks, and gives tokens of his presence for three whole years, without any appearance of religion. Here follows another instance of a ghost who manifested himself by actions alone.

They write me word from Constance, the 8th August 1748, that towards the end of the year 1746 sighs were heard, which seemed to proceed from the corner of the printing-office of the Sieur Lahart, one of the common-council-men of the city of Constance. The printers only laughed at it at first, but in the following year, 1747, in the beginning of January, they heard more noise than before. There was a hard knocking near the same corner whence they had at first heard some sighs; things went so far that the printers received slaps, and their hats were thrown on the ground. They had recourse to the Capuchins, who came with the books proper for exorcising the spirit. The exorcism completed, they returned home, and the noise ceased for three days.

At the end of that time the noise recommenced more violently than before; the spirit threw the characters for printing, whether letters or figures, against the windows. They sent out of the city for a famous exorcist, who exorcised the spirit for a week. One day the spirit boxed the ears of a lad; and again the letters, etc. were thrown against the window-panes. The foreign exorcist, not having been able to effect anything by his exorcisms, returned to his own home.

The spirit went on as usual, giving slaps in the face to one, and throwing stones and other things at another, so that the compositors were obliged to leave that corner of the printing-office and place themselves in the middle of the room; but they were not the quieter for that.

They then sent for other exorcists, one of whom had a particle of the true cross, which he placed upon the table. The spirit did not, however, cease disturbing as usual the workmen belonging to the printing-office; and the Capuchin brother who accompanied the exorcist received such buffets that they were both obliged to withdraw to their convent. Then came others, who, having mixed a quantity of sand and ashes in a bucket of water, blessed the water, and sprinkled with it every part of the printing-office. They also scattered the sand and ashes all over the room upon the paved floor, and being provided with swords the whole party began to strike at random right and left in every part of the room, to see if they could hit the ghost, and to observe if he left any footmarks upon the sand or ashes which covered the floor. They perceived at last that he had perched himself on the top of the stove or furnace, and they remarked on the angles of it marks of his feet and hands impressed on the sand and ashes they had blessed.

They succeeded in driving him from thence, and they very soon perceived that he had slid under the table, and left marks of his hands and feet on the pavement. The dust raised by all this movement in the office caused them to disperse, and they discontinued the pursuit. But the principal exorcist having taken out a screw from the angle where they had first heard the noise, found in a hole in the wall some feathers, three bones wrapped up in a dirty piece of linen, some bits of glass, and a hairpin, or bodkin. He blessed a fire which they lighted, and had it all thrown in. But this monk had hardly reached his convent when one of the printers came to tell him that the bodkin had come out of the flames three times of itself, and that a boy who was holding a pair of tongs, and who put this bodkin in the fire again, had been violently struck in the face. The rest of the things which had been found having been brought to the Capuchin convent, they were burnt without further resistance; but the lad who had carried them there saw a naked woman in the public market-place, and on that and the following days groans were heard in the market-place of Constance.

Some days after this the printer's house was again infested in this manner, the ghost giving slaps, throwing stones, and molesting the domestics in divers ways. The Sieur Lahart, the master of the house, received a great wound in his head, two boys who slept in the same bed were thrown on the ground, so that the house was entirely forsaken during the night. One Sunday a servant girl carrying away some linen from the house had stones thrown at her, and another time two boys were thrown down from a ladder.

There was in the city of Constance an executioner who passed for a sorcerer. The monk who writes to me suspected him of having some part in this game; he began to exhort those who sat up with him in the house, to put their confidence in God, and to be strong in faith. He gave them to understand that the executioner was likely to be of the party. They passed the night thus in the house, and about ten o'clock in the evening, one of the companions of the exorcist threw himself at his feet in tears, and revealed to him, that that same night he and one of his companions had been sent to consult the executioner in Turgau, and that by order of the Sieur Lahart, printer, in whose house all this took place. This avowal strangely surprised the good father, and he declared that he would not continue to exorcise, if they did not assure him that they had not spoken to the executioner to put an end to the haunting. They protested that they had not spoken to him at all. The Capuchin father had everything picked up that was found about the house, wrapped up in packets, and had them carried to his convent.

The following night, two domestics tried to pass the night in the house, but they were thrown out of their beds, and constrained to go and sleep elsewhere. After this, they sent for a peasant of the village of Annanstorf, who was considered a good exorcist. He passed the night in the haunted house, drinking, singing, and shouting. He received slaps and blows from a stick, and was obliged to own that he could not prevail against the spirit.

The widow of an executioner presented herself then to perform the exorcisms; she began by using fumigations in all parts of the dwelling, to drive away the evil spirits. But before she had finished these fumigations, seeing that the master was struck in the face and on his body by the spirit, she ran away from the house, without asking for her pay.

They next called in the Curé of Valburg, who passed for a clever exorcist. He came with four other secular curés, and continued the exorcisms for three days, without any success. He withdrew to his parish, imputing the inutility of his prayers to the want of faith of those who were present.

During this time, one of the four priests was struck with a knife, then with a fork, but he was not hurt. The son of Sieur Lahart, master of the dwelling, received upon his jaw a blow from a paschal taper, which did him no harm. All being of no service, they sent for the executioner of the neighbourhood. Two of the persons who went to fetch him were well thrashed and pelted with stones. Another had his thigh so tightly pressed, that he felt the pain for a long time. The executioner carefully collected all the packets he found wrapped up about the house, and put others in their room; but the spirit took them up and threw them into the market-place. After this, the executioner persuaded the Sieur Lahart that he might boldly return with his people to the house; he did so, but the first night, when they were at supper, one of his workmen named Solomon was wounded on the foot, and then followed a great effusion of blood. They then sent again for the executioner, who appeared much surprised that the house was not yet entirely freed, but at that moment he was himself attacked by a shower of stones, boxes on the ears, and other blows, which constrained him to run away quickly.

Some heretics in the neighbourhood, being informed of all these things, came one day to the bookseller's shop, and upon attempting to read in a Catholic Bible which was there, were well boxed and beaten; but having taken up a Calvinist Bible, they received no harm. Two men of Constance having entered the bookseller's shop from sheer curiosity, one of them was immediately thrown down upon the ground, and the other ran away as fast as he could. Another person, who had come in the same way from curiosity, was punished for his presumption, by having a quantity of water thrown upon him. A young girl of Augsburg, a relation of the Sieur Lahart, printer, was chased away with violent blows, and pursued even to the neighbouring house, where she entered.

At last the hauntings ceased, on the 8th February. On that day the spectre opened the shop door, went in, displaced a few articles, went out, shut the door, and from that time nothing more was seen or heard of it.

CHAPTER 49

Instance of a Man named Curma who was sent back into the World

St Augustine relates on this subject, that a countryman named Curma, who held a small place in the village of Tullia, near Hippo, having fallen sick, remained for some days senseless and speechless, having just respiration enough left to prevent their burying him. At the end of several days he began to open his eyes, and sent to ask what they were about in the house of another peasant of the same place, and like himself named Curma. They brought him back word, that he had just expired at the very moment that he himself had recovered and was resuscitated from his deep slumber.

Then he began to talk, and related what he had seen and heard; that it was not Curma the *curial*, but Curma the blacksmith, who ought to have been brought; he added, that among those whom he had seen treated in different ways, he had recognised some of his deceased acquaintance, and other ecclesiastics, who were still alive, who had advised him to come to Hippo, and be baptised by the Bishop Augustine; that according to their advice he had received baptism in his vision; that afterwards he had been introduced into Paradise, but that he had not remained there long, and that they had told him that if he wished to dwell there, he must be baptised. He replied, 'I am so;' but they told him, that he had been so only in a vision, and that he must go to Hippo to receive that sacrament in reality. He came there as soon as he was cured, and received the rite of baptism with the other catechumens.

St Augustine was not informed of this adventure till about two years afterwards. He sent for Curma, and learnt from his own lips what I have just related. Now it is certain that Curma saw nothing with his bodily eyes of all that had been represented to him in his vision; neither the town of Hippo, nor Bishop Augustine, nor the ecclesiastics who counselled him to be baptised, nor the persons living and deceased whom he saw and recognised. We may believe, then, that these things are effects of the power of God, who makes use of the ministry of angels to warn, console, or alarm mortals, according as His judgment sees best.

St Augustine inquires afterwards if the dead have any knowledge of what is passing in this world? He doubts the fact, and shows that at least they have no knowledge of it by ordinary and natural means. He remarks, that it is said God took Josiah, for instance, from this world, that he might not witness the evil which was to befall his nation; and we say every day, Such-a-one is happy to have left the world, and so escaped feeling the miseries which have happened to his family or his country. But if the dead know not what is passing in this world, how can they be troubled about their bodies being interred or not? How do the saints hear our prayers and why do we ask them for their intercession?

It is then true that the dead *can* learn what is passing on the earth, either by the agency of angels, or by that of the dead who arrive in the other world, or by the revelation of the Spirit of God, who discovers to them what He judges proper, and what it is expedient that they should learn. God may also sometimes send men who have been long dead to living men, as He permitted Moses and Elias to appear at the Transfiguration of the Lord, and as an infinite number of the saints have appeared to the living. The invocation of saints has always been taught and practised in the Church; whence we may infer that they hear our prayers, are moved by our wants, and can help us by their intercession. But the way in which all this is done is not distinctly known; neither reason nor revelation furnishes us with anything certain, as to the means it pleases God to make use of to reveal our wants to them.

Lucian, in his dialogue entitled *Philopseudes*, or the 'Lover of Falsehood,' relates something similar. A man named Eucrates, having been taken down to hell, was presented to Pluto, who was angry with him who presented him, saying – 'That man has not yet completed his course; his turn is not yet come. Bring hither Demilius, for the thread of his life is finished.' Then they sent Eucrates back to this world, where he announced that Demilius would die soon. Demilius lived near him, and was already a little ill.

But a moment after they heard the noise of those who were bewailing his death. Lucian makes a jest of all that was said on this subject, but he owns that it was the common opinion in his time. He says in the same part of his work, that a man has been seen to come to life again after having been looked upon as dead during twenty days.

The story of Curma which we have just told, reminds me of another very like it, related by Plutarch in his Book on the Soul, of a certain man named Enarchus, who, being dead, came to life again soon after, and related that the demons who had taken away his soul were severely reprimanded by their chief, who told them that they had made a mistake, and that it was Nicander, and not Enarchus whom they ought to bring. He sent them for Nicander, who was directly seized with a fever, and died during the day.

Plutarch heard this from Enarchus himself, who to confirm what he had asserted said to him – 'You will get well certainly, and that very soon, of the illness which has attacked you.'

St Gregory the Great relates something very similar to what we have just mentioned. An illustrious man of rank named Stephen, well known to St Gregory and Peter his interlocutor, was accustomed to relate to him, that going to Constantinople on business he died there; and as the doctor who was to embalm him was not in town that day, they were obliged to leave the body unburied that night. During this interval Stephen was led before the judge who presided in hell, where he saw many things which he had heard of, but did not believe. When they brought him to the judge, the latter refused to receive him, saying, 'It is not that man whom I commanded you to bring here, but Stephen the blacksmith.' In consequence of this order the soul of the dead man was directly brought back to his body, and at the same instant Stephen the blacksmith expired; which confirmed all that the former had said of the other life.

The plague ravaging the city of Rome in the time that Narses was governor of Italy, a young Livonian, a shepherd by profession, and of a good and quiet disposition, was taken ill with the plague in the house of the advocate Valerian, his master. Just when they thought him all but dead, he suddenly came to himself, and related to them that he had been transported to heaven, where he had learnt the names of those who were to die of the plague in his master's house; having named them to him, he predicted to Valerian that he should survive him; and to convince him that he was saying the truth, he let him see that he had acquired by infusion the knowledge of several different languages; in effect, he who had never known how to speak any but the Italian tongue, spoke Greek to his master, and other languages to those who knew them.

After having lived in this state for two days, he had fits of madness, and having laid hold of his hands with his teeth, he died a second time, and was followed by those whom he had named. His master, who survived, fully justified his prediction. Men and women who fall into trances remain sometimes for several days without food, respiration, or pulsation of the heart, as if they were dead. Thauler, a famous contemplative (philosopher), maintains that a man may remain entranced during a week, a month, or even a year. We have seen an abbess, who, when in a trance into which she often fell, lost the use of her natural functions, and passed thirty days in that state without taking any nourishment, and without sensation. Instances of these trances are not rare in the lives of the saints, though they are not all of the same kind, or duration.

Women in hysterical fits remain likewise many days as if dead, speechless, inert, pulseless. Galen mentions a woman who was six days in this state. Some of them pass ten whole days motionless, senseless, without respiration and without food.

Some persons who have seemed dead and motionless, had however the sense of hearing very strong, heard all that was said about themselves, made efforts to speak, and show that they were not dead, but who could neither speak, nor give any signs of life.

I might here add an infinity of trances of saintly personages of both sexes, who in their delight in God, in prayer remained motionless, without sensation, almost breathless, and who felt nothing of what was done to them, or around them.

CHAPTER 50

Instances of Persons who could fall into a Trance when they pleased, and remained Perfectly Senseless

Jerome Cardan says that he fell into a trance when he liked; he owns that he does not know if, like the priest Pretextatus, he should not feel great wounds or hurts, but he did not feel the pain of the gout, or the pulling him about. He adds, the priest of Calamis heard the voices of those who spoke aloud near him, but as if from a distance. 'For my part,' says Cardan, 'I hear the voice, though slightly, and without understanding what is said. And when I wish to entrance myself, I feel about my heart as it were a separation of the soul from the rest of my body, and that communicates as if by a little door with all the machine, principally by the head and brain. Then I have no sensation except that of being beside myself.'

We may report here what is related of the Laplanders, who when they wish to learn something that is passing at a distance from the spot where they are, send their demon, or their souls, by means of certain magic ceremonies, and by the sound of a drum which they beat, or upon a shield painted in a certain manner; then on a sudden the Laplander falls into a trance, and remains as if lifeless and motionless sometimes during four-and-twenty hours. But all this time someone must remain near him to prevent him from being touched, or called; even the movement of a fly would wake him, and they say he would die directly or be carried away by the demon. We have already mentioned this subject in the Dissertation on Apparitions.

We have also remarked that serpents, worms, flies, snails, marmots, sloths, etc., remain asleep during the winter; and in blocks of stone have been found toads, snakes, and oysters alive, which had been enclosed there for many years, and perhaps for more than a century. Cardinal de Retz relates in his Memoirs, that being at Minorca, the governor of the island caused to be drawn up from the bottom of the sea by main force with cables, whole rocks, which on being broken with maces, enclosed living oysters that were served up to him at table, and were found very good.

On the coasts of Malta, Sardinia, Italy, etc., they find a fish called the Dactylus, or Date, because it resembles the palm-date in form; this first insinuates itself into the stone by a hole not bigger than the hole made by a needle. When he has got in he feeds upon the stone, and grows so big that he cannot get out again, unless the stone is broken and he is extricated. Then they wash it, clean it, and dress it for the table. It has the shape of a date, or of a finger; whence its name of *dactylus*, which in Greek signifies a finger.

Again, I imagine that in many persons death is caused by the coagulation of the blood, which freezes and hardens in their veins, as it happens with those who have eaten hemlock, or who have been bitten by certain serpents; but there are others whose death is caused by too great an ebullition of blood, as in painful maladies, and in certain poisons, and even, they say, in certain kinds of plague, and when people die a violent death, or have been drowned.

The first mentioned cannot return to life without an evident miracle; for that purpose the fluidity of the blood must be re-established, and the peristaltic motion must be restored to the heart. But in the second kind of death, people can sometimes be restored without a miracle, by taking away the obstacle which retards or suspends the palpitation of the heart, as we see in timepieces, the action of which is restored by taking away anything foreign to the mechanism, as a hair, a bit of thread, an atom, some almost imperceptible body which stops them.

CHAPTER 51

Application of the Preceding Instances to Vampires

Supposing these facts, which I believe to be incontestably true, may we not imagine that the vampires of Hungary, Silesia, and Moldavia, are some of those men who have died of maladies which heat the blood, and who have retained some remains of life in their graves, much like those animals which we have mentioned, and those birds which plunge themselves during the winter in the lakes or marshes of Poland, and of the northern countries? They are without respiration or motion, but still not destitute of vitality. They resume their motion and activity when, on the return of spring, the sun warms the waters, or when they are brought near a moderate fire, or laid in a room of temperate heat; then they are seen to revive, and perform their ordinary functions, which had been suspended by the cold.

Thus, vampires in their graves returned to life after a certain time, and their soul does not forsake them absolutely until after the entire dissolution of their body, and when the organs of life, being absolutely broken, corrupted, and deranged, they can no longer by their agency perform any vital functions. Whence it happens, that the people of those countries impale them, cut off their heads, burn them, to deprive their spirit of all hope of animating them again, and of making use of them to molest the living.

Pliny, mentioning the soul of Hermotimes, of Clazomene, which absented itself from his body, and recounted various things that had been done afar off, which the spirit said it had seen, and which, in fact, could only be known to a person who had been present at them, says that an enemy of Hermotimes, named Cantandes, burned that body, which gave hardly any sign of life, and thus deprived the soul of the means of returning to lodge in its envelope; 'donec cremato corpore interim semianimi, remeanti animae velut vaginam ademerint.'

Origen had doubtless derived from the ancients what he teaches, that the souls which are of a spiritual nature take, on leaving their earthly body, another, more subtle, of a similar form to the grosser one they have just quitted, which serves them as a kind of sheath, or case, and that it is invested with this subtle body that they sometimes appear about their graves. He founds this opinion on what is said of Lazarus and the rich man in the Gospel, who both of them have bodies, since they speak and see, and the wicked rich man asks for a drop of water to cool his tongue.

I do not defend this reasoning of Origen; but what he says of a subtle body, which has the form of the earthly one which clothed the soul before death, quite resembles the opinion of which we spoke in Chapter 4.

That bodies which have died of violent maladies, or which have been executed when full of health, or have simply swooned, should vegetate underground in their graves; that their beards, hair, and nails should grow; that they should emit blood, be supple and pliant; that they should have no bad smell, etc. – all these things do not embarrass us: the vegetation of the human body may produce all these effects. That they should even eat and devour what is about them, the madness with which a man interred alive must be transported when he awakes from his torpor, or his swoon, must naturally lead him to these violent excesses. But the grand difficulty is to explain how the vampires come out of their graves to haunt the living, and how they return to them again. For all the accounts that we see suppose the thing as certain, without informing us either of the way or the circumstances, which would, however, be the most interesting part of the narrative.

How a body covered with four or five feet of earth, having no room to move about and disengage itself, wrapped up in linen, covered with pitch, can make its way out, and come back upon the earth, and there occasion such effects as are related of it; and how after that it returns to its former state, and re-enters underground, where it is found sound, whole, and full of blood, and in the same condition as a living body? This is the question. Will it be said that these bodies evaporate through the ground without opening it, like the water and vapours which enter into the earth, or proceed from it, without sensibly deranging its particles? It were to be wished that the accounts which have been given us concerning the return of the vampires had been more minute in their explanations of this subject.

Supposing that their bodies do not stir from their graves, that it is only their phantoms which appear to the living, what cause produces and animates these phantoms? Can it be the spirit of the defunct, which has not yet forsaken them, or some demon, which makes their apparition in a fantastic and borrowed body? And if these bodies are merely phantomic, how can they suck the blood of living people? We always find ourselves in a difficulty to know if these appearances are natural or miraculous.

A sensible priest related to me, a little while ago, that, travelling in Moravia, he was invited by M. Jeanin, a canon of the cathedral at Olmutz, to accompany him to their village, called Liebava, where he had been appointed commissioner by the consistory of the bishopric, to take information concerning the fact of a certain famous vampire, which had caused much confusion in this village of Liebava some years before.

The case proceeded. They heard the witnesses, they observed the usual forms of the law. The witnesses deposed that a certain notable inhabitant of Liebava had often disturbed the living in their beds at night, that he had come out of the cemetery, and had appeared in several houses three or four years ago; that his troublesome visits had ceased because a Hungarian stranger, passing through the village at the time of these reports, had boasted that he could put an end to them, and make the vampire disappear. To perform his promise, he mounted on the church steeple, and observed the moment when the vampire came out of his grave, leaving near it the linen clothes in which he had been enveloped, and then went to disturb the inhabitants of the village.

The Hungarian, having seen him come out of his grave, went down quickly from the steeple, took up the linen envelopes of the vampire, and carried them with him up the tower. The vampire having returned from his prowlings, cried loudly against the Hungarian, who made him a sign from the top of the tower that if he wished to have his clothes again he must fetch them; the vampire began to ascend the steeple, but the Hungarian threw him down backwards from the ladder, and cut his head off with a spade. Such was the end of this tragedy.

The person who related this story to me saw nothing, neither did the noble who had been sent as commissioner; they only heard the report of the peasants of the place, people extremely ignorant, superstitious and credulous, and most exceedingly prejudiced on the subject of vampirism.

But supposing that there be any reality in the fact of these apparitions of vampires, shall they be attributed to God, to angels, to the spirits of these ghosts, or to the devil? In this last case, will it be said that the devil can subtilise these bodies, and give them power to penetrate through the ground without disturbing it, to glide through the cracks and joints of a door, to pass through a keyhole, to lengthen or shorten themselves, to reduce themselves to the nature of air, or water, to evaporate through the ground – in short, to put them in the same state in which we believe the bodies of the blessed will be after the resurrection, and in which was that of our Saviour after His resurrection, who showed Himself only to whom He thought proper, and who without opening the doors appeared suddenly in the midst of His disciples?

But should it be allowed that the demon could reanimate these bodies, and give them the power of motion for a time, could he also lengthen, diminish, rarify, subtilise the bodies of these ghosts, and give them the faculty of penetrating through the ground, the doors and windows? There is no appearance of his having received this power from God, and we cannot even conceive that an earthly body, material and gross, can be reduced to that state of subtilty and spiritualisation without destroying the configuration of its parts and spoiling the economy of its structure; which would be contrary to the intention of the demon, and render this body incapable of appearing, showing itself, acting and speaking, and, in short, of being cut to pieces and burned, as is commonly seen and practised in Moravia, Poland, and Silesia. These difficulties exist in regard to those persons of whom we have made mention, who, being excommunicated, rose from their tombs, and left the church in sight of everybody.

We must then keep silence on this article, since it has not pleased God to reveal to us either the extent of the demon's power, or the way in which these things can be done. There is very much appearance of illusion; and even if some reality were mixed up with it, we may easily console ourselves for our ignorance in that respect, since there are so many natural things which take place within us and around us, of which the cause and manner are unknown to us.

CHAPTER 52

Examination of the Opinion that the Demon Fascinates the Eyes of those to whom Vampires Appear

Those who have recourse to the fascination of the senses to explain what is related concerning the apparition of vampires, throw themselves into as great a perplexity as those who acknowledge sincerely the reality of these events; for fascination consists either in the suspension of the senses, which cannot see what is passing before their sight, like that with which the men of Sodom were struck when they could not discover the door of Lot's house, though it was before their eyes; or that of the disciples at Emmaus, of whom it is said 'that their eyes were holden, so that they might not recognise Jesus Christ, who was talking with them on the way, and whom they knew not again until the breaking of the bread revealed him to them,' or else it consists in an object being represented to the senses in a different form from that it wears in reality, as that of the Moabites, who believed they saw the waters tinged with the blood of the Israelites, although nothing was there but the simple waters, on which the rays of the sun being reflected, gave them a reddish hue; or that of the Syrian soldiers sent to take Elisha, who were led by this prophet into Samaria, without their recognising either the prophet or the city.

This fascination, in what way soever it may be conceived, is certainly above the usual power known unto man, consequently man cannot naturally produce it; but is it above the natural powers of an angel or a demon? That is unknown to us, and obliges us to suspend our judgment on this question.

There is another kind of fascination, which consists in this, that the sight of a person or a thing, the praise bestowed upon them, the envy felt towards them, produce in the object certain bad effects, against which the ancients took great care to guard themselves and their children, by making them wear round their neck preservatives, or amulets, or charms.

A great number of passages on this subject might be cited from the Greek and Latin authors; and I find that at this day, in various parts of Christendom, people are persuaded of the efficacy of these fascinations. But we must own three things; first, that the effect of these pretended fascinations (or spells) is very doubtful; the second, that if it were certain, it is very difficult, not to say impossible, to explain it; and, lastly, that it cannot be rationally applied to the matter of apparitions or of vampires.

If the vampires or ghosts are not really resuscitated nor their bodies spiritualised and subtilised, as we believe we have proved; and if our senses are not deceived by fascination, as we have just seen it; I doubt if there be any other way to act on this question than to absolutely deny the return of these vampires, or to believe that they are only asleep or torpid; for if they truly are resuscitated, and if what is told of their return be true – if they speak, act, reason – if they suck the blood of the living, they must know what passes in the other world, and they ought to inform their relations and friends of it, and that is what they do not. On the contrary, they treat them as enemies; torment them, take away their life, suck their blood, cause them to die with lassitude.

If they are predestinated and blessed, whence happens it that they disturb and torment the living, their nearest relations, their children, and all that for nothing, and simply for the sake of doing harm? If these are persons who have still something to expiate in purgatory, and who require the prayers of the living, why do they not explain their condition? If they are reprobate and condemned, what have they to do on this earth? Can we conceive that God allows them thus to come without reason or necessity and molest their families, and even cause their death?

If these revenants are really dead, whatever state they may be in in the other world, they play a very bad part here.

CHAPTER 53

Instances of Persons Resuscitated, who Relate what they have seen in the other World

We have just seen that the vampires never speak of the other world, nor ask for either masses or prayers, nor give any warning to the living to lead them to correct their morals, or bring them to a better life. It is surely very prejudicial to the reality of their return from the other world; but their silence on that head may favour the opinion which supposes that they are not really dead.

It is true that we do not read either that Lazarus, resuscitated by Jesus Christ, nor the son of the widow of Nain, nor that of the woman of Shunem, brought to life by Elisha, nor that Israelite who came to life by simply touching the body of the same prophet Elisha, after their resurrection revealed anything to mankind of the state of souls in the other world.

But we see in the Gospel that the bad rich man, having begged of Abraham to permit him to send someone to this world to warn his brethren to lead a better life, and take care not to fall into the unhappy condition in which he found himself, was answered, 'They have the Law and the Prophets, they can listen to them and follow their instructions.' And as the rich man persisted, saying – 'If someone went to them from the other world, they would be more impressed,' Abraham replied, 'If they will not hear Moses and the prophets, neither will they attend the more though one should go to them from the dead.' The dead man resuscitated by St Stanislaus replied in the same manner to those who asked him to give them news of the other world – 'You have the Law, the Prophets, and the Gospel, hear them!'

The deceased Pagans who have returned to life, and some Christians who have likewise returned to the world by a kind of resurrection, and who have seen what passed beyond the bounds of this world, have not kept silence on the subject. They have related at length what they saw and heard on leaving their body.

We have already touched upon the story of a man named Eros, of the country of Pamphilia, who, having been wounded in battle, was found ten days after amongst the dead. They carried him senseless and motionless into the house. Two days afterwards, when they were about to place him on the funeral pile to burn his body, he revived, began to speak, and to relate in what manner people were lodged after their death, and how the good were rewarded and the wicked punished and tormented.

He said, that his soul, being separated from his body, went with a large company to a very agreeable place, where they saw as it were two great openings, which gave entrance to those who came from earth, and two others to go to heaven. He saw at this same place judges who examined those arrived from this world, and sent up to the right those who had lived well, and sent down to the left those who had been guilty of crimes. Each of them bore upon his back a label on which was written what he had done well or ill, the reason of his condemnation or his absolution.

When it came to the turn of Eros, the judges told him that he must return to earth, to announce to men what passed in the other world, and that he must well observe everything, in order to be able to render a faithful account to the living. Thus he witnessed the miserable state of the wicked, which was to last a thousand years, and the delights enjoyed by the just; that both the good and the bad received the reward or the punishment of their good or bad deeds, ten times greater than the measure of their crimes or of all their virtues.

He remarked amongst other things, that the judges inquired where was a certain man named Andaeus, celebrated in all Pamphylia for his crimes and tyranny. They were answered that he was not yet come, and that he would not be there; in fact, having presented himself with much trouble, and by making great efforts, at the grand opening before mentioned, he was repulsed and sent back to go below with other scoundrels like himself, whom they tortured in a thousand different ways, and who were always violently repulsed, whenever they tried to reascend.

He saw, moreover, the three Fates, daughters of Necessity or Destiny. These are, Lachesis, Clotho, and Atropos. Lachesis announced the past, Clotho the present, and Atropos the future. The souls were obliged to appear before these three goddesses. Lachesis cast the lots upwards, and every soul laid hold of the one which it could reach; which, however, did not prevent them still from sometimes missing the kind of life which was most conformable to justice and reason.

Eros added, that he had remarked some of the souls who sought to enter into animals; for instance, Orpheus, from hatred to the female sex, who had killed him (by tearing him to pieces), entered into a swan, and Thamaris into a nightingale. Ajax, the son of Telamon, chose the body of a lion, from detestation of the injustice of the Greeks, who had refused to let him have the arms of Hector, which he asserted were his due. Agamemnon, grieved at the crosses he had endured in this life, chose the form of the eagle. Atalanta chose the life of the athletics, delighted with the honours heaped upon them. Thersites, the ugliest of mortals, chose the form of an ape. Ulysses, weary of the miseries he had suffered upon earth, asked to live quietly as a private man. He had some trouble to find a lot for that kind of life; but he found it at last thrown down on the ground and neglected, and he joyfully snatched it up.

Eros affirmed also, that the souls of some animals entered into the bodies of men; and by the contrary rule, the souls of the wicked took possession of savage and cruel beasts, and the souls of just men of those animals which are gentle, tame, and domestic.

After these various metempsychoses, Lachesis gave to each his guardian or defender, who guided and guarded him during the course of his life. Eros was then led to the river of oblivion (Lethe), which takes away all memory of the past, but he was prevented from drinking of its water. Lastly, he said he could not tell how he came back to life.

Plato, after having related this fable, as he terms it, or this apologue, concludes from it that the soul is immortal, and that to gain a blessed life we must live uprightly, which will lead us to heaven, where we shall enjoy that beatitude of a thousand years which is promised us.

We see by this, 1. That a man may live a good while without eating or breathing, or giving any sign of life. 2. That the Greeks believed in the metempsychosis, in a state of beatitude for the just, and pains of a thousand years duration for the wicked. 3. That destiny does not hinder a man from doing either good or evil. 4. That he had a spirit, or an angel, who guided and protected him. They believed in judgment after death, and that the souls of the just were received into what they called the Elysian Fields.

CHAPTER 54

The Traditions of the Pagans concerning the Future Life are Derived from the Hebrews and Egyptians

All these traditions are clearly to be found in Homer, Virgil, and other Greek and Latin authors; they were doubtless originally derived from the Hebrews, or rather the Egyptians, from whom the Greeks took their religion, which they arranged to their own taste. The Hebrews speak of the *Rephaims*, of the impious giants 'who groan under the waters.' Solomon says, that the wicked shall go down to the abyss, or hell, with the Rephaims.

Isaiah, describing the arrival of the King of Babylon in hell, says, 'that the giants have raised themselves up to meet him with honour, and have said unto him, Thou hast been pierced with wounds even as we are; thy pride has been precipitated into hell. Thy bed shall be of rottenness, and thy covering of worms.' Ezekiel describes in the same manner the descent of the King of Assyria into hell – 'In the day that Ahasuerus went down into hell, I commanded a general mourning; for him I closed up the abyss, and arrested the course of the waters. You are at last brought down to the bottom of the earth with the trees of Eden; you will rest there with all those who have been killed by the sword; there is Pharaoh with all his host,' etc. In the Gospel, there is a great gulf between the bosom of Abraham and the abode of the bad rich man, and of those who resemble him.

The Egyptians called *Amenthés*, that is to say, 'he who receives and gives,' what the Greeks named Hades, or hell, or the kingdom of Hades, or Pluto. They believed that Amenthés received the souls of men when they died, and restored them to them when they returned to the world; that when a man died, his soul passed into the body of some other animal by metempsychosis; first of all into a terrestrial animal, then into one that was aquatic, afterwards into the body of a bird, and lastly, after having animated all sorts of animals, he returned at the end of three thousand years to the body of a man.

It is from the Egyptians that Orpheus, Homer, and the other Greeks derived the idea of the immortality of the soul, as well as the cave of the Nymphs described by Homer, who says there are two gates, the one to the north, through which the soul enters the cavern, and the other to the south, by which they leave the nymphic abode.

A certain Thespisius, a native of Soloe in Cilicia, well known to Plutarch, having passed a great part of his life in debauchery, and ruined himself entirely, in order to gain a livelihood lent himself to everything that was bad, and contrived to amass money. Having sent to consult the oracle of Amphilochus, he received for answer, that his affairs would go on better after his death. A short time after, he fell from the top of his house, broke his neck, and died. Three days after, when they were about to perform the funeral obsequies, he came to life again, and changed his way of life so greatly that there was not in Cilicia a worthier or more pious man than himself.

As they asked him the reason of such a change, he said that at the moment of his fall he felt the same as a pilot who is thrown back from the top of the helm into the sea; after which, his soul was sensible of being raised as high as the stars, of which he admired the immense size and admirable lustre; that the souls once out of the body rise into the air, and are enclosed in a kind of globe, or inflamed vortex, whence having escaped, some rise on high with incredible rapidity, while others whirl about in the air, and are thrown in divers directions, sometimes up and sometimes down.

The greater part appeared to him very much perplexed, and uttered groans and frightful wailings; others, but in a less number, rose and rejoiced with their fellows. At last he learnt that Adrastia, the daughter of Jupiter and Necessity, left nothing unpunished, and that she treated everyone according to their merit. He then details all he saw at full length, and relates the various punishments with which the bad are tormented in the next world.

He adds, that a man of his acquaintance said to him, 'You are not dead, but by God's permission your soul is come into this place, and has left your body with all its faculties.' At last he was sent back into his body as through a channel, and urged on by an impetuous breeze.

We may make two reflections on this recital; the first on this soul, which quits its body for three days and then comes back to reanimate it; the second, on the certainty of the oracle, which promised Thespisius a happier life when he should be dead.

In the Sicilian war between Caesar and Pompey, Gabienus, commander of Caesar's fleet, having been taken, was beheaded by order of Pompey. He remained all day on the seashore, his head only held on to his body by a fillet. Towards evening he begged that Pompey or some of his people might come to him, because he came from the shades, and he had things of consequence to impart to him. Pompey sent to him several of his friends, to whom Gabienus declared that the gods of the infernal regions favoured the cause and the party of Pompey, and that he would succeed according to his wishes; that he was ordered to announce this, 'and as a proof of the truth of what I say, I must die directly,' which happened. But we do not see that Pompey's party succeeded; we know, on the contrary, that it fell, and Caesar was victorious. But the god of the infernal regions, that is to say, the devil, found it very good for him, since it sent him so many unhappy victims of revenge and ambition.

CHAPTER 55

Instances of Christians who have been Resuscitated and Sent back to the World – Vision of Vetinus, a Monk of Augia

We read in an old work, written in the time of St Augustine, that a man having been crushed by a wall which fell upon him, his wife ran to the church to invoke St Stephen, whilst they were preparing to bury the man who was supposed to be dead. Suddenly they saw him open his eyes, and move his body; and after a time he sat up, and related that his soul, having quitted his body, had met a crowd of other souls of dead persons, some of whom he knew, and others he did not; that a young man, in a deacon's habit, having entered the room where he was, put aside all those souls, and said to him three times, 'Return what you have received.' He understood at last that he meant the Creed, which he recited instantly; and also the Lord's Prayer; then the deacon (St Stephen) made the sign of the cross upon his heart, and told him to rise in perfect health. A young man, a catechumen, who had been dead for three days, and was brought back to life by the prayers of St Martin, related that after his death he had been presented before the tribunal of the Sovereign Judge, who had condemned him, and sent him with a crowd of others into a dark place; and then two angels, having represented to the Judge that he was a man for whom St Martin had interceded, the Judge commanded the angels to send him back to earth, and restore him to St Martin, which was done. He was baptised, and lived a long time afterwards.

St Salvius, Bishop of Albi, having been seized with a violent fever, was thought to be dead. They washed him, clothed him, laid him on a bier, and passed the night in prayer by him: the next morning he was seen to move; he appeared to awake from a deep sleep, opened his eyes, and raising his hand towards heaven said, 'Ah! Lord, why hast thou sent me back to this gloomy abode?' He rose completely cured, but would then reveal nothing.

Some days after, he related how two angels had carried him to heaven, where he had seen the glory of Paradise, and had been sent back against his will to live some time longer on earth. St Gregory of Tours takes God to witness that he heard this history from the mouth of St Salvius himself.

A monk of Augia, named Vetinus, or Guetinus, who was living in 824, was ill, and lying upon his couch with his eyes shut; but not being quite asleep, he saw a demon in the shape of a priest, most horribly deformed, who, showing him some instruments of torture which he held in his hand, threatened to make him soon feel the rigorous effects of them. At the same time he saw a multitude of evil spirits enter his chamber, carrying tools, as if to build him a tomb or a coffin, and enclose him in it.

Immediately he saw appear some serious and grave-looking personages, wearing religious habits, who chased these demons away; and then Vetinus saw an angel, surrounded with a blaze of light, who came to the foot of the bed, and conducted him by a path between mountains of an extraordinary height, at the foot of which flowed a large river, in which he beheld a multitude of the damned, who were suffering diverse torments, according to the kind and enormity of their crimes. He saw amongst them many of his acquaintance; amongst others, some prelates and priests, guilty of incontinence, who were tied with their backs to stakes, and burned by a fire lighted under them; the women, their companions in crime, suffering the same torment opposite to them.

He beheld there also, a monk who had given himself up to avarice, and possessed money of his own, who was to expiate his crime in a leaden coffin till the day of judgment. He remarked there abbots and bishops, and even the Emperor Charlemagne, who were expiating their faults by fire, but were to be released from it after a certain time. He remarked there also the abode of the blessed in heaven, each one in his place, and according to his merits. The Angel of the Lord after this revealed to him the crimes which were the most common, and the most odious in the eyes of God. He mentioned sodomy in particular, as the most abominable crime.

After the service for the night, the abbot came to visit the sick man, who related this vision to him in full, and the abbot had it written down directly. Vetinus lived two days longer, and having predicted that he had only the third day to live, he recommended himself to the prayers of the monks, received the holy viaticum, and died in peace, the 31st October 824.

CHAPTER 56

The Vision of Bertholdus, as Related by Hincmar, Archbishop of Rheims

The famous Hincmar, Archbishop of Rheims, in a circular letter which he wrote to the bishops, his suffragans, and the faithful of his diocese, relates, that a man named Bertholdus, with whom he was acquainted, having fallen ill, and received all the sacraments, remained during four days without taking any food. On the fourth day he was so weak, that there was hardly a feeble palpitation and respiration found in him. About midnight he called to his wife, and told her to send quickly for his confessor.

The priest was as yet only in the court before the house, when Bertholdus said, 'Place a seat here, for the priest is coming.' He entered the room and said some prayers, to which Bertholdus uttered the responses, and then related to him the vision he had had. 'On leaving this world,' said he, 'I saw forty-one bishops, amongst whom were Ebonius, Leopardellus, Eneas, who were clothed in coarse black garments, dirty and singed by the flames. As for themselves, they were sometimes burned by the flames, and at others frozen with insupportable cold.' Ebonius said to him, 'Go to my clergy and my friends, and tell them to offer for us the holy sacrifice.' Bertholdus obeyed, and returning to the place where he had seen the bishops, he found them well clothed, shaved, bathed, and rejoicing.

A little farther on, he met King Charles, who was as if eaten by worms. This prince begged him to go and tell Hincmar to relieve his misery. Hincmar said mass for him, and King Charles found relief. After that, he saw Bishop Jessé, of Orleans, who was over a well, and four demons plunged him into boiling pitch, and then threw him into icy water. They prayed for him, and he was relieved. He then saw the Count Othaire, who was likewise in torment. Bertholdus begged the wife of Othaire, with his vassals and friends, to pray for him, and give alms, and he was delivered from his torments. Bertholdus after that received the Holy Communion, and began to find himself better, with the hope of living fourteen years longer, as he had been promised by his guide, who had shown him all that we have just related.

CHAPTER 57

The Vision of Saint Fursius

The Life of St Fursius, written a short time after his death, which happened about the year 653, reports several visions seen by this holy man. Being grievously ill, and unable to stir, he saw himself in the midst of the darkness raised up, as it were, by the hands of three angels, who carried him out of the world, then brought him back to it, and made his soul re-enter his body, to complete the destination assigned him by God. Then he found himself in the midst of several people, who wept for him as if he were dead, and told him how, the day before, he had fallen down in a swoon, so that they believed him to be dead. He could have wished to have some intelligent persons about him to relate to them what he had seen; but having no one near him but rustics, he asked for and received the communion of the body and blood of the Saviour, and continued three days longer awake.

The following Tuesday, he fell into a similar swoon, in the middle of the night; his feet became cold, and raising his hands to pray, he received death with joy. Then he saw the same three angels descend who had already guided him. They raised him as the first time, but instead of the agreeable and melodious songs which he had then heard, he could now hear only the frightful howlings of the demons, who began to fight against him, and shoot inflamed darts at him. The Angel of the Lord received them on his buckler, and extinguished them. The devil reproached Fursius with some bad thoughts, and some human weaknesses, but the angels defended him, saying, 'If he has not committed any capital sins, he shall not perish.'

As the devil could not reproach him with anything that was worthy of eternal death, he saw two saints from his own country – St Béan and St Medan, who comforted him and announced to him the evils with which God would punish mankind, principally because of the sins of the doctors or learned men of the Church, and the princes who governed the people – the doctors for neglecting to declare the word of God, and the princes for the bad examples they gave their people. After which, they sent him back into his body again. He returned into it with repugnance, and began to relate all that he had seen; they poured spring water upon his body, and he felt a great warmth between his shoulders. After this, he began to preach throughout Hibernia; and the Venerable Bede says, that there was in his monastery an aged monk who said that he had learned from a grave personage well worthy of belief, that he had heard these visions described by St Fursius himself. This saint had not the least doubt that his soul was really separated from his body, when he was carried away in his trance.

CHAPTER 58

Vision of a Protestant of York, and Others

Here is another instance, which happened in 1698 to one of the so-called reformed religion. A minister of the county of York, at a place called Hipley, and whose name was Henry Vatz (Watts), being struck with apoplexy the 15th August, was on the 17th placed in a coffin to be buried. But as they were about to put him in the grave, he uttered a loud cry, which frightened all the persons who had attended him to the grave; they took him quickly out of the coffin, and as soon as he had come to himself, he related several surprising things which he said had been revealed to him during his trance, which had lasted eight-and-forty hours. The 24th of the same month, he preached a very moving discourse to those who had accompanied him the day they were carrying him to the tomb.

People may, if they please, treat all we have just related as dreams and tales, but it cannot be denied that we recognise in these resurrections, and in these narrations of men who have come to life again after their real or seeming death, the belief of the Church concerning hell, paradise, purgatory, the efficacy of prayers for the dead, and the apparitions of angels and demons who torment the damned, and of the souls who have yet something to expiate in the other world.

We see also, that which has a visible connexion with the matter we are treating upon – persons really dead, and others regarded as such, who return to life in health and live for a long time afterwards. Lastly, we may observe therein opinions on the state of souls after this life, which are nearly the same as among the Hebrews, Egyptians, Greeks, Romans, barbarous nations, and Christians. If the Hungarian ghosts do not speak of what they have seen in the other world, it is either that they are not really dead, or more likely that all which is related of these revenants is fabulous and chimerical. I will add some more instances which will serve to confirm the belief of the primitive Church on the subject of apparitions.

St Perpetua, who suffered martyrdom in Africa in 202 or 203, being in prison for the faith, saw a brother named Dinocrates, who had died at the age of seven years of a cancer in the cheek; she saw him as if in a very large dungeon, so that they could not approach each other. He seemed to be placed in a reservoir of water, the sides of which were higher than himself, so that he could not reach the water, for which he appeared to thirst very much. Perpetua was much moved at this, and prayed to God with tears and groans for his relief. Some days after, she saw in spirit the same Dinocrates, well clothed, washed, and refreshed, and the water of the reservoir in which he was only came up to his middle, and on the edge a cup, from which he drank, without the water diminishing, and the skin of the cancer in his cheek well healed, so that nothing now remained of the cancer but the scar. By these things she understood that Dinocrates was no longer in pain.

Dinocrates was there apparently to expiate some faults which he had committed since his baptism, for Perpetua says a little before this, that only her father had remained in infidelity.

The same St Perpetua, being in prison some days before she suffered martyrdom, had a vision of the deacon Pomponius, who had suffered martyrdom some days before, and who said to her, 'Come, we are waiting for you.' He led her through a rugged and winding path into the arena of the amphitheatre, where she had to combat with a very ugly Egyptian accompanied by some other men like him. Perpetua found herself changed into a man, and began to fight naked, assisted by some well-made youths who came to her service and assistance.

Then she beheld a man of extraordinary size, who cried aloud, 'If the Egyptian gains the victory over her, he will kill her with his sword, but if she conquers, she shall have this branch ornamented with golden apples for her reward.' Perpetua began the combat, and having overthrown the Egyptian, trampled his head under her feet. The people shouted victory, and Perpetua approaching him who held the branch above mentioned, he put it in her hand, and said to her,

'Peace be with you.' Then she awoke, and understood that she would have to combat, not against wild beasts, but against the devil.

Saturus, one of the companions of the martyrdom of St Perpetua, had also a vision which he related thus: 'We had suffered martyrdom, and were disengaged from this mortal body. Four angels carried us towards the East without touching us. We arrived at a place shining with intense lustre; Perpetua was at my side, and I said unto her, "Behold what the Lord promised us."

'We entered a large garden full of trees and flowers; the four angels who had borne us thither placed us in the hands of other angels who conducted us by a wide road to a place where we found Jocondus, Saturninus, and

Artazes, who had suffered with us, and invited us to come and salute the Lord. We followed them, and beheld in the midst of this place the Almighty, crowned with dazzling light, and we heard repeated incessantly by those around Him, Holy! holy! holy! They raised us towards Him, and we stopped before His throne. We gave Him the kiss of peace, and He stroked our faces with His hand.

'We came out, and we saw before the door the Bishop Optatus and the Priest Aspasius, who threw themselves at our feet. We raised and embraced them. We recognised in this place several of our brethren and some martyrs.' Such was the vision of Saturus.

There are visions of all sorts; of holy martyrs, and of holy angels. It is related of St Exuperus, bishop of Toulouse, that having conceived the design of transporting the relics of St Saturnus, a former bishop of that Church, to place them in a new church built in his honour, he could with difficulty resolve to take this holy body from the tomb, fearing to displease the saint, or to diminish the honour which was due to him. But while in this doubt, he had a vision which gave him to understand that this translation would neither lessen the respect which was due to the ashes of the martyr, nor be prejudicial to his honour; but that on the contrary it would contribute to the salvation of the faithful, and to the greater glorification of God.

Some days before St Cyprian, Bishop of Carthage, suffered martyrdom, in 258, he had a vision, not being as yet quite asleep, in which a young man, whose height was extraordinary, seemed to lead him to the Praetorium before the Proconsul, who was seated on his tribunal. This magistrate, having caught sight of Cyprian, began to write his sentence before he had interrogated him as was usual. Cyprian knew not what the sentence condemned him to; but the young man above mentioned, and who was behind the judge, made a sign by opening his hand and spreading in form of a sword, that he was condemned to have his head cut off.

Cyprian easily understood what was meant by this sign, and having earnestly requested to be allowed a day's delay to put his affairs in order, the judge, having granted his request, again wrote upon his tablets, and the young man by a sign of his hand let him know that the delay was granted. These predictions were exactly fulfilled, and we see many similar ones in the works of St Cyprian.

St Fructueux, Bishop of Tarragona, who suffered martyrdom in 259, was seen after his death ascending to heaven with the deacons who had suffered with him; they appeared as if they were still attached to the stakes near which they had been burnt. They were seen by two Christians, who showed them to the wife and daughter of Emilian, who had condemned them. The saint appeared to Emilian himself and to the Christians, who had taken away their ashes, and desired that they might be all collected in one spot. We see similar apparitions in the acts of St James, of St Marienus, martyrs, and some others who suffered in Numidia in 259. We may observe the like in the acts of St Montanus, St Lucius, and other African martyrs in 259 or 260, and in those of St Vincent, a martyr in Spain, in 304, and in the life of St Theodore, martyr, in 306, of whose sufferings St Gregory of Nicea has written an account. Everybody knows what happened at Sebastus, in Armenia, in the martyrdom of the famous forty martyrs, of whom St Basil the Great has written the eulogium. One of the forty, overcome by the excess of cold, which was extreme, threw himself into a hot bath that was prepared just by. Then he who guarded them having perceived some angels who brought crowns to the thirty-nine who had persevered in their sufferings, despoiled himself of his garments, joined himself to the martyrs, and declared himself a Christian.

All these instances invincibly prove that, at least in the first ages of the Church, the greatest and most learned bishops, the holy martyrs, and the generality of the faithful, were well persuaded of the possibility and reality of apparitions.

CHAPTER 59

Conclusions of this Dissertation

To resume in a few words all that we have related in this dissertation: we have therein shown that a resurrection, properly so called, of a person who has been dead for a considerable time, and whose body was either corrupted, or stinking, or ready to putrefy, like that of Pierre, who had been three years buried, and was resuscitated by St Stanislaus, or that of Lazarus, who had been four days in the tomb, and already possessing a corpse-like smell – such a resurrection can be the work of the Almighty power of God alone.

That persons who have been drowned, fallen into syncope, into a lethargy or trance, or looked upon as dead, in any manner whatever, can be cured and brought back to life, even to their former state of life, without any miracle, but by the power of medicine alone, or by natural efforts, or by dint of patience; so that nature re-establishes herself in her former state, that the heart resumes its pulsation, and the blood circulates freely again in the arteries, and the vital and animal spirits in the nerves.

That the oupires, or vampires, or revenants of Moravia, Hungary, Poland, etc., of which such extraordinary things are related, so detailed, so circumstantial, invested with all the necessary formalities to make them believed, and to prove them even judicially before judges, and at the most exact and severe tribunals; that all which is said of their return to life; of their apparition, and the confusion which they cause in the towns and country places; of their killing people by sucking their blood, or in making a sign to them to follow them; that all those things are mere illusions, and the consequence of a heated and prejudiced imagination. They cannot cite any witness who is sensible, grave and unprejudiced, who can testify that he has seen, touched, interrogated these ghosts, who can affirm the reality of their return, and of the effects which are attributed to them.

I shall not deny that some persons may have died of fright, imagining that their near relatives called them to the tomb; that others have thought they heard someone rap at their doors, worry them, disturb them, in a word, occasion them mortal maladies; and that these persons judicially interrogated, have replied that they had seen and heard what their panic-struck imagination had represented to them. But I require unprejudiced witnesses, free from terror and disinterested, quite calm, who can affirm upon serious reflection, that they have seen, heard, and interrogated these vampires, and who have been the witnesses of their operations; and I am persuaded that no such witness will be found.

I have by me a letter, which has been sent me from Warsaw, the 3rd February 1745, by M. Slivisk, visitor of the province of Priests of the mission of Poland. He sends me word, that having studied with great care this matter, and having proposed to compose on this subject a theological and physical dissertation, he had collected some memoirs with that view; but that the occupations of visitor and superior in the house of his congregation of Warsaw, had not allowed of his putting his project in execution – that he has since sought in vain for these memoirs or notes, which have probably remained in the hands of some of those to whom he had communicated them; that amongst these notes were two resolutions of the Sorbonne, which both forbade cutting off the head and maiming the body of any of these pretended oupires or vampires. He adds, that these decisions may be found in the registers of the Sorbonne, from the year 1700 to 1710. I shall report by and by, a decision of the Sorbonne on this subject, dated in the year 1691.

He says, moreover, that in Poland they are so persuaded of the existence of these oupires, that anyone who thought otherwise would be regarded almost as a heretic. There are several facts concerning this matter, which are looked upon as incontestable, and many persons are named as witnesses of them. 'I gave myself the trouble,' says he, 'to go to

the fountain-head, and examine those who are cited as ocular witnesses.'
He found that no one dared to affirm that they had really seen the
circumstances in question, and that it was all merely reveries and fancies,
caused by fear and unfounded discourse. So writes to me this wise and
judicious priest.

I have also received since, another letter from Vienna in Austria, written
the 3rd August 1746, by a Lorraine baron, who has always followed his
prince. He tells me, that in 1742, his imperial majesty, then his royal
highness of Lorraine, had several verbal acts drawn up concerning these
cases, which happened in Moravia. I have them by me still; I have read
them over and over again; and to be frank, I have not found in them the
shadow of truth, nor even of probability, in what is advanced. They are,
nevertheless, documents which in that country are looked upon as true as
the Gospel.

CHAPTER 60

The Moral Impossibility of the Revenants
Coming out of their Graves

I have already proposed the objection formed upon the impossibility of
these vampires coming out of their graves, and returning to them again,
without its appearing that they have disturbed the earth, either in coming
out or going in again. No one has ever replied to this difficulty, and never
will. To say that the demon subtilises and spiritualises the bodies of
vampires, is a thing asserted without proof or likelihood.

The fluidity of the blood, the ruddiness, the suppleness of these
vampires, ought not to surprise anyone, any more than the growth of the
nails and hair, and their bodies remaining undecayed. We see every day,
bodies which remain uncorrupted, and retain a ruddy colour after death.
This ought not to appear strange in those who die without malady and a
sudden death; or of certain maladies, known to our physicians, which do
not deprive the blood of its fluidity, or the limbs of their suppleness.

With regard to the growth of the hair and nails in bodies which are not
yet decayed, the thing is quite natural. There remains in those bodies a
certain slow and imperceptible circulation of the humours, which causes
this growth of the nails and hair, in the same way that we every day see

common bulbs grow and shoot, although without any nourishment derived from the earth.

The same may be said of flowers, and in general of all that depends on vegetation in animals and plants.

The belief of the common people of Greece in the return to earth of the vroucolacas, is not much better founded than that of vampires and ghosts. It is only the ignorance, the prejudice, the terror of the Greeks, which have given rise to this vain and ridiculous belief, and which they keep up even to this very day. The narrative which we have reported after M. Tournefort, an ocular witness and a good philosopher, may suffice to undeceive those who would maintain the contrary.

The incorruption of the bodies of those who died in a state of excommunication, has still less foundation than the return of the vampires, and the vexations of the living caused by the vroucolacas; antiquity has had no similar belief. The schismatic Greeks, and the heretics separated from the Church of Rome, who certainly died excommunicated, ought, upon this principle, to remain uncorrupted; which is contrary to experience, and repugnant to good sense. And if the Greeks pretend to be the true Church, all the Roman Catholics, who have a separate communion from them, ought then also to remain undecayed. The instances cited by the Greeks either prove nothing, or prove too much. Those bodies which have not decayed, were really excommunicated, or not. If they were canonically and really excommunicated, then the question falls to the ground. If they were not really and canonically excommunicated, then it must be proved that there was no other cause of incorruption – which can never be proved.

Moreover, anything so equivocal as incorruption, cannot be adduced as a proof in so serious a matter as this. It is owned, that often the bodies of saints are preserved from decay; that is looked upon as certain, among the Greeks as among the Latins – therefore, we cannot thence conclude that this same incorruption is a proof that a person is excommunicated.

CHAPTER 61

What is Related Concerning the Bodies of the Excommunicated Leaving the Church, is Subject to very Great Difficulties

Whatever respect I may feel for St Gregory the Great, who relates some instances of deceased persons who died in a state of excommunication going out of the church before the eyes of everyone present; and whatever consideration may be due to other authors whom I have cited, and who relate other circumstances of a similar nature, and even still more incredible, I cannot believe that we have these legends with all the circumstances belonging to them; and after the reasons for doubt which I have recorded at the end of these stories, I believe I may again say, that God, to inspire the people with still greater fear of excommunication, and a greater regard for the sentences and censures of the Church, has willed on these occasions, for reasons unknown to us, to show forth His power, and work a miracle in the sight of the faithful; for how can we explain all these things without having recourse to the miraculous? All that is said of persons who being dead chew under ground in their graves, is so pitiful, so puerile, that it is not worthy of being seriously refuted. Everybody owns that too often people are buried who are not quite dead. There are but too many instances of this in ancient and modern histories. The thesis of M. Vinslow, and the notes added thereto by M. Bruhier, serve to prove that there are few certain signs of real death except the putridity of a body being at least begun. We have an infinite number of instances of persons supposed to be dead, who have come to life again, even after they have been put in the ground. There are I know not how many maladies in which the patient remains for a long time speechless, motionless, and without sensible respiration. Some drowned persons who have been thought dead, have been revived by care and attention.

All this is well known, and may serve to explain how some vampires have been taken out of their graves, and have spoken, cried, howled, vomited blood, and all that because they were not yet dead. They have been killed by beheading them, piercing their heart, and burning them; in all which people were very wrong, for the pretext on which they acted, of their pretended reappearance to disturb the living, causing their death, and maltreating them, is not a sufficient reason for treating them thus. Besides, their pretended return has never been proved or attested in such a way as to authorise anyone to show such inhumanity, nor to dishonour and put rigorously to death on vague, frivolous, unproved accusations, persons who were certainly innocent of the thing laid to their charge.

For nothing is more ill-founded than what is said of the apparitions, vexations, and confusion caused by the pretended vampires and the vroucolacas. I am not surprised that the Sorbonne should have condemned the bloody and violent executions which are exercised on these kinds of dead bodies. But it is astonishing that the secular powers and the magistrates do not employ their authority and the severity of the laws to repress them.

The magic devotions, the fascinations, the evocations of which we have spoken, are works of darkness, operations of Satan, if they have any reality, which I can with difficulty believe, especially in regard to magical devotions, and the evocation of the manes or souls of dead persons; for, as to fascinations of the sight, or illusions of the senses, it is foolish not to admit some of these, as when we think we see what is not, or do not behold what is present before our eyes; or when we think we hear a sound which in reality does not strike our ears, or the contrary. But to say that the demon can cause a person's death, because they have made a wax image of him, or given his name with some superstitious ceremonies, and have devoted him or her, so that the persons feel themselves dying as their image melts away, is ascribing to the demon too much power, and to magic too much might. God can, when He wills it, loosen the rein of the enemy of mankind, and permit him to do us the harm which he and his agents may seek to do us; but it would be ridiculous to believe that the Sovereign Master of nature can be determined by magical incantations to allow the demon to hurt us; or to imagine that the magician has the power to excite the demon against us, independently of God.

The instance of that peasant who gave his child to the devil, and whose life the devil first took away and then restored, is one of those extraordinary and almost incredible circumstances which are sometimes to be met with in history, and which neither theology nor philosophy knows how to explain. Was it a demon who animated the body of the boy, or did his soul re-enter his body by the permission of God? By what authority did the demon take away this boy's life, and then restore it to him? God may have permitted it to punish the impiety of the wretched father, who had given himself to the devil to satisfy a shameful and criminal passion. And again, how could he satisfy it with a demon, who appeared to him in the form of a girl he loved? In all that I see only darkness and difficulties, which I leave to be resolved by those who are more learned or bolder than myself.

The Folklore Society

What is folklore?   Folklore has been defined as 'traditional culture', but no one phrase can do justice to the subject. It embraces music, song, dance, drama, narrative, language, foods, medicine, arts and crafts, religion, magic and belief. Folklore is the way that people fill their lives with meaning, through the stories they share, the daily rituals they perform. Folklore can be both the expression of our individuality and the source of a sense of community. From standing stones to biker gangs, from ancient riddles to the latest joke craze, from King Arthur to the playground, from birth to death, folklore is the stuff of life.

The Folklore Society: who we are.   Since 1878 The Folklore Society has provided a meeting-ground for both academics and enthusiasts eager to learn about popular culture and traditional life. The Society promotes awareness of folklore within universities, museums, festivals, in fact wherever traditional culture is discussed and researched.

   The Society has an elected committee which aims to be responsive to its members' needs. It therefore embraces a number of specialist groups, such as the East Anglia Folklore Group, to make the Society accessible to all.

The Folklore Society: what we do.   In order to encourage awareness of folklore the Society organises events, prizes and research projects. It runs at least one conference a year, and hosts the annual Katharine Briggs memorial lecture.

   The Society publishes its own academic journal, *Folklore*, in association with Routledge. It also produces numerous monographs and pamphlets, either under its own imprint, *FLS Books*, or in conjunction with other publishers.

   In addition to the journal *Folklore*, members receive a regular newsletter, *FLS News*, through which they can call on the expertise of the entire Society. They also have access to a specialist library with both reference and lending facilities and a substantial archive. The library constitutes a unique resource for the study of folklore, old and new.

The Folklore Society: how to contact us.   For details about how to join The Folklore Society and about our forthcoming activities and publications, contact: The Folklore Society, University College London, Gower Street, London WC1E 6BT

Telephone: 020 7862 8564 (with voice mail)
E-mail: folklore.society@talk21.com
Website: www.folklore–society.com

The Folklore Society is a Registered Charity No.1074552